CONGRESS VOLUME

SALAMANCA 1983

SUPPLEMENTS

TO

VETUS TESTAMENTUM

EDITED BY
THE BOARD OF THE QUARTERLY

J. A. EMERTON - W. L. HOLLADAY - A. LEMAIRE
R. E. MURPHY - E. NIELSEN - R. SMEND
J. A. SOGGIN - M. WEINFELD

VOLUME XXXVI

LEIDEN
E. J. BRILL
1985

The President: Professor Luis Alonso Schökel, S.J.

CONGRESS VOLUME

SALAMANCA

1983

EDITED BY

J. A. EMERTON

LEIDEN
E. J. BRILL
1985

ISBN 90 04 07281 0

PRINTED IN THE NETHERLANDS BY E. J. BRILL

CONTENTS

PREFACE

The Eleventh Congress of the International Organization for the Study of the Old Testament was held from 28 August to 2 September 1983 under the Presidency of Professor Luis Alonso Schökel, S.J., of the Pontifical Biblical Institute in Rome. The Secretary of the Congress was Professor V. Collado Bertomeu, of Valencia, and the scene of the Congress was the beautiful and historic University town of Salamanca.

Those attending the Congress were saddened by the sudden death in Salamanca of Professor D. J. McCarthy, S.J., also of the Pontifical Biblical Institute. It seemed appropriate that this volume should include the address given by the President at the memorial Mass.

This volume includes all the papers read by invitation at the Congress with the exception of two, of which one will be incorporated by the author in a forthcoming book and the other was not submitted to me for publication. I am once again grateful to Dr André Lemaire, one of my colleagues on the Editorial Board of *Vetus Testamentum*, for his help in editing some of the papers written in French.

J. A. Emerton

ADDRESS IN MEMORY OF DENNIS J. McCARTHY, S.J.

Jesus Ben Sira admonishes us, "Call no one happy before his death; it is by his end that a man will be known" (xi 28). Death marks the end of a man's biography. It is the culmination, often sudden, of earthly existence.

Building upon Hezekiah's image (in Isa. xxxviii 12), we might describe a man's life as a tapestry with many scenes which are being completed even as others are beginning. A man weaves them according to his plans and as he reacts to external forces, up to the day when, peacefully or violently, he is cut off from the loom. A sudden pull which is neither planned nor foreseen interrupts the work. We human beings think that the tapestry remains incomplete; that the many possible scenes which might have been, or scenes which were begun but not completed, will always be lacking. But God, who looks on and directs the work from above, declares when the tapestry is, in fact, complete, and he pronounces his judgement.

What image of our friend and brother Dennis do we take away with us? That of a man who was dedicated to the study and service of the Word of God. He was dedicated with all his might, dedicated even beyond his natural limitations, dedicated to investigating, elucidating, expounding and preaching the Word of God. He gave all his natural talent, his philological rigour, his literary sensitivity and his gifts of explaining to this service. This is the over-all image which we have of him, but we must say that it is neither accurate nor complete.

In addition to being a servant of the Word he was a listener to the Word. Before and after his scientific work, at the base and at the summit of this service, was his humble and careful listening. The source of the energy which propelled and sustained his scientific work was his Christian faith. Out of natural modesty and respect for this mystery he did not speak about it, but those who lived with him could feel its interior presence which was discreetly active.

He answered "Here I am" to the call of the Word and thus he entered into a covenant with God the Father, a covenant sealed by the Spirit. A new and special call put him face to face with a transcendentally new step in his life and he, like Samuel, answered, "Here I am". Thus, his radical covenant of faith was established through the promises of religious life —not a second covenant, but a deepening of the same one. From then on, the successive calls which concretize the fundamental exigencies of life followed, and his life developed as a listening and responding in things large and small, in the ordinary and the special, in silence and in word. Until one night, an ordinary night which was not to be ordinary for him, when the final call came: "Come, blessed of my Father", and he answered simply, "Here I am". Here is the summary and the secret: the hearer of the Word answered it, placing himself in its service.

Now we contemplate that life, that tapestry, which has achieved its fulfilment according to the plan of God. Many of us have read Dennis's works, some of us have lived with him for years. He and his writings have formed or fostered a community of friends and acquaintances. Today we recognize, with sadness and with joy, that Dennis has brought us together by his death. We, who were brought together to this Congress in order to study the Bible or to share our work and conclusions, now by this sudden death of our colleague are united here in order to sing our common praise to God, to participate in this eucharistic thanksgiving service. We are of various Christian confessions, joined together by a common baptism, believing in the same one, true God, recognizing the religious and human values of the Bible. We are here in this chapel and represent perhaps thousands of absent colleagues. We abandon our study of the Word for an hour and we make ourselves humble listeners to that Word. I would dare to say that God, through some clever sleight of hand, has outwitted us. Through the incentive of this Congress he has brought us to Salamanca; through Dennis's death he has brought us together in this place so that we might reflect upon and experience our deep and true calling. Thus, Dennis's death was his final act of service to the Word.

We realize more now that our faith sustains and propels our work; we understand better now that our faith is actuated by listening and by responding. Now our faith is transformed into hope, and awaits the final call. When we hear, "Come, blessed of my Father", we will answer simply, "Here we are, Lord".

Luis Alonso Schökel, S.J.
Salamanca
31 August 1983

OF METHODS AND MODELS

BY

L. ALONSO SCHÖKEL

Rome

When the present site of the Congress was proposed and approved, the very name of Salamanca began to exert its charm. Here was a city with the attraction of an illustrious history, and the prospect of a trip to Salamanca implied a returning into the past from these last decades of the twentieth century.

As travellers arrive from all over the world, they can sense the attraction of this Renaissance and baroque city transformed through the centuries by the air of its dry climate. It could be a strong temptation to abandon the lecture halls, play the truant schoolboy, and fill the plazas and streets with the sound of all our different languages.

As I inaugurate this Congress, I too feel the attraction of the past, not so much in stone monuments, but rather in books and great scholars. Added to the charm of the past there is a sense of duty. We are all indebted to those great teachers and can well be aware of an obligation to recover and relive here their memory, buried, perhaps, in an unmerited oblivion.

I am afraid it is true that we can easily be satisfied with the results of our historical-critical science, and can sweep the scholars and writers of the past under the carpet we walk on. One might think of those men and their works as mouldy and dusty, as though their very presence would make the air unbreathable and the room unpresentable.

Atoning in a small way for such neglect, I should like to recall briefly the representative figure of Fray Luis de León (1528-1591), the Augustinian humanist, poet and exegete, student of illustrious Spanish-Jewish masters, and renowned teacher at Salamanca. For some while I yielded to his charm and mentally toyed with the idea of devoting this inaugural address to a portrayal of this exegete. He was a man who, when it was the fashion to turn to Greece and Rome for literary models, could savour the beauty of the OT in its original language. When the Song of Songs was being interpreted allegorically, he prepared a Spanish translation and wrote a literal commentary that manifests remarkable sensitivity. At a time when commentaries were written in Latin with citations from the Vulgate, he prepared a literary commentary on Job in beautiful

Spanish. This commentary witnessed to the empathy he had for the book of Job, an empathy derived from his own experience of suffering and persecution. He made not one but three translations of Job to accompany the commentary. Meanwhile he departed from the Schoolmen's methodology and Latin and worked out an original Christology which we might classify as "symbolic" in that he applied to Christ symbols of the OT such as Shoot of David, Mountain, Lamb, Spouse, etc. Original and far advanced as this man was, his work as a teacher flowed in the mainstream of his times. Fray Luis de León can, then, be taken as representative of a legion of scholars of his century while surpassing them in several aspects.[1]

One day it will be necessary to study this stage in the history of exegesis and to compare, in all peace, Catholic and Protestant authors. It will be seen that, despite the dogmatic and confessional differences, their methods and the results of their biblical interpretation were not so very different.

I now must beg your pardon for this confession of plans never realized. I must no longer dally with the past but pass on to the theme of my address which I hope will serve as a prologue to the Congress.

I believe that all are well agreed as to what a *method* is: a defined and controllable way of proceeding. At the present stage of biblical studies there is much discussion about methods: describing, justifying, integrating, changing. And this not merely for pedagogical reasons. Method is like a car which takes us somewhere but which we drive. Returning to this discussion might indicate that one is insecure, displeased, apprehensive or weary of one's method. When we have to speak much about our method, it could be because we are not sure of it, we want to have a check-up on it as we would on our car or our health. Or we may feel threatened as when we check to see that our wallet is still in our pocket. The appearance or the steady advance of a new method can be felt as a threat to our science or to our place in it. Finally, it may be that we are tired of the method. We feel that it has given all it had to give, we have exhausted it, and we apply ourselves to it, to see if it can carry us any further or whether we will have to trade it in for a new model.

Busy and distracted with revising methods, we can overlook a more important factor which is not dependent on method but rather directs it. This can be called a model, a paradigm (T. S. Kuhn), an hypothesis (submissively accepted), or a theory. The term hypothesis emphasizes

[1] See H. Hurter, *Nomenclator Literarius Theologiae Catholicae theologos exhibens aetate, natione, disciplinis distinctos*, I and II (Innsbruck, 1906-1907).

tentative, theory suggests systematic; model and paradigm look to the idea of exemplar. The formula "theoretical model" can effect a suitable synthesis.[2]

"Model" is a difficult term to define since models come in such a variety of forms and can be more or less generic. It may however be said that a model is a system of elements constructed to give a unified explanation to a set of observed data. Or a model may be a system already known and tested in one field which is transferred to a new field of investigation. In both cases a model contains a surplus meaning which it puts at the service of the research. For, once the model is constructed and accepted, it guides subsequent observation and explanation of data—a point which I will take up later. The model usually has an imaginative projection more or less vivid according to the imagination of the researcher. This imaginative projection is frequently the best place to analyse the adopted model.

In brief, the model, once adopted, becomes an *a priori* form of the research and its method. To the model we commit ourselves; of the method we make use.

Historians, critical or otherwise, make use of *sources* in writing their works: oral and written sources, monuments, documents. The sources may be said to give a genetic explanation of the work produced, an explanation by its causes. The way in which the sources are used reveals the vision of the historian. This is a very general model that can be realized in many different specified ways. Note the imaginative facet of the model. "Source" is originally a metaphor, a spring from which information flows. To the same imaginative vision belongs the picture of an author with his sources on his desk, analysing and selecting the documents as he prepares his work.

This generic model can be narrowed down and applied to ancient texts, e.g. the Pentateuch. The specific model presupposes pre-existing narratives which are continuous, datable and relatively complete. Moreover, it presupposes a certain homogeneity within each narrative, heterogeneity with respect to the other accounts, and the work of a redactor or author who selects, orders, and arranges the pieces of the total composition. Once this model is constructed, the methodical work begins of searching for, evaluating and cataloguing the evidence of clues: repeti-

---

[2] On models, especially in the natural sciences, see Mary Hesse, "Models and Analogy in Sciences", in *The Encyclopedia of Philosophy* (New York, 1967) V, pp. 354-8. Also Thomas Kuhn, *The Structure of Scientific Revolutions* (Chicago, 1962, 1970). Note the postcript to the second edition. And on the above see B. Barnes, *T. S. Kuhn and Social Sciences* (New York, 1982). It should be kept in mind that Kuhn is writing about the natural sciences whereas our field belongs to the humanities.

tions (the equivalent of the projection of the paradigm in the syntagm), variation of names or synonyms (the equivalent of paradigmatic alternation or substitution), constants of style, etc.

The model then is an a priori form of the method. The scholar who has chosen his model and has assimilated it as a *forma mentis* or *forma phantasiae*, will already have foreseen the global result when he sets about his work of analysis. His interest is not so much in facts as in clues, or in interpreting facts as clues. If certain data do not fit, he must, in honesty, look for another explanation of them or readjust his construct. The model with its surplus meaning is capable of assimilating or even providing a *sanatio in radice* for a reasonable number of uncertainties or unknowns, especially when these are due to the lack of external evidence.

One group of scholars took the specific model, already worked out, and transferred it to another corpus or other texts: prophets (B. Duhm), Qohelet (C. Siegfried), Jeremiah (S. Mowinckel) and so forth. Other scholars, for various reasons, refused to accept the source theory or model for the Pentateuch. When this was not for dogmatic reasons what then happened was that this group, since they did not accept the mental model, found the alleged clues to be inconclusive.

A model can be in crisis when enough data are found that do not fit into the scheme even after adjustments are made. Or a crisis can occur at the appearance and development of a rival model. It can be that a crisis of a model may be the occasion for the introduction, discussion and eventual acceptance of a new model.[3] (In the natural sciences two models are generally incompatible, so that the acceptance of the new model means the abandonment of the old. In the humanities the coexistence of two rival models is somewhat more possible.)

When Gunkel introduced research into *literary forms* (*genres*), he not only stimulated a change of method but also challenged a model. What he writes in his introduction to Genesis illustrates the imaginative side of his model. His predecessors, he says, envisioned the text as though it were a work produced in an office whereas he pictured for himself a storyteller, surrounded by his listeners, retelling old stories. He saw a community assembled for their typical, regularly recurring gatherings, making use of a repertoire of works composed for these occasions. His formula *Sitz im Leben* with the emphasis on *Leben* sounded a polemic note.[4]

---

[3] Kuhn devotes two chapters to the question of crisis: VII "Crises and the Emrgence of Scientific Theories", VIII "The response to Crisis".

[4] See Werner Klatt, *Hermann Gunkel. Zu seiner Theologie der Religionsgeschichte und zur Entstehung der formgeschichtliche Methode* (Göttingen, 1969). On Gunkel and the project of a modern literary programme see my *Treinta Salmos: Poesía y Oración* (Madrid, 1981), pp. 13-22.

Gunkel began to look at the Psalms and the stories of Genesis with new eyes, and he saw new things. So much so, that from that time the model of dated, localized sources ceased to function and a new model took over. Gunkel quite possibly was the most revolutionary moment for biblical exegesis in this century. He not only changed a method, he taught how to think and read in different way. That he encountered resistance is not surprising. Now we rejoice in his posthumous vindication.

Do the symptoms to which I referred at the beginning of this lecture indicate that today we are in a state of crisis? Some have suggested that the arrival of a literary study of the Old Testament demands a change of model, nothing less than a *confrontation with the entire historical-critical work.*[5] I personally do not think that this is quite the case. Perhaps a rigid structuralism with its purely semiotic (and not semantic) analysis of the text would have such pretensions. But if we pay attention to what the scholars who are practising literary analysis say, their intention is not to supplant or replace historical-critical study but to co-operate with it. Historical-critical work is like a lovely metropolis, well planned and maternal, neat and welcoming, which has given us our education and provides us with lodging. Historical-critical research is not exhausted.[6]

However, while not accepting this total confrontation, I venture to propose the following *proportion*: *what the study of literary forms was to the study of sources, literary analysis now is to the study of the history of redaction.* I am speaking of analogy, not identity. And I mean an analogy of relationship, or what the Schoolmen called analogy of proportionality. The area I am speaking of does not cover the whole field of our science but it does take in a large and important section of it. Some maintain that literary analysis is to be an alternative, others say that it is complementary to analysis of redaction. And although both may not cover exactly the same area, both, at the present time, must be reckoned with.[7]

What are the possible *relations between these two schools*, if I may use the term? 1. The extreme situation of *mutual condemnation* which might be violently expressed in the following terms: analysis of redaction makes the accusation, "you are analysing works which never existed"; and literary analysis would reply, "you are reconstructing a process which never took place". The cold war of mutual condemnation can easily heat up and degenerate into a desire to destroy the opponent. And in any war, hot or cold, dialogue and diplomacy are of little avail.

---

[5] David Robertson, *The Old Testament and the Literary Critic* (Philadelphia, 1977), p. 4.

[6] Edgar Krentz, *The Historical-Critical Method* (Philadelphia, 1975) pp. 63-7.

[7] Section B4.3 of the *Elenchus Bibliographicus Biblicus* lists only articles or monographs explicitly dealing with our subject. One should consult the rich bibliography in C. Conroy, *Absalom, Absalom* (Roma, 1978), brought up to date in class-notes not yet published.

2. Another extreme situation, though it may not appear to be such at first sight, would be that of *courteous non-communication*, somewhat like two neighbours who salute in passing but never stop to talk. Shyness, or exaggerated respect, a measure of fear, or perhaps a sense of self-sufficiency makes them keep at a polite distance from one another and avoid any sort of personal involvement. Does that describe our present-day situation in biblical studies?

3. A third possibility would be the relatively peaceful one of *division of labour* according to different criteria. One scholar, for example, will prefer to write a monograph within the framework of the approach that he or she finds more congenial and will be quite content to leave to another the task of studying the topic within the framework of the other approach. The division of labour could also be established along chronological lines: the text will be examined first according to one approach, then according to the other, and the question of operational priority would be the only controversial point. Or again, the approach might be varied according to the particular text being studied: many chapters of Ezekiel, for instance, might seem more amenable to an analysis of redaction, while much of Second Isaiah would offer more scope for literary analysis. Scholarly work may well be carried out in separate compartments such as those above mentioned, but one wonders whether there is any hope of a synthesis of the two approaches.[8] Must we resign ourselves to working in adjacent but sound-proof rooms?

For my part I am convinced that *dialogue* is not only possible but necessary. Even if it should lead to open controversy, that would still be preferable to a situation of polite silence. It is true that Kuhn has stressed how difficult communication can be between scholars who operate within different and incompatible paradigms; it may seem that they are talking in different languages or that they use the same words in radically different senses. Difficulty, however, does not yet mean impossibility.[9]

To begin with, we can note that *both methods imply their own model*. Redaction analysis rests on a model that we might describe figuratively by referring to the geological process of sedimentation. The original, usually short, oracle or narrative can be seen as the bedrock upon which successive strata have been deposited, until the text has acquired its present form. Each stratum is homogeneous in itself and heterogeneous with respect to the others. Literary sedimentation cannot, however, be taken simply as a process of superimposition, since there is interaction between

[8] The synthesis should be made in works of exegesis and particularly in text-books and reference works such as Introductions. Kuhn highlights the influence of textbooks: pp. 136 ff.

[9] Kuhn, p. 149.

the older and the recent strata. The final product is not regarded as a poem or literary text as we understand those terms now; it is rather the trace and outcome of a process that was in part governed by deliberate decisions, in part by chance circumstances. The scholar's task, then, will be to assign each portion of the text to its appropriate stratum on the basis of clues still visible in the text, and to explain each portion in terms of its own stratum and its interacton with the preceding ones.[10]

Another possible image for the model underlying redaction analysis would be the projection of a horizontal (synchronic) text on a vertical (diachronic) scale. This image might even give a better idea of the dynamics of the method.

The work of redaction analysis is governed by two distinct orders of stimuli. First, there is the discovery of various tensions and incoherencies in the text, which are then explained by diachronic separation of strata. Secondly, there is the postulate that the author's deliberate intention completely determines the meaning of the text. While the latter postulate exercises its influence independently of the particular nature of the text being studied, the stimulus given by the discovery of tensions and incoherencies is not really an autonomous one. It is only because one has previously accepted the sedimentation model that tensions have to be taken as pointing to the existence of textual strata.[11]

Literary analysis too has its model, which is that of the literary work and its author. The coherence one expects to find in such a work is specifically poetical or literary, not necessarily logical. It can take the form of an organizing pattern, a central symbol or field of imagery, a dominant emotion, or a situation that provides a framework for the characters.

The literary work can be governed simultaneously by several systems whose mutual relationship may be harmonious or laden with tension. If the author should happen to make use of pre-existing material, this will be shaped and transformed according to the purposes of the new work. What the author consciously intended to communicate is indeed a main factor in the meaning of the work but it is by no means the only one. The work can often transcend the intention of the author.

---

[10] At times the stratum is restricted to the text being analysed. At other times the later level belongs to a wider stratum present in various texts or oracles, for example, the Deuteronomistic redaction. In the latter case sooner or later it becomes necessary to study the wider stratum in itself.

[11] Note the difference. In one case frequent and serious inconsistencies demand a diachronic separation of verses: the investigation proceeds *a posteriori*. In other cases it is not inconsistency that starts the process; we ourselves look for evidence and clues to reconstruct a process. Here the model sets the research in motion and directs it.

The existence of the model is shown by scholars of both schools, when they state their positions without presenting adequate reasons: on the one hand, by those who insist that the primary task is to reconstruct the growth-process of the text, and on the other, by those who claim that all one has to do is study the text itself.

Since, then, both methods imply an underlying set of presuppositions with their own principles and axioms, mutual condemnation would seem to be quite out of place. But we must ask whether real dialogue is now possible.[12]

The following examples and critical reflections are offered as first or further steps in such a dialogue. We can start by considering the stylistic feature of concentric structure whose frequent recurrence in Hebrew literature is now an established fact. A scholar intent on discovering the different strata within a text will probably overlook the presence of a concentric structure. In fact, since operational priority has been given to redaction analysis and stylistic analysis is left for later, the analytical fragmentation of the text (which necessarily destroys the concentric structure) may well prevent one from seeing the structure in the subsequent literary analysis. In other words, while the model may sharpen one's vision for some features of the text, it may also prevent one from noticing other aspects.[13]

The use of textual data as analytical clues affords another example. The formula *bayyôm hahûʾ* in its ordinary sense is simply an adverbial expression for "then" or (with some emphasis) "in that day". Used in narrative or in poetry it can connect sub-units, signal the temporal continuation of an utterance, or function as an ordering particle in anaphoric series—such as the *ʾl tʾmr* or *bṭrm* series in Sirach. As well as that, however, it can also be used by a redactor or glossator to join a new portion of text to older material. The formula itself, in brief, is functionally polyvalent, and this explains why one scholar can take it in a particular case as a connective phrase, while another will read it as indicating a later addition to the text. The latter option can even be generalized into the assertion that the formula in question is a criterion of general validity for identifying a later addition to a text. It is clear, however, that this criterion rests on a subjective decision. A genetic theory that prescinds from the possible literary functions of this particular linguistic feature can only be termed unconvincing. Much the same, with rather more caution, can be said of arguments based on the occurrence of the particle *gam*. In

[12] R. Polzin is treating more of the scientific approval that one approach should grant to the other: R. Polzin, *Moses and the Deuteronomist* (New York, 1980), p. 4.

[13] We could cite the way Siegfried divided Qohelet into an author, a ḥakam and a ḥasid, and thus destroyed much of the internal tension of this book.

such cases it is the underlying model that determines the interpretation of textual data as clues and criteria for the chosen approach.

Similarly, features such as changes of person, or number, or imagery cannot be taken without further argument as signs of later additions to a text. The literary analyst will insist that these features must be first studied systematically before a univocal judgement is pronounced about their function and before building a theory upon that judgement.

A further point concerns the homogeneity and monotony of the several diachronic strata into which the text has been divided by redaction analysis. Faced with such results, the experienced literary analyst may well feel the absence of that dramatic tension which characterizes so many literary works. Contrasting visions, hope struggling with depression, triumph after apparent despair—all these have been systematically separated into academically coherent strata.

Of course, there is a certain amount of exaggeration in these remarks. No one will dispute the fact that redactional analysis of a text can at times restore the splendour of the original literary work from which later accretions have been removed: "Take away the dross from the silver, and the smith has material for a vessel" (Prov. xxv 4 *RSV*).

The two models can now be compared from the point of view of the literary scholar, taking into account the axioms and peculiar requirements of each model.

1. The ideal of *objectivity*. The literary model appears to have the advantage here thanks to its concentration on the given biblical text, while the sedimentation model obliges its adherents to go behind the textual data by a series of conjectures in order to discover the supposed stages of development of the text. The question could be raised, however, whether the objectivity of the literary model in this case is genuinely such or whether it may not really be simply a disguised form of fundamentalism. In reply it can be pointed out that contemporary practitioners of literary analysis have all had a solid training in historical-critical methodology. Furthermore, it is significant that literary analysis itself can often identify additions to a text, for instance the speeches of Elihu in Job, the last verses of Ps. li, perhaps the end of Ps. cxxxvi, and so on.

What of the assertion that study of the *author's intention* provides a sound criterion of objectivity? The literary model does not deny the primary value of the author but it concentrates on the text because, in the last analysis, our only means of access to the author's intention is precisely by way of the text (unless we possess some external evidence on the matter). Since, however, the biblical authors have not given us separate formulations of their intentions and since authors in general are not always the best interpreters of their own work (for one thing they struggle directly with language and lack familiarity, in many cases, with the metalanguage of criticism), it must be concluded that the text itself offers a more objective basis for study than the alleged intention of its author.[14]

2. The aspect of *pluralism*. The sedimentation model is obliged by its axioms to assign each part of the text to a specific stratum, and this means that it cannot admit more than one explanation for each of the parts. The literary model, on the contrary, is not only able to accept but can even welcome a plurality of explanations. Specified verses within a prophetic oracle, for example, cannot simultaneously be assigned to the original prophet and to the activity of a redactional school two centuries later. One of the proposals will be true and the others false, or all will be false, or all will be merely probable to a greater or lesser extent. And it is to be noted that the limited degree of probability attainable in such cases is not attributed to the lack of skill in the practice of the method but simply to the absence of reliable information from independent sources. The compilers of Jeremiah's oracles, for example, sometimes noted carefully the precise historical setting of the oracle, in other cases they apparently showed no concern at all for this. The two attitudes existed at the same time. It follows that many of our questions about historical settings cannot, by the very nature of the evidence, hope to receive a sure or even solidly probable answer. If, then, the understanding of a text depends on knowledge of the author's intention, it is inevitable that our interpretation will very often fail to reach even a modest degree of probability.

The literary model, on the other hand, does justice both to the complexity of the psychological factors involved in literary creation and to the complexity of structures that constitute the finished work. The work itself can thus give rise to a variety of interpretations, all of them legitimate so far as they are faithful to the text. It would appear, then, that the literary model enjoys an advantage over the other in this question of pluralism. It might be objected that such talk about a plurality of interpretations simply throws open the gates to a completely arbitrary reading of texts; if every sort of reading is possible, it might be urged, then none has any real value. In reply it must be stated quite firmly that not everything is possible in a literary analysis: the text itself remains the arbiter of the situation and can easily disqualify inappropriate readings.

3. *Wealth of insights*. Here too the literary model seems preferable. By its very nature it tends to maximalize the possibilities of a text, while

[14] Two uses of "intention" must be kept apart. One usage refers to "meaning"; another to the "purpose" or "aim" of an author, for example "this is written that you may believe".

redaction analysis has to remain at a minimalistic level of statement due to its need to define precisely the author's intention. It is good to remember too that the Bible has been able to inspire millions of people for many generations. Redaction analysis can point in reply to the rich insights gained by seeing how successive generations of readers confronted the matter of the text and left in it the mark of their reflections in stratum after stratum.

4. Other aspects. With respect to the actualization of ancient texts, redaction analysis remains at a loss since its concern is to anchor each element of the text firmly in its original period and setting; literary analysis, on the other hand, is able to cast the text loose and let it set out on its voyage down through the centuries. While redaction analysis may boast of the scientific exactitude of its constructions, literary analysis can offer the aesthetic satisfaction of a penetrating explanation that can find coherence amid complexity and present a finely phrased exposition of the text.

Finally, we can ask whether this brief confrontation of the two models obliges us to conclude that a change of model is now imperative. It is clear that my presentation has been too one-sided to justify any such conclusion; besides, forty-five minutes are hardly enough to persuade people that a paradigm shift is called for. Nor have my reflections given adequate treatment to the whole question of dialogue between the two models. The case for redaction analysis needs to be argued at greater length. But I will not set about that task now: partly because I do not wish to inflict another talk on you, partly because dialogue needs more than one speaker and there are others who can present the case for redaction analysis in a more competent way.

The rules of the Congress give me the first word, but not the second nor the last! I make no claim to have resolved a dilemma that does not in fact exist, nor to have laid the definitive foundations for a discussion that ought indeed to exist; my hope is rather that I have encouraged a dialogue between the two models, which will certainly be more fruitful than polite non-communication. And in this context disagreement can be just as valuable as agreement: "He who states his case first seems right, until the other comes and examines him" (Prov. xviii 17 *RSV*).

THE TARGUMIM AND THE RABBINIC RULES FOR THE DELIVERY OF THE TARGUM

BY

P. S. ALEXANDER

Manchester

Correct interpretation of any literary work depends on an understanding of its *Sitz im Leben*, by which I mean the circumstances in which it came into being, the functions it was meant to perform, and the literary genre to which it belongs. This is as true for the Aramaic Targumim as for any other document. Yet in the spate of publications on the Targumim over the past thirty years it is hard to find any that give more than a glance at the problem of the literary setting of the Targum. So long as this setting remains unclear any conclusions drawn from analysis of the text, language and content of the Targumim are bound to lack concreteness and give the impression of being out of focus. In defining the *Sitz im Leben* of the Targumim we must consider two lines of evidence: (1) the testimony of the Targumim themselves as to their form and genre, and (2) Rabbinic statements on the function and setting of the Targum. Let us consider each of these in turn.

I. Genre and Form of the Targumim

As to genre Targum is translation. This is the basic meaning of the term Targum itself, and most scholars accept this general classification, though some, feeling it does not do justice to the expansive nature of the Targumim, prefer to speak of "paraphrase", or "paraphrastic translation". Such refinements are of little use. The only way forward to a more precise definition of the genre of the Targumim is to consider them in the light of ancient translation theory and the ancient typology of translation.

Writing to Pammachius Jerome asserts (Ep. LVII 5): "Ego enim non solum fateor sed libera uoce profiteor, me in interpretatione Graecorum absque scripturis sanctis, ubi et uerborum ordo mysterium est, non uerbum e uerbo sed sensum exprimere de sensu." As Sebastian Brock has shown, Jerome here neatly distinguishes the two main types of translation prevalent in antiquity.[1] The one, which rendered *uerbum e uerbo*, was

[1] "Aspects of Translation Technique in Antiquity", *Greek, Roman and Byzantine Studies* 20 (1979), pp. 69-87.

very literal and followed the original word for word, even to the detriment of the natural order and syntax of the target language. The other, proceeding *sensus de sensu*, rendered the meaning of the original, rather than its words, and paid attention to good style and syntax in the target language. The *sensus de sensu* type of translation was favoured by literary men such as Cicero in their versions of the Greek classics. The *uerbum e uerbo* approach was characteristic of legal documents (e.g. *senatus consulta*) where verbal accuracy was very important and where, in the nature of the case, the documents would be subjected to explanation by experts. Jerome confesses that his normal approach is *sensus de sensu*, save in the case of Scripture, because in Scripture "et uerborum ordo mysterium est". By implication the only proper way to render Scripture is *uerbum e uerbo*. This view was evidently held by many of the early Bible translators, and because literal translation was used for Holy Writ, it came to be regarded in the Middle Ages as the normal way to render any work into another language.

Because of its paraphrastic character, Targum at first sight appears to fall into the *sensus de sensu* category. A little thought, however, will lead us to reject this conclusion, for it is clear that there is in many of the Targumim an element (the base translation) which has all the hallmarks of a literal version of the original, even to the point of forcing the syntax and vocabulary of the Aramaic into unnatural agreement with the Hebrew. This element fulfills all Brock's criteria for the *uerbum e uerbo* type of translation. Seen from this angle the Targumim do not differ significantly from the other ancient versions of the Bible. But there is another component in the make-up of the Targumim—explanatory paraphrase. This is hard to parallel in other ancient translations, whether biblical or non-biblical. To be sure, a certain amount of paraphrase and "midrash" has been detected in the Septuagint,[2] but it is meagre compared to what we find in the Targumim. In terms of early translation theory the meturgeman has acted (to borrow Latin terminology) both as *interpres* and as *expositor*: he has combined in one flowing, seamless text both literal translation and explanatory glossing. This combination of *fida interpretatio* and *expositio* in one and the same document makes the Targumim typologically unique.

Targum may be *sui generis* as translation, but it was intended as translation nonetheless, and the meturgemanim went to great lengths to preserve its translational appearance. This point can be brought out by

---

[2] See D. W. Gooding, "Problems of Text and Midrash in the Third Book of Reigns", *Textus* 7 (1969), pp. 1-29; R. P. Gordon, "The Second Septuagint Account of Jeroboam: History or Midrash?", *VT* 25 (1975), pp. 368-93.

comparing Targum with a closely related genre—midrash. Targum, as has often been observed, is midrashic as to its exegetical method. What has not been sufficiently stressed is that it is not midrashic as to its literary form. If we compare the Targumim with a classic midrash, such as the Mekilta of Rabbi Ishmael, the following significant differences emerge:

(1) The Targumim never cite Rabbinic authorities by name. The interpretations which they offer can often be found attributed elsewhere in Rabbinic literature to well-known Rabbis, but Targum never acknowledges any exegetical debts. This contrasts sharply with the midrashim which make a point of naming their authorities.

(2) The midrashim often quote verses of Scripture introduced by citation-formulae such as *šenne'ĕmar*. In the Targumim Scripture may be tacitly quoted or implied, but never (or almost never) do we find explicit quotations of Scripture clearly demarcated by the use of citation-formulae.

(3) The midrashim are argumentative in style: they are at pains to set out the steps by which their conclusions have been reached. The Targumim give the conclusions and are careful to conceal the bones of the exegetical logic.

(4) The midrashim are happy to introduce variant and often conflicting interpretations, prefaced by some such formula as *dābār 'aḥēr*. It is certainly possible to find multiple interpretations of the same biblical item in the Targumim, but the meturgemanim are careful to smoothe away any conflicts and certainly never resort to formulae such as *dābār 'aḥēr* to demarcate different interpretations.

(5) The basic literary form of midrash, at least of the Mekilta of Rabbi Ishmael type, is biblical lemma + comment. Unlike Qumran *pēšer*, Rabbinic midrash makes no formal demarcation between lemma and comment. Yet confusion between these two entities is usually impossible. The Targumim, at least those belonging to our type A (see below), have an analogous structure: their base translation corresponds to the lemma, their explanatory plusses to the commentary. But there is an important difference to be noted. While in the midrashim lemma and comment are simply juxtaposed, transition from one to the other being abrupt and syntactically discontinuous, in the Targum every effort is made to smoothe the transitions between the base translation and the explanatory plusses. The meturgemanim tried very hard to fuse translation and comment together, so that without a knowledge of the Hebrew it would often be difficult to resolve the text into its two basic components.

It is clear, then, that midrash and Targum, though similar exegetical phenomena, show subtle and significant differences of presentation. These differences can best be explained from the desire of the meturgemanim to avoid introducing anything that manifestly could not have been written by the author of the original. They worked to precise, preset literary guidelines, which differed from those observed by the darshanim, and they had a clear idea of the conventions of the genre to which their work belonged.

As to their literary form, the Targumim may be divided into two broad types. Type A consists of a base translation + explanatory additions. The base translation follows the Hebrew very closely, and corresponds on the whole one-to-one with it. It represents the *uerbum e uerbo* style of translation, as I have already stated. The explanatory plusses are carefully and skilfully inserted into this base in such a way that they can normally be bracketed out, leaving behind a linguistically viable, non-expansive version of the original.

As an illustration of type A Targum we may take Gen. xviii 1-5 in Targum Pseudo-Jonathan (BL Add. 27031):

M.T.	*Targum*
1. The Lord appeared to him at the Terebinths of Mamre, while he was sitting at the door of the tent in the heat of the day.	*The Glory of the Lord appeared to him at the Plains of Mamre, while*, suffering from the pain of the circumcision, *he was sitting at the door of the tent in the strength of the day.*
2. He lifted up his eyes and looked, and behold three men were standing before him. When he saw (them) he ran from the door of the tent to meet them, and bowed down to the ground.	*He lifted up his eyes and looked, and behold three* angels in the form of *men were standing before him.* They had been sent to accomplish three things, for it is not possible for the ministering angels to be sent for more than one thing. One had come to announce that Sarah was going to bear a male child; one had come to rescue Lot; and one had come to destroy Sodom and Gomorrah. *When he saw them he ran from the door of the tent to meet them, and bowed down to the ground.*
3. He said: "O Lord, if now I have found favour in your eyes, do not depart from your servant.	*He said*: "I beseech you, by the mercies before you, *O Lord, if now I have found favour before you, let not the Glory of your Shekhinah depart from your servant,* while I receive these travellers."
4. Let now a little water be brought, and wash your feet, and recline beneath the tree.	(Then) Abraham turned and said to those men: "*Let now a little water be brought, and wash your feet, and recline beneath the tree.*
5. I will bring you a portion of bread, so that you may sustain your hearts. Afterwards you may go on your way. For it was for this reason you passed by your servant." They said: "Do according as you have spoken."	*I will bring you sustenance of bread, so that you may sustain your hearts* and give thanks to the Name of the Memra of the Lord, *and after this you may go on your way. For it was for this reason you* chanced to come along at meal-time, and *passed by your servant,* so that you might be sustained." *They said*: "You have well spoken. *Do according to your word.*"

Targum experts have always been aware of the existence of these two components in the Targumim. They are, for example, more or less clearly distinguished in R. Le Déaut's and J. W. Bowker's versions of the

Palestinian Targumim by the use of different kinds of print. The phenomenon, however, merits much more attention than it has received. The decision as to what belongs to the base and what to the plus can be a matter of fine judgement. In the passage just quoted I have assigned to the base "the Glory of the Lord" in *v.* 1, and "the Glory of your Shekhinah" in *v.* 3, even though neither of these expressions corresponds one-to-one with the Hebrew. I am obliged to do so in order to achieve a detachable non-expansive version. I doubt if anyone will object to such a move in this instance. The base translation, though literal, does not have to be ultra-literal, and the circumlocutions for God involved here are so characteristic of Targumic style that it is easy to admit them to the base translation. However, in resolving the Targumim into their two constituents, more controversial cases will arise, though it must be stated they are few in number, and for the most part detaching base from plusses is a simple task.

It is natural to assume that the base translation will represent *pᵉšāṭ* exegesis. Often it will, but it would be a mistake to suppose that it must necessarily do so. As G. Vermes demonstrated for Targum Onqelos, an apparently simple translation of the Hebrew can reflect *dᵉrāš* and may contain allusive aggadah.[3] All we can safely say to characterize the base translation is that it aims to follow the Hebrew as closely as doctrinal presuppositions will allow, and to provide one-to-one equivalents for it.

Type A Targum is normal in the Pentateuch, though it must be conceded that it is not carried through there absolutely consistently. Cases where it is not possible to isolate successfully base from plusses range from single verses (e.g. Pseudo-Jonathan to Gen. xxii 14) to chapter-length sections (e.g. Pseudo-Jonathan to Deut. xxxiv 1-12). These deviations from type may be put down to failure of technique. It is hardly surprising to find such occasional lapses, given the difficulty of what the meturgemanim were trying to do. That they maintained their technique for such long periods is something of a *tour de force*. It is also possible, at least in the case of the longer passages, that the departure from the norm is due to deliberate reworking of a Targum which was originally in pure type A form.

How is this curious phenomenon of base and detachable plusses to be explained? The most obvious suggestion (one favoured by nineteenth century scholars) would be to suppose that the Targum was originally short and more or less literal, but that, as time went by, it was augmented

---

[3] "Haggadah in the Targum Onkelos", *JSS* 8 (1963), pp. 159-69. Further, J. W. Bowker, "Haggadah in the Targum Onkelos", *JSS* 12 (1967), pp. 51-65.

by material drawn in from the midrashim. This explanation has much to commend it, and should not be dismissed out of hand, as some modern scholars seem inclined to do. It must surely account for some of the expansions in the Palestinian Targumim, especially in Pseudo-Jonathan. However, this cannot be the whole story. A case has been successfully made out for abbreviation in the Targumim: an originally expansive Targum has been shortened to bring it into closer conformity to the Hebrew text. We must beware of facile evolutionary models: the shorter and simpler—the earlier; the longer and more complex—the later.[4]

There may originally have been a liturgical reason for the carefully contrived structure of base translation plus detachable additions. The minimum Targum which the meturgeman could recite in synagogue was the base translation, but it lay in his discretion how much explanatory material to weave in from the store of traditional Bible exegesis. His decision may have been influenced by whether or not a sermon was to be included in the service. The practice of shortening the Haftarah if there was either a Targum or a sermon is attested in a number of Babylonian and Palestinian texts.[5] The point appears to have been to avoid wearying the congregation by unduly lengthening the service. Similar considerations may have dictated the length of the Targum. If there was a sermon, only the basic Targum would be delivered; if not, then the Targum could be expanded. Such shortening would also avoid any possible overlap between the content of the Targum and the content of the sermon.

Type B Targum consists of free-running paraphrase in which the original is more or less "dissolved" in the expanded translation, so that it is difficult, if not impossible, to extract a simple and grammatically viable base translation from the mass of plusses. To use a musical analogy, type B Targum is a fantasia, or, perhaps, a set of variations on the theme of Scripture.

To illustrate the type B Targum we may take Targum Lam. i 1 as printed in P. de Lagarde's edition, which represents a western recension of the text.

M.T.	*Targum*
How does the city sit alone, that was full of people! She has become	Jeremiah the prophet and high priest said: *How* is it decreed against Jerusalem and her people

[4] See the articles of Vermes and Bowker cited in n. 3. Further, A. van der Heide, *The Yemenite Tradition of the Targum of Lamentations* (Leiden, 1981), pp. 23-36; M. H. Goshen-Gottstein, "The 'Third Targum' on Esther and Ms. Neofiti 1", *Biblica* 56 (1975), pp. 301-29.

[5] See J. Mann, *The Bible as Read and Preached in the Old Synagogue* I (New York, 1940), p. 9; Mann, *Collected Articles* I (Gedera, 1971), p. 339 (= *Tarbiṣ* 1 [1930] no. 3, p. 6). The latter contains an interesting passage from *Sēper ma ʿăśîm libnê ʾereṣ yiśrāʾēl.*

as a widow, she that was great among the nations and a mistress over provinces, how has she become tributary!

that they should be condemned to banishment and that lamentation should be made for them, just as Adam and Eve were condemned to banishment from the Garden of Eden and the Lord of the World made lamentation for them? The Attribute of Justice answers and says: Because of the multitude of her sin and rebellion that is in her midst. Therefore *she sits alone*, as a man in whose flesh is the plague of leprosy sits alone. And *the city that was full of crowds* and many peoples is emptied of them *and has become like a widow*; *and she that was great among the peoples and rules over provinces*, and they offered tribute to her - *she in turn* has been brought low and *pays tribute* to them after (all) this!

It is tempting to classify type B Targum with the "rewritten Bible" texts—Pseudo-Philo's *Liber Antiquitatum Biblicarum*, the Genesis Apocryphon, and Jubilees. Certainly it is typologically close to these works, but I feel there are small but significant differences to be noted. The most important of these is that type B Targum, for all its expansiveness, remains closer to the Bible than any of these other works. The whole of the Bible is usually there somewhere in it—as well as much else. It covers every verse of the Bible, in strict order, and within each verse it will try to represent every word. This point may be illustrated from our example: note the words italicized. The "rewritten Bible" texts, however, are more selective: they skip whole sections of Scripture, they omit verses and change round the order of the biblical narrative from time to time. Even when they are following the Hebrew closely they tend to omit a word here and a phrase there, and are generally freer than the Targumim.

Type B Targum is common in the Five Megillot. One of its most remarkable representatives is Targum Sheni to Esther. A. Sperber classifies this as "Targum a misnomer for Midrash",[6] but I think he may be going too far. The influence of the genre midrash on the Targumim of all the Megillot can certainly be seen, but it should be observed that it is confined largely to two features: (a) the extreme length of the works in comparison to the original Hebrew, and (b) the occasional direct quotation of other Scriptures introduced by citation formulae (see Targum Cant. i 1). Even at their most exuberant these Targumim still usually manage to incorporate the whole of the biblical text. It is curious to observe how exhaustion seems gradually to overtake the meturgeman. This tendency is well illustrated by Targum Lam., which, having started out as wildly expansive, sobers up towards the end, becoming shorter

[6] *The Bible in Aramaic*. IV A (Leiden, 1968), Table of Contents.

and closer to the Hebrew, and increasingly offering examples of more or less straightforward translation.

II. Rabbinic Evidence on the Setting of the Targum

There are many statements scattered throughout classic Rabbinic literature as to the function and setting of the Targum. They constitute our sole external evidence on the Targum's *Sitz im Leben.*[7] These references deserve much more attention than they have received. With few exceptions modern Targum experts' knowledge of them appears to be derived from the summaries of nineteenth century scholars such as A. Berliner.[8] In assessing the Rabbinic material two major problems must be faced. First, we must bear in mind the dangers of producing an artificial synthesis out of widely scattered statements. Our sources are very diverse as to date and provenance, and we must not assume that uniform practice in the use of the Targum prevailed through space and time. Second, we must remember that Talmudic pronouncements are essentially prescriptive, not descriptive: they state what ought to happen, not necessarily what actually happened. Reconstructing historical events from legal documents is an extremely tricky business.

Unfortunately, space does not permit me to tackle these complex problems here. I must content myself with offering a synchronic digest of the Rabbinic sources, and simply leaving the problems on the record —to show I am aware of them, and to indicate the limitations of my conclusions. I really have no other option. I doubt if the text-, form-, and literary criticism of the Rabbinic corpus has gone far enough to allow us to treat the Rabbinic dicta on the Targumim in proper diachronic fashion. In the end the damage done by, in effect, ignoring the problems may not be great. The fact is that the various dicta require little harmonizing, and a remarkably consistent view as to the setting and function of the Targum emerges from all the diverse Rabbinic sources.

The Rabbinic texts envisage three distinct settings for the Targum: (1) private devotion, (2) school, and (3) synagogue. Let us consider each of these separately.

---

[7] The Targum remained in liturgical use in the Yemen down to modern times. See Van der Heide, *Yemenite Tradition*, pp. 11-14. The Yemenis were simply putting into effect the Talmudic rulings on the Targum, or, rather, Maimonides' summary of those rulings in *Yad*: Hilkot Tepillah XII 10-14.

[8] The one notable exception is A.D. York's useful study, "The Targum in the Synagogue and in the School", *JSJ* 10 (1979), pp. 74-86.

1. *Private Devotion*

Evidence for the use of the Targum in private devotion comes from a famous passage in B. Ber. 8a (end): "Rab Huna bar Judah said in the name of Rabbi Ammi: A man should always complete his *pārāšiyyôt* with the congregation—twice in the Hebrew and once in the Targum." The situation envisaged here is quite clear. A man should make sure to study beforehand in the privacy of his own home the set lection from the Torah for the coming Sabbath by reading it through twice in the original Hebrew and once in the Targum. The double reading of the original neatly highlights the greater importance of the Hebrew over the Targum. The Targum does not exist in and of itself, but only as an aid to the understanding of the Hebrew. This use of the Targum, I understand, has continued among observant Jews down to modern times, though some Rabbinic authorities now consider it acceptable to replace the Targum with some other exegetical work such as the J. H. Hertz *Ḥumaš* (cf. Šulḥan ᶜAruk, *'Oraḥ Ḥayyim* 285).

2. *School*

Scripture was the basis of Jewish elementary education, and there is evidence to suggest that the Hebrew Bible was studied in the Bet ha-Sefer in conjunction with a Targum. Targum is mentioned immediately after *miqrā'* in accounts of the Jewish educational curriculum: "Rabbi Aqiba went to the schoolhouse and began to read from a student's tablet, he and his son. He studied Scripture, Targum, Midrash, Halakhah and Aggadah, (arcane) speech and parables; he studied everything" (Abot deRabbi Natan, Recension B XII, ed. S. Schechter p. 29).[9] It is interesting to note that in a story recorded in Y. Meg. 74d we find a schoolmaster in possession of a written copy of the Targum. It is possible that in the smaller communities the schoolmaster would have been the custodian of the Targum and would normally have acted as meturgeman in synagogue. The *uerbum e uerbo* character of the type A Targum would make it particularly useful for teaching purposes. Brock well observes: "In very general terms the *sensus de sensu* approach can be seen as bringing the original to the reader, whereas in the *verbum e verbo* translation the original acts, as it were, as Aristotle's unmoved mover, and the psychological effect is to bring the reader to the original."[10] The Targum could have formed a bridge by which the pupil crossed from his ver-

[9] I quote here A. Saldarini's translation, *The Fathers According to Rabbi Nathan* (Leiden, 1975), pp. 95-6. See his notes ad loc.
[10] (n. 1), p. 73.

nacular (Aramaic) to a knowledge of the sacred tongue (Hebrew). Here may be the key to the problem of how Jews in Talmudic times acquired a knowledge of Hebrew without grammars and dictionaries. Similar "cribs" were in use in Greek schools to assist students in the acquisition of Latin. Note especially the bilingual editions of Vergil in which the Latin is rendered into Greek with slavish literalness, line by line and word by word.[11]

3. *Synagogue*

The primary setting for the Targum was the synagogue, where it was used to render the biblical lections into Aramaic. The vast majority of Rabbinic pronouncements on the Targum relate to its liturgical role. The following points will serve to summarize this Rabbinic evidence.

(1) The Targum was not an obligatory element in the service, but if it was included it had to be recited according to strict rules (Y. Meg. 74d; cf. B. Meg. 23a-b and Y. Meg. 75a). It is not clear under what circumstances it could be omitted, but one may speculate that in a congregation learned enough to follow the original and versed in traditional exegesis it would have been optional. Though not obligatory, it was presumably normal to recite the Targum. Since it was taught in the Bet ha-Sefer, and since even a minor was allowed to translate in synagogue (see below), it would have been a very impoverished congregation that could not have enjoyed the benefit of an Aramaic paraphrase of the lesson.

(2) The Targum belongs to *tôrāh šebb*^{e}*ʿal peh* (Pesiqta Rabbati V, ed. Friedmann p. 14a-b; Tanḥuma Buber II 87-8 = *Wayyera'* 6), and the manner of its recitation in synagogue expresses liturgically the Rabbinic view of the relationship between Oral and Written Torah. (a) The Scripture reader could not at the same time act as translator; two different people had to perform the two different functions (Y. Meg. 74d; cf. the rulings in T. Meg. IV (III) 20, Y. Ber. 9c, B. Meg. 21b, where this idea is implicit). (b) The Scripture-reader must *read* from the written text: he must not recite it orally. He must not raise his eyes from the written text and recite even a few verses of it from memory, no matter how well he thinks he knows it. Conversely, the meturgeman must not, under any circumstances, read the Targum in public from a written text (Y. Meg. 74d; Pesiqta Rabbati V, ed. M. Friedmann p. 14a-b; Tanḥuma S. Buber II 87-8 = *Wayyera'* 6). (c) The Scripture-reader was not allowed to prompt

[11] The texts may be found conveniently in R. Cavenaile, *Corpus Papyrorum Latinarum* (Wiesbaden, 1958).

the translator, nor was the translator allowed to glance at the biblical text —"lest the people should say that the translation is written in the Torah" (B. Meg. 32a; Pesiqta Rabbati V, ed. Friedmann p. 14a-b; Tanḥuma Buber II 87-8 = *Wayyera'* 6). (d) The reading and translation were not simultaneous: the reader had to complete the verse of Scripture before the translator began and vice versa. On the other hand there were to be no long pauses between reading and translation (B. Soṭ. 39b; M. Meg. IV 4; cf. B. Soṭ. 41a). (e) The Targum was recited after Scripture, and a difference in practice was observed in the case of the Torah and the Haftarah. In the case of Torah, one verse of Scripture was followed immediately by one of Targum; in the case of the Haftarah, it was three verses of Scripture against three of Targum. However, if those three verses constituted three separate sections, then they were to be read and translated singly (M. Meg. IV 4; cf. B. Soṭ. 41a). Behind these cleverly contrived rules are two clear, if rather contrary, aims: the first is to thrust Targum and Scripture apart, to demarcate rigorously between them and preserve their independence; the second is to bring them as closely as possible together, so that Targum can illuminate Scripture and form a means of passing over to it. Again and again we are brought back to this basic fact: it was not envisaged that Targum should be studied as an end in itself, but that Scripture should be studied with the aid of the Targum.

(3) The translator was known as the *m^e^turg^e^mān* or *turg^e^mān*, or simply as "he who translates" (*hamm^e^targēm*). It is important to realise that there are two quite separate offices in Rabbinic texts covered by the term *m^e^turg^e^mān*. First, there was the meturgeman who acted as the spokesman of a scholar. This person was also called an amora. When a sage lectured to his students it was customary for him not to address them directly but through a meturgeman. He whispered his words to the meturgeman who then proclaimed them aloud to the audience. The meturgeman did not necessarily repeat the sage's words verbatim, but elaborated on them, and so had to be something of a scholar in his own right (B. Soṭ. 40a; B. Ber. 27b; B. MQ 21a). This curious practice was probably influenced by the Biblical picture of the relationship between Moses and Aaron: the sage took the place of Moses, his amora-meturgeman that of Aaron (cf. Exod. R. VIII 3). Second, there was the meturgeman who rendered the Biblical lesson into Aramaic in synagogue. This sort of meturgeman was quite different from the other. Unlike the sage and his amora, one of whom whispered and the other spoke out loud, the Bible-reader and translator were enjoined to adopt the same tone and volume of voice: there could be no question of whispering Scripture (B. Ber. 45a). And in contradistinction to the amora-meturgeman, no particular skill or erudition would have been required of the Bible-translator, only knowledge of

the Targum. That this was so may be deduced from the fact that even a minor was allowed to recite Targum liturgically (M. Meg. IV 6; cf. T. Meg. IV(III) 21). The minor's knowledge of the Targum comes as no surprise in view of the evidence that the Targum was taught in the Bet ha-Sefer. However, a minor may have been called upon to act as meturgeman only in exceptional circumstances, and, as I suggested earlier, the role was probably normally taken by the schoolmaster.

(4) It is not clear whether the Targum was passed on orally or in written form. As we have seen the use of a written Targum in synagogue was strictly forbidden. There is evidence to suggest that some authorities tried to extend this prohibition to cover the use of written texts even in private study and teaching (B. Shabb. 115a; T. Shabb. XIII(XIV) 2-3; Y. Shabb. 15c; Soferim V 15). The theory was that Targum as *tôrāh šebbeᶜal peh* should be learned orally and transmitted orally: "Those who write down *hălākôt* are like those who burn the Torah, and he who learns from written texts receives no reward" (B. Tem. 14b). But this represents something of an ideal. There evidently were copies of Targum in circulation, just as there were written collections of aggadah and halakah (B. Yeb. 22a; B. Tem. 14a). The existence of Targum texts is clearly implied by a number of Rabbinic stories and rulings.

(5) The meturgeman was not free to translate just as he pleased. It is a fair guess that the translation was always to a large degree predetermined and traditional. To describe Targum as "a spontaneous phenomenon of Jewish exegesis" is rather misleading.[12] Besides the force of tradition, there was the pressure exerted by the religious authorities to regulate the content of the Targum. This took a variety of forms. There was general advice on how to translate, as in the famous, but alas, unclear dictum of Judah bar Ilai: "He who translates a verse according to its form is a liar, and he who adds (to it) is a blasphemer" (T. Meg. IV 41).[13] There was also criticism of certain specific translations (cf. M. Meg. IV 9, where a Targum of Lev. xviii 21, still found in Pseudo-Jonathan, is condemned). In addition the religious authorities issued lists of passages which could, or could not, be rendered into Aramaic in synagogue (M. Meg. IV(III) 31-38; B. Meg. 25a-b). As I have demonstrated elsewhere,[14] form-critical analysis of these lists shows that they have undergone revision and modification over a considerable period of time. They represent a signifi-

---

[12] I allude to the title of R. Le Déaut's article, "Un phénomène spontané de l'herméneutique juive ancienne: le 'targumisme'", *Biblica* 52 (1971), pp. 505-25.

[13] For a summary of Rashi's and Rabbenu Ḥanan'el's attempts to explain this dictum see S. Lieberman, *Tosefta Ki-Fshuṭah*, Part V (New York, 1962), p. 1223.

[14] "The Rabbinic Lists of Forbidden Targumim", *JJS* 27 (1976), pp. 171-91.

cant attempt by the Rabbinic authorities, going back to early Tannaitic times, to control the content of the Targum. The supervision of the Targum was undertaken by leading Rabbis. Thus T. Meg. IV(III) 35 records an incident in which, while acting as Scripture-reader, Rabbi Ḥananiah b. Gamliel instructed the meturgeman not to translate one of the forbidden passages. Again in T. Meg. IV(III) 34 (cf. B. Meg. 25b) a case is cited in which Rabbi Eliezer publicly rebuked someone for "reading" (*editio princeps*: "reading and translating") another of the forbidden passages (Ezek. xvi 1ff.) as a Haftarah. Normally, however, censure appears to have been in the hands of the congregation. The religious leaders relied on educating the people at large in their ideas and securing their co-operation in putting them into effect. In most congregations not only the acting meturgeman would have known the Targum, but at least some of the adult males as well. Members of the congregation were encouraged instantly and publicly to silence or rebuke an erring meturgeman (M. Meg. IV 9-10).

III. The Sitz im Leben of the Targumim

I have surveyed the two main lines of evidence as to the *Sitz im Leben* of the Targum. It is now time briefly to draw some conclusions. First, however, a very important caveat. It would be wrong for us simply to assume that the extant Targumim are simple and direct transcripts of the oral Targum delivered in the old synagogue. As Goshen-Gottstein has rightly insisted, the *Gestalt* of the old synagogue Targum remains intensely problematic, despite the discovery of Codex Neofiti 1.[15] This point was well-enough understood by nineteenth century scholars, but I feel the present generation of Targum experts tends to ignore it. The fact is that the Targum had a purely literary life of its own in the Middle Ages, and all our extant Targumim have gone through a literary phase of development, divorced from their original setting. They were valued by the mediaeval exegetes as midrashic sources, and copied (and doubtless augmented and changed) long after their synagogue use had come to an end. We do not know when the Targum fell into liturgical desuetude, nor when the Targumim were first committed to writing, nor what effect transition from oral, or predominantly oral, to written transmission would have had on their form and content. However, it would be hypersceptical to deny that our extant Targumim are in some way descended from works of the Talmudic era. This is unquestionably true of Onqelos and Jonathan, but, I believe, holds good for the Palestinian Targumim as

[15] Goshen-Gottstein (n. 4), p. 313.

well. Certain peculiarities of the Targumim (particularly of type A) make good sense in the light of the Rabbinic pronouncements on the setting and function of the Targum. This convergence of internal and external evidence must surely go some way towards reassuring us that our extant texts give us access to the old synagogue Targum.

So then, the *Sitz im Leben* of the extant Targumim may be defined as follows:

(1) In origin they are liturgical versions intended to be read side by side with Scripture: they were not meant in any sense to replace Scripture. "Targumizing" was an activity which took place in the presence of Scripture, and which set up a continuous dialectic between the translation and the original Hebrew. The Targumim were not meant to be read on their own, to be regarded as self-referent entities.

(2) The Targumim were recited publicly before the assembled congregation. This public use may be reflected *inter alia* in the way in which they tend to modify indelicate expressions which might prove offensive or embarrassing to the congregation.

(3) The Targumim were addressed primarily not to scholars, but to the mass of the unlearned. This may account for their emphasis on aggadah, often of a folkloristic character. It is also possible that their extremely reverential tone and elaborate anti-anthropomorphism reflect their liturgical setting, and spring from a desire to avoid expressions that could be misunderstood by the uninstructed. The frequent and often startling anthropomorphisms of the Talmud stand in striking contrast. However, though Targum was intended for popular consumption, it would be a grave error to suppose that the meturgemanim responsible for these versions were unlearned or uneducated people. It required scholarship and skill to produce a Targum.

(4) The Targumim were meant both to give a full and more or less one-to-one rendering of Scripture, while at the same time to interpret Scripture in such a way as to make it accessible to the people.

(5) Despite efforts to do so, the Rabbis never brought the Targumim fully under their control. They succeeded best in the case of Onqelos and Jonathan. The Palestinian Targumim, however, were a different matter. As has often been observed, it is possible to find in these texts old material which has not been "revised" into line with current Rabbinic doctrine.[16] The home of the Targum was the Bet ha-Keneset. In a very real sense it represents popular religion, and brings us close to the themes and interests of popular preaching.

---

[16] See J. Heinemann, "Early Halakhah in the Palestinian Targumim", *JJS* 25 (1974), pp. 114-22.

Taken as a whole these features define for the Targumim a unique position on the spectrum of early Jewish literature and thought. Their nearest neighbours would be the great daily prayers of the *Siddur*. The integrity of the Targumim must be respected, their ideas analysed and expounded in their own right. They must not be treated as pale reflections of the great Yeshivah texts, such as the Babli and the Yerušalmi, nor even of the sophisticated, highly academic midrashim of Bet ha-Midrash origin.[17]

[17] For the form-critical significance of the distinction between Bet ha-Keneset and Bet ha-Midrash see J. Heinemann, *Prayer in the Talmud* (Berlin, 1977), pp. 251-2.

ZUR DEUTERONOMISTISCHEN KONZEPTION VON FREIHEIT UND FRIEDEN

VON

GEORG BRAULIK

Wien

Über Freiheit und Frieden zu sprechen dürfte heute ebenso aktuell wie schwierig sein. In meinem Referat führt der "lange Marsch" dazu über den Aufweis eines Aussagensystems. Es findet sich innerhalb des Alten Testaments nur im Deuteronomistischen Geschichtswerk (= DtrGW), auf das ich mich im folgenden beschränke, ferner in dem davon abhängigen Chronistischen Geschichtswerk. Seine Schlüsselwörter lauten erstens *nwḥ*-hi. I "Ruhe verschaffen", dessen Subjekt immer Jahwe und dessen indirektes Objekt entweder Israel oder sein König sind; zweitens *m^enûḥâ* "die Ruhe", die von Jahwe gegeben wird. Meine Ausführungen möchten auch einen Beitrag liefern zu den neueren Diskussionen, denen es im Gefolge von F. M. Cross[1] oder R. Smend[2] um die verschiedenen Redaktionsschichten des DtrGW geht. Ich knüpfe besonders an jene Untersuchungen an, die nicht mehr mit M. Noth Dtn. v-xxx als einen dem/den Deuteronomisten bereits vorgegebenen Block ansehen, sondern wie zuletzt N. Lohfink[3] auch innerhalb dieser Kapitel Spuren mehrerer deuteronomistischer (= dtr) Redaktionen entdeckt haben. Aus methodologischer Vorsicht spreche ich zunächst nur von einem Aussagensystem, präjudiziere damit also keine Schichtenbestimmung der einzelnen Stellen.

Die Bedeutung des "Ruhe"-Themas ist von der Forschung erkannt worden, seit G. v. Rad im Jahr 1933 seinen bahnbrechenden Artikel "Es ist noch eine Ruhe vorhanden dem Volke Gottes"[4] geschrieben hat. Seither sind ihm begriffs-, motiv- und traditionsgeschichtliche Beiträge und

---

[1] "The Themes of the Book of Kings and the Structure of the Deuteronomistic History", in *Canaanite Myth and Hebrew Epic. Essays in the History of the Religion of Israel*, (Cambridge, Mass., ⁴1980), pp. 274-89; R. D. Nelson, *The Double Redaction of the Deuteronomistic History* (Sheffield, 1981).

[2] *Die Entstehung des Alten Testaments* (Stuttgart, ²1981), pp. 111-25.

[3] "Kerygmata des Deuteronomistischen Geschichtswerks", in J. Jeremias/L. Perlitt (Hrsg.), *Die Botschaft und die Boten. Festschrift H. W. Wolff* (Neukirchen-Vluyn, 1981), pp. 87-100.

[4] "Es ist noch eine Ruhe vorhanden dem Volke Gottes (Eine biblische Begriffsuntersuchung)", *Zwischen den Zeiten* 11 (1933), pp. 104-11 (= *Gesammelte Studien zum Alten Testament* [München, ³1965], pp. 101-8).

eine redaktionskritische Studie verschiedener Autoren gefolgt.[5] Keiner von ihnen hat jedoch das Funktionieren jenes Aussagensystems wirklich in den Griff bekommen. Somit erscheint eine neuerliche Analyse angebracht zu sein.

1. Den Ansatzpunkt bildet Dtn. xii 9-10. Die Verse stehen innerhalb der Kultzentralisationsgesetze zu Beginn des dtn Kodex. Sie umreißen die geschichtlichen Voraussetzungen für das Inkrafttreten der Opferbestimmungen, die zur Zeit der mosaischen Gesetzespromulgation noch nicht gelten können.

Denn bis jetzt seid ihr noch nicht zu der Ruhe und dem Erbbesitz gekommen,
die Jahwe, dein Gott, dir gibt.
Wenn ihr aber den Jordan überschritten
und euch in dem Land angesiedelt habt,
das Jahwe, euer Gott, an euch als Erbbesitz verteilt,
und (wenn) er euch Ruhe verschafft hat vor allen euren Feinden ringsum,
sodaß ihr sicher wohnt (V.9-10),

dann soll Israel — so setzen die V.11-12 fort — seine Opfer zu der erwählten Stätte bringen und sich dort vor seinem Gott freuen.

V.9 nennt "die Ruhe" (*hammᵉnûḥâ*) und "den Erbbesitz" (*hannaḥᵃlâ*) als Konstitutiva der Existenz Israels. Die beiden Heilsgaben Gottes dürfen nicht miteinander identifiziert werden. Denn *bwʾ ʾel hammᵉnûḥâ* "zu der Ruhe kommen" meint vom Kontext her den Zug zum Jerusalemer Tempel. In xii 4-28, also den Gesetzen über das einzige legitime Heiligtum, ist *bwʾ*-q. immer auf *ʾel-hammāqôm* "die(se) Stätte" bezogen (V.5,26) und verweist *bwʾ*-hi. durch die Verbindung mit *šāmmâ* "dorthin" zurück (V.6,11; vgl. V.5). Der einzige weitere Beleg für "die Ruhe, die Jahwe gibt", findet sich in 1 Kön. viii 56 im Zusammenhang der Tempelweihe Salomos. Er wird dieses Verständnis von der *mᵉnûḥâ* als dem Jerusalemer Zentralheiligtum noch bestätigen.

Es besteht freilich auch ein philologisch und theologisch wichtiger Unterschied zwischen *ntn* mit dem abstrakten Substantiv *mᵉnûḥâ* als Objekt

[5] J. Frankowski, "Requies, Bonum Promissum populi Dei in VT et in Judaismo (Hebr 3,7-4,11)", *VD* 43 (1965), pp. 124-49, 225-40; G. Braulik, "Menucha — Die Ruhe Gottes und des Volkes im Lande", *BiKi* 23 (1968), 75-8; A. R. Hulst, "De Betekenis van het Woord *mᵉnūḥa*, in *Schrift en uitleg. Festschrift W. H. Gispen* (Kampen, 1970), pp. 62-78; W. C. Kaiser, "The Promise Theme and the Theology of Rest", *Bibliotheca Sacra* 130/518 (1973), pp. 135-50; W. Schulz, *Stilkritische Untersuchungen zur deuteronomistischen Literatur* (Diss. Tübingen, 1974, Mschr.), pp. 111-62; W. Roth, "The Deuteronomic Rest Theology: A Redaction-Critical Study", in *Papers of the Chicago Society of Biblical Research* 21 (Chicago, 1976), pp. 5-14; F. Stolz, "*nūᵃḥ* ruhen", in *THAT* II, Sp. 43-6.

einerseits und dem stammverwandten Verb *nwḥ* im hi. andererseits.[6] So sind Gott, der Geber, und die *m^enûḥâ* eng aufeinander bezogen, während Israel als ihr Empfänger ziemlich passiv bleibt. Wenn aber Jahwe seinem Volk Ruhe verschafft, dann ist es in *nwḥ*-hi. miteinbezogen, wird gleichsam zum Untersubjekt der Handlung. Diese zweite Formulierung begegnet nun in Dtn. xii 10.

Der Vers bildet die historisierende Einleitung zum anschließenden Opfergesetz. Seine fünf Verbalsätze sind alle als w=qatal-x gestaltet. Diese syntaktische Formation bezeichnet vor allem einen fortschreitenden Progreß. So ergibt sich ein linearer Geschichtsablauf: Jordanüberschreitung, erste Ansiedlung, jetzt erst "Zur-Ruhe-gebracht-werden", und als Konsequenz ein sicheres Wohnen. Diese Geschehensfolge ist jedoch nicht die einzige Möglichkeit, die Satzreihe zu verstehen. w=qatal-x kann nämlich auch bei resümierender Wiederaufnahme zukünftiger Sachverhalte stehen. Die Wiederholung von *yšb* legt sogar eine Art Parallelismus zwischen V.10a und 10b nahe, wobei das zweite Glied die Aussage des ersten wiederholen, aber auch steigern würde (*yšb beṭaḥ*). Also: Ihr werdet den Jordan überschreiten und euch ansiedeln, ja, der Herr wird euch Ruhe verschaffen und ihr werdet euch in Sicherheit ansiedeln. In diesem Fall liegt somit die mit *nwḥ*-hi. bezeichnete Handlung nicht nach, sondern *vor* der Ansiedlung. Eine Entscheidung zwischen diesen Alternativen der Syntax läßt sich nur von den anderen Belegen von *nwḥ*-hi. her treffen. Die Ambivalenz könnte allerdings, wie sich zeigen wird, intendiert sein.

2. Dtn. xii 9-10 hat programmatische Funktion. Das beweisen die folgenden drei Texte: xxv 19 bezieht sich terminologisch auf beide Verse zurück; Jos. xxi 43-45 und 1 Kön. viii 56 stellen den Zusammenhang zu Dtn. xii 10 bzw. V.9 durch eigene Rückverweise her.

Nur im Amalekitergesetz, dem "politischen Testament" des Mose am Ende des dtn "Zivilrechts", wird in Dtn. xxv 19 wie in xii 9-10 *nwḥ*-hi. mit *naḥ^alâ* bzw. *nḥl*-hi. verknüpft. Das Ruhemotiv fungiert dadurch als Rahmenelement des dtn Gesetzeskorpus, seiner Kult- und Sozialordnung.

Eroberung und Verteilung des Verheißungslandes werden in Jos. xxi 43-45 durch ein Geschichtssummarium samt Erfüllungsnotiz abgerundet. *nwḥ*-hi. bildet in den V.43-44a den letzten von vier, mit wayyiqtol formulierten Sätzen. Die Inbesitznahme des Landes und die Ansiedlung sind also vorausgegangen, ehe Israel zur Ruhe gebracht wird. Damit hat sich Jahwes Schwur an die "Väter", das heißt die Mosegeneration, er-

---

[6] C. J. Labuschagne, "*ntn* geben", in *THAT* II, Sp. 117-41, besonders 128-9.

füllt. Zwar bezieht sich der Gotteseid in Dtn. i 8,39 ausdrücklich bloß auf die Übereignung des Landes. Nach Jos. xxi 43-44 aber vollendet sich die Landgabe erst in der Ruhe, die Jahwe gewährt. Deshalb interpretiert dieser Text mit einer im Alten Testament singulären Aussage Jahwes Ruheschaffen als Verwirklichung seines Vätereides. Darüber hinaus ist aber jetzt auch vollbracht, was Dtn. xii 10 angekündigt hat. Jos. xxi 43-44a deutet den Rückbezug darauf zunächst durch die Verbindung von *yšb* mit *nwḥ*-hi. an, die sich sonst nur noch in Dtn. xii 10 findet. Allerdings folgt dann bloß *missābîb*. Trotzdem fehlt auch der zweite Präpositionalausdruck *mikkol-ʾōyebîm* nicht, der aus Dtn. xii 10 erwartet wird. Jos. xxi 44b trägt ihn sogar mit zwei Sätzen nach: Keiner von all den Feinden konnte Widerstand leisten, alle Feinde hat der Herr in die Gewalt Israels gegeben. Diese beiden Feststellungen im (w=)x-qatal brechen die vorausgehende Reihe von Progressen ab und schildern den Hintergrund der Landnahme und des Ruheverschaffens. Die Wendung *ntn yhwh*, von der die V.43-44 gerahmt werden, deutet die ganze Geschichte Israels als vom Wirken Gottes umgriffene Gnadengabe, wie auch die gottgegebene *menûḥâ* eine bildet. Schließlich verweist auch V.45 auf den Zukunftsentwurf von Dtn. xii 10 zurück. Voll Pathos proklamiert der Vers das Eintreffen des "ganzen guten Wortes", das Jahwe zu Israel gesprochen hat.

Diese Erfüllungsnotiz findet sich auch 1 Kön. viii 56. Hier wird sie jedoch nicht von *nwḥ*-hi., sondern von *menûḥâ* ausgesagt. Führt Dtn. xii 9 sie im Rahmen der Opfergesetzgebung als noch fehlende Voraussetzung für die Beobachtung dieser Gesetze an, so preist Salomo sie am Ende der Tempelweihliturgie in 1 Kön. viii 56 als nun von Jahwe gegeben. Mit der *menûḥâ* ist der eigentliche Höhepunkt der Verheißungsgeschichte Israels erreicht. So wird hier die Erfüllung der Ruhezusage Jahwe als Doxologie zugesprochen. Sie enthält zwei Rückverweise. Der erste in V.56a nennt keinen Adressaten oder Mittler der Verheißung. Wäre eine durch Mose ergangene Zusage gemeint, würde damit nur der zweite Rückverweis unpräzis vorweggenommen. Mit dem Jahwewort in V.56a ist daher höchstwahrscheinlich die Natanprophetie anvisiert, konkret 2 Sam. vii 13a. Um diese Ankündigung in die Tat umzusetzen, hat nämlich Gott in 1 Kön. v 18-19 dem Salomo Ruhe vor allen seinen Gegnern verschafft. Ähnliches hatte nach 2 Sam. vii 1 und 11 sogar schon für David gegolten. Ich werde auf diese Stellen später noch kurz zurückkommen. Jedenfalls wird so verständlich, warum der erste Rückverweis in 1 Kön. viii 56a keinen Namen nennt: Der unmittelbare Empfänger der Verheißung war David, letzlich zugesprochen aber wurde sie Salomo. *menûḥâ* bezeichnet also den salomonischen Tempel. V.56a klammert dann die (Anspielung auf die) Natanweissagung über das Jerusalemer Heiligtum an den mosaischen Ursprung zurück. Gemeint ist Dtn. xii 9, der einzige Beleg für *m^e^nûḥâ* im Mund des Mose. Was Mose dort implizit als Gabe zusagt, wird nun in 1 Kön. viii 56 als Erfüllung eines von Mose vermittelten Jahwewortes expliziert. In ähnlicher Weise hat ja auch Jos. xxi 45 die Voraussage des Mose in Dtn. xii 10 reinterpretiert. Beide Erfüllungstexte profilieren Israels Geschichte somit theo-logisch. Im übrigen erscheint in 1 Kön. viii 56 die *m^e^nûḥâ*, für die Jahwe gepriesen wird, als Medium des Segens, den Salomo nach V.55 über die ganze Versammlung Israels spricht. Es macht eine Erhörung der Bitten der V.57-58 und die Paränese von V.61 möglich. Die Funktion des Tempels als "der Ruhe" wird zwar nicht weiter konkretisiert. Aber durch ihn wird Jahwe mit Israel wie mit seinem König sein und die Herzen zu sich hinlenken. Dann können sie "seine Gebote, seine Gesetze und Rechtsvorschriften", das heißt die Bundesverpflichtungen des Dtn., beobachten (vgl. 1 Kön. viii 58b mit Dtn. xxvi 17).

Das *nwḥ*-hi./*m^e^nûḥâ*-System periodisiert in Jos. xxi 43-45 und 1 Kön. viii 56 die Geschichte Israels. Die Ruhe, die Jahwe verschafft bzw. die er gibt, begrenzt die Epoche der Landnahme unter Josua und die davidisch-salomonische Ära des Tempelbaues. Das "ganze gute Wort, von dem nichts hinfällig geworden ist", aber faßt das gesamte, zwischen Verheißung und Erfüllung ausgespannte historische Geschehen zur Einheit einer Heilsgeschichte zusammen. Mit der *m^e^nûḥâ* ist das Zentralheiligtum gegeben, die Forderung der Kultzentralisation tritt nach Dtn. xii jetzt in Kraft. Die Kön.-Bücher können nun ihr kultisches Hauptthema entwickeln. Von *nwḥ*-hi. und *m^e^nûḥâ* wird nach der Einweihung des Tempels freilich im DrtGW nicht mehr gesprochen. Denn alle weitere Geschichte könnte und müßte ja ein Leben gehorsamer Treue zu Jahwe aus diesem Heilszustand heraus sein. 1 Chr. xxii 9 wird ihn später im Zusammenhang mit *m^e^nûḥâ* und *nwḥ*-hi. ausdrücklich als *šālôm*, hier "Friede" im umfassenden Sinn, charakterisieren.

3. Neben dem eben beschriebenen strengen Bezugssystem gibt es freilich im DtrGW noch andere Texte, die an Dtn. xii 9-10 zurückgebunden sind. Wenn Gott in ihnen Königen Ruhe verschafft, dann wegen der *m^e^nûḥâ* von V.9. Wird ohne *nwḥ*-hi. formuliert, dann knüpfen die Stellen zumeist an die Präpositionalausdrücke *mikkol-ʾōy^e^bîm* und/oder *missābîb* bzw. an die Wendung *yšb beṭaḥ* an, die in V.10 dem Ruheverschaffen folgen. So ergibt sich im Ablauf der Geschichte Israels eine Reihe gezielter Anspielungen auf Dtn. xii 9-10 als den Programmtext einer Ruhetheologie. Keinerlei Zusammenhang besteht jedoch mit der Vorstellung eines öfteren "Ruhens", die *šqṭ* ausdrückt. Sie wird erst im Chronistischen Geschichtswerk mit *nwḥ*-hi. verknüpft werden.

Jahwe hat Israel unter Josua Ruhe vor allen Feinden ringsum verschafft. Diese Aktion wird später nie mehr wiederholt, ist also offenbar nicht völlig rückgängig gemacht worden. Wenn Gott wiederum Ruhe verschafft, dann nicht mehr dem Volk, sondern seinen Königen, konkret David und Salomo. Freilich kann Israel auch nach seiner Ansiedlung in Feindesnot geraten. Doch hängt das, wie Josua in seiner "Abschiedsrede" am Ende des vorrichterlichen Zeitalters verdeutlicht, einzig von Israels Gottesverhältnis ab (Jos. xxiii). Tatsächlich fällt Israel dann in der Richterperiode immer wieder von Jahwe ab. Dadurch verkehren sich seine früheren Erfolge gegenüber den Feinden ins Gegenteil. Der "Leitartikel" für die Richterzeit Ri. ii 14 wendet die Feindaussagen von Jos. xxi 44 wörtlich gegen Israel an. Nur die von Jahwe eingesetzten Richter konnten es aus Feindesgewalt befreien (vgl. Ri. ii 18). So stellt Samuel am Höhepunkt des historischen Rückblicks seiner "Abschiedsrede" in 1. Sam. xii 11 fest: Von Gott bevollmächtigte Männer, allen voran Jerubbaal/Gideon (s. auch Ri. viii 34), retteten die Israeliten "aus der Gewalt ihrer Feinde ringsum (*miyyad ᵓōyᵉbîm missābîb*), sodaß sie sicher wohnen konnten (*yšb beṭaḥ*)." Keines dieser zwei Geschichtssummarien am Anfang (Ri. ii) und am Ende (1 Sam. xii) der Richterepoche spricht freilich von *nwḥ*-hi. Nur Neh. ix 28 wird die zeitlich begrenzte Befreiung Israels aus jener Feindbedrängnis mit diesem Verb interpretieren. Im DtrGW aber ist davon erst wieder 2 Sam. vii 1 die Rede, also genau dann, wenn David in seinem Palast zu residieren beginnt und einen Tempelbau plant. Gerade durch diese Ruhe "ringsum vor allen Feinden", und zwar nun des Königs, unterscheidet sich nach V.11 die Ära Davids von der Richterzeit. Beide Belege von *nwḥ*-hi. aber sind eigentlich auf die Zusage eines "Hauses für Jahwes Namen" in V.13a und damit auf die *mᵉnûḥâ* in 1 Kön. viii 56 ausgerichtet. Das macht endgültig 1 Kön. v 17-19 klar: Salomo möchte die Natanprophetie verwirklichen, nachdem Jahwe ihm ringsum Ruhe verschafft hat. V.18 gebraucht in diesem Zusammenhang freilich andere Feindtermini als alle übrigen Stellen bisher. Geht es dabei doch nicht mehr um nationale Feinde, sondern um außen- wie innerpolitische Widersacher des Königs. Israel kann jetzt nicht nur wie zur Richterzeit sicher wohnen (1 Sam. xii 11), sondern dieses Leben auch in Prosperität genießen. Denn nach 1 Kön. v 4b-5 hatte Salomo "Frieden (*šālôm*) von allen Seiten ringsum (*mikkol- … missābîb*); Juda und Israel aber wohnten in Sicherheit (*yšb lābeṭaḥ*), jeder saß unter seinem Weinstock und seinem Feigenbaum". Friedensherrschaft und nationaler Wohlstand werden durch den Tempelbau gekrönt. Zwar bildet er nirgends syntaktisch die Konsequenz von *nwḥ*-hi. Dennoch tendiert das Verb bei David und Salomo — anders als bei Israel — letztlich auf die *mᵉnûḥâ* von 1 Kön. viii 56, in der sich Dtn. xii 9 erfüllt.

4. Ein zweites Textsystem (nur) mit *nwḥ*-hi. bilden Dtn. iii 20; Jos. i 13,15; xxii 4. Die vier Stellen sind Teile von Reden, mit denen sich Mose oder Josua an die zweieinhalb im Ostjordanland ansässigen Stämme wenden. In ihnen geht *nwḥ*-hi. stets der Inbesitznahme (*yrš* q.) des Landes, das Jahwe gibt (*ntn*), voraus. Dtn. iii 20 und Jos. i 15 zeigen offenkundig diese Abfolge. In xxii 4 wird verkürzt gesprochen. Die Rückverweise auf die anderen Texte lassen jedoch erkennen, daß hier ebenso gedacht wird. Diesen drei Stellen zufolge gewährt Jahwe den westjordanischen Stämmen zunächst Ruhe und verleiht ihnen dann das Land, das sie in Besitz nehmen. Schwieriger ist der Halbvers i 13b gebaut, der die Ostjordanier betrifft. Er enthält zwei Sätze. Der erste verwendet *nwḥ*-hi. im Partizip, das im deuteronomistischen sprachlichen Kontext zumeist die unmittelbar bevorstehende Zukunft bezeichnet. Der zweite Satz schließt Jahwes Landgabe im w=qatal-x an, was am einfachsten als Zukunftsaussage mit Progreß gegenüber der vorausgehenden Handlung erklärt wird. Das heißt aber: Nach dem in Jos. i 13b zitierten Mosewort wird Jahwe auch den Ostjordaniern zuerst Ruhe verschaffen und ihnen dann das Land geben. Für Dtn. iii 20 (s. V.18) und Jos. i 15 liegt dieses Geschehen, das i 13b referiert, bereits in der Vergangenheit.[7] Sie können deshalb die Zukunft der Westjordanier mit der Vergangenheit der Ostjordanier vergleichen: Jahwe wird an den westjordanischen Brüdern handeln, wie er an den ostjordanischen Stämmen bereits gehandelt hat.

Wenn *nwḥ*-hi. vor *yrš* q. und *ntn hāʾāreṣ* gereiht wird, was ist dann mit "Ruhe verschaffen" gemeint? Es muß hier entweder heißen "der Wanderexistenz ein Ende bereiten" oder "die Bedrohung durch Feinde beseitigen". Im zweiten Fall wären damit die Könige anvisiert, deren Besiegung sowohl im Ost- wie im Westjordanland der Inbesitznahme des Landes durch Israel vorausging, wovon in Dtn. ii-iii bzw. Jos. ii-xii berichtet wird. Jedenfalls ist ein sachlicher Unterschied zu dem Gebrauch von *nwḥ*-hi. in Dtn. xii 10 und Jos. xxi 44 vorhanden. Denn dort liegen die Eroberungskriege schon lange zurück, Israel hat sein Land bereits in Besitz genommen (*yrš* q.) und sich angesiedelt (*yšb*). *nwḥ*-hi. bezeichnet dort eine fundamentale Sicherheit gegenüber dem Ansturm der Feinde von außen, von dem dann das Richterbuch mehrfach erzählt.

Daß es sich in den zwei Stellenreihen bei *nwḥ*-hi. nicht um die gleiche Sache handeln kann, legen auch Unterschiede im Wortfeld nahe. Während nämlich in Dtn. xii 10; Jos. xxi 44 usw. Jahwe Ruhe "vor allen Feinden ringsum" verschafft, wird in Dtn. iii 20; Jos. i 13,15, xxii 4

---

[7] Während sich die Rede Josuas in Jos. i 13a,14-15 an die Moserede von Dtn. iii 18-20 anlehnt, ist das in Jos. i 13b erwähnte Mosewort in Dtn. i-iii nirgends überliefert. Es muß in dem dort berichteten Geschehen spätestens vor Dtn. ii 32 angesetzt werden.

keine solche Präzisierung hinzugefügt. Fehlt aber jeder Feindhinweis, dann ist vielleicht auch die Deutung von *nwḥ*-hi. als Beendigung einer Wanderexistenz vorzuziehen.

5. Wie lassen sich aber die beiden unterschiedlichen Textsysteme miteinander vereinen? Die Frage wird drängend, wenn man mit Lohfink eine Deuteronomistische Landeroberungserzählung (= DtrL) annimmt, die von Dtn. i bis Jos. xxii reicht und in der dann *nwḥ*-hi. auf zweifache Weise verwendet wird. Folgende Antworten scheinen mir vertretbar zu sein, je nach dem, ob man die Belege einer einzigen Schicht oder verschiedenen Schichten zuteilt.

Rechnet man beide Ruhesysteme zur gleichen Schicht, dann hat sie *nwḥ*-hi. in unterschiedlichen Zusammenhängen für zwei verschiedene, einander jedoch ähnliche Sachverhalte gebraucht: einmal für die Besiegung von Feinden vor der Inbesitznahme ihres Landes oder neutraler für das Beenden der Wanderexistenz (Dtn. iii 20; Jos. i 13,15, xxii 4); dann aber für die Sicherheit vor den umliegenden Völkern nach der Besiedlung des Landes (Dtn. xii 10, xxv 19; Jos. xxi 44). Die differenzierte Gestaltung — *nwḥ*-hi. ohne bzw. mit den erwähnten Zusätzen — und der entsprechende Kontext verdeutlichen zur Genüge, was gemeint ist. Wegen der *m^{e}nûḥâ*-Aussagen in Dtn. xii 9 und 1 Kön. viii 56 könnte freilich diese Schicht nicht nur bis Jos. xxii reichen.[8]

Für wahrscheinlicher halte ich freilich eine Lösung, die den unterschiedlichen Gebrach von *nwḥ*-hi. als schichtenspezifisch ansieht. Dann hat Lohfink's DtrL *nwḥ*-hi. ohne weitere Bestimmung für etwas verwendet, was vor der Ansiedlung Israels liegt. Eine spätere Redaktionsschicht aber hat jene Stellen, in denen *nwḥ*-hi. durch weitere Umstandsangaben ergänzt wird, eingetragen, und zwar für etwas, das nach der Ansiedlung liegt. Beide Schichten wurden in Jos. xxi 43-45 miteinander verwoben. Dabei könnten die V.43,44b aus der DtrL stammen, während die spätere Redaktion die V.44a.45 hinzugefügt und damit die ganze Passage in das Hauptsystem von *nwḥ*-hi./*m^{e}nûḥâ* integriert hat. Diese Theorie könnte erklären, warum die beiden Präpositionalausdrücke *mikkol-ʾōy^{e}bîm* und *missābîb* in V.44 nicht wie in Dtn. xii 10; xxv 19 zusammenstehen, sondern in V.44a nur *missābîb* an *nwḥ*-hi. angehängt wird. Der Ausdruck *mikkol-ʾōy^{e}bîm* wurde ja bereits im vorgegebenen V.44b, wenn auch in anderem Sinn, verwendet. Vielleicht läßt sich jetzt sogar die zu Beginn in

---

[8] Zur Not läßt sich auch eine Phase des DtrGW denken, in der dieses noch keine Einheit bildete, sondern erst in Teilstücken wie Dtn.-Jos., Ri., Kön., freilich vom selben Autorenkreis, geschaffen wurde. Dann könnte man bei einer DtrL bleiben und annehmen, sie habe in Dtn. xii 9 auf ein Werk der gleichen Schule über die Königszeit verwiesen.

Dtn. xii 10 beobachtete Ambivalenz in der Ereignisabfolge einordnen. Die syntaktische Formation könnte nämlich wegen der Vereinigung der beiden Bezugssysteme bewußt eine doppelte Verständnismöglichkeit offen gehalten haben: Ruhe verschaffen einmal in fortschreitendem Progreß der Handlungen als Konsequenz des Ansiedelns wie in Jos. xxi 44; aber auch Ruhe verschaffen in resümierender Wiederaufnahme des vorausgehenden Geschehens und damit als Voraussetzung für die Ansiedlung Israels wie in Dtn. iii 20 usw. Damit wäre auch *nwḥ*-hi. im Sinn einer Beseitigung von Feindbedrohung im Programmtext xii 10 erkennbar und somit dort verankert.

6. Weist man die beiden Textreihen verschiedenen Schichten zu, dann kann es bei einer DtrL bleiben, die mit Jos. xxii endet. Das in der Schlüsselstelle Dtn. xii 9-10 einsetzende Ruhesystem gehört dann zu einer Redaktion des DtrGW, die mindestens schon 1 Kön. viii einschließt. Möglicherweise handelt es sich dabei um die älteste Konstruktion des Gesamtwerkes. Weil in ihr alles auf die Kultproblematik der Kön.-Bücher vorbereitet, die in der Kultreform des Joschija gipfelt, könnte sie durchaus zu seiner Zeit entstanden sein. Mit Cross ginge es also um die erste, vorexilische Ausgabe. Wenn man aus anderen Gründen jedoch mit Smend annimmt, ein DtrGW habe es erst im Exil oder danach gegeben, läßt sich auch dies vom aufgezeigten System her wohl nicht ausschließen. In beiden Fällen aber wäre die ältere Schicht der DtrL in das jüngere, erweiterte Werk eingegliedert worden.

Entscheidet man sich freilich für die Zugehörigkeit der beiden Textsysteme zu einer einzigen Schicht, dann hat sie ein einheitliches Geschichtsschema konzipiert, in dem Israel vor und nach der Landnahme "Ruhe gewährt" und ihm schließlich "die Ruhe" gegeben wird. Sie hätte allerdings keinen Schlüsseltext verfaßt. Denn als solcher funktioniert Dtn. xii 9-10 nur, wenn man auch eine spätere Redaktion annimmt, die darin ihre Anliegen auf einmal und in zentraler Position vorstellt.

Weiterer Überlegung bedürfte jetzt noch die Zuordnung der Belege von *nwḥ*-hi. in 2 Sam. vii 1,11 und 1 Kön. v 18, die auf die *m*[e]*nûḥâ* von 1 Kön. viii 56 abzielen. Meines Erachtens gehören auch sie zu jener Schicht, die ihr Programm in Dtn. xii 9-10 formuliert hat. Auch das redaktionelle Verhältnis von Jos. xxiii 1, einem gewiß spätdeuteronomistischen Text, zu den anderen Ruhestellen wäre zu bestimmen. Schließlich müßten auch die Anspielungen in Ri. ii 14, viii 34; 1 Sam. xii 11; 1 Kön. v 5, die wohl zu verschiedenen Zeiten verfaßt worden sind, redaktionsgeschichtlich geortet werden. Ich kann diese Fragen hier freilich nur andeuten und zu ihrer Beantwortung wie auch zur weiteren Begründung meiner Thesen auf eine umfassende Studie verweisen, deren Veröffentlichung ich plane. In ihr habe ich alle Ruhetexte ausführlich exegetisiert und ihre Systematik theologisch ausgewertet.

Auf der Stufe der Endredaktion wird jedenfalls die Geschichte Israels vom Aufbruch am Horeb bis zur Errichtung des Tempels auf dem Zion durch das Aussagensystem von *nwḥ*-hi. I/*m*^{e}*nûḥâ* als eine Geschichte gottgewirkter Befreiung und gottgewährten Friedens charakterisiert, bis sich das Volk schließlich im Zentralheiligtum der kultischen Gemeinschaft mit seinem Gott erfreuen darf. Dieses Ziel der Geschichte Jahwes mit Israel aber wird nach der vorliegenden deuteronomistischen "Ruhe-Konzeption" in vier Phasen erreicht:

1. "Beruhigung" Israels vor der Inbesitznahme des Landes, wobei *nwḥ*-hi. die Beendigung seiner Wanderexistenz oder die Beseitigung der Bedrohung durch im Land ansässige Feinde anzeigt (Dtn. iii 20; Jos. i 13, 15, xxii 4).

2. "Beruhigung" Israels nach der Besiedlung des Landes; *nwḥ*-hi. garantiert eine letzte Sicherheit gegenüber Feinden von außen (Dtn. xii 10, xxv 19; Jos. xxi 44; ferner xxiii 1 und die Anspielungen ohne das Verb in Ri. ii 14; viii 34; 1 Sam. xii 11 sowie 1 Kön. v 5).

3. "Beruhigung" Davids durch Unterwerfung seiner, also des Königs, Feinde (2 Sam. vii 1, 11) und "Beruhigung" Salomos durch Ausschalten seiner außen- wie innenpolitischen Gegner (1 Kön. v 18). *nwḥ*-hi. aber dient hier als Voraussetzung für

4. die Gabe "der Ruhe", der *m*^{e}*nûḥâ* als des Tempels von Jerusalem (Dtn. xii 9; 1 Kön. viii 56), mit dem die Kultzentralisation des Dtn ihre Gültigkeit erlangt.[9]

---

[9] Für hilfreiche Bemerkungen zu diesem Referat sei N. Lohfink herzlich gedankt.

Der Gebrauch von *nwḥ*-hi. I und *m^{e}nûḥâ* im Deuteronomistischen Geschichtswerk

DtrGw	*m^{e}nûḥâ*	*nwḥ*-hi. I syntaktische Formation	indirektes Objekt	*mikkol-ʾōy^{e}bîm*	*missābîb*	*yšb* (*beṭaḥ*)	*yrš*-q.	*ntn hāʾāreṣ*	Er-füllungs-notiz	Rück-verweis
Dtn iii 20		x	West-jordanier				nach *nwḥ*	nach *yrš*		
xii 9	x		Israel							
xii 10		w=qatal-x	Israel	x	x	vor/nach *nwḥ* (+*beṭaḥ*)				
xxv 19		x	Israel	x	x					
Jos. i 13		Partizip	Ost-jordanier					nach *nwḥ*		nicht referiert
i 15		x	West-jordanier				nach *nwḥ*	nach *yrš*		
xxi 44		wayyiqtol-x	Israel	V.44b	V.44a	vor *nwḥ*		V.43	V.45	auf Dtn. xii 10
xxii 4		w=x-qatal	West-jordanier							auf Dtn. iii 20 usw.
xxiii 1		x	Israel	x	x				V.14	x
Ri. ii 14				*miyyad ʾōy^{e}bîm*	*x*					
viii 34				*miyyad kol-ʾōy^{e}bîm*	*x*					
1 Sam. xii 11				*miyyad ʾōy^{e}bîm*	*x*	*yšb beṭaḥ*				
2 Sam. vii 1		w=x-qatal	David	x	x	V.1a				
vii 11		w=qatal-x	David	x						
1 Kön. v 5						*yšb lābeṭaḥ*				
1 Kön. v 18		w=x-qatal	Salomo	(vgl. V.18b)	x					V.19: auf 2 Sam. vii 13b
1 Kön. viii 56	x		Israel						x	auf 2 Sam. vii 13b Dtn. xii 9

GENESIS L 15-21: A THEOLOGICAL EXPLORATION

BY

WALTER BRUEGGEMANN

Saint Louis

The study of the Joseph narrative has been dominated by the work of Martin Noth[1] and Gerhard von Rad.[2] But their work has led to a *cul-de-sac*. Noth has been interested only in the "great themes" of the Pentateuch and so has paid little attention to this narrative. Von Rad, with his "wisdom hypothesis", has also disregarded this narrative in his study of the Hexateuch, and has treated the internal character of the narrative in something of a vacuum. Neither Noth's concern for external function nor von Rad's attention to internal character has opened a way for a theological understanding of the narrative.

I

Scholarly work since von Rad and Noth includes the following: D. B. Redford[3] and G. W. Coats[4] seek to find the core story which has been subsequently expanded. But both of them are interested in the internal literary character of the narrative and focus on the intent of the present

[1] *Überlieferungsgeschichte des Pentateuch* (Stuttgart, 1948), esp. pp. 226-32, E. tr. *A History of Pentateuchal Traditions* (Englewood Cliffs, N.J., 1972), pp. 208-13.

[2] Von Rad has treated the text in a variety of places. See *Theologie des Alten Testaments* 1 (Munich, 1957), pp. 175-7, E. tr. *Old Testament Theology* 1 (Edinburgh, London, and New York, 1962), pp. 172-5; "Josephsgeschichte und ältere Chokma", *Congress Volume: Copenhagen 1953, SVT* 1 (1953), pp. 120-7, reprinted in *Gesammelte Studien zum Alten Testament* (Munich, 1958), pp. 272-80, E. tr. "The Joseph narrative and ancient Wisdom", *The Problem of the Hexateuch and Other Essays* (Edinburgh, London, and New York, 1966), pp. 292-300; *Das erste Buch Mose: Genesis* (5th edn, Göttingen, 1958), pp. 303ff., E. tr. *Genesis* (revised edn, London and Philadelphia, 1972), pp. 347ff.; "Die Josephsgeschichte", *Gottes Wirken in Israel* (Neukirchen-Vluyn, 1974), pp. 22-41, E. tr. "The Story of Joseph", *God at Work in Israel* (Nashville, 1980), pp. 19-35.

[3] *A Study of the Biblical Story of Joseph*, *SVT* 20. Redford (much more than Coats) attempts to identify the stages through which the story has expanded.

[4] *From Canaan to Egypt* (Washington, D.C., 1976). See also Coat's discussions in "The Joseph Story and Ancient Wisdom: a Reappraisal", *CBQ* 35 (1973), pp. 285-97, and "Redactional Unity in Genesis 37-50", *JBL* 93 (1974), pp. 15-21.

text very little. Rolf Rendtorff[5] seeks to take the text as it stands without dissection. His work has the merit of letting the text be a discrete "cluster", and he has paid attention to the promise motif, thus opening the way for a theological analysis. B. S. Childs[6] and D. J. A. Clines[7] from the perspective of canonical criticism have tried to see the narrative in its present canonical setting. Childs presents the narrative in terms of the promise under threat. Clines suggests that the narrative is a reversal of the disastrous flow of Gen. i-xi. Both see the promise still unresolved and open-ended. It appears that the work of Rendtorff, Childs and Clines helps in moving our work out of the sharp contrast of internal and external foci, left by Noth and von Rad.

One result of this shift in perspective is that von Rad's sapiential interpretation is increasingly disregarded and denied, for it does not seem to take the narrative on its own terms in its present context. The part of von Rad's understanding which likely will endure is the portrayal of the "deep hiddenness" of God and God's plan fulfilled through suffering.[8]

The Joseph story is lodged here, not simply as a "formal bridge", (though it may be that) or as a convenient place for a wisdom narrative (other places may have been equally convenient), but because Israel at this point in the narrative needed not so much a great Pentateuchal theme as a reflective moment concerning how the promise could be trusted and kept credible against the reality of non-fulfillment. The inscrutability of Yahweh is not simply a literary technique for bridging (so Noth), nor simply a cultural advance reflective of an Enlightenment (so von Rad), but an experiential reality in the faith of Israel, as presented in this literature. From whatever source it may have been taken, the Joseph Narrative now serves to meet a religious need in the experiential faith of Israel. The "redescribed" character of Israel's faith is created and made available by this literature.[9] My point is that the more recent scholarship may provide a legitimate way to pose again a theological issue which has been prevented by the hardening of scholarly constructs and the rigidity of analytical categories. Thus the theological issues on which the nar-

---

[5] *Das überlieferungsgeschichtliche Problem des Pentateuch*, *BZAW* 147 (Berlin, 1977); cf. "Der 'Jahwist' als Theologe? Zum Dilemma der Pentateuchkritik", *Congress Volume: Edinburgh 1974*, *SVT* 28 (1975), pp. 158-66, E. tr., "The 'Yahwist' as Theologian? The Dilemma of Pentateuchal Criticism", *JSOT* 3 (1976), pp. 2-10.

[6] *Introduction to the Old Testament as Scripture* (London and Philadelphia, 1979), pp. 150-8.

[7] *The Theme of the Pentateuch* (Sheffield, 1978).

[8] *Theologie des AT* 1, pp. 175-6, E. tr., pp. 172-3.

[9] Paul Ricoeur has most helpfully presented the idea of "redescribing" as the work of revelatory literature. Cf. "Biblical Hermeneutics", *Semeia* 4 (1975), p. 31 and *passim*; "Imagination in Discourse and in Action", in Anna-Teresa Tymieniecka (ed.), *Action, The Irreducible Element in Man II* (Boston, Mass., 1978).

rative turns are not those of credal theology or sapiential reflection from the Solomonic Enlightenment (the issues left for us by Noth and von Rad). Rather, the issues are those of the revelatory character of God and the hiddenness of God, the sense that in the hiddenness God still governs, but that the hiddenness opens toward new disclosure that is stunning in its power and yet not unambiguous in its meaning. Posing the question this way permits us to think about theological claims and religious needs, issues which our scholarly constructs have excessively subordinated to matters of cultural history and more analytic questions of date and source.[10] That disclosure, as we shall see, is carried by the character of Joseph in our text, who is both stunning and, up to a point, not unambiguous. It is the ambiguity of the person of Joseph that points to the ambiguity of God in this moment of historical ambiguity.

The part of the narrative to be considered here is the conversation of the brothers with Joseph after the death of father Jacob. It is introduced by lamentation and burial of their father (xlxix 28-l 14).[11]

II

In what follows, we consider l 15-21 as a piece of carefully wrought theology. Our discussion will address itself to two points:

A. This exchange is a theological statement drawing upon those theological motifs that Israel found most useful in contexts of fear and hopelessness, of which exile is a primary example.[12]

---

[10] It is beyond the scope of this article to consider the Joseph narrative from the perspective of "The New Literary Criticism", though there are important gains to be made through such an approach. For efforts in that direction, see Donald A. Seybold, "Paradox and Symmetry in the Joseph Narrative", in Kenneth R. R. Gros Louis, James Ackerman and Thayer S. Warshaw (ed.), *Literary Interpretations of Biblical Narrative* (New York, 1974), pp. 59-73, and Mary Savage, "Literary Criticism and Biblical Studies: A rhetorical Analysis of the Joseph Narrative", in Carl D. Evans, William W. Hallo and John B. White (ed.), *Scripture in Context* (Pitssburgh, 1980), pp. 89-100. And see the discerning treatment of Robert Alter, *The Art of Biblical Narrative* (New York, 1981), especially pp. 157-76. However, on two points, that kind of literary criticism is inadequate for our question. It tends to screen out theological issues, and to take the text apart from the community. On both these points, I judge the method to be important, but by itself inadequate.

[11] For both Redford, pp. 163-4, 186, and Coats, "Redactional Unity", pp. 15, 21, this passage falls outside the principal narrative. Coats does allow that this is a "supporting satellite narrative" which functions as a "recapitulation", so that his judgement is not as radical as that of Redford. But neither of them addresses the crucial placement and function of this piece. The judgement of Westermann, *Genesis 3* (37-50) (Neukirchen-Vluyn, 1982), pp. 230-1, is not different.

[12] Such an argument may appear to support the late dating generally taken by the "Toronto School". Cf. John Van Seters, *Abraham in History and Tradition* (New Haven, Conn., and London, 1975). But our concern here is not chronology but a characteristic, if not paradigmatic, response to exile. I mean to beg the question of dating.

B. The Joseph story is now shaped for the primary purpose of staging this speech which is carefully placed at the seam between Exodus and Genesis. But the careful placement is not simply to make a literary or historical linkage, but to articulate a theological affirmation. The chapter functions typologically for a religious seam or crisis in Israel's life.

The unit portrays an exchange between Joseph and the other sons of Jacob. Absent now is the third party to the triangle, the father who had always played a decisive, mediating role. And when that third party is removed, relations between the two remaining parties must be reconfigured, and not without risk.[13] It is that reconfiguration[14] which is now reported. The space between Joseph and the others is ominous and ill-defined, filled with terror for the brothers. All parties know that the absence of their father matters enormously. And no doubt the terror consists largely of unresolved guilt. At the same time, Joseph is non-committal. When he is passionate with weeping and not at all cool (e.g., Gen. xlv 14, xlvi 29), we are not sure what it means. All parties are now set in a dangerous situation of rawness. Old guarantees, protections and conventions are removed. Now all parties must face the danger. And none knows beforehand how it will turn out. The risk in the family without the controlling presence of Jacob is not unlike every exile in which old systems of support have been lost.

III

The encounter is initiated from the side of the brothers, the admittedly guilty party. The subject is now retribution, the settling of accounts that could not happen while the father lived (*v.* 15).

1. It is as though the subject of retaliation and the settlement of accounts was not a clear and present danger while Jacob was alive. For the brothers, Jacob embodies something of a barrier against retribution which has now been removed. Now everything is at risk.

2. The device of sending a message (a messenger is not mentioned) in *vv.* 16-17a is marvelously ambiguous, as everything in this interaction is ambiguous. The commentaries speculate on whether Jacob had in fact commissioned such a message.[15]

---

[13] On "triangling" as a characteristic of dynamic of family interaction, see Murray Bowen, *Family Therapy in Clinical Practice* (New York, 1978).

[14] Such social "reconfiguring" should be seen as related to the literary act of "redescribing", mentioned above. Literary "redescribing" serves and permits social reconfiguring.

[15] Von Rad, *Genesis*, p. 377, E. tr., p. 432, takes the trouble to say it is a "false assumption" that the brothers are lying in this act. But we do not know. The narrator does not intend us to know.

But we must not speculate. We must stay inside the story. And inside the story everything is ambiguous for all parties. Thus whether Jacob gave such a directive is intended to be uncertain. We are not told. And likely the brothers do not know if it is true. We do not know how Joseph will respond. If it is a true word from the father, the brothers do not know if Joseph will remember it, or if he will think (with the commentaries) that it is a device. Or if Joseph remembers, we do not know if he will honor it. Thus the literary mode of a message serves to delay the encounter and to heighten the suspense and risk. The situation with Joseph is now quite new, one of discontinuity. The brothers want to cling to their old support, even if it means claiming too much for Jacob. They hope the old support by Jacob still has force. But of course they do not know.

3. But the appeal to Jacob is almost diversionary to the movement of the encounter. In *v.* 17b, the brothers' initiative moves to the present petition: *weᶜattāh.* In that moment of confrontation, neither the terror of the brothers nor the injunction of the dead father counts for anything. The brothers must stand helpless before the great ruler who may or may not act like a remembering kinsman. The petition is bold, accompanied only by a definitional term "servants".

The petition is simple and massive: "forgive transgressions". The request is first in the mouth of Jacob and then in the mouths of the brothers. The formula is used in a telling way in Ex. x 17 where Pharaoh petitions Moses and Aaron for forgiveness. Here the situation is exactly reversed. Here it is needy Israel come to the great Egyptian officer. There it is the Pharaoh himself come in need to Israel. Perhaps the two uses together attest the general inversion. But for our purposes, perhaps the most interesting use is that made in a lament Psalm. In the petition of Ps. xxv 18 there are a cluster of terms for seeking relief from a situation of trouble:

> Turn thou to me, and be gracious to me;
> for I am lonely and afflicted,
> Relieve the troubles of my heart,
> and bring me out of my distresses.
> Consider my affliction and my trouble,
> and forgive all my sins.
> (cf. 1 Sam. xv 25, xxv 28)

The language of petition used by the brothers is the standard language of the lament Psalm. In the Psalm the petition is, of course, addressed to God. Here the petition is addressed to Joseph, and not to God. In each case it is addressed to the one who has power to act to extricate the guilty. And here that is undoubtedly Joseph.

The way in which the petitioners identify themselves is important. In *v.* 17, where Jacob said it for them, they are "your brothers". Now they say only "servants of the God of your father". Two times, here and in *v.* 16, it is "your father", not "our father". So the brothers have moved a distance from brother to servant. They do not yet say directly "your servant", but "servant of God". They are not yet ready for full capitulation. But they are on the way. In their fear, they have abandoned the brother-talk their father thought appropriate. They still want to make a case of family binding, but dare to do it only by making a general theological reference. Thus far in the narrative, we have no clue about how the petition will be received. We do not know if they act in good faith or deviously. We do not know how the great man will respond. And the brothers do not know either.

IV

The narrative might have moved directly to Joseph's definitive response in *v.* 19. But it does not. The narrative holds off as long as possible. So in *vv.* 17b-18 there is an intermediate stage, a parrying between brothers, a dramatic delay. When one comes to such a staggering confrontation, one must not rush to resolve what cannot be resolved in a rush.

1. So first there is Joseph's initial response, which is profoundly ambiguous. Joseph wept when they spoke to him. Joseph's characteristic response to family matters is weeping. The response seems obvious. But we are not told at all what the weeping might mean. We are apparently free to speculate in any way we choose. We are told nothing of Joseph's motives or feelings. The narrative is disciplined in that regard. The action functions to slow the conversation. And we must still wait to find out Joseph's response to his brothers. It could be a mocking. Or it could be that Joseph is deeply moved. Or if our assignment of the petition to a lament form is correct, it could be that Joseph stands in solidarity with their grief, recognizing that he also has transgressions that await forgiveness. It is, in any case, recognized as an occasion proper for weeping.

This situation includes a) loss of conventional support; b) emergence of questions concerning retribution; and c) acknowledgement of fear and displacement. This is the situation in which all parties find themselves. And the narrator invites the listening Israelite into that situation as well. The crying perhaps characterizes not only Joseph but all who participate in the narrative, its actors and its listeners.

2. The other element in this intermediate section is the response of the brothers to the weeping of Joseph in *v.* 18. They fall before him, a motif

we have watched steadily in the entire narrative since the initial dream of chapter xxxvii. So the encounter now has intentional binding with the beginning of the entire family narrative.

What interests us more is the way in which the brothers refer to themselves. They are no longer "brothers" as in *v.* 17, nor are they "servants of God", as in *v.* 18. Now it is an act of unambiguous political deference. They say simply "your servants" (*v.* 18). In two careful moves, the term has gone from "brothers" to "servants of the God of your father", to "your servants", all the way from kinship to political realism and submission.

The speech is not of familial embrace, but the working out of power relations. The brothers have acknowledged their guilt. Now they abase themselves completely. They are helpless petitioners, without a bargaining chip. And that perhaps is precisely what is desired by Joseph, as the narrative offers him to us. There is no talk of brothers or of father or of forgiveness. But there is a complete abandonment of every other help, reference and resource. The narrative has moved carefully to this radical act of self-abasement.

V

Only now are we ready for the third element, Joseph's lordly response (*vv.* 19-20). The exchange has begun from the side of the brothers with their guilt and fear. The exchange concludes with Joseph's carefully crafted response. Nothing is conceded. The brothers have it right. They are servants. Joseph is lord. No one in the meeting is unclear about that.

1. The speech begins, "Do not fear." Of course we have here the salvation oracle which Begrich has studied in such detail. Taken by itself, it is clear that this is a response directly to the petition, "forgive!" We have seen that it is a situation of fear and guilt, in which questions of retribution and retaliation are on the table, a situation of weeping when all old supports have failed and there is utter abasement along with complete helplessness.

In response, the salvation oracle, "Do not fear", is perhaps the most appropriate answer available among the formularies of Israel. The salvation oracle marks a radical break, a move from the other side, a beginning again out of radical discontinuity. It is the characteristic way in which Israel experiences the overcoming of fear, the termination of retribution, the eradication of weeping, the raising up after complete abasement. The word uttered by Joseph is the best word Israel has to offer. None of the old modes of relation is pertinent, not the devices of the brothers, not the protective oversight of the father, not the calculations of

Joseph. The situation is resolved in the only way it can be, by a new generative act permitting life, spoken by the one with all the power.

2. But who is Joseph to speak such a word? The formula is characteristically the speech of God.[16] How dare Joseph speak such a word? So the marvelous announcement is followed by a most curious rhetorical question: "Am I in the place of God?" Again the narrator leaves us with a remarkable ambiguity. What is the intended answer to the rhetorical question? If one answers the question, "yes", it suggests that Joseph can speak a "fear not", and implicitly that he can forgive sin because he has placed himself in God's place. That may be the intention, because all through the narrative the brothers perceive him as acting as though he were God, or as though he thought he was God. Conversely, if one answers, "no", then it means that Joseph is not in God's place, cannot really forgive sin, and thus his "fear not" is not ultimately believable.[17] The question may preclude Joseph's capacity to forgive, or his capacity to retaliate.

We do not know which way the narrator intends the question to be answered. We do not even know if an answer is intended. I suggest, rather, that the darkness and ambiguity of the encounter is here maintained and intensified by this enigmatic statement. Joseph's initial response does not alleviate the fear or offer any assurance. The brothers still have the burden of guilt and therefore of fear. The brothers are here given no clear assurance of forgiveness, even though it appears so on the surface. The petition which seeks forgiveness receives a response "fear not", but it is a response short of resolution. The following rhetorical question places the salvation oracle in a position of jeopardy, and seems immediately to take back what has been so wondrously given.

3. Finally, the delaying tactics of the narrative lead to the well-known formula of *v.* 20, "You meant it for evil, God meant it for good." The most influential interpretation is that of von Rad who regards the statement as a summary of wisdom teaching, which he several times relates to Prov. xvi 2, 9, xix 21, xx 24, xxi 30.[18] Von Rad[19] calls this formulation "a bold mixture of divine activity and guilty human deeds." That is, the plans of God are wrought through the guilty actions of the brothers.

---

[16] See the comprehensive analysis of the formula by Thomas M. Raitt, *A Theology of Exile* (Philadelphia, 1977), ch. 6.

[17] The most obvious parallel rhetorical question is that of Jacob in Gen. xxx 2, which requires a negative answer.

[18] *Theologie des AT* 1, pp. 437-8, E. tr., pp. 439-40; *Gottes Wirken*, p. 38, E. tr., p. 33; "Josephsgeschichte und ältere Chokma", pp. 124-5/277-8, E. tr., pp. 297-8.

[19] Von Rad, *Weisheit in Israel* (Neukirchen-Vluyn, 1970), p. 258, E. tr., *Wisdom in Israel* (London, 1972), p. 200.

We may suggest three objections to the relation of this statement to wisdom:

a) The verse is often, and even by von Rad, taken by itself, without reference to its context. When the statement is taken in its context, we have seen that it is surrounded not by sapiential marks, but by characteristics of the Psalms, the petition, the weeping and the salvation oracle. Thus, we would do better to look at the Psalms for illumination.[20]

b) It is telling that in the set of Proverbs regularly cited in this regard (Prov. xvi 2, 9, xix 21, xxi 2, xx 24, xxi 30)[21] never does the word *ḥāšab* occur twice, as in our formula, and only two times (xvi 9, xix 21) does it occur even once. I shall suggest that the parallels in the Psalms are much more pertinent.

c) Faithful to the claims of wisdom, von Rad tends to view the "meant" of the brothers and the "meant" of God as somehow continuous, as though the one is wrought out of the other. I suggest that such a reading of the relation of the two elements is not in keeping with the text. In the Proverbs cited, the contrast is one of discernment and mystery but that does not approach the moral crises surfaced in l 20. Rather the two "meant" statements here are adversative and what is asserted is that the plan of God defeats the plan of the brothers, not that it is a mixture of the two or a use of one by the other. If that is correct, then the statement finds a better habitat in the conflictual, adversative language of the Psalms than in the accommodating, embracing language of wisdom.[22]

On all three grounds, I suggest that the resolution of this entire encounter is more likely to be understood in the tradition of the Psalms. This statement about good and evil is not a general statement, but is the cry of the righteous one who has been or is about to be vindicated against the evil wrought by the wicked. Thus, the context requires that Joseph's speech is not a statement of cool reconciliation, but it is a victory assertion in which the brothers must indeed be servants and not brothers because God gives well-being to his righteous one. The relation between Joseph and his brothers is not that of family members at a love-feast, but litigants appearing before the throne. No wonder Joseph is not in the place of God. He takes his place before God and claims vindication. Joseph is pictured, not as forgiving, for there is no hint of that, but as a righteous man who is vindicated. The wisdom interpretation, I should

---

20 See the comments of Westermann, p. 283.

21 See von Rad, *Theologie des AT* 1, p. 437, E. tr., p. 439.

22 See the counter use of *ḥšb* in Micah ii 1-3, and cf. Patrick D. Miller, Jr, *Sin and Judgment in the Prophets* (Chico, California, 1982), pp. 29-31. Miller's entire analysis presumes an adversative relationship, which is what we have in our text.

argue, with its propensity for harmonization, misses the abrasive, threatening tone used here.

I suggest that the double use of *ḥāšab* here functions in the same way as in the Psalms of lament. Note especially Pss. xxxv 4, 20, xxxvi 5, xl 6, 18, lvi 6, but see also x 2, xxi 12, xli 8, lii 3-4, xcii 6-7, cxl 2-3, 5. The sum of this evidence is that the Psalmists trust the plans of God to defeat the plans, schemes and plots of evil persons. The language occurs in several genre, but the primary usage is in the complaint Psalm which appeals to the plan of God against the destructive plans of the evil.

This contrast is most clearly expressed in Ps. xxxiii 10-11:

> The Lord brings the counsel of the nations to nought;
> he frustrates the *plans* of the peoples.
> The counsel of the Lord stands for ever,
> the *thoughts* of his heart to all generations.

To be sure, this Psalm is not without reminiscences of wisdom, but the language is much closer to lament than to any of the proverbs cited by von Rad.

The formula of *v.* 20 serves as a vindication of Joseph. And conversely it is an indictment of the brothers who are rightly not more than servants. Their way or ordering the life of this family (and the future of Israel) has been defeated. The language of vindication and indictment is a way of appropriate entry into the Exodus narrative, and a reflection of the tenor of the entire Joseph narrative. The reference to *ʿam rab* in *v.* 20 indicates a readiness to move on into the public history of Israel (cf. Ex. i 9).

4. We come now to the last structural element in the encounter of Joseph and his brothers who have become his slaves. I have suggested that the text falls into two primary parts, *vv.* 15-17a, an approach by the brothers, and *vv.* 19-21, the resolution by Joseph, with a transitional element in *vv.* 17b-18. The two main parts are structurally complementary, each dominated by an assertion that is reiterated after *w^{e}ʿattāh*. For the brothers, it is:

> Forgive, I pray their transgressions...
> *w^{e}ʿattāh* forgive the transgressions...

This matched in the response of Joseph:

> Fear not...
> *w^{e}attāh* do not fear...

In each case, the reasserted element after *w^{e}ʿattāh* is much more forceful. In each case, the preliminary statement seems dramatically less secure. The concluding response of Joseph following the *w^{e}ʿattāh* consists in three parts:

a) There is the reiterated "do not fear". Now there is no rhetorical question to qualify.

b) This is followed by a self-assertion, governed by the imperfect verb, "I will provide". This formula is in the position of completing the salvation oracle, although the usual particle *kî* is absent. This statement offers the ground for not fearing. And in this usage, Joseph operates with godlike authority (cf. Gen. xli 38-41).

c) The final element contains two factors of great interest. First the verb *nāḥam* (piᶜel), "Joseph comforted his brothers." The text still does not say that he forgave or that he felt affection. Perhaps the earlier rhetorical question is honored, i.e., only God can forgive. The use of the word *nāḥam* cannot be accidental. The *piᶜel* usage is widespread and diverse. But we may observe its use in four clusters that sustains my thesis concerning parallels in the Psalms. The term is used in lament Psalms lxix 21, lxxi 21, lxxxvi 17, cxix 76, 82). It is used in the poetry of the book of Lamentations i 2, 9, 16, 17, 21, ii 13), in the speeches of Job (vii 13, xvi 2, xxi 34, xxix 25) and in II Isaiah (xl 1, xlix 13, li 3, 12, 19, lii 9) with which we my associate Jer. xxxi 13; Ezek. xiv 23, xvi 54; Isa. lxi 2, lxvi 13. All these usages refer to situations of distress, either hoping for or rejoicing in an act of rescue and intervention which makes all things new.

Dramatically speaking, as related to the lament Psalms and II Isaiah, we may conclude that the salvation oracle is the decisive factor in being comforted. That is, the use of *nāḥam* is made possible by the "do not fear" which precedes. As nearly as we can place these various uses, they refer to situations of exile, if not the specific situation of sixth-century exile. Joseph's speech and action are presumably exile-ending acts by speaking a word that lets the past be past and moves on to the promises of *ᶜam rab* and the provisions for that future.

Second, the use of the verb *nāḥam* is supported by the final statement, "He spoke with words that touched their hearts" (*wayᵉdabbēr ᶜal-libbām*) (*Jerusalem Bible*). Again the phrase "speak to the heart" is widely used. It may mean "to remember" (Jer. iii 16, xii 11; Isa. xlvi 8), "to take seriously" (Isa. xlii 25, lvii 1; Mal. ii 2), or "to determine" (Dan. i 8). But the closest parallels would suggest that it is language of intimacy, care and embrace (Gen. xxxiv 3; Judg. xix 3; Ruth ii 13).[23] This last usage in Ruth ii 13 is of special interest for us because the full statement that Ruth speaks to Boaz is:

> You are most gracious to me, my Lord,
> for you have comforted me and spoken kindly...

[23] Hans Walter Wolff, *Dodekapropheton 1: Hosea* (Neukirchen Kreis Moers, 1961), p. 50 says that it "bleibt ganz in der Sprache der Liebe eines Mannes zu seiner Frau"; E. tr. *Hosea* (Philadelphia, 1974), p. 42: "belongs to the language of courtship".

This speech combines *dibber ʿal-lēb* with the *piʿel* of *nāḥam*, closely paralleling our passage. Here Boaz has performed an act of inordinate power and kindness which permits a hopeless person to begin a new life.

But the phrase of Joseph's statement points, I suggest, especially to Hos. ii 16 and Isa. xl 2. In Hos. ii 16, the speech of Yahweh "to the heart" has the effect of permitting Israel to begin again, again after the death sentence of *vv.* 4-15. The object of the speech "is to overcome sorrow and resentment (cf. also 2 Chr 32:6), obstinacy and estrangement."[24] In the decisive passage of Isa. xl 2, the great exile-ending speech which seems to answer to the hopelessness of lamentations, again *ʿal lēb* is closely linked to *nāḥam*.

Thus, Joseph's speech after the *weʿattāh* consists of four elements: a) salvation oracle, b) promise of provision, c) comfort, and d) speaking to the heart. All together, they are about ending the terror and guilt expressed in *vv.* 15-17a.

VI

Our analysis may yield these conclusions:

The theological motifs used are those regularly used by Israel in *situations of fear and hopelessness*. More specifically this piece reflects the motifs used in the theological crisis of Lamentations and II Isaiah.

a) The *loss of the support and safeguard* of a father is not unlike the loss of all conventional social props in 587 which are grieved for in the book of Lamentations.

b) The overriding *response of Israel* to the situation of 587 is one of guilt and fear (cf. Lam. i 8-9, 14, 18, 20 and especially 22). The brothers are here portrayed in a like situation, in dread because they are justly subject to retaliation.

c) The *response of Joseph* with a salvation oracle is not unlike salvation oracles generally in response to laments. Specifically, II Isaiah has used the form to provide hope and comfort to the exiles (cf. Isa. xli 10, 13, 14, xliii 1, xliv 1, cf. Jer. xxx 10-11; Lam. iii 57). In both cases the speech is exile-ending.

d) The decisive statement of *v.* 20 in which the *plans of Yahweh* override the destructive plans of the brothers is parallel to two exile-ending assertions in Jer. xxix 11,[25] Isa. lv 6-9.

---

[24] Wolff, p. 51, E. tr., p. 42.

[25] The *šālôm/raʿ* contrast here is not unlike the *ṭôb/raʿ* contrast in our text. Indeed, the Deuteronomic tradition of Jeremiah plays with the motif. Cf. Jer. xliv 27, xxxix 16, xxiv 6. The claims of our text sound very different when set in the abrasive context of exile.

e) The final formulation of "comfort/speak to the heart" functions as an *anticipation of "homecoming"* when illuminated by the intimacy of Ruth ii 13 and the proclamation of Isa. xl 2.

Thus, the piece draws primarily from the language used in laments and oracles in the Psalter, and not that of the wisdom literature. The language is that which comes closest to exilic speech of despair and new possibility. In both senses, our text is paradigmatic for what Israel characteristically says in such contexts. The Joseph narrative, featuring the brothers as desperate Israel and Joseph as a giver of the future, is not artificially linked to the Pentateuch but integrally, an entry point to the book of Exodus.[26] We meet Israel in the book of Exodus, precisely at the point of despair. In Gen. l 15-21 (22-26), important promises have been made which have not yet been fulfilled. This moment of the brothers before Pharaonic Joseph presents Israel in its utter helplessness, waiting for a new word, a word spoken in Egypt by Moses and in Babylon by II Isaiah. The culmination of the Joseph narrative shows that the promise of Genesis has its own life. It still may be fulfilled. But it has not yet been fulfilled. We may thus find a way beyond that methodological impasse to see that the intimate conflict of Joseph's family and the larger sweep of Israel's tradition are not two separated phenomena. They partake of the same continuing interaction of lament and assurance. The substantive theological judgement is that this exchange foreshadows the Exodus and indeed offers a succint articulation of the main theological paradigm for Israel's faith. It is placed here just as the saving narrative of Israel begins. Scholarly treatment of the Joseph narrative has tended to split the external function of the narrative (so Noth) from a study of its internal character (so von Rad). The present article suggests that attention to the issue of helplessness (expressed as lament) and to response of assurance (expressed as salvation oracle) releases us from the impasse. That is, ap-

---

[26] Cf. Rendtorff, p. 75. He notes especially the use of *pāqad* which is used in Ex. iii 16, iv 31. Note the same word in Jer. xxix 10, with reference to return from exile. P. D. Miller, Jr, "Psalms and Inscriptions", *SVT* 32 (1980), pp. 330-2, observes tht *pqd* is a word used in prayer of petition in time of distress. This fact is yet another small point which links our text (cf. *vv.* 22-26) to the Psalms and to the exilic situation. Hartmut Gese, *Zur biblischen Theologie: Alttestamentliche Vorträge* (Munich, 1977), p. 34, E. tr. *Essays on Biblical Theology* (Minneapolis, 1981), p. 37, appeals to the entire scene of the death of Jacob: "In Genesis 50 we read about how the great funeral of Jacob, the eponymous hero of Israel, was performed in reverse analogy to the exodus. All the Egyptian court and the army of chariots and horsemen accompanied the deceased to the Holy Land. This becomes a symbol in reverse of the exodus, but in an anticipation that corresponds to the truth. Life in the land first became possible through a grave; through a grave the group put down roots in the land." While Gese's comment is correct, he does not comment upon the decisive role played by the speech-exchange of Joseph and his brothers. It is the speech that turns the history of Israel toward the land.

peal to a primary formulary pattern of Israel's faith lets us see the character and function of the narrative in a new way. The resolution of the relation of the brothers given in the narrative may use sapiential motifs. But its main appeal is to forms found in the Psalms which place it at the center of Israel's faith. Life begins again for the guilty and hopeless when a word is spoken by the one who can forgive the guilt and make provision for the future. The family of Joseph is indeed a bearer of this understanding of historical vocation, always troubled, regularly addressed in exile-ending ways.

A LITERARY ANALYSIS OF 1 KINGS I 41-53, WITH METHODOLOGICAL REFLECTIONS

BY

CHARLES CONROY

Rome

After some brief remarks on the challenge posed to current exegetical practice by the newer approaches inspired by developments in linguistics and literary study, the paper will analyse features of the literary dimension of 1 Kgs i 41-53 and conclude with some comments on a recent redaction-critical proposal about part of that pericope.[1]

I

The emergence of what is broadly called the literary approach to the Bible can perhaps best be viewed as an attempt at interdisciplinary dialogue with the expanding and influential fields of general linguistics and literary studies (theory and criticism). Interdisciplinary dialogue is by no means a new phenomenon in biblical study. To mention just one example: the pioneers of the historical-critical approach worked under the stimulus of the growing influence of modern critical historiography,[2] and the results of almost two centuries of historical-critical analysis are there to show how energetically that challenge was met. Today's challenge, however, comes rather from the critical study of language and literature, and biblical scholars are called upon to respond with the same open-mindedness as that shown by the pioneers of the historical-critical approach in the cultural situation of their time.

To accept this new challenge does not at all entail the abandonment of the historical-critical approach. On the contrary, a thorough consideration of the literary dimension of a biblical text will inevitably bring up the question of its original communicative situation, just as serious literary

---

[1] At the Congress this paper was presented together with that of Professor T. Ishida; a public discussion followed on the respective contributions of the historical and literary approaches.

[2] See R. A. Oden, "Hermeneutics and Historiography: Germany and America", in P. J. Achtemeier (ed.), *SBL Seminar Papers 1980* (Chico, 1980), pp. 135-57. That the historians learned something too from the biblical scholars has been noted by H. Butterfield, *Man on his Past. The Study of the History of Historical Scholarschip* (Cambridge, 1969: first publ. 1955), pp. 15, 36, 57.

study of a Shakespearian play will inevitably bring up the question of the original audience and stage-practice. In the case of many biblical texts, moreover, it will be necessary to distinguish the original communicative situation from successive communicative situations to which the texts were variously adapted. And for all this the techniques of historical criticism remain essential.

It is not a question, then, of "literary versus historical" in the sense of an either/or antagonism, but rather of working towards a responsible integration of the two areas of scholarly endeavour, while taking into account the particular nature of the text one happens to be studying. Just as historical criticism has been, and remains, essential for biblical study, so too a reasonable acquaintance with the theoretical and practical aspects of linguistics and literary study should be seen as indispensable in today's cultural situation. It will no longer do to regard such matters as harmless eccentricities or as subjective and non-scientific aberrations. Indeed, to persist in ignoring the possible literary dimension of a biblical text is profoundly contrary to the scholarly spirit, since it means closing one's eyes to an aspect of the reality one is studying. Certain biblical texts are narratives, not by a subjective decision of the interpreter but by their literary nature. To take account of this is not an optional extra, and to take account of it responsibly calls for a familiarity with contemporary discussion on narrative in general.[3]

II

An adequate discussion of the literary dimension of 1 Kgs i-ii would require far more space than is available here.[4] Rather than touch superficially on a large number of points or on general thematic questions, the following analysis will limit itself to an important pericope (1 Kgs i 41-53), which happens to have played a crucial part in recent historical-

[3] Two useful English-language works can be selected from the extensive international bibliography on narrative: S. Chatman, *Story and Discourse. Narrative Structure in Fiction and Film* (Ithaca and London, 1978); G. Prince, *Narratology. The Form and Functioning of Narrative* (Berlin, New York and Amsterdam, 1982). There are two recent general treatments of classical Hebrew narrative: J. Licht, *Storytelling in the Bible* (Jerusalem, 1978); R. Alter, *The Art of Biblical Narrative* (New York and London, 1981).

[4] Recent literary studies that discuss 1 Kgs i-ii include: D. M. Gunn, *The Story of King David. Genre and Interpretation* (Sheffield, 1978); J. P. Fokkelman, *Narrative Art and Poetry in the Books of Samuel. A Full Interpretation based on Stylistic and Structural Analyses* I: *King David (II Sam. 9-20 & I Kings 1-2)* (Assen, 1981); B. O. Long, "A Darkness between Brothers: Solomon and Adonijah", *JSOT* 19 (1981), pp. 79-94; K. K. Sacon, "A Study of the Literary Structure of 'The Succession Narrative'", in T. Ishida (ed.), *Studies in the Period of David and Solomon, and other essays* (Tokyo, 1982), pp. 27-54. Valuable literary observations can also be found in some more historically-oriented studies, especially those of F. Langlamet (cf. n. 16).

critical discussion of the two chapters in question. This limitation means that wider literary questions such as the analysis of the personages or the bearing of the pericope on the thematic statements of the literary context to which it belongs cannot be treated here.

After a short note on the place of the pericope within the action of 1 Kgs i, the analysis will focus on the narrative structure and linguistic texture of the pericope. These matters, it must be stressed, are being studied here for their own sake, not simply to supply data for a historical-critical analysis. It is in fact methodologically incorrect to pose the question of a possible stratification within the pericope before one has examined at length the degree of narrative coherence that can be seen in the existing form of the text.[5]

a) *The action of 1 Kgs i*

The basic plot-structure of the chapter is that of problem/solution. The problem is the urgent need of a successor to David; hence the stress on David's age and infirmity (*vv.* 1-4, 15) and the repeated thematic question *my yšb ʿl ksʾ ʾdny hmlk ʾḥryw* (*vv.* 20, 27). There are two possible solutions for this problem: Adonijah who takes the initiative himself (*vv.* 5-10), and Solomon who remains in the background and is presented by others (*vv.* 11-27). The climax comes with David's decision to have Solomon anointed as his successor on the throne. This narrative element is presented three times in the text: the royal decision and its sequel (*vv.* 28-37), the fulfilment of the royal command told in the narrator's own voice (*vv.* 38-40), and then the same fulfilment and its sequel described by one of the personages (*vv.* 43-48).[6] The closing verses of the chapter, dealing with the dispersal of the defeated party (*vv.* 49-50) and the submission of the defeated leader (*vv.* 51-53), round off the conflictual aspect of the solution and bring the narrative movement to a point of relative repose.[7]

The chapter provides a fine example of skilful handling of the time-dimension of narrative. Two time-sequences run simultaneously in the

[5] The principle underlying this statement, fundamental in general linguistics since the work of F. de Saussure, is slowly becoming recognized in biblical scholarship too: see e.g. M. Theobald, "Der Primat der Synchronie vor der Diachronie als Grundaxiom der Literarkritik. Methodische Erwägungen an Hand von Mk 2,13-17/Mt 9,9-13", *BZ*, N.F. 22 (1978), pp. 161-86.

[6] The importance of the technique of repetition in 1 Kgs i has often been noted: see e.g. G. Ridout, *Prose Compositional Techniques in the Succession Narrative (2 Sam. 7, 9-20; 1 Kings 1-2)* (Diss. Berkeley, 1971), pp. 112-16; Alter (cf. n. 3), pp. 98-100.

[7] With Long (cf. n. 4), p. 87, it must be stressed that the narrative repose is only relative, for the alternatives stated in *v.* 52 most probably point ahead to further narrative about Adonijah. Contrast the position of M. Noth, *Könige* 1 (Neukirchen-Vluyn, 1968), pp. 8-11, 29; and J. Kegler, *Politisches Geschehen und theologisches Verstehen. Zum Geschichtsverständnis in der frühen israelitischen Königszeit* (Stuttgart, 1977), pp. 121-2, 196-201.

world of the text—Adonijah's feast (*vv.* 9-10, 41-49) and the manoeuvres of Solomon's supporters (*vv.* 11-40). The narrator, however, places in the foreground now the one, then the other, now the first one again, and finally brings them together in the meeting of Adonijah and Solomon told in *vv.* 51-53.

b) *Narrative structure of 1 Kgs i 41-53*

The micro-structure message/reaction occurs twice here (*vv.* 41-50, 51-53), and the general liking for binary articulation of the material is a noteworthy feature of the pericope.[8]

First message/reaction: The message element (*vv.* 41-48) comprises a narrative introduction (*vv.* 41-42) and the delivery of the message (*vv.* 43-48). Each of these in turn has two parts: the introduction first describes the tumult heard by Adonijah's party (*v.* 41) and then tells of the arrival of the messenger (*v.* 42); Jonathan's message begins with information already known to the reader (*vv.* 43-45: cf. *vv.* 38-40) and goes on to what has not yet been recounted (*vv.* 46-48). The first part of the message is linked to the first part of the introduction (*v.* 41) by the reference to noise and uproar in *v.* 45. The second part of the message has an ironic lexical connection with the second part of the narrative introduction: *wṭwb tbśr* (*v.* 42) and *yyṭb ᵓlhyk ᵓt šm šlmh* (*v.* 47): what is "good" in the course of events has to do with Solomon, not with Adonijah. The reaction element (*vv.* 49-50) also has two parts: the first tells of the panic-stricken departure of Adonijah's party (*v.* 49), the second focuses on Adonijah's own reaction (*v.* 50).

Second message/reaction: The message element (*v.* 51) is closely connected on the verbal level to the preceding verse; this argues for treating the two message/reaction units as one pericope. The reaction element (*vv.* 52-53) is more developed than the message part in this case (in contrast to *vv.* 41-50); this is not surprising, for it is King Solomon's reaction that is described here. The reaction has two parts: the royal decree (*v.* 52: itself set out as two alternatives), and the subsequent scene of mute submission by the defeated Adonijah (*v.* 53), which terminates in a brusque two-word command by Solomon, *lk lbytk*.

c) *Linguistic texture of 1 Kgs i 41-53*

Verse 41 skilfully conveys an impression of the growing awareness by Adonijah and his guests of the tumult of popular exultation at Solomon's

---

[8] See C. Conroy, *Absalom Absalom! Narrative and Language in 2 Sam 13-20* (Rome, 1978), pp. 93-95, 124.

anointing (cf. *vv.* 39b-40): one notes the double occurrence both of *ŠMᶜ* (*vv.* 41a, 41b: anaphora) and of *qwl* (twice in *v.* 41b). The first *ŠMᶜ* has no direct object in its own sentence; though translations often supply a pronoun object "it", the elliptic formulation of the Hebrew has the useful effect of establishing a close cohesive link between *v.* 41a and what precedes. It is Joab, the old general, who hears the sound of the trumpet (*v.* 41b). The reader recalls that he had often sounded the trumpet as commanding officer in the course of his successful military career (2 Sam. ii 28, xviii 16, xx 22). Now the initiative has passed to others. Joab belongs to the defeated party, and the text conveys this dramatically by putting a baffled question on his lips, *mdwᶜ qwl hqryh hwmh*.

All this happened just as Adonijah's party had finished their meal (*whm klw lʾkl*: *v.* 41a): a neat effect of contrast, for the ending of a meal is normally a time of peace and quiet. In the context the verb *KLH* takes on a deeper connotation: the feast is at an end, and so too is the cause of Adonijah. The reader knows more than the personages at this point, which opens up possibilities for linguistic irony. One notes also the alliterative repetition of the consonants /k/ and /l/ (*wkl...klw...lʾkl*: all in *v.* 41a), which is then re-echoed by the recurrence of /q/ and /l/ in the double *qwl* of *v.* 41b; the sounds coming from the city do, in fact, mean the end of all Adonijah's hopes (*qwl* - *KLH* - *kl*).

Verse 42 suggests the urgency of the situation by stressing that Joab's question coincided with Jonathan's arrival. The formula *ᶜwd* + *DBR* piel part. + *BWʾ* is used here for the third time in the chapter. The previous occurrences (*vv.* 14, 22) referred to Nathan's coming to David, which proved decisive for the succession of Solomon; this third occurrence is decisive too, but in the opposite direction, for it is set in a scene dealing with the defeated rival of Solomon. Adonijah greets Jonathan with what may have been a conventional formula for greeting messengers (*v.* 42b: cf. the similar wording at 2 Sam. xviii 27), but the conventional phrases acquire an added nuance of dramatic irony here in view of the reader's knowledge that what Jonathan has to announce will be anything but "good news" for Adonijah (*wṭwb tbśr*).

Verse 43 begins with a quotation formula of the type *ᶜNH* + *ʾMR*, which in the present material signals a particularly important speech (cf. 1 Kgs i 28, 36, ii 22). Jonathan's speech is addressed directly to Adonijah (*lʾdnyhw*: *v.* 43a with the MT against the Old Greek). Though Jonathan is shown as having overheard Joab's question of *v.* 41b (cf. *ᶜwdnw mdbr* at *v.* 42a, and also *v.* 45b), his words are hardly meant to be taken simply as a reply to that question, which after all was not addressed directly to him. The message is for Adonijah and the whole party (cf. *šmᶜtm*: *v.* 45). The opening adversative *ʾbl* (*v.* 43b),[9] though unrelated etymologically to *ʾBL* "mourn, be dried up", takes on something of the latter's connotations in the context; Jonathan's message will indeed be a cause of mourning for Adonijah. The solemn title given to David, *ʾdnynw hmlk* (*v.* 43b), seems to echo in an ironic way the *ʾādôn* element in Adonijah's own name (*v.* 43a).[10] The statement of *v.* 43b summarizes the main point of Jonathan's message; details are developed then in *vv.* 44-48 (the anointing, the enthronement, David's reaction).

Verses 44-45a present information about the anointing of Solomon that is already known to the reader from *vv.* 33-35 and 38-40. The several close verbal similarities between *vv.* 38-40 (the narrator's own voice) and *vv.* 44-45 (Jonathan's voice) show clearly that Jonathan's message should not be taken as a piece of realistic reportage, as if it were the sound-track (so to speak) of the scene at En-rogel. On the contrary, it is the narrator who has chosen Jonathan's words for his own narrative purposes. It would be naive to limit the narrator's presence in this type of narrative to items given in the narrator's own voice, though of course his stance towards the material is usually clearer in the latter case. As regards Jonathan's speech, it is important to realize that communication is taking place on two levels here: (1) in the textual world, between Jonathan and Adonijah's party; (2) in the narrative situation, between the narrator and the readers. On the latter level, the readers hear for the third time that Solomon's anointing is the outcome of David's command; the legitimacy of Solomon's succession is thus hammered home in an unmistakable way. The end of the first part of Jonathan's speech is signalled by the nominal sentence of *v.* 45b, whose vocabulary (*qwl, ŠMʿ*) takes up the terminology that dominated *v.* 41 (the narrator's own voice, as well as Joab's). One can note that there are seven principal sentences in this first part of the speech, six verbal (*hmlyk*, *wyšlḥ*, *wyrkbw*, *wymšḥw*, *wyʿlw*, *wthm*) and one nominal (*hwʾ hqwl*...).

Verses 46-48 present the second part of Jonathan's speech. Two structural devices can be noted: (1) the inclusion on the thematic phrase *YŠB ʿl ksʾ* (*vv.* 46, 48); (2) the triple anaphora in *wgm* (vv. 46, 47, 48). As regards the latter feature, the occurrence of double (not triple) *wgm* within quoted messages at 1 Sam. iv 17 and 2 Sam. i 4 may indicate that the usage belonged to the conventions of messenger speech. In any case, the first effect of the triple *wgm* here is to lay heavy stress on the enthronement of Solomon (the term *ksʾ* occurs with different nuances in each of the three

[9] See N. Kilwing, "ʾ*BL*: 'ja, gewiss'—'nein, vielmehr'?", *Biblische Notizen* 11 (1980), pp. 23-8.

[10] See Ridout (cf. n. 6), p. 170.

wgm units). Secondly, from the reader's point of view at least, one can also speak of a crescendo effect here. The information given by *v.* 46, though new (Solomon's enthronement was not narrated at *vv.* 38-40), is not altogether unexpected, for it represents the fulfilment of David's order given at *v.* 35. Then *v.* 47 gives the courtiers' reaction to Solomon's enthronement together with a wordless gesture of acknowledgement by David, while *v.* 48 goes on to present David's own words in the form of a prayer of thanksgiving. Since it was David's words that decided the question of the succession (*vv.* 28ff.), it is fitting that the climax of Jonathan's message should be David's words of thanksgiving.

Verse 47 is given its solemn tone by two rhetorical features: the use of the full designation *ʾdnynw hmlk dwd* in Jonathan's introduction (which forms a verbal link with the beginning of his speech in *v.* 43b), and the phrasing of the courtiers' congratulations in two sentences that exhibit syntactical and, to a large extent, semantic parallelism: (1) precative verbs with God as subject (*yyṭb, wygdl*); (2) direct object referring to Solomon's royal status (*šm, ksʾ*); (3) comparative *min* and the same substantive (*šm, ksʾ*) with reference to David's status. The resemblance between the second sentence (*GDL* + *ksʾ* + *mksʾ*) and Benaiah's words at *v.* 37 creates something of a refrain effect; Benaiah's words after David's decision are re-echoed by all the courtiers after the carrying-out of the king's orders. On the narrator-reader level, this way of shaping the text results in a heavy stress on Solomon's position as David's fully legitimate successor in whom the fame and greatness of the Davidic line can continue to increase (which redounds to the greater glory of David too).[11]

David's gesture of acknowledgement (*v.* 47b) presents an interesting contact with a death-bed scene in the Patriarchal narratives:

1 Kgs i 47b: *wyšthw hmlk ʿl hmškb*
Gen. xlvii 31: *wyšthw yśrʾl ʿl rʾš hmṭh*

When Joseph has sworn to bring Israel's bones out of Egypt in order to bury them with his fathers, the dying Israel bowed "upon the head of his bed", a wordless gesture of acknowledgement and probably of gratitude too. Just as the dutiful son Joseph has fulfilled his father's last wish, so too Solomon's succession has fulfilled David's last desire and he can now utter his *Nunc dimittis* (*v.* 48). On the synchronic level of reading, the Patriarchal allusion adds to the present scene a tone of pathos and an

[11] For a different interpretation see T. Ishida, "Solomon's Succession to the Throne of David—A Political Analysis" (cf. n. 4), pp. 175-87: on p. 181. The interpretation I have preferred is more in line with that proposed earlier by Ishida, *The Royal Dynasties in Ancient Israel. A Study on the Formation and Development of Royal-Dynastic Ideology* (*BZAW* 142; Berlin and New York, 1977), pp. 105-6.

association with venerable tradition (with all the consequent benefits for the image of Solomon as well as of David).

Verse 48 goes on to present the king's words, which begin with the same root *BRK* used of the courtiers in *v.* 47 but now referred to the Lord (*brwk yhwh ʾlhy yśrʾl*: the divine designation links back to David's words in *v.* 30 where the succession problem was decided). The importance of this great day is underlined by the third use of *hywm* in the chapter (*vv.* 25, 30, 48). Though Nathan the prophet may have played a notable part in the preliminaries to David's decision, the real "giving" (*nātan*: *v.* 48) of David's successor has been the work of the Lord God of Israel. The last phrase of David's prayer (*wʿyny rʾwt*: *v.* 48b) recalls Bathsheba's words earlier (*ʿyny kl yśrʾl ʿlyk*: *v.* 20), and it may also be possible to see another Patriarchal allusion here. In Gen. xlviii 10-11 there is a rather insistent reference to the eyes of the dying Israel (*wʿyny yśrʾl kbdw mzqn lʾ ywkl lrʾwt ... whnh hrʾh ʾty ʾlhym gm ʾt zrʿk*): God has granted Israel the favour of seeing the sons of Joseph. Admittedly the contact here is less immediate than that of *v.* 47 above, but in matters of literary allusion one need not expect precise correlation of all the details. The Israel-allusion of *v.* 47 encourages the reader to perceive something of a Patriarchal tonality in David's words at *v.* 48 as well.

Jonathan's speech ends on this high note of religious interpretation of the preceding events: the Lord is the giver, David is the grateful spectator. The gift is that of kingship over Israel,[12] and it is interesting to note that forms of the root *MLK* occur ten times in the speech (*melek* 8x; *MLK* hif 1x; *mlwkh* lx). Is it simply a coincidence that there were also ten occurrences of the root *MLK* in the decisive pericope of *vv.* 32-37?

Verses 49-50 bring the reader back to the action of the story. They describe the reaction to Jonathan's message in a sequence of seven verbs arranged in a largely parallel pattern:

v. 49 (Adonijah's guests): *ḤRD QWM HLK*
v. 50 (Adonijah himself): *YRʾ QWM HLK ḤZQ*

The seventh item (*ḤZQ*) leads on to *vv.* 51-52. While the semantic pattern can thus be described as 3 + 3 + 1, the syntactical pattern is different (3 wyqtl + 1 x-qtl + 3 wyqtl)—another instance of variation. The opening verb of *v.* 49 (*ḤRD*) with its connotations of physical trembling and general panic makes a violent contrast with the calm tone of the preceding verses. The reader's attention is concentrated still more on the verb by the device of delayed identification, its subject being specified only after the following verb *wyqmw*. The subject *kl hqrʾym ʾšr lʾdnyhw* recalls the opening verse of the scene (*v.* 41: *ʾdnyhw wkl hqrʾym ʾšr ʾtw*);

[12] On the themes of gift and giving see Gunn (cf. n. 4), esp. chap. 5.

while Adonijah was associated with his guests there, he is set apart here by the x-qtl inversion at the start of *v.* 50. Defeat entails isolation.

Verse 51 shifts the scene to Solomon by means of a second message/reaction pattern. The text of the message is made more vivid by the use of *hnh* ... *whnh*. The first *hnh* sentence repeats the verb *YRʾ* used in *v.* 50 but now makes explicit (as *vv.* 49-50 did not) the reason for Adonijah's fear: *hmlk šlmh*. In the second sentence the verb *ʾḤZ* replaces its near-synonym *ḤZQ* of *v.* 50 (variation accompanying repetition again). The quoted words of Adonijah use *hmlk šlmh* for the second time in the verse; one notes the reversal of his first words in the chapter (*v.* 5: *ʾny ʾmlk*). It is curious that the only other occurrence of "swear to me first" (*ŠBʿ* nif + *ly* + *kywm*) is at Gen. xxv 33 in a context of rivalry between brothers (Jacob and Esau); on a synchronic level of reading at least, it may not be too far-fetched to see yet another allusion to the Patriarchal traditions here (cf. *vv.* 47 and 48 above), even though the Solomon/Adonijah situation is not exactly the same as the Jacob/Esau one.

Verse 52 presents Solomon's reply to Adonijah's request. There may be some ironic significance in the fact that the reply is not phrased explicitly as an oath (cf. *yšbʿ ly* in *v.* 51): Solomon owes his kingship to David's oath (*vv.* 29-30), but his first royal decision is a refusal to bind himself by oath. It must be added, however, that the solemn public statement of a king may have been regarded as equivalent to an oath (cf. 1 Kgs ii 36-38 with 42-43).[13] Solomon wisely envisages two possibilities. If the defeated rival acts as a *bn ḥyl*, not a hair of his head will be harmed (a similar phrase is found at 1 Sam. xiv 45 and 2 Sam. xiv 11, in both cases as part of an oath). The use of *bn ḥyl* may carry ironic overtones for the reader who recalls that Adonijah had used a similar expression (*ʾyš ḥyl*) as a greeting to his subordinate Jonathan at *v.* 42. An uncommon phrase is used in the second possibility: *MṢʾ* nif + *rʿh* as subject (elsewhere only at 1 Sam. xxv 28; for *MṢʾ* qal + *rʿh* as object see 1 Sam. xxix 6 and Jer. xxiii 11). The passive form is ominous; the reader can already suspect that the "finding" of wickedness in Adonijah will be the prerogative of King Solomon (as ii 22ff. will confirm).[14]

Verse 53 finishes off the Adonijah affair for the time being with a rapid series of five narrative verbs, one of which (*wyštḥw*) occurs for the fifth time in the chapter (cf. *vv.* 16, 23, 31, 47). The only one to speak in the brief face-to-face encounter of the brothers is King Solomon who utters a

---

[13] See the discussion by G. Giesen, *Die Wurzel ŠBʿ "schwören". Eine semasiologische Studie zum Eid im Alten Testament* (Königstein/Ts. and Bonn, 1981), p. 97 with n. 171.

[14] Similarly Gunn (cf. n. 4), p. 106.

curt command *lk lbytk*. No mention is made of Adonijah's reaction or of his departure; his name does not even occur in *vv.* 52-53. The once proud prince (cf. *v.* 5) has been reduced to a nonentity,[15] while Solomon exercises his unopposed power. It may be significant that the personal name "Solomon" is used seven times in *vv.* 51-53. Solomon has been a passive figure in 1 Kgs i up to this point, simply the object of other people's initiatives; now he suddenly emerges having full and perfect control of events, and the seven occurrences of his name help to symbolize this linguistically.

III

Though the redaction-critical problems of 1 Kgs i-ii have been much debated in recent years, no scholarly consensus has as yet emerged.[16] The purpose of these concluding remarks is not to outline a general hypothesis about the genesis of the text but simply to suggest, with the help of an example, that a sharper awareness of literary possibilities can contribute to a more critical use of redaction-critical argumentation. Specifically, the suggestion is that narrative analysis in general, and debate about tensions and incoherence in particular, would profit by paying closer attention to the narrator-reader dimension and to the active role of the reader in processing the text. These matters have been amply discussed within literary studies by scholars associated with "reader-response criticism",[17] and a more theoretical elaboration can be found in some presentations of the developing discipline of text linguistics.[18]

---

15 Compare Fokkelman (cf. n. 4), p. 379.

16 The redactional problems of 1 Kgs i-ii have recently been discussed by: E. Würthwein, *Die Erzählung von der Thronfolge Davids — theologische oder politische Geschichtsschreibung?* (Zürich, 1974); T. Veijola, *Die ewige Dynastie. David und die Entstehung seiner Dynastie nach der deuteronomistischen Darstellung* (Helsinki, 1975); F. Langlamet, "Pour ou contre Salomon? La rédaction prosalomonienne de I Rois, i-ii", *RB* 83 (1976), pp. 321-79, 481-528 (see also his lengthy review of the studies of Würthwein and Veijola in the same volume, pp. 114-37); T. N. D. Mettinger, *King and Messiah. The Civil and Sacral Legitimation of the Israelite Kings* (Lund, 1976); E. Würthwein, *Das Erste Buch der Könige, Kapitel 1-16* (Göttingen, 1977); F. Crüsemann, *Der Widerstand gegen das Königtum. Die antiköniglichen Texte des Alten Testaments und der Kampf um den frühen israelitischen Staat* (Neukirchen-Vluyn, 1978); H. Seebass, *David, Saul und das Wesen des biblischen Glaubens* (Neukirchen-Vluyn, 1980); J. Trebolle, "Testamento y muerte de David. Estudio de historia de la recensión y redacción de I Rey., ii", *RB* 87 (1980), pp. 87-103; P. R. Ackroyd, "The Succession Narrative (so-called)", *Interp* 35 (1981), pp. 383-96; P. K. McCarter, Jr., "'Plots, True or False'. The Succession Narrative as Court Apologetic", ibid., pp. 355-67; J. Conrad, "Der Gegenstand und die Intention der Geschichte von der Thronfolge Davids", *TLZ* 108 (1983), cols 161-76.

17 The useful anthology edited by J. P. Tompkins, *Reader-Response Criticism. From Formalism to Post-Structuralism* (Baltimore and London, 1980), has an annotated bibliography that includes references to scholars associated with *Rezeptionsästhetik*.

18 See e.g. R.-A. de Beaugrande and W. U. Dressler, *Introduction to Text Linguistics* (London and New York, 1981).

To illustrate the point, let us return to 1 Kgs i 46-48. Timo Veijola and François Langlamet, to mention two of the foremost redaction-critics in this area, agree that *vv.* 46-48 violate the requirements of temporal realism.[19] A glance at the context will show why. Since Jonathan's arrival at En-rogel is contemporaneous with the sounding of the trumpet that hails Solomon's anointing at Gihon (cf. *vv.* 42a, 41, 39), Jonathan could not have known what happened later in the court after Solomon's enthronement on his return from Gihon; *vv.* 46-48, however, present us with Jonathan's description of those events. Should one conclude, with Veijola and Langlamet, that this state of affairs points to the secondary nature of *vv.* 46-48? In my opinion, not necessarily, at least on the basis of the foregoing argumentation.

It is useful to recall here the existence of two levels of communication. On the level of the textual world, where communication takes place between the personage Jonathan and the personages of Adonijah's party, there is undoubtedly an incoherence or lack of realism as regards the temporal dimension. But if we also consider the narrative situation, where communication takes place between the (implied) narrator and the (implied) reader, it may be possible to arrive at a higher form of coherence that, as it were, neutralizes the temporal incoherence and allows the reader to process *vv.* 46-48 quite spontaneously as a textual unity with the preceding verses. This could be the case, for instance, if we suppose that the primary intention of the text is not limited to realistic description of the scene (why should it be?) but consists above all in giving the reader an understanding of what it means that Solomon has been enthroned with the full approval of David. The temporal incoherence would then be offset by the interpretational coherence.

One might ask, however, why the author should have admitted the temporal incoherence at all. In reply, it can be pointed out that, while the predominantly interpretational material of *vv.* 46-48 could have been communicated in the narrator's own voice (thus eliminating the temporal incoherence), it gains immensely in dramatic force by being presented as a speech of one of the personages to the members of the defeated party. This dramatic appropriateness is undoubtedly more evident to readers than the temporal incoherence. Indeed, seeing that the vast majority of readers of the text (including those trained in historical-critical analysis) have overlooked the temporal incoherence noted by Veijola and Langlamet, it is hardly rash to propose (at least as a possibility) that the original author, guided by his interpretational aim and by his instinct for dramatic effect, did not notice the temporal incoherence either. Similar

[19] Veijola (cf. n. 16), p. 16; Langlamet (cf. n. 16), pp. 493-94.

cases of lower-order incoherence or inconsistency are by no means infrequent in some of the masterpieces of world literature.[20]

Furthermore, one can note that there are other instances of direct speech in Hebrew narrative that are obviously not intended to be taken as realistic on the level of the textual world but are meant simply as devices for communication on the narrator-reader level. At 2 Sam. xvii 15, for example, we read the spoken words of Hushai: *kzʾt wkzʾt yʿṣ ʾḥytpl* ... *wkzʾt wkzʾt yʿṣty ʾny.*[21] Realistically in the textual world, it is impossible to visualize Hushai actually saying *kzʾt wkzʾt*; he would have had to specify the content of the advice he is talking about, since the priests whom he is addressing are supposed not to have been present at the preceding audience scene. That is to say, the form *kzʾt wkzʾt* functions solely on the narrator-reader level of communication, even though presented as the spoken words of Hushai. The reader already knows what advice was given, so the narrator uses the abbreviated form to convey the urgency of the situation and thus increase the reader's suspense. If, then, factors of appropriateness on the narrator-reader level take precedence over factors of realism at 2 Sam. xvii 15, one cannot exclude the possibility of an analogous situation at 1 Kgs i 46-48 in the original stratum of the text.

To conclude: consideration of the narrator-reader dimension and of the reader's processing activity, whereby aspects of the text that are problematic on one level can be integrated into a higher-order coherence, has shown that one of the arguments adduced for the secondary nature of 1 Kgs i 46-48 is not cogent (on its own, at least). Other arguments would

---

20 There are numerous examples in Shakespeare: see, for instance, J. Dover Wilson (ed.), *Hamlet* (The New Shakespeare; Cambridge, 1954), pp. xlvi-xlviii; P. Brockbank (ed.), *Coriolanus* (The Arden Shakespeare, new edn; London, 1976), p. 160. In the present context there is a particularly interesting case in *Othello* where "...Desdemona's suspected adultery may have been impossible in real time, but it was technically perfect in the tempo of the theatre" (J. L. Styan, *The Shakespeare Revolution. Criticism and Performance in the Twentieth Century* [Cambridge, 1977], p. 31). Cervantes, *Don Quixote*, part I, chap. XXIII, tells of the stealing of the ass by Gines de Pasamonte; a few pages later Sancho is riding the ass again as if nothing had happened, but a little further on he is again without his mount. Even Flaubert, a realist if ever there was one, can supply an example: at various points in *Madame Bovary*, the colour of Emma's eyes is said to be brown, blue, and black (noted by P. Thody, *Roland Barthes. A Conservative Estimate* [London, 1977], pp. 142-3). In brief, there is empirical evidence that oversights and inconsistencies can be found in the original work of authors; consequently, it is simply wrong to postulate that *every* such case in biblical narrative *must* be attributed to later hands. This is not to say that some, perhaps many, cases may not find their most convincing explanation in the hypothesis of a later reworking of the text; the point is that each case must be examined on its own in the light of all the relevant factors of textuality.

21 For the purposes of the argument here it is irrelevant whether *v.* 15b is redactional or not; see F. Langlamet, "Ahitofel et Houshaï. Rédaction prosalomonienne en 2 S 15-17?", in Y. Avishur and J. Blau (ed.), *Studies in Bible and the Ancient Near East presented to Samuel E. Loewenstamm* (Jerusalem, 1978), pp. 57-90: esp. pp. 67-74.

have to be examined, of course, before a final decision could be reached about the verses in question,[22] but that is not the scope of the present remarks. The point has been to suggest that historical-critical analysis (not only in the case of 1 Kgs i-ii) has much to gain, within its own legitimate field of enquiry, by remaining open to relevant insights from literary theory and criticism as well as from text linguistics.

---

[22] For further discussion of the arguments adduced by Veijola and Langlamet see Gunn (cf. n. 4), p. 117; Seebass (cf. n. 16), p. 31; Long (cf. n. 4), pp. 80-1.

L'HERMÉNEUTIQUE BIBLIQUE EN FACE DES MÉTHODES CRITIQUES: DÉFI ET PERSPECTIVES

PAR

J. SEVERINO CROATTO

Buenos Aires

Ce que je vais dire sur le défi de l'herméneutique biblique peut paraître doublement paradoxal. D'un côté, il y a la formulation de l'exégèse scientifique qui nous parvient de l'Atlantique Nord. Elle n'épuise pas, selon notre perspective, toutes ses possibilités. On pourrait dire qu'elle prend un biais avant d'atteindre son but. La prodigieuse réussite des méthodes historico-critiques, en lutte contre une exégèse fondamentaliste (au fond, rationaliste), provoqua le repli de ces méthodes sur elles-mêmes, se considérant sans doute comme la seule façon d'interpréter.

D'un autre côté, l'herméneutique existentielle transposa l'accent de l'"histoire" sur l'interprète, provocant de cette façon un nouveau conflit. Mais cette herméneutique existentielle, individualiste et ahistorique, nous a très peu servi pour reformuler la Parole de Dieu dans notre propre contexte, comme si, elle aussi, n'avait pas atteint son but.

De meilleures perspectives nous sont ouvertes par la sémiotique et les sciences linguistiques, qui prennent la Bible telle qu'elle est, c'est-à-dire, comme un *texte*. Mais nous pensons que ce moment de l'exégèse biblique, très fécond d'ailleurs et qui suppose aussi un énorme progrès, s'épuise en soi, dans sa propre clôture textuelle et synchronique. La *sémiotique* peut ainsi se retrouver avec son opposant, l'exégèse *historico*-critique, si elle ne se dépasse pas critiquement; c'est-à-dire qu'avec diverses approches et différents résultats interprétatifs, il reste encore le danger de demeurer dans le passé. Il nous semble encore une fois que la sémiotique n'a pas atteint son but. Ce n'est pas sa faute, mais plutôt celle des exégètes et des théologiens.

Voilà donc le premier paradoxe: ceux qui ont formulé une exégèse scientifique ne sont pas arrivés à son terme.

La formulation d'une herméneutique de la Bible, comme nous voulons l'exposer ensuite, offre une certaine nouveauté dans l'expression, mais elle ne cherche pas une explication originelle du phénomène, qui est le présupposé qui éclaircit la formation de la Bible comme livre sacré.

Le paradoxe est qu'on est en face d'un phénomène scientifiquement reconnaissable, en même temps que faisant partie du kérygme. Ce qui est décisif pour nous, c'est que toutes les méthodes exégétiques puissent arriver à leur but, afin que le kérygme biblique soit précisement kérygme et non pas histoire. Il n'y a pas d'autre façon de faire la théologie. C'est pour cette raison que nous sommes étonnés de la résistance à accepter toutes les implications de l'herméneutique biblique, et donc à la relecture des textes et à leur recontextualisation. Très souvent cette résistance vient de ceux qui nous ont donné les instruments d'analyse et le vocabulaire de l'herméneutique.

I. A LA RECHERCHE DU SENS

1) Les méthodes historico-critiques de l'exégèse biblique ont ouvert de nouveaux sentiers d'approche vers la Bible. Lorsqu'elles nous ont redécouvert l'horizon historique et culturel dans lequel la Bible s'est développée, elles nous ont donné la possibilité d'une meilleure contextualisation du sens originel de chaque passage. L'exégèse critique a brisé les lectures naïves, "historicistes" et concordistes de la Bible qui nous ont détournés du sens réel du texte. Mais surtout, elle amplifie significativement l'exploration des textes.

Pourtant, il ne faut pas oublier qu'il y a un certain réductionisme propre à ces méthodes qui offre des dangers. D'une part, elles montrent ce qui est "derrière", c'est-à-dire l'archéologie du texte actuel de telle façon qu'elles détournent l'attention de l'exégète et du lecteur, en la plaçant dans un niveau pré-canonique. Le Pentateuque, par exemple, peut-être interprété selon les traditions J, E, P, D ou autres. On souligne ainsi le *pré*-texte.

D'autre part, en partant de la critique littéraire, qui permet d'identifier les empreintes de la formation du texte, les autres méthodes conduisent jusqu'aux lointaines origines (très souvent à travers d'une chaîne d'hypothèses, qui servent d'appui à d'autres hypothèses) et reconduisent, à travers l'histoire de la rédaction, jusqu'à l'état présent d'une oeuvre ou d'un texte. On parcourt ainsi un arc très étendu qui part du texte et retourne; pourtant il s'agit d'une histoire du texte plutôt que d'une exploration de son sens; en tout cas, on identifie le sens avec celui des couches antérieures, lorsqu'elles nous sont accessibles.

Mais on ne peut pas faire, par exemple, l'interprétation du Pentateuque en se limitant à identifier la théologie (incomplète, comme on le sait) de J ou des autres traditions subjacentes. En effet, le Pentateuque n'est pas l'addition de certaines traditions, mais une oeuvre nouvelle qui a un sens en soi plutôt que par le sens de ses fragments. Tout ce qu'on peut dire de ces derniers appartient à l'histoire de la composition du Pentateuque plutôt qu'au Pentateuque même. Le niveau de lecture de celui-ci se trouve impliqué dans sa forme, sa structure et son contenu transmis par la tradition.[1]

La critique de la rédaction réduit en partie cette déficience, mais quand on se réfère au "rédacteur" au lieu de l'"auteur", et quand on considère la rédaction comme une "histoire de la rédaction", on met alors l'accent sur la formation du texte en partant d'origines lointaines ou de son *Sitz im Leben* pré-textuel qui, le plus souvent, est hypothétique.

La critique classique de la rédaction laisse au "rédacteur" une marge d'originalité très étroite vis-à-vis des traditions qu'il recueille (on peut éclaircir cela avec n'importe quel livre prophétique dans sa forme actuelle) ou met l'accent sur l'intention du rédacteur comme le moment dernier de la formation du texte et de la totalisation de son sens. De cette façon, on court le risque d'enfermer dans le passé le message de la Bible, prise comme "dépôt" d'un sens achevé qui coïncide avec la pensée de son rédacteur, ou peut-être, de ses pré-rédacteurs.

Malgré l'importance de ces méthodes, et malgré son retour au texte par la voie de la critique de la rédaction, nous sommes convaincus que la possibilité de signification d'un texte n'aboutit pas ici.

Nous allons remarquer que le sens d'un texte ne peut jamais s'épuiser dans l'intention, même explicite, de son auteur. Autrement, il n'y aurait pas interprétation, mais répétition ou explication. Ceci est extrêmement important pour la théologie; c'est le premier pas pour partir d'une théologie des ouvrages vers une théologie de la vie. C'est pour cela que nous répétons, encore une fois, qu'il faut passer par les méthodes historico-critiques, mais en dépassant nécessairement leur réductionisme "historique" et leur fascination pour l'histoire du texte. "Passer" exige le "dépassement". Le but, le terme se trouve au delà.

2) La plus récente contribution aux études bibliques, qui vient des sciences linguistiques, en particulier de la littérature et de la sémiotique narrative, constitue un excellent complément des méthodes historico-critiques. La genèse et la diachronie du texte sont ainsi complétées par l'analyse de sa structure synchronique. L'étude de ce qu'on appelle structure profonde, soit narrative (actants, fonctions) ou bien discursive (rôles thématiques, axes de sens, etc.) nous aide à "centrer" le sens d'un texte, indépendamment de la diversité ou de l'hétérogénéité de ses parties. Elle nous aide aussi à percevoir qu'un texte est toujours cohérent, malgré les incohérences que la critique littéraire ou des traditions met en évidence.

---

[1] L'excellente *Introduction critique à l'Ancien Testament* (Paris, 1973) de H. Cazelles constitue un cas typique: le chapitre sur le contenu et la théologie du Pentateuque finit avec des considérations très exactes mais sans nous offrir une théologie *du Pentateuque* en sa structure actuelle.

Mais, cette analyse risque aussi de tomber dans le ''réductionisme'', comme si le sens d'un texte pouvait se trouver dans sa structure profonde, alors que la fonction de cette analyse est de montrer comment fonctionne un texte et d'orienter la lecture comme production d'un nouveau sens.

Plus féconde encore est l'étude de la structure de surface et son complément, la rhétorique du texte.[2] Découvrir la codification d'un texte c'est avoir les clefs de sa lecture en nous permettant de pénétrer et d'approfondir tout le texte jusqu'à ses sémas minimes. Même en étant très féconde, cette méthode (surtout si elle reçoit, avant ou après, l'appui des méthodes historico-critiques) peut, comme celles-ci, rester dans le passé.

3) C'est pour celà qu'il est indispensable de tenir compte du nouveau complément de l'herméneutique. Mais, avant tout, je veux éclaircir le chemin. Premièrement de façon négative, en disant que ce n'est pas l'herméneutique existentielle qui nous intéresse, parce qu'elle est générique et ambigüe; moins encore dans son expression bultmannienne, nuancée d'individualisme et d'effectivisme (remarquons que la ''décision existentielle'' est aussi générique qu'imprécise). Ce qu'on peut retenir de l'herméneutique existentielle c'est la clarification du concept de ''précompréhension'', tel que nous pouvons le reformuler en termes moins teintés de subjectivité et plus linguistiques (v. gr. ''relecture'', ''eiségèse'', etc.).

Deuxièmement, et de façon positive, il me semble qu'après la contribution des sciences linguistiques, particulièrement de la sémiotique, nous devons inscrire — d'une certaine manière — l'herméneutique dans la sémiotique ou, au moins, nous croyons qu'elle doit faire un détour par la sémiotique. L'opposition apparente qui se présente (entre la synchronie de la linguistique et la diachronie de l'herméneutique) se résout dans un enrichissement et une fécondation mutuels. La sémiotique nous donne les clefs de lecture intérieures au texte. L'herméneutique c'est l'exercice de la lecture orientée par ces clefs. Ainsi diminue le danger de subjectivité qui est l'accusation typique qu'on dresse contre l'herméneutique.

Toutefois, l'herméneutique incorpore d'autres clefs (d'où l'insuffisance de la linguistique seule) controlées à leur tour par les règles de la sémiotique. Notre lecture, qui est toujours herméneutique, sera d'autant plus féconde que nous respecterons le texte comme texte et comme un texte, en particulier, dont la structure et la compétence de production de sens ont été explorées préalablement par la science des signes.

---

[2] Cf. M. Kessler, ''A Methodological Setting for Rhetorical Criticism'', dans D. J. A. Clines (ed.), *Art and Meaning: Rhetoric in Biblical Literature* (Sheffield, 1982), pp. 1-19.

II. Éléments linguistiques de l'herméneutique

L'herméneutique c'est l'interprétation des événements, ou l'interprétation des textes qui recueillent sa lecture. Étant donné que l'herméneutique biblique dit rélation avec un texte, elle nous situe en plein dans le domaine de la linguistique.

1) *Polysémie.* Du point de vue de la linguistique, un texte quelconque possède une qualité intrinsèque qui est la polysémie. L'alternance polysémie/monosémie ou clôture du sens, se trouve au sein même du phénomène du langage. Si la langue, en tant que système de signes, est polysémique; la "parole" (l'acte d'utiliser la langue dans un discours), au contraire, a tendance à clôturer le sens: le locuteur qui sélectionne les signes, l'interlocuteur qui les déchiffre, l'un et l'autre qui dialoguent dans un contexte ou horizon concret, ces trois éléments ferment monosémiquement le sens du discours. Autrement, on ne pourrait pas parler. Or, quand le discours cristallise dans un "texte" qui se transmet (oralement ou par écrit, peu importe pour le moment) le locuteur et l'interlocuteur s'évanouissent et l'horizon de référence du discours parlé est modifié. La même situation se produit quand un texte adressé à quelqu'un de bien déterminé, est lu par d'autres personnes dans des circonstances différentes. La clôture du sens que l'auteur avait donné au texte (dont les seules traces se trouvent dans le texte même) s'ouvre de nouveau à la polysémie. Il n'est pas difficile d'admettre que le nouveau lecteur apporte au texte de nouvelles questions quand il le lit sous une autre perspective ou avec un autre horizon de compréhension. Ceci serait déjà impossible si le sens restait immobilisé dans sa première lecture.

2) *De l'auteur au texte.* Ce que les exégètes n'admettent pas volontiers, c'est le fait, encore plus clair, que l'auteur — aussi bien que le locuteur dans l'acte de "parler" — meurent au moment même où ils codifient leur message: l'inscription d'un sens, dans un récit ou dans un texte quelconque, est un acte créatif dans lequel on peut dire symboliquement qu'on perd la vie. Mesurer les conséquences de ce phénomène est essentiel pour l'herméneutique qui fait le détour par la linguistique. Ceci invalide les anciennes formulations de l'herméneutique (cf. Schleiermacher) qui cherchaient à identifier la lecture interprétative avec la pensée de l'auteur d'un texte; on invalide aussi la prétention des méthodes historico-critiques de récupérer et de faire revivre l'auteur ou rédacteur du texte (v. gr. la Redaktions*geschichte*). On n'interprète pas un auteur mais un texte. Il y aura toujours quelqu'un qui écrit ou raconte, mais c'est seulement dans le texte qu'il est possible de le reconnaître. Ce n'est jamais lui seul la clef de la lecture. Le narrateur est le texte même et non quelqu'un du dehors à qui on pourrait demander ce qu'il voulait dire. Le

texte parle en tant que texte. Quand nous lisons une oeuvre littéraire, quand nous voyons un film (qui est un texte!) ou écoutons une musique, il ne nous vient pas à l'esprit l'idée de nous diriger vers l'auteur pour lui demander qu'est-ce qu'il voulait dire ou quel est le sens exact de sa pensée.

Seule une préoccupation historiciste ou psychologiste peut identifier le sens d'un texte avec la pensée de son auteur ou producteur. Certes, on ne peut pas nier que le contexte historique, le *Sitz im Leben*, les traditions, l'intention rédactionnelle, aident à clarifier le sens. Mais celui-ci se trouve codifié dans le texte. La critique historique, culturelle, sociologique, philologique nous rapproche du moment de la production du texte afin de comprendre la "langue" (les mots, les phrases) et le référent extralinguistique du texte et donc, le sens global du texte à ce moment là: sens historique, en dernière instance. Mais, à part le fait que ceci nous amène irrémédiablement à des lectures hypothétiques[3] et que cette méthode signifie chercher hors du texte les clefs de sa lecture, finalement on n'aboutit qu'à une "histoire" du sens du texte en question. Ce n'est pas mal, mais ce n'est pas tout et ce n'est peut-être même pas la question principale. Le texte est là, avec ses propres clefs de lecture identifiables par la critique littéraire et rhétorique, par la sémiotique et la linguistique. Pour une lecture théologique de la Bible qui soit herméneutique, cette constatation est capitale. Si on reste attaché à l'auteur d'un texte, on ne fait pas un acte herméneutique mais une répétition. Parce que les textes de la Bible ont été écrits en d'autres époques et pour d'autres hommes, une exégèse seulement historique (comme d'ailleurs l'exégèse concordiste ou fondamentaliste) les rend peu pertinents. Il ne reste que l'application à notre situation; mais je considère que celle-ci est un aspect secondaire de l'interprétation.

Dans la naissance d'un texte quelconque se produit nécessairement une distantiation entre celui-ci et son auteur, ce qui implique une polysémie du texte et le besoin d'entreprendre sa lecture comme une relecture. Voilà un mot suspect dans certains milieux théologiques mais qui vise un phénomène qui ne peut être contesté: il n'y a pas de lecture qui ne soit relecture. Quand on le nie, on le pratique en même temps. Il n'est pas possible de faire autrement. Même la lecture historico-critique est une relecture atténuée, malgré sa prétendue identification avec la pensée de l'auteur (ou mieux de ses pré-rédacteurs).

---

[3] Ceci est visible dans l'interprétation des cantiques du Serviteur de Yahvé. Est-ce que notre lecture peut être conditionnée par l'identification préalable de l'ʿ*ebed* avec Yoyakîn ou avec une autre figure historique?

3) *La réserve-de-sens.* Une conséquence de la distantiation déjà signalée entre l'auteur et le texte qu'il produit[4] et du phénomène de la transformation de toute lecture en relecture, c'est la réserve-de-sens impliquée dans chaque texte et qui est explorée et développée en chaque lecture. En effet, le sens d'un texte ne s'identifie pas avec l'intention de son auteur (contextuelle, fugace, irréversible et irrécupérable dans sa pureté). Nous l'avons déjà signalé. De la même manière, l'intention de l'auteur ne se trouve guère dans le texte comme dans un dépôt qui demeure immobile et permanent à travers les générations. La sémiotique, en effet, nous a enseigné définitivement que le sens ne se trouve pas dans l'auteur mais dans le texte, bien qu'il ne soit pas possible de le trouver dans celui-ci comme une substance, comme un contenu bien renfermé. La sémiotique nous enseigne plutôt que le sens est codifié dans la structure du récit, dans un "tissu" (= texte!) de relations, différences et oppositions (des actants, fonctions, rôles thématiques, images, figures rhétoriques, structures littéraires, etc.). La lecture, alors, c'est une "décodification", c'est l'oeuvre de déchiffrer. Grâce au croisement des clefs, la lecture peut choisir les unes ou les autres comme dans un jeu inépuisable qui sera mis à profit par la perspective herméneutique, comme nous allons voir.

4) *La lecture comme production du sens.* La lecture donc, est en réalité la production d'un discours et en conséquence, d'un sens a partir d'un texte. Ce qu'on lit ce n'est pas un sens mais un texte, dont, chaque fois qu'on le lit, jaillit un sens. Ceci n'est pas relativiser le sens de la Bible. S'il y a une certaine relativisation, c'est vis-à-vis d'une conception fixiste et historiciste que nous croyons erronée du point de vue de la sémiotique et de l'herméneutique: du point de vue de la sémiotique, ce que nous venons d'affirmer s'exprime en disant que la lecture c'est une production de sens. Du point de vue de l'herméneutique, ceci signifie que tout texte qui fait référence à la réalité humaine et non aux lois physiques ou mathématiques, comporte une réserve-de-sens. En d'autres mots, le sens actuel d'un texte, qui est celui de la lecture, amplifie, approfondit, réévalue, fait croître le sens originel inscrit par son auteur ou aussi par une lecture normative préalable. Encore une fois, interpréter (comme dans la musique, comme dans le théâtre, comme dans toute praxis), ce n'est pas répéter. S'il y a quelque chose que je veux faire remarquer au long de cette exposition, c'est ce phénomène essentiel de l'interprétation, qui est en même temps la meilleure définition d'une herméneutique liée à la

---

[4] Il faut signaler ici que les textes religieux (mythes, écritures saintes), d'ordinaire, sont anonymes. Leur attribution à un "auteur" est un fait postérieur qui résulte à son tour d'un phénomène herméneutique: non seulement parce qu'ils sont la création d'une communauté, mais plutôt par le fait qu'ils sont significatifs à cause de ce qu'ils disent plutôt que par celui qui le dit.

sémiotique (même si elle reste différente d'elle): toute lecture est herméneutique, et elle est une relecture, et celle-ci implique chaque fois un accroissement du sens d'un texte. Nous sommes très loin de l'idée d'un "dépôt" du sens (au niveau linguistique) aussi bien que d'un "dépot" de la Révélation (au niveau théologique).

L'image de l'exégèse biblique que nous venons d'esquisser fait la convergence des méthodes historico-critiques (étape introductoire), de la sémiotique narrative (avec son accent sur le texte tel qu'il est, non comme il était) et de l'herméneutique comme relecture à partir de l'horizon de l'interprète et comme accumulation de sens dans un texte. Ce qui ressort à chaque instant c'est l'intime connexion entre herméneutique et sémiotique, généralement traitées séparément ou en opposition. Nous verrons encore d'autres aspects de cette corrélation.

5) *Sens et référence d'un texte.* Maintenant, nous allons introduire un autre élément linguistique, la distinction entre sens et référence d'un texte, en considérant ses implications herméneutiques. Les méthodes historico-critiques de l'exégèse biblique nous aident à identifier le référent d'un texte, par exemple Isa. liii: s'agit-il de Yoyakîn? de Zorobabel? d'un prophète? d'un sage? d'un roi? ou d'Israël? Le texte d'Isaïe n'identifie pas ce personnage, et il serait digne de louange, peut-être enrichissant et quelquefois fascinant, de vouloir le faire maintenant par le moyen de la critique historique.[5] Il faut, sans doute, le faire. Mais il arrive que le texte d'Isa. liii ne se préoccupe pas de nous indiquer le référent historique originel. Pourquoi? Parce qu'il était évident pour ses destinataires, qui pourra l'affirmer? Est-ce que ce ne serait pas parce qu'au moment où il fut écrit ce qui vraiment intéressait était la figure du Serviteur de Yahvé (dépeint par des traces symboliques fortement marquées d'attributs royaux) plutôt que son identité? Le texte est ainsi doublement polysémique: par ses qualités littéraires et symboliques, et parce qu'il n'explicite pas son référent. Le texte a un sens en soi, comme tel texte, et non par tout le contenu que la critique pourrait découvrir derrière lui. Même quand le référent historique reste explicite dans un texte, en soulignant ainsi la clôture du sens contextuel, la transmission ultérieure du texte affaiblit peu à peu le référent (ce qui peut être arrivé dans Isa. liii, s'il ne s'agit pas d'un texte purement littéraire!) en faveur du sens, donné par la position et la structuration de ses signifiants linguistiques, lesquels font référence à des significations qui demeurent à l'intérieur du récit.

Or, les relectures d'un texte s'originent à partir de son sens, pas à partir de son référent, ce qui est évident dans le cas d'Isa. liii. De la polysé-

[5] Cf. P. Grelot, *Les Poèmes du Serviteur. De la lecture critique à l'herméneutique* (Paris, 1981), pp. 67-73.

mie de ce texte, transmis dans la tradition d'Israël comme prophétique, ont surgi des interprétations aussi diverses que celles de la LXX, du NT et du Targum. En Amérique Latine, nous lui donnons un nouveau référent, dans la ligne christologique, fait qui ne doit pas nécessairement coïncider "historiquement" avec celui du NT, parce que chaque interprétation est une clôture du sens ouvert qui vient d'un texte antérieur.

6) *Intertextualité et intratextualité.* Maintenant nous devons voir la relation entre l'intertextualité et l'intratextualité. Le sens d'un texte se produit par la lecture, grâce aux codes et aux clefs que le texte même possède en soi comme structure signifiante. Mais il est vrai qu'un texte se clarifie aussi par un autre texte qui se trouve à côté, comme un mythe se comprend par d'autres mythes dans la même cosmovision. Celle-ci crée une "pertinence" textuelle qui permet de supposer dans un texte plusieurs choses qui se trouvent sous-entendues. Alors, le sens du texte (l'intratextualité) se trouve amplifié par le con-texte littéraire ou cosmovisionel (l'intertextualité). Mais cette tension conduit à un autre phénomène d'un grand relief herméneutique, c'est-à-dire, que l'intertextualité devient une intratextualité nouvelle. En d'autres mots, plusieurs textes qui se réfèrent à une "pertinence" commune, deviennent un texte.

Ce principe explique en partie la formation du Pentateuque, ou du livre actuel d'Isaïe et, plus spécialement, nous aide à comprendre le NT comme une relecture globale de l'AT compris comme un seul texte.

J'ai déjà dit que ce phénomène a des conséquences herméneutiques. Avant tout, c'est le résultat d'un travail herméneutique. Dans le processus d'interprétation des traditions et des textes qui les ont thématisées, on trouve que l'accumulation du sens est chaque fois plus grande en vertu de sa polysémie et de la nécessité de nouvelles clôtures. À distance, les textes antérieurs sont vus comme une totalité dans laquelle on remarque les grands axes sémantiques et diminuent — encore une fois — les référents du passé. C'est pour cela que le Pentateuque est une oeuvre, dans laquelle les différences des diverses traditions, surtout au niveau des codes, passent au second plan dans la nouvelle intratextualité qui, il faut le dire, se finit dans la structure du Pentateuque. Constituer une nouvelle intratextualité qui renferme aussi le livre de Josué (Hexateuque) est un aspect de ce même phénomène herméneutique, mais, cette fois, il ne trouve pas d'appui dans la tradition juive et ne répond pas à la structure sémiotique du Pentateuque même.[6] Par la transposition de l'intertextualité à l'intratextualité, on peut s'expliquer que l'Église primitive ait

[6] Voir, pour une critique de l'hypothèse d'un Hexateuque, "Una promesa aun no cumplida. Algunos enfoques sobre la estructura literaria del Pentateuco", *Revista Biblica* 44:4 n. 8 (1982), pp. 193-206.

conservé tout l'AT sans considérer comme impérative la pratique de la Thora de la façon dont nous la trouvons légiférée dans les codes du Pentateuque.

7) *Axes sémantiques.* Ce que nous avons établi jusqu'ici nous permet de considérer toute la Bible comme un seul texte, dans lequel on doit interpréter chaque passage dans son propre contexte littéraire, mais tout en cherchant aussi les grands axes sémantiques et kérygmatiques. Ceci est un travail que la science exégétique n'a pas encore entrepris, mais qui nous concerne de façon angoissante.

La Bible est un ensemble de textes énormément étendu et qui permet les lectures les plus variées. On pourrait dire qu'il y a un texte pour chaque plaisir. Il y a des théologies et des traditions très diverses. Peut-on se contenter des ''théologies bibliques'' qui se limitent généralement à l'Ancien ou au Nouveau Testament et dont la plupart sont centrées sur des concepts (tels par exemple: Dieu, l'homme, le roi, le péché, etc.) et sur leur évolution historique? (Remarquons encore une fois la préoccupation historique dont nous avons déjà parlé.) Chaque mot, chaque tradition, n'offre un vrai sens que dans un récit qui les clôture. De la même façon, reprendre la Bible comme un texte devra nécessairement enrichir les lectures fragmentaires des livres et des péricopes, qui d'ailleurs sont indispensables.

Dans la lecture de la Bible comme une totalité narrative, il y a une nouvelle production de sens. Dans cette perspective, le sens de certaines idées ou de certains vocables, sans perdre son propre contexte littéraire, se structure de telle façon qu'il produit un effet-de-sens nouveau. Ceci permet, par exemple, d'identifier l'exode comme ''axe sémantique'' et donc ''kérygmatique'' qui structure les grands thèmes théologiques de toute la Bible. Celle-ci se présente alors comme un grand projet historico-salvifique qui nous interdit d'isoler et de mettre au premier plan les textes qui peuvent justifier l'oppression d'autres peuples, la concentration du pouvoir, etc., et démasque les fausses théologies anti-humaines construites sur la Bible.

Aussi bien, la tendance spiritualisante du NT se trouve-t-elle incluse dans la totalité sémiotique de la Bible comme un macro-récit et alors celle-ci ne conserve plus la signification ''évolutioniste'' qu'on lui a prêté (d'après cette conception, le NT serait la culmination de l'AT, ce qui à mon avis, est une erreur, pas seulement sémiotique, mais aussi herméneutique, et par conséquent théologique). Le NT est un grand effort herméneutique de relecture de l'AT, comme un grand texte dans lequel on reconnaît des grandes centres de gravitation. Il est la relecture par laquelle on *interprète* l'événement de Jésus comme l'Envoyé de Dieu. Cette lecture était située spontanément dans une intratextualité produisant de nouveaux textes (le NT). Avec ces textes s'est formé, à son tour, une nouvelle intertextualité; et c'est à nous de reprendre l'Ancien et le Nouveau Testaments comme une nouvelle intratextualité. Pour les pays opprimés, ceci est extrêmement important, parce que la Bible porte les empreintes (marquées dans sa propre structure littéraire) de profondes expériences de souffrance et d'oppression, de libération et de grâce, où la foi israélite a su reconnaître le Dieu sauveur dans une dimension libératrice.

8) *Praxis et interprétation.* Jusqu'à présent nous nous sommes placés sur un registre linguistique, pour ainsi dire. Les méthodes historico-critiques, la sémiotique et l'herméneutique, les trois travaillent sur des textes. Pourtant, l'herméneutique est liée, de façon explicite et essentielle, à une certaine forme de praxis. Celle-ci comprend deux moments: celui de la constitution du texte même; et celui de la lecture/interprétation.

La Bible (en tant que texte surtout religieux) est le résultat d'un long processus herméneutique dont le point de départ se trouve dans certains événements. Tout événement est, de soi, polysémique: le récit qui le recueille est toujours interprétation, et une interprétation parmi d'autres possibles. La lecture de l'événement est, en son temps, une clôture de son sens. Mais, plus tard, le déplacement des facteurs linguistiques (locuteur/interlocuteur, ou auteur/destinataire) et contextuels, que nous avons analysés un peu plus avant, a fait que cette lecture (convertie en récit, tradition ou texte plus ou moins fixe) redevient polysémique, suscitant une nouvelle clôture de sens par le jeu de nouvelles interprétations, et ainsi de suite. Le processus se fait à plusieurs étages, en passant aussi par la constitution d'un "canon" normatif, lequel, à son tour, doit être réinterprété par de nouveaux récits ou discours (Mišna/Talmud en face de la Thora; Pères de l'Église en face de l'Ancien et du Nouveau Testaments comme nouvelle totalité).[7] Mais ce qui détermine et oriente la réinterprétation, c'est le texte (d'après la perspective de la sémiotique) et c'est surtout la vie, les situations nouvelles d'Israël, la nécéssité de recueillir le sens des événements nouveaux et interpellants.

Bref, la clef de la lecture des textes c'est une certaine forme de praxis humaine. C'est pour cela que la Bible a été formée par un long processus herméneutique. Elle est la lecture permanente des situations; quand il y a déjà des traditions et des textes, la lecture des situations et des textes (ceux-ci étant la lecture de situations précédentes) se fait en forme circulaire (= circularité herméneutique). Les événements du passé et ses lec-

---

[7] Ce point a été développé dans le ch. II de *Hermeneutica Biblica. Para una teoria de la lectura como produccion de sentido* (Buenos Aires, 1984).

tures interprétatives éclaircissent les nouveaux événements, et, ainsi, ils acquièrent graduellement le caractère de fondateurs. Ils sont fondateurs à leur tour parce que leur sens ne fut jamais épuisé à leur première lecture, tout en étant plutôt l'accumulation du sens d'autres événements qui avaient été lus herméneutiquement dans leur horizon ou dans leur continuum sémantique. C'est pour cela que l'exégèse purement "historique" appauvrit les textes bibliques, surtout quand elle se tourne hors de l'horizon biblique, en cherchant de cette manière à identifier le sens d'un texte. Le fait historique est important en tant qu'interprété par de nouvelles pratiques socio-historiques, mais pas comme un fait nu et extérieur que l'historien cherche à récupérer.

Une fois que l'événement a été lu dans un texte, son sens se trouve dans ce texte, non dans sa reconstruction artificielle. Mais cet événement produit aussi des effets au niveau de la praxis, de la vie, et ici encore nous nous trouvons une nouvelle fois dans l'optique du sens, pas dans la répétition du fait.

Alors, en dernière instance, c'est le sens d'un événement recueilli et agi dans de nouveaux événements qui fait que la lecture des textes (lesquels à son tour sont le sens d'événements ou de situations) est toujours une certaine forme de relecture. Il y a toujours un contexte vital qui fait progresser la lecture comme exploration d'une réserve-de-sens d'un texte.

9) *Exégèse et eiségèse.* Ce que nous venons de dire suppose que l'exégèse et l'eiségèse sont corrélatives, comme la montée et la descente d'un même chemin. Il ne serait pas nécessaire d'inventer le mot "eiségèse" si l'exégèse n'avait la prétention d'être seulement une "sortie" à partir du texte. La formation de la Bible comme processus herméneutique — qui appartient à son propre message! — suppose que l'interprétation des événements, des traditions et des textes a toujours été un processus "eiségétique". Dans toute lecture, quelque chose de nouveau "entre" dans le texte ou dans l'événement qu'on lit. Si on prend le cas d'un peuple ou d'une communauté qui ont leur propre identité cosmovisionelle, tant au niveau politique que sociologique, culturel ou religieux, ceci est un principe herméneutique fondamental. D'autre part, comme nous l'avons vu, ce principe se base aussi sur la structure du langage, dont le jeu de clôture/polysémie de sens fait que toute lecture est une production (et pas une répétition) du sens.

Aussi bien, dans la lecture/interprétation de la Bible que fait le spécialiste, il y a une certaine forme de praxis, de conditionnement historico-culturel ou religieux, qui oriente la lecture. Il n'existe pas un travail exégétique neutre, même s'il se présente de la façon la plus académique. Ni le *midrāš*, ni le *pēšer*, ni le commentaire mishnique de la Thora n'ont été un produit de la spécialisation rabbinique ou des docteurs de la Loi. Ils furent engendrés au sein d'une communauté, à l'intérieur de courants théologiques, de groupes religieux socio-historiquement situés.

L'aspiration de l'exégéte — quelquefois explicitée — à chercher le sens objectif, historique, du texte biblique, est une illusion. Ceci pour des raisons que nous, exégètes, avons expérimentées. Ce qu'on recueille, ce sont des résidus ou bien des hypothèses. Très souvent, on trouve ce qui disent (c'est-à-dire, le sens) d'autres textes, qu'on peut rapporter au texte biblique, obtenant ainsi des résultats positifs, quelquefois spectaculaires. Mais, en définitive, le sens du texte biblique qu'on analyse, est donné par ses propres codes, dans une structure narrative et discursive et dans une disposition littéraire. Ces éléments engendrent l'interprétation, et celle-ci entraine une partie de la vie de l'exégète ou de la communauté à laquelle il appartient, c'est-à-dire son propre monde.

Toute exégèse, même académique, est une eiségèse. On entre dans le texte de plusieurs manières, avant d'en sortir triomphalement avec le sens. Si le spécialiste arrive à reconstituer le contexte originel d'un texte, s'il peut établir le sens exact d'un mot avec l'aide de la philologie sémitique, sa tâche d'éclaircissement est à peine commencée. La connaissance qu'il obtient est encore "historique" ou plutôt "pré-historique" à l'égard du texte même.

Il reste encore le travail inévitable d'aborder le texte en tant que structure linguistique, par exemple à la lumière de la sémiotique narrative. Et il faut faire encore une autre démarche, cette fois herméneutique: il faut "ouvrir" le texte en avant, vers la vie, en montrant sa féconde polysémie qui pousse vers la relecture, vers une nouvelle clôture du sens, qui sera faite par le lecteur ou par celui qui utilise son travail scientifique.

Conclusion

Il est habituel de dire que l'herméneutique est subjective et pour cela ne mérite pas l'attention de l'exégète historico-critique. En tenant compte de ce que nous avons dit, il reste établi que *toute* lecture de textes est herméneutique et partant eiségétique, même quand on ne le reconnaît pas.

Mais, d'autre part, l'accusation de subjectivité est valable pour une herméneutique qui s'approche seulement du texte, sans entrer dans le cercle de son poids sémantique. Nous avons souligné déjà l'insertion de l'herméneutique dans la sémiotique. L'herméneutique des textes bibliques se trouve par conséquent conditionnée par le contexte de l'interprète et, de façon simultanée, *par les textes mêmes*. En effet, c'est *le texte* qui indique la limite du sens, quel qu'en soit son ampleur. Polysémie du texte ne signifie pas n'importe quoi. *Un texte dit ce qu'il permet de dire.* Sa polysémie surgit d'une clôture préalable. C'est pour cela qu'il est nécessaire de le situer dans son propre contexte par le moyen des méthodes historico-critiques et d'explorer alors sa capacité à produire du sens (lois de la sémiotique) afin de faire surgir, de la vie, son "avant". La critique historique, la sémiotique et l'herméneutique socio-historique (mieux qu' "existentielle") doivent être convergentes, en se soutenant mutuellement pour une étude féconde de la Bible qui soit reflexion de la foi et par conséquent théologie, c'est-à-dire, discours sur Dieu: jamais le Dieu du passé mais le Dieu qui se manifeste dans *notre* histoire.

JESAJA LVI 1-7:
EIN ABROGATIONSFALL INNERHALB DES KANONS— IMPLIKATIONEN UND KONSEQUENZEN

VON

HERBERT DONNER

Kiel

Am Anfang des tritojesajanischen Corpus steht die Verbindung eines prophetischen Mahnwortes (lvi 1-2) mit einer Thora über die Zulassung von Nichtisraeliten und Eunuchen zur Gemeinde des Jerusalemer Tempels (lvi 3-7).[1] Der Text lautet folgendermaßen:

(1) Also hat Jahwe gesprochen:
Pflegt das Recht und tut die Gerechtigkeit!
Denn mein Heil kommt bald, und meine Gerechtigkeit wird offenbar.
(2) Wohl dem Menschen, der das tut, und dem Menschenkind, das sich daran festhält:
der den Sabbath hält, ohne ihn zu entweihen,[2] und der seine Hand hütet, ohne alles Böse zu tun!
(3) Und der Fremde, der sich Jahwe angeschlossen hat,[3] soll nicht sagen:
''Jahwe trennt mich völlig von seinem Volke ab'';
und der Eunuch soll nicht sagen: ''Ich bin ja ein trockener Baum.''
(4) Denn also hat Jahwe gesprochen:
Den Eunuchen, die meine Sabbathe halten und vorziehen, was mir gefällt, und die sich an meinem Bunde festhalten,
(5) denen gebe ich in meinem Tempel und in meinen Mauern ''Hand und Namen''[4] — besser als Söhne und Töchter! —;

---

[1] In der Regel wird V.8 zu diesem Spruchgebilde hinzugerechnet. Stil und Inhalt des Verses lassen jedoch eher an einen interpretierenden Zusatz denken.

[2] 1QIs[a] *mḥllh* behandelt den Sabbath als nomen fem.; vgl. Ex. xxxi 14 und Lev. xxv 6. LXX τὰ σάββατα μὴ βεβηλοῦν scheint *šabbātōt mᵉḥallēl* vorauszusetzen; dagegen Vulg. *sabbatum ne polluat illud.*

[3] *hannilwā* ist 3. Pers. m. sg. perf. Nif. mit relativ. Artikel; daran ist gegen GK § 138k (*BH*, *BHS*) festzuhalten, obgleich part. m. sg. Nif. *hannilwæ* (vgl. LXX, Theodotion, Peschiṭta, Targume) ebenfalls einen guten Sinn ergäbe.

[4] Vgl. dazu M. Delcor, ''The Special Meanings of the Word *yād* in Biblical Hebrew'', *JSS* 12 (1967), pp. 230-40; S. B. Frost, ''The Memorial of the Childless Man'', *Interpreta-*

einen ewigen Namen gebe ich "ihnen"[5], der nicht ausgetilgt wird.
(6) Und die Fremden, die sich Jahwe anschließen,[6] indem sie ihm dienen und Jahwes Namen lieben, indem sie ihm Knechte werden, jeder, der den Sabbath hält, ohne ihn zu entweihen, und die sich an meinem Bunde festhalten,
(7) die bringe ich zu meinem heiligen Berge und erfreue sie in meinem Bethaus.
Ihre Brandopfer und ihre Schlachtopfer "werden" wohlgefällig "aufsteigen"[7] auf meinen Altar;
denn mein Tempel wird ein Bethaus für alle Völker heißen.

Hauptinhalt dieser prophetischen Thora[8] ist die von Jahwe verfügte Zulassung von Nichtisraeliten und Eunuchen zur Jerusalemer Tempelgemeinde, und zwar unter der Bedingung, daß sich diese Gruppen, "an Jahwe anschließen", d.h. seinen Willen tun und sich an seinen "Bund" halten — was gewiß nicht ausschließlich, aber auch und vornehmlich in der Sabbathheiligung seinen Ausdruck findet. Damit setzt die Thora eine Situation voraus, in der die Zugehörigkeit von Nichtisraeliten und Eunuchen zur Tempelgemeinde problematisch geworden war, mehr noch: in der diese bereits zugehörigen Gruppen ausgeschieden, von der Gemeinde abgetrennt wurden (*bdl* Hif.).

Man hat längst bemerkt, daß diese Situation innerhalb der nachexilischen Geschichte Israels präzise lokalisiert werden kann: im Zusammenhang der Neugestaltung der Gemeinde von Jerusalem zur Zeit Nehemias und Esras.[9] Die vielfältigen und schwierigen literarischen und histori-

---

tion 26 (1972), pp. 437-50; G. Robinson, "The Meaning of *yād* in Is. 56,5", *ZAW* 88 (1976), pp. 282-4; H. A. Brongers, "Miscellanea Exegetica", *Übersetzung und Deutung, Festschrift A. R. Hulst* (Nijkerk, 1977), pp. 35-7.

[5] L. mit 1QIs^{a} (*lhmh*) und den Vers. (LXX αὐτοῖς, Vulg. *eis*) *lāhæm* oder *lāmō*.

[6] Zwar steht hier part. m. pl. Nif., was dazu verleiten könnte, auch in V.3 part. anzunehmen. Aber V.6 steht im Verdacht, zumindest teilweise Zusatz zu sein, wofür auch die merkwürdig schwankende Textüberlieferung spricht: 1QIs^{a} *ʾl yhwh* (wie MT V.3) und *lhywt lw lʿbdym wlbrk ʾt šm yhwh wšmrym ʾt hšbt* statt MT *l*^{e}*šār*^{e}*tō* bis *šabbāt*; LXX: εἰς δούλους καὶ δούλας.

[7] Mit Jes. lx 7 und 1QIs^{a} ist *ya*^{ʿa}*lū* einzufügen.

[8] Abgesehen von den Jesaja-Kommentaren sind an neueren Bearbeitungen zu nennen: Th. Lescow, "Die dreistufige Tora", *ZAW* 82 (1970), pp. 362-79; K. Pauritsch, *Die neue Gemeinde: Gott sammelt Ausgestoßene und Arme (Jesaja 56-66)* (Rome, 1971), pp. 31-51; G. Robinson, "The Idea of Rest in the OT and the Search for the Basic Character of Sabbath", *ZAW* 92 (1980), pp. 32-42; H. Klein, "Die Aufnahme Fremder in die Gemeinde des Alten und des Neuen Bundes", *Theol. Beiträge* 12 (1981), pp. 21-34. — Noch immer sehr nützlich und viel zu wenig beachtet ist die gründliche Analyse von H. Odeberg, *Trito-Isaiah. A Literary and Linguistic Analysis* (Uppsala, 1931), pp. 7f., 33-62.

[9] Vgl. z.B. K. Marti, *KHC* X (1900), p. 362; B. Duhm, *HKAT* III,1 (1914^{3}), pp. 391f.; C. Westermann, *ATD* 19 (1970), pp. 249f. Zweifel äußerte A. Dillmann, *KeH* 5 (1898^{6}), p. 474. Die Auffassung von Pauritsch, p. 44f., dem Spruch liege eine auf Grund von Dt. xxiii 2-9 abschlägig beschiedene Thora-Anfrage von Eunuchen und Fremden aus Babylonien kurz nach 515 v.Chr. zugrunde, hat m.E. keine Wahrscheinlichkeit für sich.

schen Probleme der Reform Nehemias und Esras sollen hier nicht ausgebreitet werden. Es genügt die Auflistung der Stellen, die den negativen Hintergrund der prophetischen Thora von Jes. lvi 1-7 bilden. Das sind die folgenden:

1. Neh. ix 1-2: (1) Am 24. dieses Monats versammelten sich die Israeliten mit Fasten und Trauerkleidern und Erde auf ihren Häuptern. (2) Die Nachkommenschaft Israels (*zæraᶜ yiśrāʾēl*) trennte sich (*wayyibbādᵉlū*) von allen Fremden (*bᵉnē nēkār*). Dann traten sie hin und bekannten ihre Sünden und die Übertretungen ihrer Väter.

2. Neh. x 29-32: (29) Und der Rest des Volkes — die Priester, die Leviten, die Torhüter, die Sänger, die Tempelsklaven und jeder, der sich von der Landbevölkerung (*ᶜammē hāʾᵃrāṣot*) hin zur Thora Gottes abgetrennt hat (*hannibdāl*), ihre Frauen, ihre Söhne, jeder Verständige 'und' Einsichtige[10] — (30) die halten sich (*maḥᵃzīqīm*) zu ihren vornehmen Volksgenossen und treten ein in Fluch und Eid, zu wandeln in der Thora Gottes, die durch den Gottesknecht Mose gegeben ist, und alle Gebote, Rechtssätze und Satzungen unseres Herrn Jahwe zu beachten und zu tun: (31) besonders daß wir unsere Töchter der Landbevölkerung nicht geben und ihre Töchter für unsere Söhne nicht nehmen. (32) Wenn die Landbevölkerung am Sabbathtage Waren und allerlei Getreide zum Verkauf bringt, dann werden wir ihnen am Sabbath oder an einem heiligen Tage nichts abnehmen...[11]

3. Neh. xiii 1-3: (1) An jenem Tage wurde dem Volke aus dem Buche des Mose vorgelesen, und darin fand sich geschrieben: "Kein Ammoniter und Moabiter darf jemals zur Gemeinde Gottes gehören; (2) denn sie sind den Israeliten nicht mit Brot und Wasser entgegengekommen, und er mietete gegen es den Bileam, es zu verfluchen, aber unser Gott drehte den Fluch in Segen um." (3) Als sie die Thora gehört hatten, trennten sie (*wayyabdīlū*) alle Mischlinge (*ᶜēræb*) von Israel ab.

4. Esra ix 1-2: (1) Und als das vollendet war, traten die Beamten zu mir (und erklärten): "Das Volk — Israel, die Priester und die Leviten — hat sich von der Landbevölkerung nicht getrennt gehalten (*lōʾ-nibdᵉlū*), gemäß ihren Greueln, (nämlich) der Kanaanäer, Hittiter, Pheresiter, Jebusiter, Ammoniter, Moabiter, Ägypter und Amoriter;[12] (2) denn sie haben Töchter von ihnen für sich und für ihre Söhne genommen, so daß sich der heilige Same (*zæraᶜ haqqōdæš*) mit der Landbevölkerung vermischt hat (*wᵉhitᶜārᵉbū*). Die Beamten und Vorsteher sind Anstifter zu diesem Frevel gewesen."

---

[10] L. mit LXX und Peschitta *ūmēbīn*.
[11] Der Versschluß ist korrumpiert, kann aber hier auf sich beruhen bleiben.
[12] LXX, Aquila, 1 MS: Edomiter!

5. Esra x 11: Jetzt aber, legt Jahwe, dem Gott eurer Väter, ein Dankbekenntnis ab und tut seinen Willen! Trennt euch (*hibbādᵉlū*) von der Landbevölkerung und von den fremden Frauen!

Die historischen Einzelheiten der Ausscheidung von Fremden und Mischlingen aus der Gemeinde bleiben ebenso undeutlich wie die Modalitäten des Mischehenverbots. Aber eines ist ganz deutlich: die nachexilische theokratische Gemeinde am Tempel zu Jerusalem verstand sich als "Israel" im Sinne einer Blutsgemeinschaft, obwohl sie das faktisch schon lange nicht mehr war und genau genommen weder je gewesen war noch hatte sein können. Sie schied jedenfalls alle Fremden aus und "reinigte" sich unter ausdrücklicher Berufung auf die "Thora Gottes", d.h. auf das Gemeindegesetz des Deuteronomiums (Dt. xxiii 2-9). Damit schuf sie die Situation, in der der *bæn-hannēkār* sagen mußte: "Jahwe trennt mich völlig von seinem Volke ab!" (Jes. lvi 3). Diese Formulierung ist ganz wörtlich zu nehmen: Jahwe, nicht etwa die geistlichen Leiter der Gemeinde! Denn die Berufung auf Dt. xxiii 2-9 bedeutete Berufung auf heiliges, autoritatives Gotteswort — und also mußte Jahwe selbst als Initiator jenes Trennungsvorganges angesehen werden.

Natürlich kann man die Verbindung der Stellen aus den Büchern Nehemia und Esra mit Dt. xxiii 2-9 in Zweifel ziehen. Der Umstand, daß das Deuteronomium zitiert wird,[13] könnte auf das Konto einer nachchronistischen, harmonisierenden Redaktion gehen, der daran gelegen war, das inzwischen zu kanonischer Würde aufgestiegene Deuteronomium als Grundurkunde der Reformen Nehemias und Esras in Anspruch zu nehmen. Die Erklärung der Verbindung als sekundär würde an Überzeugungskraft gewinnen, wenn sich zwei Annahmen mit einem ausreichenden Grade von Wahrscheinlichkeit vertreten ließen: 1. daß das Gemeindegesetz Dt. xxiii 2-9 ein später, nachexilischer Zusatz zum Deuteronomium ist,[14] und 2. daß das Deuteronomium selbst erst im Laufe der ersten nachexilischen Jahrhunderte kanonische Bedeutung gewann und diese jedenfalls um und nach 450 v. Chr. noch nicht unbestritten hatte.

Beide Annahmen stoßen freilich auf Schwierigkeiten. Das deuteronomische Gemeindegesetz ist gewiß nicht in seiner ursprünglichen Gestalt überliefert, sondern im Laufe der Zeit durch Zusätze angereichert worden.[15] Das ist mit Blick auf die singularische Einschaltung über Bileam in

---

[13] Neh. xiii 1-3 zitiert Dt. xxiii 4-5. In Esra ix 10-12 werden kombinatorisch und frei zitiert: Dt. vii 1-3, xi 8, xxiii 7; Lev. xviii 24f., 27.

[14] So mit Nachdruck A. Bertholet, *Die Stellung der Israeliten und der Juden zu den Fremden* (Freiburg i.B. und Leipzig, 1896), pp. 142-5.

[15] Literaturübersicht: S. Mowinckel, "Zu Dt. 23,2-9", *Acta Orientalia* (Leiden) 1 (1922/23), pp. 81-104; K. Galling, "Das Gemeindegesetz in Dt. 23", *Festschrift A. Bertholet* (1950), pp. 176-91; D. R. Hillers, "A Note on Some Treaty Terminology in the OT", *BASOR* 176 (1964), pp. 46f.; Y. Freund, "Verachte den Edomiter nicht, denn er ist dein

V.5b/6 unbestritten. Darüber hinaus sind allerdings nur Vermutungen möglich. So kann man z.B. erwägen und hat erwogen (s. die Kommentare), ob nicht vielleicht die Paränese des V.7 und die Formel von der "zehnten Generation" in V.3f. Zusätze sein könnten. Ferner ist möglich, daß die mit *lōʾ-yābōʾ* eingeleiteten Sätze (V.2,3,4) überlieferungsgeschichtlich von denen getrennt zu halten sind, die mit *lōʾ-tᵉtaʿēb* beginnen (V.8,9). Es will jedoch nicht gelingen, einen sicheren Grundbestand des Gemeindegesetzes kritisch zu rekonstruieren, der als Ausgangspunkt für nachinterpretierende Erweiterungen gelten könnte. Ebenso unsicher ist die Datierung des zu vermutenden Grundbestandes und der Zusätze. Für gewöhnlich betrachtet man den Grundbestand als sehr alt: er ist "ein prächtiges Stück altjahwistischen Sakralrechtes"[16] und spiegelt "die geschichtliche Erfahrung der mittelpalästinischen Stämme in der Zeit zwischen Landnahme und Staatenbildung" (Kellermann, p. 37). Doch sind auch spätere Ansätze vorgeschlagen worden, bis hin zu der Auffassung, der Satz über die bevorzugte Behandlung der Edomiter sei überhaupt erst nach der Eroberung Idumäas durch Johannes Hyrkanus I. 128 v.Chr. möglich und verständlich (Diebner-Schult, p. 11). In die Debatte darüber soll hier nicht eingetreten werden. Denn für den Zweck dieser Betrachtung genügt folgende einfache, bisher nicht überzeugend widerlegte Annahme: das ursprüngliche Deuteronomium — also der Grundbestand von Dt. xii bis xxvi — enthielt ein Gemeindegesetz, das die Zugehörigkeit von Eunuchen und Fremden zur Gemeinde Jahwes verbot oder erschwerte. Mehr ist nicht notwendig, und die Einzelheiten können auf sich beruhen bleiben.

Was andererseits die qualitative Kanonizität des Deuteronomiums betrifft, so hat sie sich gewiß nicht erst im Laufe der Zeit ergeben, sondern war von allem Anfang an gegeben. Das Urdeuteronomium — welchen Umfang es immer gehabt haben mag — ist mit dem Geburtsadel einer heiligen Schrift in die Welt getreten, und die späteren Bearbeitungen und Ergänzungen haben diesen Charakter bewahrt und verstärkt. Man findet eine beachtliche Anzahl der Merkmale, welche Heilige Schriften als solche qualifizieren,[17] bereits in ihm selbst und in der Geschichte seiner

Bruder...", *Beth Mikra* 11,3 (1965), pp. 117-21 (hebr.); W. A. Sumner, "Israel's Encounters with Edom, Moab, Ammon, Sihon, and Og According to the Deuteronomist", *VT* 18 (1968), pp. 216-28; B. Diebner—H. Schult, "Edom in alttestamentlichen Texten der Makkabäerzeit", *Dielheimer Blätter zum AT* 8 (1975), pp. 11-17; U. Kellermann, "Erwägungen zum deuteronomischen Gemeindegesetz", *BN* 2 (1977), pp. 33-47.

[16] G. v. Rad, *ATD* 8 (1964), p. 104 im Anschluß an K. Galling.

[17] Vgl. dazu J. Leipoldt—S. Morenz, *Heilige Schriften. Betrachtungen zur Religionsgeschichte der antiken Mittelmeerwelt* (Leipzig, 1953).

Auffindung und Promulgation unter König Josia von Juda.[18] Natürlich ist nicht zu erwarten, daß die klassischen Charakteristika des späteren jüdischen und christlichen qualitativen Kanonbegriffes[19] auf das Deuteronomium einfach und ausnahmslos angewendet werden könnten, so daß man gewissermaßen nur "abzuhaken" brauchte. Das kommt schon deshalb nicht in Betracht, weil das Deuteronomium vor Beginn des eigentlichen Zeitalters der Heiligen Schriften entstanden ist. Aber der Anspruch, mit dem es auftritt, und die Begleitumstände, die es sich selbst zuschreibt oder die ihm alsbald zugeschrieben werden, lassen deutlich erkennen: das Deuteronomium ist eine Frühform dessen, was später einmal Heilige Schrift sein und so genannt werden wird. Bereits die Verbindung mit der Offenbarung am Gottesberg in der Wüste[20] und der Charakter als Abschiedsrede des Mose[21] sind Hinweise darauf, daß Jahwes und Mosis Autorität im Deuteronomium nachhaltig und verpflichtend Gestalt gewonnen haben. Das ist fraglos eine der hauptsächlichen Bedingungen dafür, daß Schriften heilig werden, aber es ist noch kein eindeutiges Kennzeichen einer Heiligen Schrift. Anders liegen die Dinge jedoch bei den folgenden, im Deuteronomium selbst und im Auffindungsbericht anzutreffenden Merkmalen:

1. der Geburtsadel, d.h. der Ursprung in grauer Vorzeit — vor Beginn der Landnahme — und die Zurückführung auf eine große Gestalt der Vergangenheit (Leipoldt-Morenz, pp. 24ff.);
2. die geheimmnisvollen Umstände der Entdeckung oder Auffindung: 2 Reg. xxii (Leipoldt-Morenz, pp. 28f.);
3. die Schriftlichkeit, d.h. der Sachverhalt, daß die Schriftform von allem Anfang an gegeben ist und selbst durch die Fiktion der Rede deutlich hindurchscheint: Dt. vi 7, xi 19, xvii 18f., xxvii 3, 8, xxviii 58,61, xxx 10, xxxi 9-13,24f.;
4. die kanonische Formel zur Sicherung der Textintegrität (die sog. *Ptahhotep*-Formel): Dt. iv 2, xiii 1 (Leipoldt-Morenz, pp. 56ff.);
5. die öffentliche Bekanntmachung: 2 Reg. xxiii 2 (Leipoldt-Morenz, p. 101);
6. die Einrichtung des Raumes für die öffentliche Bekanntmachung,

---

[18] Gegen die Verbindung des Dt. mit der josianischen Reform: E. Würthwein, "Die josianische Reform und das Dt.", *ZThK* 73 (1976), pp. 395-423; M. Rose, "Bemerkungen zum historischen Fundament des Josia-Bildes nach II Reg 22f.", *ZAW* 89 (1977), pp. 50, 63; O. Kaiser, *Einleitung in das AT* (Gütersloh, 1978[4]) § 11.

[19] Vgl. dazu H. Donner, "Gesichtspunkte zur Auflösung des klassischen Kanonbegriffes bei Joh. Sal. Semler", *Fides et Communicatio, Festschrift M. Doerne* (Göttingen, 1970), pp. 56-68.

[20] Dt. i 6ff., iv 12-14, v 20-30, xviii 16-19, xxviii 69.

[21] Dt. iii 23-28; iv 21f., xxxi, xxxiv.

das Vorhandensein eines Lesepodestes o.dgl.: 2 Reg. xxiii 3 (Leipoldt-Morenz, pp. 105f.);

7. die Aufbewahrung an heiliger Stätte, z.B. im Tempel: Dt. xvii 18, xxxi 26; 2 Reg. xx 8 (Leipoldt-Morenz, pp. 165ff.);

8. die Neuinterpretation der Prophetie als heilige Schriftstellerei und des Propheten als des Autors heiliger Texte, damit verbunden die Einrichtung einer prophetischen Sukzessionskette während des kanonischen Offenbarungszeitraumes: Grundlage dafür ist das Prophetengesetz Dt. xviii 9-22.[22] Mit einem Wort: es gibt keine ausreichenden Gründe für die Annahme, daß das Deuteronomium um 450 v.Chr. die Qualität einer Heiligen Schrift noch nicht hatte, d.h. noch nicht in kanonischer Geltung stand. Es ist ferner nicht zu widerlegen, daß zumindest der nicht mehr sicher rekonstruierbare Grundbestand des Gemeindegesetzes zu dieser Zeit Bestandteil des Deuteronomiums war. Also ist die Berufung auf das Gemeindegesetz während der Reform Nehemias und Esras nicht das Werk nachinterpretierender Redaktoren, sondern ursprünglich und sachgemäß — wobei offenbleiben kann, ob das vom vollen Umfang der mit der Endgestalt der Texte gegebenen Bezugnahmen auf Dt. xxiii 2-9 gilt.

Dann aber ergibt sich eine bemerkenswerte und m.W. bisher nicht genügend beachtete Konsequenz für Jes. lvi 1-7. Wenn der Prophet im Namen Jahwes die Zugehörigkeit von Nichtisraeliten und Eunuchen zur Gemeinde am Jerusalemer Tempel proklamiert, dann befindet er sich nicht nur im faktischen Gegensatz zur Fremden- und Mischehenpraxis der Zeit Nehemias und Esras, sondern setzt im Namen Jahwes Dt. xxiii 2-9 außer Kraft. Er tut das im Zeichen des Eschaton: "denn mein Heil kommt bald, und meine Gerechtigkeit wird offenbar!" (V.1b). Vor dem Anbruch des Eschaton verändert die Gemeinde ihre Gestalt: aus der Blutsgemeinschaft, die sie hatte sein sollen und wollen, wird eine Bekenntnisgemeinschaft, deren Glieder am Halten des Gesetzes, insbesondere der Sabbathheiligung, erkannt werden können. Die Frage, ob dem Propheten in der Situation der Neugestaltung der Gemeinde durch Nehemia und Esra irgendein "Erfolg" beschieden war, ist zweitrangig und kann hier auf sich beruhen bleiben. Sehr viel wichtiger ist, daß genau genommen nicht der Prophet das dt. Gemeindegesetz außer Kraft setzt, sondern Jahwe selbst. Das geht aus der Gestaltung von Jes. lvi 1-7 als Gottesrede eindeutig hervor und ist der Sache nach vollkommen schlüssig und konsequent. Denn niemand anderes als Jahwe hatte das Gemeindegesetz dereinst durch Mose offenbart und in Kraft gesetzt — also

[22] Vgl. H. Donner, "Prophetie und Propheten in Spinozas Theologisch-politischem Traktat", *Theologie und Wirklichkeit, Festschrift W. Trillhaas* (Göttingen, 1974), pp. 31-50.

konnte auch kein anderer als Jahwe seine Gültigkeit unter veränderten Bedingungen für erloschen erklären. Es handelt sich um nicht mehr und nicht weniger als um eine Korrektur der Hl. Schrift durch den göttlichen Autor derselben: ein Fall von Abrogation eines hl. Textes durch die Autorität Gottes.

Das ist — wie sich zeigen wird — zwar einmalig im Alten Testament, jedoch nicht einmalig innerhalb der Buchreligionen. Wer Genaueres über die Abrogation hl. Texte erfahren will, sieht sich vornehmlich an den Koran gewiesen. Der Grundsatzvers steht in Sure 2,106: "Wenn wir einen Vers (aus dem Wortlaut der Offenbarung) tilgen oder in Vergessenheit geraten lassen, bringen wir (dafür) einen besseren oder einen, der ihm gleich ist. Weißt du denn nicht, daß Gott zu allem die Macht hat?"[23] Derselbe Sachverhalt, bereichert um Angaben über ein mögliches Motiv der Abrogation, findet sich in Sure 16,101-103: "(101) Und wenn wir einen Vers anstelle eines anderen eintauschen — und Gott weiß (ja) am besten, was er (als Offenbarung) herabsendet —, sagen sie (d.h. die Ungläubigen): 'Es ist ja eine (reine) Erfindung von dir (wörtl. du heckst ja nur (etwas) aus).' (Das ist nicht wahr). Aber die meisten von ihnen (d.h. den Menschen) wissen nicht Bescheid. (102) Sag: Der heilige Geist hat ihn (d.h. den Koran) von deinem Herrn mit der Wahrheit herabgesandt, um diejenigen, die glauben, zu festigen, und als Rechtleitung und Frohbotschaft für die, die sich (Gott) ergeben haben. (103) Wir wissen wohl, daß sie (d.h. die Ungläubigen) sagen: 'Es lehrt ihn (d.h. Mohammed) (ja) ein Mensch, (was er als göttliche Offenbarung vorträgt).' (Doch) die Sprache dessen, auf den sie anspielen (?), ist nichtarabisch. Dies hingegen ist deutliche arabische Sprache." Es ist also möglich, daß Allah, der hier im Wir-Stile spricht, einen Koranvers abrogiert, indem er ihn durch einen anderen ersetzt. Der abrogierte Vers (arab. *ʾal-mansūḫ*) verschwindet aus der schriftlichen oder doch zur Schriftlichkeit bestimmten Koranoffenbarung. Die Ursache für diese Abrogationstheorie besteht darin, daß veränderte Bedingungen und Verhältnisse eine neue Willenskundgabe Allahs nötig machen können, die zu früherer Offenbarung im Widerspruch steht. Es läßt sich denken, daß die Gegner des Propheten den Widerspruch gegen ihn selbst wandten: als werde damit die Unglaubwürdigkeit seiner Behauptung erwiesen, der Koran sei von Allah herabgesandt. Er *ist* von Allah herabgesandt: der abrogierende Vers (arab. *ʾal-nāsiḫ*) und der abrogierte (*ʾal-mansūḫ*) haben denselben göttlichen Autor. Als ältester konkreter Abrogationsfall wird im Islam die Änderung der Gebetsrichtung (arab. *ʾal-qibla*) von Jerusalem nach Mekka

[23] Alle Koranzitate nach R. Paret, *Der Koran. Uberarbeitete Taschenbuchausgabe* (Stuttgart, 1979). Was in Klammern steht, ist Zusatz von R. Paret zum besseren Verständnis.

angesehen, die im Jahre 2 d.H. = 623 n.Chr. erfolgt sein soll. Diese Auffassung gründet sich auf Sure 2,142-150:[24] "(142) Die Toren unter den Leuten werden sagen: 'Was hat sie (d.h. die Muslime) von der Gebetsrichtung, die sie (bisher) eingehalten haben, abgebracht?' Sag: Gott gehört der Osten und der Westen ... (143) ... Wir haben die Gebetsrichtung, die du (bisher) eingehalten hast, nur eingesetzt, um (die Leute auf die Probe zu stellen und) in Erfahrung zu bringen, wer dem Gesandten folgt, und wer eine Kehrtwendung vollzieht (und abtrünnig wird...) (144) Wir sehen, daß du unschlüssig bist, wohin am Himmel du dich (beim Gebet) mit dem Gesicht wenden sollst. Darum wollen wir dich (jetzt) in eine Gebetsrichtung weisen, mit der du gern einverstanden sein wirst: Wende dich mit dem Gesicht in Richtung der heiligen Kultstätte (in Mekka)! Und wo immer ihr (Gläubigen) seid, da wendet euch mit dem Gesicht in diese Richtung! ..." Das ist in der Tat ein höchst charakteristischer Abrogationsfall, und zwar einer, der in die Zeit der Koranoffenbarung selbst zurückgeht. Nirgendwo im Koran wird auch nur angedeutet, daß die ursprüngliche Gebetsrichtung der Muslime nach Allahs Willen Jerusalem gewesen war. Es steht nur geschrieben, daß Allah früher eine andere *qibla* als die gegenwärtige und von nun an gültige "eingesetzt" hatte (V.143). Mit anderen Worten: nur der abrogierende V.144 (*ʾal-nāsiḫ*) ist Heilige Schrift geworden, der abrogierte (*ʾal-mansūḫ*) dagegen ist "getilgt oder in Vergessenheit geraten" (Sure 2,106). Damit ist eine zweite Bedingung jeder Abrogation gegeben: Gott ist nicht nur der Autor von *ʾal-nāsiḫ* und *ʾal-mansūḫ*; er verfährt darüber hinaus so, daß er sich selber nicht zitiert. *ʾAl-nāsiḫ* enthält nicht den Wortlaut von *ʾal-mansūḫ*, sondern ändert nur die Sache. Das Abrogierte gilt im Wortsinne als getilgt oder vergessen.

Es ist begreiflich, daß der in Sure 2,106 gegebene Abrogationsgrundsatz der nachfolgenden islamischen Theologie ein notwendiges und wertvolles Interpretationsmittel an die Hand gab. Denn jede Buchreligion steht vor dem Problem, wie sie den verpflichtenden hl. Text ihres Kanons veränderten Bedingungen anpassen soll, oder auch: wie sie die veränderten Verhältnisse aus ihrem Kanon begründen kann. Die Buchreligionen haben dafür verschiedene exegetische Techniken ausgebildet, die einander nicht ausschließen, sondern ergänzen. Die vornehmste unter ihnen ist die Allegorese, die von dem Grundgedanken ausgeht, der hl. Text meine etwas anderes als er sage, d.h. sein eigentlicher Sinn sei hinter dem Wortlaut verborgen und müsse durch exegetische Kunst ans Licht gebracht werden. Die Allegorese wie auch die Typologie stehen nicht selten in Verbindung mit heilsökonomischen und heilspädagogi-

[24] Der Text im Auszug.

schen Denkmodellen, in denen von der Akkomodation des göttlichen Autors der Schrift an die jeweiligen menschlichen Verhältnisse gesprochen wird. In die Reihe dieser exegetischen Techniken tritt nun, besonders in der islamischen Theologie, die Abrogation.[25] Ihr sind in den Blütezeiten des Islam scharfsinnige exegetische Werke gewidmet worden: z.B. und vor allem *ʾAbū ʾl-Qāsim Hibat-ʾAllāh b. Salāma* (†410 d.H. = 1019 n.Chr.), *Kitāb ʾal-nāsiḫ wal-mansūḫ*. In Werken dieser Art wird die exegetische Terminologie begründet und ausgebaut; ferner werden Regeln aufgestellt, die einen sachgemäßen Umgang mit eben dieser Terminologie ermöglichen sollen. Dabei verfielfachen sich die Fälle, in denen Abrogation angenommen wird: *Hibat-ʾAllāh* zählt 239 Abrogationen in 71 Suren, wobei allein Sure 9,5 nicht weniger als 124 Mal abrogiert, d.h. als *ʾal-nāsiḫ* auftritt. Das führt dann zu dogmatischen Datierungstheorien innerhalb des Koran; denn der abrogierende Text muß logischerweise stets jünger sein als der abrogierte. Auch wird die Abrogation selber zum Gegenstand kategorisierender Unterscheidungen gemacht. Abgesehen von dem Fall, daß der Koran die Offenbarungen früherer, d.h. alt- und neutestamentlicher Propheten abrogiert,[26] differenziert *Hibat-ʾAllāh* folgende möglichen Fälle: 1. ein Vers ist dem Sinne nach aufgehoben, aber im Wortlaut erhalten; 2. ein Vers ist dem Wortlaut nach aufgehoben, aber dem Sinne nach gültig; 3. ein Vers ist nach Sinn und Wortlaut aufgehoben. Zur Illustration diene eine kleine Auswahl von Beispielen, die in der islamischen Theologie bis heute gelten und erörtert werden. Die relativ milden Bestimmungen über das Weintrinken und das Losspiel in den Suren 2, 219 und 4,43 sind durch das strenge Verbot von Sure 5,90f. abrogiert. Die Vorschriften über die Bestrafung von Unzucht (4,15f.; 65,1) unterliegen der Abrogation durch Sure 24,2. Bei einander widersprechenden Zahlenangaben abrogiert der spätere Vers den früheren; so setzt z.B. 8,66 den unmittelbar vorhergehenden Vers 8,65 außer Kraft. Von besonderem Interesse — und wahrscheinlich nicht ausschließlich exegetischer Natur — ist die Theorie über die sog. "satanischen Verse" in Sure 53,19-25. Es handelt sich um die Haltung des frühen Islam gegenüber den in Mekka verehrten Göttinnen *ʾal-Lāt*, *ʾal-ʿUzzā* und *Manāt*, die als "Töchter Allahs" galten.[27] In der Endgestalt der 53. Sure wird diese Auffassung na-

---

[25] Vgl. grundsätzlich: Th. Nöldeke—Fr. Schwally, *Geschichte des Qorāns* 1 (Leipzig, 1909²), pp. 52-4; F. Buhl, *Enzyklopaedie des Islam* II (1927), Sp. 1141f. (s.v. *al-Ḳorʾān*); A. T. Welch, *The Encyclopaedia of Islam*, New Edition, V (1981), Sp. 415f. (s.v. *al-Ḳurʾān*).

[26] Nach Nöldeke-Schwally, p. 52, vergleichbar der christlichen Abrogation des Gesetzes — bes. des alttestamentlichen Zeremonialgesetzes — durch das Evangelium; vgl. z.B. Eph. ii 15 und Kol. ii 14.

[27] Vgl. J. Wellhausen, *Reste arabischen Heidentums* (Berlin, 1927³, Nachdruck 1961), pp. 24-45.

türlich abgewiesen. Aber es hat sich eine Tradition erhalten,[28] nach welcher der Satan dem Propheten nach 53,19f. folgende Forsetzung einflüsterte: "Das sind die erhabenen Kraniche (?). Auf ihre Fürbitte darf man hoffen."[29] Danach hat Muḥammad in einer Unsicherheitsphase, wahrscheinlich noch während seiner mekkanischen Wirksamkeit, erwogen, den im Sinne des Monotheismus unmöglichen Allahtöchtern eine leidlich positive Rolle im Islam zuzuweisen. Kann man das erfinden? Man kann es kaum, umso weniger als selbst noch in der kanonischen Gestalt der 53. Sure ein schwacher Nachhall dieser positiven Rolle spürbar ist. Es heißt in V.23: "Das sind bloße Namen, die ihr und eure Väter aufgebracht habt..." — und nicht "das sind Götzen, deren Verehrung verboten ist" o.ä. Jedenfalls gelten die "satanischen Verse" den Exegeten durch Sure 22,52 als abrogiert: "Und wir haben vor dir keinen Gesandten oder Propheten (zu irgendeinem Volk) geschickt, ohne daß ihm, wenn er etwas wünschte, der Satan (von sich aus etwas) in seinen Wunsch unterschoben hätte. Aber Gott tilgt dann (jedesmal), was der Satan unterschiebt. Hierauf legt Gott seine Verse fest. Er weiß Bescheid und ist weise." Diese Art der Abrogation hatte zur Folge, daß der Wortlaut der "satanischen Verse" im Koran nicht erhalten ist. Die Aufzählung der Beispiele ließe sich fortsetzen. Den z.T. sehr komplizierten Einzelheiten der exegetischen Abrogationstheorien braucht hier weiter nicht nachgegangen zu werden.[30] Notwendig ist aber der Hinweis darauf, daß alle diese Theorien den abgeschlossenen kanonischen Koran voraussetzen und sich auf ihn beziehen.

Eben hier liegt der Unterschied gegenüber Jes. lvi 1-7 und seinem Verhältnis zu Dt. xxiii 2-9. Denn dabei handelt es sich gerade nicht um einen Fall von "exegetischer Abrogation", d.h. um die von nachgeborenen Auslegern vollzogene Außerkraftsetzung einer Stelle des hl. Textes durch eine andere Stelle desselben hl. Textes, unter der Voraussetzung, daß beide kanonische Würde genießen. Es handelt sich vielmehr um einen Fall von "aktueller Abrogation". Für diese gilt, in der Terminologie des Islam: nur *ʾal-mansūḫ* ist Heilige Schrift, noch nicht *ʾal-nāsiḫ*! Ein Passus des schriftgewordenen Gotteswillens — in unserem Falle das deuteronomische Gemeindegesetz — wird durch einen von Jahwes Autorität erfüll-

[28] Einzelheiten bei R. Paret, *Der Koran. Kommentar und Konkordanz. Taschenbuchausgabe* (Stuttgart, 1980), z.St. p. 461.

[29] Varianten: "ihre Fürbitte ist (Gott) genehm" oder "auf ihre Fürbitte darf man hoffen. Ihresgleichen wird nicht vergessen".

[30] Das Material, freilich verbunden mit eigenwilligen Deutungsversuchen, ist aufgearbeitet von J. Wansbrough, *Quranic Studies. Sources and Methods of Scriptural Interpretation* (London, 1977), bes. pp. 150f., 192-202; J. Burton, *The Collection of the Qurʾān* (Cambridge, 1977), bes. pp. 46-104.

ten und getragenen Prophetenspruch außer Kraft gesetzt: Jahwe korrigiert sich auf der Strecke der Kanonbildung noch selbst. Dabei sind die Merkmale, die später auch die "exegetische Abrogation" kennzeichnen, bereits vorhanden: 1. nur Gott selbst kann seinen eigenen, früher offenbarten Willen abrogieren; 2. der abrogierte Text wird nicht zitiert, es wird nur auf ihn angespielt — dies allerdings auffallend deutlich. Denn daß auch das Problem der Eunuchen während der Reform Nehemias und Esras eine nennenswerte Rolle gespielt haben könnte, ist aus den Texten nicht zu erkennen; der Fall dürfte überhaupt selten gewesen sein. Dennoch werden sie genannt, sozusagen gleichberechtigt neben den Fremden, wenn auch nach ihnen (Jes. lvi 3) — und zwar deswegen, weil auch das Gemeindegesetz von ihnen handelt (Dt. xxiii 2). Die aktuelle Situation, in der die Abrogation erfolgte, hatte es nur mit den Fremden zu tun: deshalb stehen sie in Jes. lvi 3 zuerst. Das Gemeindegesetz ist der abrogierte Text: wo ihn der Prophet durch den neuen Gotteswillen ersetzt, nennt er die im Gemeindegesetz an erster Stelle stehenden Eunuchen zuerst (Jes. lvi 4f.). Bezogen auf die Verhältnisse im Islam kann man sagen, daß diese "aktuelle Abrogation" am ehesten der Abrogation der Gebetsrichtung nach Koran Sure 2,142-150 entspricht (s. O. S. 89): mit dem Unterschiede freilich, daß die *qibla* nach Jerusalem im Koran nicht mehr vorkommt, während das deuteronomische Gemeindegesetz im Kanon verblieb.

Jes. lvi 1-7 ist der einzige Abrogationsfall im Alten Testament. Es gibt noch drei weitere Stellen, bei denen man allenfalls erwägen kann, ob sie nicht in denselben Zusammenhang gehören.

1. Mal. ii 13-16 scheint das deuteronomische Ehescheidungsgesetz Dt. xxiv 1-4 zu abrogieren. Der sehr schlecht erhaltene und schwerverständliche Text lautet in V.15b-16: "So hütet euch für euer Leben! Und an der Frau deiner Jugend 'handle nicht treulos'![31] Denn 'ich hasse'[32] die Scheidung — hat Jahwe, der Gott Israels, gesprochen — und 'das Bedecken'[33] seines Gewandes mit Gewalttat — hat Jahwe Zebaoth gesprochen. So hütet euch für euer Leben! Handelt nicht treulos!" Die vorauszusetzende historische Situation ist nicht sicher zu erkennen; doch hat die Vermutung eine gewisse Wahrscheinlichkeit für sich, daß die Heiratspolitik der aus dem Exil zurückgekehrten judäischen und Jerusalemer Oberschicht gemeint ist.[34] Entscheidend ist jedenfalls der Satz, daß Jahwe die Ehescheidung haßt: also ist sie nicht erlaubt. Dieses Gottes-

[31] L. mit zahlreichen MSS, LXX, Vulg. und den Targumen *tibgōd* statt MT *yibgōd*.
[32] L. vielleicht *śānōʾ śānēʾtī*; Schreibfehler (dittogr.)?
[33] L. *wᵉkassē*.
[34] So die Kommentare; vgl. z.B. F. Horst, *HAT* 14 (1938), pp. 261f.; K. Elliger, *ATD* 25 (1950), p. 192.

wort würde Dt. xxiv 1-4 dann abrogieren, wenn dort die Ehescheidung ausdrücklich erlaubt oder — unter bestimmten Bedingungen — gar geboten wäre. Das aber ist nicht der Fall. Dt. xxiv 1-4 ist kein Gesetz über die Ehescheidung, sondern regelt den Fall der Wiederverheiratung des Mannes mit einer von ihm bereits einmal geschiedenen oder nach dem zweiten Manne verwitweten Frau. Dabei wird das Rechtsinstitut der Ehescheidung nicht eingesetzt, sondern vorausgesetzt. Daß die spätere Deutung — beginnend mit LXX und wirksam in Matth. v 31-32, xix 7 u.ö.[35] — den deuteronomischen Passus dann doch als gesetzliche Regelung der Ehescheidung verstanden hat, steht auf einem anderen Blatt und ändert nichts am Sachverhalt.

2. Jes. xxiii 17-18 scheint Dt. xxiii 19 zu abrogieren. Es handelt sich um einen Zusatz zum Tyrus-Orakel,[36] wahrscheinlich aus der Zeit nach 274 v.Chr., als Ptolemaios II.Philadelphos die Autonomie der Hafenmetropole wiederhergestellt hatte:[37] "(17) Und nach 70 Jahren wird Jahwe Tyrus heimsuchen, so daß es wieder zu seinem Hurenlohn kommt und mit allen Königreichen der Welt auf der Erdoberfläche hurt. (18) Dann wird sein Gewinn und sein Hurenlohn heilige Gabe (*qōdæš*) für Jahwe sein. Es darf nicht aufgehäuft und nicht gespeichert werden, sondern sein Gewinn wird denen, die vor Jahwe wohnen, zu reichlicher Nahrung und stattlicher Kleidung dienen." Demgegenüber verordnet Dt. xxiii 19: "Du darfst keinen Hurenlohn und kein Hundegeld in den Tempel deines Gottes Jahwe bringen für irgendein Gelübde; denn ein Greuel für deinen Gott Jahwe sind sie beide." Die sakrale Verwendung des Hurenlohnes (*ʾætnan*) scheint einmal erlaubt, das andere Mal verboten zu sein. Aber Dt. xxiii 18-19 ist ein Verbot der Hierodulie: der "Hurenlohn" ist hier wörtlich gemeint, während das Wort in Jes. xxiii 17-18 metaphorisch für den tyrischen Handelsgewinn steht, der der Jerusalemer Tempelgemeinde zufallen soll. Beide Texte reden von verschiedenen Tatbeständen; also kann nicht einer der anderen abrogieren.

3. In der großen Rekapitulation der Heilsgeschichte Ez. xx scheint Jahwe in V.25 seinen eigenen, früher offenbarten Gotteswillen zu abrogieren: "Auch gab ich ihnen Satzungen, die nicht gut waren, und Rechte, durch die sie nicht leben konnten." Dieser in der Tat erstaunliche Satz kontrastiert mit V.11/13/21 und bezieht sich vielleicht auf das Erstgeburtsopfer.[38] Mann kann Zimmerlis Auffassung teilen, der dazu bemerkt: "Die paulinische Erkenntnis vom Wesen des Gesetzes (Rö. 5,20; 7,13; Gal. 3,19) ist hier in einer eigentümlich begrenzten Formulierung

---

[35] Vgl. Strack-Billerbeck I, pp. 303-21.
[36] Vgl. H. Wildberger, *BK* X, 11-12 (1978), pp. 879f.
[37] O. Kaiser, *ATD* 18 (1973), pp. 139f.
[38] Vgl. W. Zimmerli, *BK* XIII,6 (1959), pp. 449f.

von ferne zu ahnen." Aber Abrogation liegt nicht vor; denn es handelt sich nicht um die Gültigkeit des mit dem Gesetz gegebenen Gotteswillens, sondern um seine Wirkung. Es gilt, aber es wirkt zum Bösen, nicht zum Guten. Der Gedanke, es könne außer Kraft gesetzt sein, liegt außerhalb des Horizontes dieses Textes.

Es bleibt also dabei: Jes. lvi 1-7 ist der einzige Fall einer aktuellen Abrogation im Alten Testament. Dabei ist zu beachten, daß die Aktualität der Abrogation der späteren Entstehung einer exegetischen Abrogationstheorie hinderlich gewesen ist. Als der abrogierende Text selber Heilige Schrift geworden war, mußte das Problem entstehen, wie man *ʾal-nāsiḫ* und *ʾal-mansūḫ* mit den Mitteln der vorkritischen Exegese zueinander in Beziehung setzen konnte. Man hatte zwei einander entgegengesetzte hl. Texte innerhalb desselben Kanons. Es war das gerade nicht eingetreten, was die aktuelle Abrogation hatte bewirken wollen: die Ausscheidung von Dt. xxiii 2-9 durch Außerkraftsetzung. Vielmehr war das deuteronomische Gemeindegesetz gültig und im Kanon verblieben. Die aktuelle Abrogation war geschichtlich gescheitert. Da Gott aber weder scheitert noch sich widerspricht, konnte das Abrogationsmodell auf der Ebene der Exegese nicht einfach wiederholt werden. Aus diesem exegetischen Dilemma half der Umstand, daß der abrogierende Text den abrogierten nicht wörtlich zitiert. Das eröffnete die Möglichkeit zu erklären, es handle sich beidemale um ganz verschiedene Sachverhalte. Dt. xxiii 2-9 redet nicht — wie Jes. lvi 1-7 — von "Fremden" (*b^enē-hannēkār*), sondern von Ammonitern und Moabitern, die selbst noch in der 10. Generation nicht zur Jahwegemeinde gehören dürfen (V.4), ferner von Edomitern und Ägyptern, denen der Eintritt in die Gemeinde bis zur 3. Generation versagt ist (V.8f.). Diese konkreten Menschengruppen sind in Jes. lvi 1-7 nicht genannt, also auch nicht gemeint.[39] Ähnliches gilt für die Eunuchen: sie heißen in Dt. xxiii 2 *p^eṣūaʿ-dakkāʾ ūk^erūt šåpkā* "ein durch Zerquetschung (der Hoden) Entmannter und einer mit abgeschnittener Harnröhre", in Jes. lvi 3f. dagegen einfach *sārīsīm* "Eunuchen, Kastraten". Man konnte exegetisch davon ausgehen, daß den Sonderfällen von Dt. xxiii 2 der Eintritt in die Jahwegemeinde ebenso verboten blieb wie den Ammonitern, Moabitern, Edomitern und Ägyptern, jeweils unter den angegebenen Bedingungen.

Abschließend ist eine Überlegung zum Verhältnis von Jes. lvi 1-7 zu den anderen Überlieferungseinheiten der tritojesajanischen Prophetie notwendig. Dabei soll die Diskussion über die Probleme der Entstehung, der Einheitlichkeit und der Datierung von Jes. lvi-lxvi nicht aufgenom-

[39] Dieses Interpretationsmodell hat bis in die kritische Exegese des 19. Jahrhunderts gewirkt; vgl. A.Dillmann, *KeH* 5 (1898^6), p. 475.

men und weitergeführt werden. Es genügt folgende, im großen und ganzen unstrittige Feststellung: die tritojesajanische Prophetie ist in außergewöhnlich starkem Maße auf vorgegebene heilige Überlieferung bezogen. Man kann das durch Leitbegriffe wie Schülerschaft, Aktualisierung und Nacharbeit zu verstehen suchen. Man kann freilich auch davon ausgehen, daß Tritojesaja zu Beginn, wahrscheinlicher noch auf der Strecke des Zeitalters der Heiligen Schriften im nachexilischen Judentum entstanden ist. Dann müßte die schon immer beobachtete Beziehung auf vorgegebene Überlieferung als Beziehung auf heilige, qualitativ kanonische Texte verstanden werden. In der Tat machen zentrale Stücke der tritojesajanischen Sammlung den Eindruck auslegender, schriftgelehrter Prophetie (*scribal prophecy*). Das gilt, wie ich anderwärts zu zeigen hoffe, besonders für Jes. lx-lxii, aber auch für lix, lxiii 7-lxiv 11, lxvi 10-15 u.a. Es gilt ganz eindeutig nicht für Jes. lvi 1-7.[40] Zwar bezieht sich dieser Text auf Dt. xxiii 2-9, aber eben so, daß er das deuteronomische Gemeindegesetz durch das Mittel lebendiger prophetischer Autorität außer Kraft setzt. Der Gotteswille ist nicht schon in einem hl. Texte kristallisiert, aus dem er erhoben und auslegend aktualisiert werden könnte. Er tritt vielmehr in der Weise der klassischen prophetischen Wortoffenbarung direkt — nicht auf dem Umweg über einen hl. Text — in Erscheinung. Die Flamme der lebendigen, situationsgebundenen Prophetie strahlt kurz vor ihrem Erlöschen noch einmal auf und zeigt an, daß sich der Übergang in das Zeitalter der Heiligen Schriften, in die Buchreligion, nicht ohne "Rückfälle" in die vorkanonische Art der Offenbarung des Gotteswillens vollzogen hat. Für Jes. lvi 1-7 gilt der fundamentale Grundsatz aller Buchreligionen nicht: "Sucht in der Schrift Jahwes und lest!" (Jes. xxxiv 16). Der Gotteswille wird nicht gelesen, sondern gehört, so wie ihn Gott ausweislich der Botenformel (V.1,4) gesprochen hat.

Die wissenschaftliche Untersuchung des Übergangs von der vorexilischen Kultreligion zu der sich in nachexilischer Zeit bildenden Buchreligion ist zwar schon seit langem im Gange,[41] hat aber m.E. noch immer nicht die gebührende Aufmerksamkeit gefunden. Wir alle setzen Wesen und Wirkung heiliger Texte viel zu wenig als Faktoren in unsere exegetischen Rechnungen ein. Hier liegt ein weites Feld für künftige Arbeiten, auch und besonders über den Charakter und über das Zustandekommen des alttestamentlichen Kanons, der mehr und vor allem noch etwas anderes ist als eine Sammlung synagogal oder kirchlich approbierter Schriften gegenüber den sog. Apokryphen.

---

[40] Auch lxiii 1-6 fällt heraus und hat deutlich anderen Charakter als die umgebenden Stücke.

[41] Vgl. z.B. R. Hanhart, *Drei Studien zum Judentum* (München, 1967).

LA CONDESCENDANCE DIVINE (SYNKATABASIS) COMME PRINCIPE HERMÉNEUTIQUE DE L'ANCIEN TESTAMENT DANS LA TRADITION JUIVE ET DANS LA TRADITION CHRÉTIENNE

PAR

FRANÇOIS DREYFUS

Jérusalem

I. Définition

Le premier à avoir attiré l'attention sur la condescendance divine comme principe herméneutique de l'A.T.[1] est le théologien anglican John Spencer (1620-1693) dans son ouvrage *De legibus Hebraeorum ritualibus et earum rationibus* (La Haye, 1686). On peut résumer sa doctrine, éparse dans son volumineux traité, dans les propositions suivantes:

1. Dieu a exprimé sa révélation, non seulement dans le langage des hommes mais aussi dans leur univers mental, leurs conceptions, leurs coutumes.
2. Dieu a révélé aux hommes d'une époque donnée, non pas tout ce qu'ils étaient capables de comprendre, mais ce qu'ils étaient capables d'accepter, étant donné leur faiblesse et leur péché.
3. Dieu a prescrit aux hommes des choses qu'il ne voulait pas car, étant donné leur faiblesse et leur péché, c'était le seul moyen possible pour obtenir ce qu'il voulait.
4. C'est dans cette perspective qu'il faut comprendre et expliquer la présence dans la loi de Moïse de rites, de coutumes et d'institutions empruntées au paganisme ambiant.

II. LA CONDESCENDANCE DIVINE DANS LA TRADITION CHRÉTIENNE

1. *Le Nouveau Testament.* Une parole de Jésus a certainement joué un rôle prédominant dans l'élaboration de la doctrine chrétienne de la

---

[1] Bibliographie: H. Pinard, "Les infiltrations païenne dans l'ancienne loi d'après les Pères de l'Eglise: la thèse de la condescendance", *Recherches de Sciences Religieuses* 9 (1919), pp. 197-221. Cet article a été beaucoup utilisé dans la présente étude. K. Duchatelez, "La condescendance divine et l'histoire du salut", *Nouvelle Revue Théologique* 95 (1973), pp. 593-621 (bibliographie étendue p. 593, n.2). B. de Margerie, *Introduction à l'histoire de l'exégèse, 1. Les Pères orientaux* (Paris, 1980), pp. 125 s., 214-39. Dans la Constitution *Dei Verbum* sur la révélation divine, du II° concile du Vatican, un paragraphe est consacré à la

condescendance divine, c'est Marc x 5 (= Mt. xix 8) à propos du divorce: "C'est à cause de la dureté de votre coeur (σκληροκαρδία) qu'il (= Moïse) vous a écrit cette loi". Autrement dit, le péché oblige le législateur à donner des commandements imparfaits, car des commandements plus parfaits auraient pu être compris, ils n'auraient pas été acceptés.

2. *Les Pères de l'Eglise.* Cette doctrine est commune à la plupart des Pères, bien que le mot lui-même de condescendance (συγκατάβασις) n'apparaisse qu'avec S. Jean Chrysostome.

a) *S. Justin* (mort vers 165), dans son dialogue avec le Juif Tryphon, affirme que, dans sa législation, Dieu s'est adapté (ἁρμοσάμενος) au peuple juif. Les sacrifices ont été ordonnés par Dieu afin qu'ils soient offerts à son nom et non pas aux idoles (ch. 19).

b) *S. Irénée* (mort vers 200) mérite une mention spéciale, car il est un des rares Pères de l'Eglise à mettre en rapport la condescendance divine avec une conception évolutive du peuple hébreu passant progressivement de l'état d'enfance à l'état adulte; le monde moderne est familiarisé avec cette idée, lui pour qui l'évolution de l'humanité est une évidence; mais il n'en était pas ainsi dans le monde antique. Irénée apparaît donc comme une exception: pour lui l'homme a été créé petit enfant; il grandit peu à peu pour atteindre la perfection de l'homme adulte; et Dieu, pour l'éduquer, a dû se faire enfant comme lui (*Adv. Haer.* IV 38,1-3). A côté de cette vue, Irénée présente une conception voisine de l'Evangile et de S. Justin: Certains préceptes de la loi de Moïse s'expliquent comme une concession accordée au peuple pécheur (Id., IV 15,2). Et il ajoute que cela se retrouve même dans le Nouveau Testament (Id., ibid.). Les lois sur les sacrifices n'ont été données par Dieu qu'après l'adoration idolatrique du veau d'or (Id., IV 15,1), mais il précise que ces prescriptions, et d'autres analogues, sont adaptées à l'éducation du peuple (Id., IV 16,5). Terminons enfin en signalant que c'est dans cette perspective que S. Irénée situe l'Incarnation: "Dans les derniers temps, quand il récapitula tout en lui, notre Seigneur vint à nous, non tel qu'il le pouvait, mais tel que nous étions capables de le voir (...) Ce fut sa venue comme homme" (Id., IV 38,1).

c) *Tertullien* (mort vers 220) reprend les mêmes thèmes et apporte d'autres exemples. La loi: "oeil pour oeil, dent pour dent" limitait la violence par la crainte salutaire des représailles, en attendant une loi plus parfaite où la vengeance était réservée à Dieu. Il en est de même pour les sacrifices: "Dieu ne les voulait pas pour lui, mais il était mû par sa sollicitude à l'égard d'un peuple enclin à l'idolâtrie et à la désobéissance. Il

---

doctrine de la condescendance (Chap. III § 13). Je remercie mon ami Meir M. Bar Asher pour l'aide qu'il m'a apportée pour l'élaboration de cet article.

voulait l'attacher à son culte par des prescriptions analogues à celles en vigueur dans la paganisme contemporain, mais afin de les détourner de l'idolâtrie. En effet, il prescrivait que ces sacrifices soient offerts à lui seul, comme s'il les désirait, afin que le peuple ne pèche pas en offrant des sacrifices aux idoles'' (*Contre Marcion* II 18).

d) *Origène* (mort vers 255) ajoute à ses prédecesseurs quelques précisions intéressantes: les consultations par certains rites divinatoires (Ephod, Urim et Tumim), certains prodiges opérés par les prophètes à l'appui de leurs oracles, toutes ces réalités n'étaient pas voulues pour elles-mêmes; elles étaient une concession au peuple, afin qu'à leurs yeux leur religion ne soit pas moins bien pourvue que celle de leurs voisins (*Contre Celse* I 36 et III 2). De même le choix des animaux à immoler à Dieu était déterminé par la lutte contre l'idolâtrie: on ne pouvait pas adorer des animaux qu'on égorgeait (*Fragments sur le Lév.*, PG 12,400). On verra chez Maïmonide une conception analogue.

e) *S. Grégoire de Nazianze* (mort vers 390) présente une idée nouvelle que l'on retrouvera également chez Maïmonide: la pédagogie divine doit se faire progressive, par des perfectionnements successifs et des suppressions également graduelles. De cette façon, Dieu ne contraignait pas son peuple, et obtiendrait de son peuple un progrès librement consenti (*Discours XXXI*, PG 36,160 ss.).

f) *S. Jean Chrysostome* (mort en 407) est le grand théologien de la condescendance, qu'il rattache, comme S. Irénée, à l'économie générale du dessein salvifique de Dieu: Dieu s'est mis à la portée de l'homme en parlant le même langage que lui dans l'Ecriture, en devenant homme comme lui dans l'Incarnation (*Sur l'épitre à Tite*, III 2, *Sur la Genèse*, XVIII 3; *sermon sur Matth. xxvi 39.* PG 62,678; 53,152; 51,36). Pour lui, l'attitude de Dieu s'apparente souvent au stratagème, à la ruse. Il ordonne certaines pratiques pour éviter de plus grands maux et pour obtenir plus tard des plus grands biens: *Adv. Judaeos* IV 3; *Sur Col.*, IV 3; *Sur Tite*, III 2; *Sur Hébr.*, XVIII 1 (PG 48, 879 ss.; 62,328 ss.; 62,678; 63,135). ''Il autorisa les sacrifices qu'il ne voulait pas, pour assurer le succès de ce qu'il voulait'' (Sur Isa., I 4, PG 56,19).

g) *S. Jérôme* (mort en 420) reprend dans ce domaine la doctrine de ses prédecesseurs, en particulier la conception de S. Irénée qui affirme que Dieu n'a pas ordonné de sacrifices avant l'idolâtrie du veau d'or. Ceux-ci sont une concession au penchant idolâtrique du peuple. Le rituel des sacrifices ''non erat per se bonum et nequaquam malum quia Deo offerebantur, et tamen non bonum quia boni auctorem offenderant''. S. Jérôme écrit cela en commentant Ez. xx 25: ''je leur donnai des lois qui ne sont pas bonnes'', texte qu'il explique en fonction de la doctrine de la condescendance: ''pas bonnes'' équivaut à: ''moins bonnes'' (Sur Ezechiel, PL 25, 194). Voir aussi son commentaire sur Jér. vii 22 (Sur Jérémie, PL 24, 733). Mais surtout, il présente une idée neuve et hardie pour son temps: le sacerdoce est un emprunt fait par les Juifs aux païens, et non l'inverse comme le disaient les anciens apologistes chrétiens: "...ut non Gentes ex Judaeis, sed Judaei a Gentibus sacerdotium acceperint..." (Lettre 73, PL 22, 678).

On pourrait sans peine allonger la liste des Pères de l'Eglise développant des idées analogues. On s'est borné aux plus importants, et aux idées majeures développées par eux.

3. *Caractéristiques générales.* On pourrait les résumer ainsi:

a) Le cadre est très souvent celui de la polémique anti-juive. Pour ne donner qu'un seul exemple: la permission du divorce était un moindre mal, car sinon ils auraient tué leurs femmes pour pouvoir en épouser une autre (Chrysost., *de virgin.* 41, PG 48,563; S. Jér., *comm. de Matth.* xix 8, PL 26, 134). D'autres positions sont encore moins défendables: ainsi certaines lois de l'AT étaient présentées comme une punition éducative pour un peuple que le péché avait réduit à la condition d'esclave, en invoquant Ez. xx 25 ("je leur donnai des lois qui n'étaient pas bonnes"). Ainsi S. Justin, *Dialogue* 21; S. Irénée, *Adv. Haer.* IV 15,1, et d'autres. Cf. aussi *Didascalie des apôtres* VI 18 (éd. Funk). Le N.T. a toujours évité de pareils excès. S. Paul affirme très clairement que la loi est bonne (Rom. vii 12).

b) Le principe fondamental est celui d'une pédagogie progressive de Dieu pour éduquer un peuple pécheur. On trouve chez S. Irénée l'idée d'une pédagogie fondée sur l'idée d'un peuple enfant passant progressivement à l'âge adulte, conception qu'on retrouve chez Chrysostome: *Sur Col.*, IV 3; PG 62,328.

c) L'explication par la condescendance n'est pas la seule. La loi n'est pas seulement un pédagogue; elle révèle de façon cachée, symbolique et allégorique, les mystères du Christ et du monde à venir. L'exégèse allégorique de type philonien, mais orientée vers le mystère chrétien est déjà presente dans le Nouveau Testament (cf. Héb. ix 9). Les références patristiques sont innombrables. Notons seulement que l'école exégétique d'Antioche (Théodore de Mopsueste, Diodore de Tarse, S. Jean Chrysost.) met davantage l'accent sur la condescendance, tandis que celle d'Alexandrie (Origène, Cyrille d'Alexandrie, etc...) insiste davantage sur l'allégorie.

4. *Les théologiens du Moyen-Age* ont repris la doctrine des Pères de l'Eglise. Au XIII° siècle, S. Thomas d'Aquin en fait un usage abondant dans sa Somme Théologique, au traité de la loi ancienne.[2] Mais ses pré-

[2] Voir surtout ST 1-2, 94,5, co (= Somme théologique, Prima Secundae, question 94, article 5, corps de l'article); et toujours dans la Prima Secundae: 98, 1, co.; 98, 2, co. et ad 1°; 101, 3, co. et ad 3°; 107, 2, co.

decesseurs immédiats, Alexandre de Halès et Guillaume d'Auvergne l'utilisent également.[3] Ils avaient comme devanciers, aux siècles précédents Walafrid Strabon, et Anselme de Havelberg.[4] Mais tous ces écrivains soulignent fortement que la condescendance divine n'est pas l'unique raison d'être des préceptes de la loi de Moïse. Ils ont aussi une signification symbolique, annonçant le mystère du Christ.[5] La pensée générale du Moyen-Age chrétien est bien résumée par cette formule de la *glose ordinaire* sur Lév. xvii 7: "Lex ergo, quasi paedagogus eorum praecepit Deo sacrificare ut in hoc occupati abstinerent se a sacrificio idolatriae. Tamen sanctificavit sacrificia quibus mysteria significantur futura".[6]

Mais une nouveauté importante sera introduite par les théologiens chrétiens du XIII° siècle, l'idée de *loi naturelle.* Pour eux, de nombreux préceptes moraux de la loi de Moïse, ainsi que certains préceptes rituels de cette même loi, étaient conforme à la loi naturelle, c'est-à-dire à la nature de l'homme. S. Thomas expliquera qu'il est conforme à la nature de l'homme d'offrir des sacrifices à Dieu.[7]

III. La condescendance divine dans la tradition juive

1. *Maïmonide* (mort en 1204). Le texte très connu du *Guide des égarés* sur les sacrifices (III 32) a marqué de façon très profonde la pensée juive sur le sujet qui fait l'objet de notre étude. Après lui, c'est à ce texte qu'on se réfère, explicitement ou non. Disciples et adversaires de Maïmonide, tous ont fouillé la tradition pour trouver des arguments pour ou contre sa thèse. Maïmonide s'exprime ainsi:

> Quand Dieu envoya Moïse pour faire de nous un royaume de prêtres et un peuple saint (...) afin de nous rendre dévoués à son culte, c'était une habitude universelle (...) d'offrir diverses espèces d'animaux en sacrifice dans les temples des idoles (...). La sagesse de Dieu ne jugea pas convenable de nous ordonner le rejet de ces espèces de culte (...) car cela aurait paru inadmissible à la nature humaine qui aime toujours ce qui lui est habituel. (...) C'est pourquoi Dieu laissa subsister ces différentes espèces de culte (...) mais il les a transférés à son nom (...). Il nous ordonna donc de bâtir un temple (...) d'élever un autel à son nom (...) et de lui offrir des sacrifices...

---

[3] Voir A. Funkenstein, "Gesetz und Geschichte, zur historisierenden Hermeneutik bei Moses Maimonides und Thomas von Aquin", *Viator* 1 (1970), pp. 147-78; voir en particulier pp. 167 ss. et les notes. D'ailleurs les théologiens chrétiens du XIII° siècle dépendent au moins autant de Maïmonide que des Pères de l'Eglise, sur ce sujet.

[4] Id., ibid. p. 116 et nn. 75 et 76.

[5] Il s'agit là d'un lieu commun de la théologie du Moyen-Age. Voir en particulier l'exposé de Saint Thomas: ST 1-2, 101, 2; 104, 2, etc.

[6] PL 113, 344 s. (début du XII° siècle au plus tard).

[7] C'est surtout S. Thomas qui développera ce point. Pour les préceptes moraux, cf. ST 1-2, 100, 1; pour les sacrifices, cf. 2-2, 85, 1.

Il ajoute encore que "Dieu ne change pas par miracle la nature des individus humains"; mais il agit progressivement. Ces sacrifices, étaient offerts en un lieu unique, en des temps fixés, par les seuls prêtres, "tout cela pour restreindre ce genre de culte".

Dans un chapitre suivant (*Guide* III 46), où Maïmonide expose en détail la raison d'être des différentes lois sur les sacrifices, il montre comment ce dessein de Dieu s'est réalisé. L'idolâtrie était combattue précisément par le fait qu'on offrait des animaux qui étaient tenus en grand honneur chez les païens parce qu'ils étaient plus ou moins divinisés.

Ce texte de Maïmonide a eu un grand retentissement, non seulement dans le monde juif, mais aussi dans le monde chrétien (le *Guide* a été traduit en latin dès le début du XIII° siècle). Il est utilisé par la plupart des théologiens scolastiques du XIII° siècle; Guillaume d'Auvergne, Alexandre de Halès, S. Albert, S. Thomas. Dans son *Pugio Fidei* (vers 1270), le dominicain Raymond Martin cite integralement ce chapitre 32 en hébreu et en latin. Et on sait que ce livre a été longtemps la grande source où les chrétiens puisaient leur connaissance de la pensée juive.

Mais malgré l'appui que Maïmonide paraissait apporter aux thèses chrétiennes sur le caractère imparfait, pédagogique et provisoire de la loi de Moïse, sa doctrine n'a été reçue par les théologiens chrétiens que comme une explication *partielle* en conformité avec la pensée des Pères.[8]

2. *Les successeurs de Maïmonide.* Il faut en dire autant des nombreux penseurs juifs qui ont commenté et discuté ce texte du *Guide*. Certains refusent energiquement cette manière de voir. Naḥmanide (mort en 1270) n'hesite pas à la qualifier d'ineptie, d'absurdité (*dbry hbʾy*) en son commentaire de Lév. i 9. Isaac Arama (mort en 1515) en fait une critique serrée, lui reprochant, entre autres, de donner des armes aux chrétiens.[9] Il faut se rappeler que la fameuse controverse de Tortosa (1414) n'est pas loin; et au cours des débats, ce texte de Maïmonide avait été invoqué par les théologiens chrétiens à l'appui de leur position.[10] Parmi les défenseurs les plus ardents de Maïmonide, il faut citer I. Abravanel (mort en 1509) qui cherche à prouver la justesse de la position de Maïmonide en montrant qu'elle est traditionnelle (cf. *infra*, III 3a). Voir l'introd. à son comment. du Lévitique, § 4. Dans son commentaire de Jér. vii 22, il reprend

---

[8] Ainsi Guillaume d'Auvergne (mort en 1249), *Tractatus de fide et legibus* (Paris, 1874), II, p. 29: "septem de causis ante legem et etiam sub lege sacrificia hujusmodi offeri voluit Deus, non solum propter consuetudinem idolatriae ut quidam (sûrement Maïmonide) opinati sunt. Haec enim causa in Cain et Abel locum non habuit". Nahmanide (comm. sur Lév. i 9) utilisera contre Maïmonide le même argument, assez faible: Dieu n'a pas *commandé* un sacrifice à Caïn et à Abel.

[9] On trouvera tous les détails et les références chez S. Heller Wilensky, *The Philosophy of Isaac Arama* (Jérusalem-Tel Aviv, 1956), pp. 109-13 (en hébreu).

[10] Voir I. Beer, *A History of the Jews in Christian Spain* (Philadelphia, 1978) II, p. 194.

l'idée des Pères et de S. Thomas pour qui les sacrifices n'ont été prescrits qu'après l'idolâtrie du veau d'or (ce qui paraît assez contestable, du moins selon l'ordre actuel du texte biblique: cf. Ex. xx 24). Citons aussi parmi les défenseurs de Maïmonide David Qimḥi (Radaq: 1160-1235) qui, dans son commentaire de Jér. vii 22, approuve et résume l'enseignement de Maïmonide. On trouvera son texte plus bas, § IV. Mais la plupart des auteurs ont une position plus nuancée. Personne ne nie que les sacrifices soient un remède à l'idolâtrie, car les textes bibliques sont clairs: Lév. xvii 7; de façon générale, on ne conteste pas la doctrine de la condescendance, bien attestée dans la littérature rabbinique ancienne (cf. *infra* III 3). Mais on dit que ce n'est pas la seule raison d'être des sacrifices, ni même la plus importante.

Pour Naḥmanide (comm. sur Lév. i 9), — qui reprend une opinion d'Ibn Ezra (mort en 1163) dans son commentaire sur Lév. i 1, — le sacrifice pour le péché substitue la mort d'un animal à la place de la mort qu'a mérité le pécheur. Il y a peut-être là une influence chrétienne, mais ce n'est pas sûr.[11] Pour Isaac Arama,[12] il est le signe du don total que l'homme doit faire à Dieu de lui-même. D'autres insistent sur la valeur "sacramentelle" des sacrifices, réalisant la proximité de l'homme avec Dieu (*qorbān* vient de *qārōb*, proche). Ainsi Albo,[13] le Maharal de Prague,[14] qui s'inspirent peut-être de Juda Halevi (mort vers 1140).[15] Dans la Kabbale se manifeste une autre conception: le sacrifice réalise l'union des puissances célestes (*s^e^pīrōt*).[16]

3. *La doctrine de la condescendance avant Maïmonide.*

a) *Le Midrash.* Dans l'introduction à son commentaire sur le Lévitique, § 4, Abravanel défend Maïmonide contre ses adversaires en montrent que sa doctrine est traditionnelle. Et il cite dans le Midrash *Levitique Rabba* XXII 8, parasha *Aḥare mot*, sur Lév. xvii 3, une parabole de R. Levi, amora palestinien (vers 310):

> Un roi a un fils qui a l'habitude de manger des morceaux de viande impropre à la consommation. Le roi dit: "Qu'il *les* mange (*y'klm*) toujours à ma table et il perdra vite son habitude." Ainsi en est-il pour Israël, passionnément attaché au culte des idoles, qui portait ses sacrifices aux satyres malgré l'interdiction divine. Le Saint, béni soit-il, dit: "Qu'ils offrent leurs sacrifices dans la tente de la Rencontre, et ils se débarrasseront de leur idolatrie."

---

[11] Cette idée se trouve déjà dans la Septante. En Lev. xvii 11, *bnpš* est traduit par ἀντὶ τῆς ψυχῆς. Dans la littérature rabbinique ancienne, elle est très rare: *Pesiqta Rabbati*, éd. Friedmann (Vienne, 1880), p. 194b: *šeyy^e^kappēr dam ʿal dam* (Simeon bar Yoḥaī). Cette rareté provient sans doute de l'usage abondant de cette idée chez les chrétiens: les sacrifices de l'A.T. préfiguraient le sacrifice du Christ.

[12] Voir n. 9.

[13] *Iqqarim* III 25 (début du XV° siècle).

[14] *Gevurot ha-Shem*, chapitre 69 (fin du XVI° siècle).

[15] *Kuzari*, III 53.

[16] *Zohar* I 206b. Cf. Joseph Albo, *Iqqarim* III 25.

Le texte d'Abravanel a: "qu'il *les* mange toujours à ma table", tandis que l'édition critique[17] porte: "qu'il *soit* (*yhyh*) toujours à ma table". Cette variante n'est pas passée inaperçue, mais elle est considérée comme fausse par D. Hoffmann et N. Leibowitz.[18] Ces exégètes considèrent qu'il est impossible qu'un amora ait pu comparer à de la viande avariée les sacrifices offerts au vrai Dieu. Mais d'après les règles de la critique textuelle: *lectio difficilior, lectio potior*; et on comprend mieux, bien sûr, la naissance du texte actuel par correction de celui d'Abravanel (pour la raison indiquée par Hoffmann et Leibowitz) plutôt que l'inverse. Et le texte dans la version d'Abravanel a un parallèle intéressant dans le texte de Jérôme cité plus haut (*supra*, II 2 g); et on sait que S. Jérôme était assez familier avec l'exégèse rabbinique. Cependant, il ne faut pas exagérer l'importance de cette divergence entre les deux textes: dans une parabole, tous les détails n'ont pas nécessairement une signification religieuse; et dans la suite du texte où R. Levi explique clairement le sens de la parabole, la divergence disparaît.

L'existence de ce texte du Midrash Rabba rend douteuse l'hypothèse de S. Pines selon lequel, sur ce point, Maïmonide dépendrait des Pères de l'Eglise par l'intermédiaire des écrivains arabes.[19] Certes, il y a des formules presque identiques chez S. Jean Chrysostome et chez Maïmonide; et l'idée était si répandue chez les penseurs chrétiens que Maïmonide a pu en avoir connaissance d'une manière ou d'une autre. Mais la pensée exprimée dans le *Guide* peut s'expliquer suffisemment par les sources juives et par le génie de l'auteur et sa méditation de la Bible.

b) *Le Talmud.* Il y a un cas bien connu de condescendance divine dans le Talmud, le cas de la "belle captive": B. Qid. 21b, interprétant Deut. xxi 10-14. Le conquérant peut avoir des relations sexuelles avec sa prisonnière avant qu'elle ne se soit convertie au judaïsme. C'est une concession au mauvais instinct (*yéṣer hāraᶜ*) dit le texte du Talmud (cf. les comm. de Rashi sur le texte biblique et sur le texte talmudique, et voir *Guide* III 41).

c) *La Torah parle selon le langage des hommes* (*dibbᵉrāh tōrāh kilᵉšōn bᵉnê ʾādām* Midr. Sifré sur Num. xv 31; B. Ber. 31b; B. Ketub. 67b; B. Yebam. 71a, etc.). Ce texte correspond au point n° 1 de la définition de la condescendance (*supra*, I). Il faut cependant noter que, dans la littéra-

---

[17] *Midrash Wayyikra Rabbah*, éd. M. Margulies (2° éd., Jérusalem, 1972), p. 517, qui ne cite pas cette variante.

[18] D. Hoffmann, *Das Buch Leviticus* (Berlin, 1906). Je n'ai pu consulter que la traduction hébraïque de ce livre (Jérusalem, 1976), pp. 40 ss. N. Leibowitz, *Studies in Wayikra (Leviticus)* (Jerusalem, 1980), p. 17.

[19] S. Pines, *Some Traits of Christian Theological Writing in Relation to Moslem Kalam and to Jewish Thought*, The Israel Academy of Sciences and Humanities Proceedings, V, 4 (Jerusalem, 1973), pp. 4-6.

ture talmudique et midrashique, il ne s'agit pas de condescendance divine, mais d'interprétation des textes bibliques. R. Aqiba affirmait que tout mot apparemment superflu était significatif dans l'Ecriture (présence du *ʾet* de l'accusatif, "mourir il mourra" au lieu de simplement "il mourra". Au contraire, R. Ismael dit: ce qui est sans signification dans le langage courant est aussi sans signification dans le texte biblique: la Torah parle le langage des hommes. Mais ultérieurement, cette formule a pris un sens plus large pour désigner la condescendance divine qui se met à la portée, non seulement des sages, mais aussi des gens simples et sans culture. Maïmonide l'emploie souvent dans ce sens (*Mišneh Torah, Yesode Torah* I 9; *Guide* I 26, 33, 46) mais il a été précédé par Bahya ibn Pakuda (XI° siècle), *Devoirs des coeurs* I 10; Judah Halevi (début du XII° siècle), *Kuzari* V. 27. W. Bacher[20] cite encore de nombreux auteurs des IX°, X° et XI° siècle qui emploient cette formule en ce sens élargi: Ibn Koreish, Dunash ibn Labrat, Jacob ben Nissim, Menachem ibn Saruk, Tobia ben Eliezer. Il faut cependant noter qu'il ne s'agit pas d'une vue évolutive de l'histoire religieuse du peuple juif passant d'un état primitif (où cette formule s'appliquerait) à un état plus parfait. C'est une idée peu connue des anciens (S. Irénée est une exception). Il s'agit d'une vue synchronique: A toutes les époques, il y a eu des simples et des savants. Dieu se met à la portée des simples.

IV. Origine de la doctrine de la condescendance divine dans l'*A. T.*

Nous avons rapidement retracé les étapes de la doctrine de la condescendance dans la tradition juive et dans la tradition chrétienne. Peut-on remonter jusqu'à leur source commune, l'Ecriture?

Pour le problème des sacrifices, que nous avons rencontré si souvent au cours de cette étude, la Bible nous présente deux séries de textes: le rituel des sacrifices du Lévitique, présenté comme ordonné par Dieu, et les textes prophétiques bien connus condammant la pratique concrète des sacrifices sans conversion. Pour qui considère la Bible comme parole de Dieu, il faut concilier des deux séries de textes. Et on ne peut se contenter de dire que seules les déviations du culte sacrificiel sont condamnées: le culte sans justice, sans amour et sans pénitence. Des textes comme Amos v 25; Jér. vii 22 vont plus loin. La solution de ce problème ne doit-elle pas être cherchée dans la doctrine de la condescendance? Nous avons vu que beaucoup d'exégètes anciens, tant juifs que chrétiens, ont interprété en

---

[20] *Die Bibelexegese der jüdischen Religionsphilosophen des Mittelalters vor Maimuni* (Budapest, 1896), p. 72, n.1; *Die Bibelexegese Moses Maimunis* (Budapest, 1896), p. 19, n.4.

ce sens Jér. vii 21-23. Cette manière de voir a été récemment adoptée par M. Weinfeld,[21] et elle semble parfaitement exacte. Il écrit:

> Dans ces paroles de Jérémie, il y a une vérité théologique qui, dans une certaine mesure, correspond à la manière de voir de Maïmonide sur les sacrifices. A propos de ce verset, Redaq (= David Qimhi, 1160-1235) a dit justement: "Dans tout le décalogue, qui est le coeur de la Loi, il n'y a pas de référence ni à l'holocauste quotidien, ni au temple bâti pour le culte divin. La raison est celle qu'a donnée notre maître Rabbi Moïse: ces réalités étaient destinées à déraciner les coutumes étrangères et à assigner au culte de Dieu les temples bâtis pour les idoles, afin que le nom même de l'idolâtrie soit supprimé".

Weinfeld pense avec raison que Jérémie suivait la chronologie du Deutéronome pour qui le Décalogue seul avait été donné au peuple sur le mont Sinaï, tandis que le reste de la législation, reçu par Moïse au Sinaï, n'avait été promulgué par lui qu'avant sa mort, dans les plaines de Moab.

V. Perspectives actuelles

1. *Le problème.* Le problème auquel la doctrine de la condescendance s'efforce de répondre, est toujours actuel. Les progrès des sciences historiques et de l'étude comparée des religions ont rendu évident à tous un grand nombre de données inconnues des auteurs qui ont été mentionnés.

a) L'univers mental des hommes de la Bible est structuré par la mentalité, la culture propre à leur époque et à leur milieu. Les mots de la Révélation ne peuvent se faire entendre d'eux qu'en revêtant cette mentalité, cette culture. La Parole de Dieu fera évoluer et progresser cette mentalité, mais très lentement, progressivement. Il y a là un donné qui n'est pas seulement lié au péché comme le croyaient beaucoup des auteurs qui ont été cités ici, encore que son influence soit grande. Il y a là une conséquence inéluctable de l'historicité de l'homme.

b) Il y a donc évolution, changement des cultures et des mentalités, qui n'est ni progrès continuel, ni décadence généralisée, mais progrès dans certains domaines, décadence dans d'autres.

Dans cette perspective, la doctrine de la condescendance apparaît comme un des tout premiers essais d'herméneutique au sens précis du mot: un effort pour dégager pour nous, aujourd'hui, la portée des textes anciens solidaires d'une mentalité qui n'est plus la nôtre, en cherchant à manifester l'intention de l'auteur divin de l'Ecriture au-delà d'une formulation liée à une mentalité dépassée.

---

[21] "Jeremiah and the Spiritual Metamorphosis of Israel", *ZAW* 88 (1976), pp. 17-56. Voir surtout pp. 53 ss. Le texte cité est p. 54.

2. *Risques d'une théologie de la condescendance.*

a) *Rationalisme.* Il y a incontestablement un risque de rationalisme à expliquer la Bible, et en particuliers les commandements divins, uniquement par la situation de l'époque où ces textes ont été écrits. Maïmonide explique un grand nombre de lois bibliques par les moeurs de l'époque où elles ont été promulguées (*Guide* III 36-49). Le lecteur peut être porté à conclure que, ces moeurs n'existant plus, le commandement n'a plus de raison d'être. Maïmonide ne dit jamais cela; au contraire, il condamne sévèrement ceux qui mépriseraient un commandement parce qu'ils n'en comprendraient pas ou plus la raison (*Mišneh Torah, Meᶜila* VIII 8). Le danger n'est pas moins réel. Il ne peut être écarté que par la conviction que le sens des paroles de la Bible dépasse celui que la raison peut établir. A la célèbre controverse de Tortosa (1414), c'est ce que répondaient les docteurs juifs aux théologiens chrétiens qui voulaient leur prouver le caractère périmé de la loi de Moïse à l'aide du texte de Maïmonide sur les sacrifices: Ce que dit Rabbi Moïse est vrai, répondaient-ils en substance, mais il n'a pas tout dit. Il y a une autre dimension des sacrifices, mystérieuse, inaccessible à la raison (cf. n. 10).

b) *Risque de la subordination de la Révélation à une philosophie.* C'est le reproche que l'on a fait à Maïmonide: Le culte idéal, sans temple ni sacrifice, c'est cela que Dieu avait en vue, selon lui, quand Israël a été élu pour être un peuple saint et un royaume de prêtres (cf. *Guide* III 32). Mais ce culte idéal, où le trouve-t-il? Dans la Bible où dans la philosophie?

Ici, un parallèle intéressant peut être fait entre Maïmonide et Bultmann. Ce dernier veut dégager l'intention des textes, au delà d'une formulation dans une mentalité dépassée, marquée par le mythe. A lui aussi, on a reproché de chercher cette intention non dans la Bible, mais dans une conception de l'homme issue d'une certaine philosophie, celle de Heidegger.

En fait, les deux écueils que l'on vient de signaler sont de toutes les époques. Ils se présentent dans toutes les religions chaque fois que l'on essaie de désolidariser le message du livre saint d'une culture qui n'est plus la nôtre pour l'inscrire dans celle d'aujourd'hui.

3. *A la recherche d'un critère.*

On le voit, ce qui apparaît clairement, c'est la nécessité d'un critère objectif permettant de faire cette réinterprétation de la pensée biblique dans une mentalité actuelle, sans se faire l'esclave de cette mentalité et en conservant intacte la fonction critique et contestatrice que la pensée biblique peut et doit exercer à l'égard de la mentalité et de la culture d'une époque donnée.

Pour la foi chrétienne, le Nouveau Testament constitue partiellement un tel critère: Le Christ est l'intention finale de l'auteur divin de l'Ancien

Testament. Mais aussi juste que soit cette réponse pour le chrétien, elle ne fait que déplacer le problème: car le message du Nouveau Testament s'exprime lui aussi dans une mentalité qui n'est plus la nôtre.

Il semble que la tradition juive comme la tradition chrétienne fournit un tel critère: c'est la vie de la communauté. Dans le judaïsme, c'est le principe: "sors et vois comment le peuple se comporte" (B. Ber. 45a et parallèles: *pūq ḥăzī maʾy ʿammāʾ dᵉbar*). Dans la tradition chrétienne, c'est le consensus des fidèles, le *sensus fidelium*, notion commune à toutes les branches de la tradition chrétienne, quoiqu'avec des différences notables. Donnons quelques exemples en nous bornant aux lois.

Dans la tradition chrétienne, les décrets du concile de Jérusalem (en 48) sont tombés très rapidement en désuétude sans qu'ils aient jamais été abolis par aucune autorité. Ils ont été pourtant promulgués dans le N.T. et présentés comme étant d'origine divine: Act. xv 28: "Il a plu à l'Esprit Saint et à nous". C'est l'attitude de la communauté qui a fait comprendre qu'il s'agissait, non d'une loi permanente, mais d'une concession provisoire, une condescendance divine causée par une situation particulière: la coexistence, dans la communauté primitive, de chrétiens d'origine juive et de fidèles issus du paganisme.

Dans le judaïsme, la loi des eaux amères données à la femme soupçonnée d'adultère (Num. v 11-31) a été abolie par Joḥanan ben Zakkaï au début de notre ère (M. Soṭah ix 9). Les raisons données pour cette suppression sont différentes dans la Michnah et dans B. Sotah 47b. Mais il est clair que la décision de Joḥanan ben Zakkaï ne fait qu'entériner un état de choses: cette loi était tombée en désuétude, car liée à une mentalité qui n'était plus celle du début de notre ère. On peut dire la même chose de l'abolition de la polygamie par Gershom de Mayence (X° siècle). Dans ces différents cas, il y a eu la conviction informulée du peuple croyant que ces lois étaient uniquement le reflet d'une mentalité périmée. Mais dans d'autres cas où, semble-t-il, la situation était analogue, on a conservé, et dans la tradition juive et dans la tradition chrétienne, des lois apparemment solidaires, elles aussi, d'une mentalité dépassée. C'est que, dans la conviction du peuple fidèle, ces lois avaient une dimension plus profonde, bien que difficilement conceptualisable; et leur suppression aurait mutilé gravement l'héritage spirituel de la communauté croyante.

On peut dire, en conclusion, que la doctrine de la condescendance, commune aux deux traditions juive et chrétienne, peut et doit être considérée encore aujourd'hui comme un principe valable d'herméneutique biblique, mais en précisant bien qu'il s'agit d'un principe partiel, et que le critère de son application doit être la vie de la communauté croyante, dans sa relation vivante avec les sources de sa foi.

JÉRÔME ET LES PROPHÈTES

HISTOIRE, PROPHÉTIE, ACTUALITÉ ET ACTUALISATION DANS LES COMMENTAIRES DE NAHUM, MICHÉE, ABDIAS ET JOËL

PAR

YVES-MARIE DUVAL

Poitiers

Lorsque Jésus replie le Livre d'Isaïe qu'on lui a donné à lire dans la Synagogue de Nazareth, il déclare: "Aujourd'hui s'accomplit à vos oreilles ce passage des Écritures" (Luc iv 22). Lorsqu'au soir de la Résurrection il chemine sur la route d'Emmaüs, il "parcourt les prophètes et interprète aux voyageurs tout ce qui dans les Écritures le concernait" (Luc xxiv 25-27). La connaissance, même bien imparfaite, des cycles de lectures synagogales, de l'exégèse juive à l'époque intertestamentaire, permet de mieux situer et comprendre de tels propos. Malheureusement, si nous avons bien un Targum des prophètes, il ne nous est parvenu que des bribes de "commentaire", ou de péshèr, consacré à l'un ou l'autre prophète. Quant à l'exégèse chrétienne, au delà du Nouveau Testament, elle procède longtemps par *testimonia*, et non par Commentaire continu d'un livre. En gros, on ne voit apparaître ce type d'interprétation continue qu'avec Hippolyte et Origène. Encore ce dernier — même s'il sera beaucoup question de lui dans les pages qui suivent — est-il loin d'avoir couvert l'ensemble des 15 ou 16 Prophètes. Lorsqu'un bon siècle plus tard, Jérôme s'intéresse aux Prophètes et s'engage en 393 dans leur commentaire, il le fait au terme d'une longue préparation personnelle.[1] Avec des interruptions sur lesquelles je vais revenir, il mènera cette oeuvre pendant près de 25 ans et sera près de terminer ce grand-oeuvre par le Commentaire de Jérémie, commencé en 414 et laissé inachevé. Pour lui aussi, comme il le dit à la fin de l'*In Malachiam*, dernier des petits prophètes, "La Loi et tout le Choeur des prophètes annoncent la Passion du Christ".[2]

---

[1] On trouvera sur ce point quelques éléments dans le début de l'Introduction que j'ai écrite à une nouvelle édition de l'*In Ionam* de Jérôme, sous presse dans la Collection des *Sources Chrétiennes*.

[2] Jérôme, *In Malachiam*, iv 5-6 (Éd. M. Adriaen, *CCL* 76 A [Turnhout, 1969], p. 941, l. 90-1). Tous les renvois seront faits à cette édition, meilleure que celle de Vallarsi (reprise par Migne - *PL* 25), mais perfectible, ne serait-ce que pour la clarté de la présentation. Voir de même *In Matthaeum* III, xvii 3 (*CC* 77, p. 148, l. 260-2); *In Marcum*, ix 1-7 (*CC* 78, p. 481, l. 170-1).

La nouveauté, et la difficulté, de l'entreprise de Jérôme tient tout d'abord au fait qu'il se veut de commenter à la fois l'hébreu et les Septante, dont les deux traductions sont données en lemme, de manière ordinaire.[3] Ces deux traductions ne se juxtaposent ni ne se substituent l'une à l'autre, d'ordinaire. Même lorsque les textes sont voisins, elles se superposent le plus souvent. A l'hébreu est confiée la tâche de révéler les circonstances historiques dans lesquelles a été délivrée la prophétie. Celles-ci sont souvent confirmées par les commentaires ou traditions obtenus, plus ou moins directement, auprès de Juifs.[4] La traduction du Grec délivre, elle, ce que Jérôme appelle souvent "l'intelligence spirituelle",[5] qui permet au chrétien de se sentir directement concerné, soit par les événements de la vie passée d'Israël, soit par les annonces et promesses des prophètes. Nombre de problèmes ne pouvaient manquer de surgir de cette superposition. D'une part, celle-ci n'est pas totale, puisque les textes présentent des différences parfois inconciliables; mais, d'autre part, les ressemblances sont également assez fréquentes pour qu'il n'y ait pas quelque artifice à opérer une telle répartition des "sens". Quoi qu'il en soit — et contrairement à ce qui est dit parfois, à ce qui semble aussi ressortir, à première vue, d'une explication apparemment émiettée —, le commentaire de Jérôme se développe en une vaste polyphonie, où chaque "voix" décrit ou doit décrire une ligne mélodique complète, fût-elle dissonante. C'est l'un des points que je voudrais essayer de montrer dans les pages qui suivent.[6]

---

[3] Sans compter les leçons qu'il cite des divers autres traducteurs grecs. Souvent, les remarques textuelles figurent en tête de la section. Ensuite, Jérôme explique la traduction de l'hébreu, puis celle du grec, en suivant pas à pas le texte, de part et d'autre.

[4] Il est difficile de faire la part entre ce que Jérôme a appris lui-même et ce qu'il ne connaît qu'à travers Origène. Il ne peut être question de faire la distinction ici, mais elle doit toujours être latente. Sur Origène et les Juifs, voir, entre autres, G. Bardy, "Les traditions juives dans l'oeuvre d'Origène", *RBi* 34 (1925), pp. 217-52, qui donne le dossier; N. de Lange, *Origen and the Jews. Studies in Jewish-Christian relations in third-century Palestine* (Cambridge, 1976). Sur Jérôme, voir G. Bardy, "Saint Jérôme et ses maîtres hébreux", *RBen* 46 (1934), pp. 145-64. Quant à la connaissance que Jérôme a d'Origène, et en particulier de ses Commentaires sur les petits prophètes dont il sera surtout question dans les pages qui suivent, il suffit de renvoyer à la joie qu'il exprime de les posséder (*De uiris illustribus*, 75). A Césarée, Jérôme pouvait exploiter les ressources de la Bibliothèque épiscopale; il pouvait sans doute également avoir des rapports avec l'importante communauté juive.

[5] Sur le vocabulaire multiple de cette intelligence spirituelle, v. mon Introduction au *Sur Jonas*.

[6] A sa mesure, je l'ai fait pour l'*In Ionam*, en essayant de reconstituer trois lignes de développement du Commentaire de Jérôme et de les replacer dans l'histoire de l'interprétation antique de ce Livre: *Le Livre de Jonas dans la littérature chrétienne grecque et latine. Sources et influence du Commentaire sur Jonas de saint Jérôme* (Paris, 1973). J'essaie de donner ici une esquisse, qui se limite à Jérôme et insiste sur l'unité profonde de chaque Commentaire. La matière est loin d'être épuisée dans cette étude, qui a dû être fortement réduite. Le tra-

Mais je voudrais également expliquer la raison pour laquelle telle ou telle "voix" se tait à un moment ou à un autre: il faut tenir compte de la chronologie des Commentaires. Commencée avant la querelle origéniste, l'interprétation de Jérôme adopte tout d'abord certaines des théories les plus aventureuses d'Origène, comme on peut le constater dans les cinq premiers Commentaires de petits prophètes rédigés en 393 (Nahum, Sophonie, Aggée, Michée, Habacuc). Survient la querelle origéniste, qui stoppe le travail commencé. Lorsqu'en 396 Jérôme revient à son entreprise avec Jonas et Abdias, il est beaucoup plus sur ses gardes. Une nouvelle interruption de dix ans ne modifie plus profondément la façon de faire.

Je ne prendrai ici que quatre exemples: les Commentaires de Nahum et Michée, en 393, celui d'Abdias de 396, celui de Joël en 406. On peut facilement étendre l'enquête et la vérification aux autres Commentaires, jusqu'en 415; à condition de les lire, tout d'abord, non pas dans l'ordre des canons hébreu ou grec, mais dans celui où Jérôme les a composés. Chaque livre présente, certes, des caractéristiques propres qui influencent l'interprétation. Mais il prend aussi place dans un ensemble, dont Jérôme s'efforce de suivre la progression, à la suite d'Origène, pour ce qui concerne l'enseignement spirituel, à la suite de ses maîtres hébreux pour ce qui concerne le contexte historique. Même si les quatre exemples choisis ne couvrent pas tout cet enseignement, ni toute cette histoire, ils peuvent déjà permettre d'esquisser un certain nombre de "règles", à condition de ne pas donner à ce mot un sens trop strict.

I. Les premiers Commentaires: l'In Nahum

Dans le premier groupe, composé en 393, je prendrai donc ici tout d'abord l'exemple de l'*In Nahum*, le premier sans doute des petits prophètes commentés en ce début d'année. Il a l'avantage de concerner Ninive, comme l'*In Ionam* de 396, mais l'inconvénient, pour qui veut lire les prophètes d'Israël à la lumière du Nouveau Testament, de ne pas avoir été utilisé de manière importante par le Christ ou un Apôtre. Jérôme donne la plus large place à une interprétation qu'on ne peut simplement appeler morale, tant elle donne de place aux êtres spirituels; nous essaierons d'en mettre en lumière quelques éléments et de montrer d'où Jérôme les tient. Celui-ci ne veut pas moins expliquer les faits narrés ou annoncés par le prophète. Il le fait en exploitant intelligemment le texte lui-même, mais

---

vail peut être étendu aux autres petits prophètes, et adapté à Isaïe, Ézéchiel et Jérémie. Les différentes "prophéties messianiques" ont été regroupées et étudiées par F. M. Abel, "Saint Jérôme et les prophéties messianiques", *RBi* 13 (1916), pp. 423-40; 14 (1917), pp. 247-69. L'esprit du présent essai est différent.

aussi en recourant à l'enseignement de Juifs, mentionnés plusieurs fois. Ceux-ci l'ont aidé à situer — plus ou moins bien — le prophète dans l'histoire d'Israël.

Nahum ne nous est en effet connu que par son livre. Il ne semble pas que les Hébreux se soient beaucoup intéressés à sa personne, bien que, dans sa Préface, Jérôme rapporte une tradition qui fait d'Elcesaeus le nom de son père, non celui de son village. En un sens, la prophétie de Nahum était claire et immédiate: elle annonçait, de la manière la plus nette, la ruine de l'ennemi de toujours, l'Assyrien: "Iuxta litteram, *manifestus* est sensus",[7] dit Jérôme. La plupart des péricopes sont accompagnées d'un commentaire qui souligne l'évidence et la clarté du récit.[8] L'absence de difficulté historique du texte a pour conséquence la rapidité même du "commentaire historique". Celui-ci ne tient souvent qu'une place minime dans le texte qui est consacré à chaque péricope.

Cependant, si l'échéance immédiate de la prophétie ne fait pas de doute, il est d'autres considérations historiques qui découlent de la date à laquelle Nahum formule son annonce. Le livre, en réalité, ne fournit d'autre coordonnée que celle de l'annonce — future — de la prise de Ninive. Jérôme ne dit pas comment il a établi que Nahum parlait peu après la prise de Samarie, au moment où Sennachérib assiège Jérusalem. Sans doute tient-il cette chronologie d'une tradition juive. Mentionnée dès la Préface,[9] on la retrouve tout au long de la première partie du Commentaire, en particulier lorsque surgit une petite difficulté. En i 9, il est dit: "la tribulation ne se lèvera pas *deux fois*". Un Hébreu a expliqué (à Jérôme?) qu'Israël avait été puni en 721 par la prise de Samarie, mais que Juda serait épargnée sous Sennachérib.[10] La suite contient plusieurs autres références à l'époque et à la vie du même Sennacherib.[11]

L'Hébreu, qui a fourni à Jérôme toutes ces précisions historiques et qui a tenté de lui expliquer ce qu'était la No Amon de iii 8-12,[12] ne semble pas lui avoir fait connaître d'interprétation actualisée du Livre de Nahum, telle qu'on en saisit quelques traces dans le fragment du Pésher de la Grotte 4 de Qumran. Faute de référence néo-testamentaire, ce qui intéresse le plus Jérôme, c'est l'enseignement ascétique, qu'il découvre grâce à l'interprétation du nom même de la capitale assyrienne: Ninive la

[7] *In Nahum*, i 12-13 (*CCL* 76 A, p. 537, l. 357-8).

[8] *Ibid.*, ii 3-7 (p. 545, l. 121-2), 8-9 (p. 547, l. 211), 10 (p. 549, l. 295 sq.), 11-12 (p. 551, l. 354-5); etc.

[9] *Ibid.*, *Praef.* (p. 525, l. 9-18).

[10] *Ibid.*, i 9 (p. 535, l. 283-8).

[11] *Ibid.*, i 11 (p. 536, l. 333 sq.), 14 (p. 539, l. 419-25), 15 (p. 540, l. 453-66: en réalité, les Paralipomènes invoqués ne disent rien d'aussi précis, pas plus que les Chroniques, les Rois, ni Isaïe).

[12] *Ibid.*, iii 8-12 (p. 562, l. 274 sq.).

Belle n'est autre que le Monde.[13] Donc, "tout ce qui est dit contre Ninive est annoncé de manière figurée de ce monde".[14] Aussi la Préface peut-elle conclure: "Selon l'*anagogé*, la prophétie concerne la fin du monde pour la consolation des saints: ainsi, tout ce qu'ils aperçoivent dans le monde, le mépriseront-ils comme passager et caduc et se prépareront-ils au jour du Jugement, où le Vengeur contre les véritables Assyriens ne sera autre que le Seigneur."[15] Dès lors, la lecture du Livre de Nahum n'est que l'inventaire des faux biens que le chrétien, et en particulier l'ascète, doit rejeter, des tentations qui l'assaillent, des ennemis — persécuteurs, hérétiques ou démons — qui l'attaquent, mais dont le châtiment final est annoncé. Le commentaire devient plus d'une fois une exhortation au combat spirituel.

Cette parénèse se retrouve dans tous les Commentaires, qui ne sont jamais, chez Jérôme, une simple explication savante. On pourrait en dire autant de la présence des démons, si la nature du Commentaire et la date à laquelle il a été composé n'invitaient à donner à quelques affirmations un sens qui devait être plus accentué encore dans le modèle de Jérôme. Le rôle des puissances mauvaises est mainte fois rappelé au long du Commentaire. Elles interviennent continuellement dans la vie du chrétien, ne serait-ce que par l'intermédiaire des hérétiques,[16] ou des idoles.[17] Elles prennent surtout les traits du "lion de Ninive", dont Nahum annonce l'anéantissement et dont il énonce les rapines et les meurtres. Si Jérôme hésite à deux reprises, dans la datation de cette destruction, entre le premier et le second avènement du Christ,[18] il se rappelle lui-même à l'ordre et opte pour la fin du monde et le Jugement dernier. Plusieurs fois, il parle, pour ces puissances mauvaises, d'un châtiment, dont rien ne laisse entrendre qu'il ne soit définitif.[19] A la fin du Commentaire, il s'adresse au Diable qu'est le Roi d'Assur. Il célèbre sa dérision, en montrant que ce monde — jusqu'ici au pouvoir du Malin — est détruit. Mais on notera que cette apostrophe au Diable ne figure, selon Jérôme, que dans le texte hébreu,[20] tandis que le texte des Septante, et surtout l'interprétation qui

---

[13] Même utilisation au long de l'*In Ionam*, en particulier en i 1-2.

[14] *In Nahum, Praef.* (p. 525, l. 18-22).

[15] *Ibid.* (p. 526, l. 37-42).

[16] *Ibid.*, i 12-13 (p. 538, l. 395-401), ii 12-13 (p. 553, l. 392 sq.).

[17] *Ibid.*, i 15 (p. 540, l. 467-74).

[18] *Ibid.*, ii 3-7 (p. 546, l. 165-72) et ii 11-12 (p. 552, l. 365-80).

[19] *Ibid.*, i 7-8 (p. 553, l. 224-31). Mais, un peu plus haut, il a dit *sola apparente clementia* (p. 221) et parlé d'un nouveau déluge "quod pertranseat, non quod permaneat" (l. 215); ii 3-7 (p. 546, l. 157-202), immense combat apocalyptique, où le Monde finit par se soumettre au Christ et à participer à son triomphe. Cf. *In Sophoniam*, iii 14-18 (p. 707, l. 524 sq.), de cette même année 393.

[20] *Ibid.*, iii 18-19 (p. 575, l. 732-64).

en est donnée, est beaucoup moins radical.[21] Selon celle-ci, la multitude de Ninive, le "peuple mêlé"[22] ne peut recouvrer la santé et le salut que s'il abandonne son orgueil: "S'il s'humilie, s'il se soumet au Christ, Dieu ne méprise pas un coeur contrit et humilié..."[23] Nous avons là, sans tambour, mais sans grande réserve, l'énoncé de la doctrine origénienne de l'apocatastase.

Présente tout au long du Commentaire, elle est clairement exprimée dans la longue explication de ii 10, où l'assaut contre Ninive est, selon le grec et selon un sens plus élevé (*altius*), décrit comme un traitement médical, destiné à expurger le mal qui subsiste, non seulement dans les pécheurs, mais aussi dans les anges mauvais et même dans leur chef.[24]

On pourrait ajouter bien d'autres développements, plus ou moins anodins, de coloration origénienne eux aussi. Lorsque, par exemple, Jérôme déclare que les âmes des saints, "qui s'étaient alourdies par leur union avec la chair, une fois emportées vers le ciel, deviendront d'une substance plus légère et, amenées au pied du trône divin, le serviront au milieu des anges en certaines fonctions subalternes...",[25] il reprend des thèses qu'il rejetera avec vigueur quelques mois plus tard lorsqu'éclate la querelle origéniste. Lorsqu'en 396 Jérôme reprend ses Commentaires par le Livre de Jonas qui concerne également Ninive et son roi, Jérôme dénonce avec violence la doctrine d'Origène qui enseigne, dit-il, la conversion du Diable à la fin du monde.[26] Il est désormais beaucoup plus attentif à tout ce qui fleure l'origénisme.

---

21 *Ibid.* (p. 576, l. 764 sq.).

22 Il rapproche le σύμμικτος de Na. iii 17 LXX du σύμμικτος d'Ex. xii 38 (comme il le dit, p. 572, l. 632 sq.). Origène s'était lui aussi intéressé à ce peuple mêlé qui accompagne les Hébreux à leur sortie d'Égypte (v.g. *PG* 12, c. 272 B-C).

23 *Ibid.* (p. 577, l. 799-807). Cf. *In Sophoniam*, iii 14-18 (p. 707, l. 507 sq.).

24 *Ibid.*, ii 10 (p. 550, l. 300-p. 551, l. 343). Cette longue page peut être éclairée et confirmée par plusieurs autres pages de l'*In Sophoniam* en particulier (v.g. i 6-7; p. 663, l. 290 sq.). Voir "La cure et la guérison ultime du Monde et du Diable dans l'In Nahum de Jérôme", *Augustinianum* 24 (1984), pp. 471-94. La meilleure description parallèle de ce traitement médical se trouve dans le ch. 27 de la *Philocalie*, extrait du Commentaire d'Exode x 27, sur l'endurcissement de Pharaon. Voir en particulier *PG* 12, c. 269C-272C. Ces pages ont été commentées par M. Harl, "La mort salutaire du Pharaon selon Origène", *SMSR* 38 (1967), pp. 260-8. Sur les prophètes comme médecins de l'âme, voir *infra*, p. 130 et n. 136-7.

25 *Ibid.*, i 3b (p. 529, l. 72-7). De même l'idée que Dieu ne châtie pas deux fois la même faute (i 9-p. 534, l. 247-p. 535, l. 283), dirigée contre les Marcionites. Voir v.g. *In Matthaeum*, 15, 15 (*PG* 13, c. 1297 A-B), sur Ananie et Saphire, punis en cette vie, pour sortir plus purs de ce monde — et ne pas subir un châtiment plus dur, ou *In Ezechielem h.* 1, 2 (*PG* 13, c. 669 A-C), qui cite Nahum.

26 Voir "Saint Cyprien et le roi de Ninive dans l'*In Ionam* de Jérôme: la conversion des lettrés à la fin du IVe siècle", *Epektasis* (Mélanges J. Daniélou) (Paris, 1972), pp. 551 sq., et mon annotation à l'*In Ionam*, iii 6-9 en particulier.

Il n'en était pas de même dans les premiers Commentaires. Car l'*In Nahum* n'est pas un "accident". La même "démonstration" pourrait être menée à partir de l'*In Sophoniam* ou de l'*In Aggaeum.*[27] Inversement, les commentaires de 393 montrent que l'intérêt pour l'exégèse historique et pour les interprétations juives n'est aucunement dû à ce tournant doctrinal. L'*In Michaeam* de cette même année 393 fait une large place au contexte historique dans lequel vivait Michée. Il prend soin de démarquer l'exégèse chrétienne de l'exégèse juive au sujet de l'accomplissement déjà effectué ou à venir des promesses de Michée. Il n'en consacre pas moins, lui aussi, une très large place à l'aventure de l'âme ou de la Jérusalem céleste, tombées du Paradis spirituel dans ce monde matériel, ou au sort du Diable promis à un châtiment qui le fera réfléchir, et se convertir.

II. Le Commentaire sur Michée

Tel qu'il se présente à nous, le Livre de Michée répète, *grosso modo*, un double mouvement: l'annonce d'un châtiment, consécutif à une série de fautes, est suivie d'une promesse de restauration et de renouvellement: i-v (i-iii + iv-v), vi-vii (vi 1-vii 7 + vii 8-20). Le premier ensemble, nettement plus long que le second, a peut-être en partie masqué ce parallélisme. L'ordre et l'enchaînement des oracles à l'intérieur de chaque partie ne sont cependant pas toujours très nets. Ne nous étonnons donc pas que les deux livres du Commentaire ne correspondent pas aux deux "parties" du texte sacré, mais soient sensiblement égaux; les exigences de l'édition l'emportent sur celles de la composition de l'ouvrage commenté. Nous verrons toutefois que Jérôme ne termine sans doute pas gratuitement son premier livre par une attaque contre l'interprétation juive.

Jérôme est également gêné par les différences importantes entre le texte hébreu et celui des Septante. Il en vient même, pour la première fois dans des Commentaires sur les prophètes, à suspecter la valeur et l'origine de la traduction grecque, en invoquant le témoignage de Josèphe: les Soixante-dix n'auraient traduit que le Pentateuque.[28] Cela le conduit un certain nombre de fois, dans les premiers chapitres, à ne pas donner les deux textes en lemme et à ne fournir l'explication du grec que dans un second temps, de façon morcelée souvent. Dans la suite du Commentaire, les différences entre les deux textes deviennent moins fréquentes ou sont moins fortement soulignées, tant et si bien qu'il faut être très

---

[27] Par ex., *In Aggaeum*, ii 21-24 (p. 745, l. 704-32). L'origine de cette page peut être établie à l'aide de l'*Ep.* 30, 13-14 d'Ambroise, qui part de la même source.

[28] *In Michaeam* I, ii 9-10 (pp. 446-7), l. 272-7). Cf. *Hebraïcae Quaestiones in Genesim, Praefatio* (*CC* 72, p. 2, l. 27 sq.).

attentif pour apercevoir quelle est la traduction que Jérôme est en train d'utiliser. Les deux traductions peuvent d'ailleurs être entrelacées[29] ou une seule et même explication valoir explicitement pour les deux interprétations.[30] Fait exceptionnel même,[31] l'une des dernières péricopes, tout entière expliquée selon le texte grec, se termine par cette remarque: "Tout cela selon les Septante. Mais, puisque, dans ce passage du moins, notre traduction n'est pas très différente de la leur, ce qui a été dit de cette traduction, considérons que cela l'a été également de la nôtre".[32]

Il faut noter que dans ce passage de Michée vii 14-17, c'est Dieu qui parle à son Fils, selon Jérôme. La distinction des deux traductions est assurément plus importante lorsque, selon le commentateur, le prophète, ou Dieu, s'adresse à Samarie, à Jérusalem, ou aux deux à la fois. Le début du livre fournit en effet des coordonnées précises du ministère du prophète. De l'indication des trois règnes successifs de Joathan, Achaz et Ézéchias, Jérôme ne tire cependant qu'une indication globale et générale, sans essayer de distinguer les époques, même s'il trouve une allusion à la levée du siège de Jérusalem par Sennachérib, événement qu'il mentionne si souvent.[33] Pour lui, l'ensemble du livre concerne la destruction de Samarie, par les Assyriens, *et* celle de Jérusalem, par les Babyloniens.[34] Le fait ne laisse aucun doute à Jérôme. "Le sens est manifeste", déclare-t-il plusieurs fois;[35] ce qui le conduit plusieurs fois à comprendre des deux royaumes ce qui semble annoncé d'un seul,[36] ou à appliquer à l'ensemble ce qui s'adresse à Juda.[37] Inversement, il applique à Samarie ce qui devrait être entendu de Juda.[38]

Il n'est pas sûr qu'il faille imputer toutes ces "erreurs" à Jérôme. Elles auraient d'ailleurs l'excuse de textes parfois difficiles à cerner. C'est justement lorsque le texte devient trop obscur que Jérôme invoque ses auteurs. La première fois, il est en train d'expliquer la complainte sur les villes du Bas-Pays qui joue sur le "sens" du nom de ces cités. Il ne s'est pas trouvé de Juif, semble-t-il, pour lui expliquer ces jeux de mots, mais c'est aux *Hebraei* qu'il attribue les précisions qu'il donne sur les circons-

---

29 *Ibid.* II, vi 1-2 (pp. 493-4).

30 *Ibid.* II, vi 8 (p. 499, l. 230-6).

31 On le trouve cependant en d'autres commentaires, v.g. *In Sophoniam*, iii 19-20 (p. 711, l. 661-3).

32 *In Michaeam* II, vii 14-17 (p. 522, l. 650-3).

33 *Ibid.* I, i 10-15 (p. 432, l. 340-5).

34 *Ibid.* I, i 1 (p. 422, l. 5-14).

35 *Ibid.* I, i 2 (p. 423, l. 52-4), iii 1-4 (p. 457, l. 11-12); II, iv 10 (p. 477, l. 361-2) ...

36 *Ibid.* I, i 3-5 (p. 424, l. 89 sq.), i 6-9 (p. 427, l. 169 sq.; 187 sq.; 203-4) ...

37 *Ibid.* II, vi 3-5 (p. 496, l. 130-1); II, vi 3-7 (p. 497, l. 185 sq.); II, vi 8 (p. 499, l. 231 sq.).

38 *Ibid.* II, vi 9 (p. 500, l. 283 sq.); II, vi 10-16 (p. 502, l. 338 sq.).

tances historiques de cet oracle.[39] De même, au chapitre ii 11-13, pour un passage où les deux textes à commenter s'écartent trop l'un de l'autre.[40] Ces *Hebraei* ne reparaîtront plus que deux autres fois dans le deuxième livre,[41] mais ils seront précédés et suivis, à quatre ou cinq reprises, par des *Iudaei*, à propos de promesses de restauration, que ces Juifs interprètent à leur avantage et situent, à la fin des temps, dans une prospérité matérielle de rêve, perspectives que Jérôme qualifie de chimères.[42]

La situation est rendue plus complexe par le fait suivant. Sans qu'il le relève ici explicitement,[43] Jérôme considère que les paroles du prophète ont une double échéance: il n'annonce pas seulement la prochaine captivité de Samarie ou Jérusalem par les Assyriens ou les Chaldéens, mais aussi celle que les Juifs subiront de la part des Romains. Cette seconde perspective, d'abord présentée comme possible,[44] devient évidente tout au long de la première série de menaces. Plus même, elle est présentée comme le châtiment des mauvais traitements infligés au Christ.[45]

Le début du chapitre iv, promesse de renouveau, est au contraire interprété comme la suite de ce qui précède: "La Loi sortira de Sion". Et de citer les textes de Josèphe sur l'abandon du Temple, en 70, par les Puissances célestes.[46] Quant à la paix universelle promise par le prophète, Jérôme la voit réalisée au moment de la naissance du Christ, par la fin des guerres civiles romaines et l'avènement de la *monarchia* de Rome, qui ont permis aux Apôtres de se répandre à travers le monde.[47] Cette opinion, que Jérôme n'a pas inventée, sera reprise dans l'oracle correspondant de l'*In Isaiam*, en 408. Dès cet *In Michaeam*, il renvoie à Isaïe ii 1-4, mais surtout pour en critiquer l'interprétation qu'en donnent les *Iudaei* et leurs héritiers, les millénaristes.[48] C'est l'une des mentions annoncées plus haut. Il est remarquable qu'elle termine le premier livre du Commentaire, en vouant les Juifs qui ont renié le Christ à une condamnation sans excuse.[49]

---

[39] *Ibid.* i 10-15 (p. 433, l. 374-6): "...ut ab Hebraeis audiuimus...".

[40] *Ibid.* I, ii 11-13 (p. 451, l. 401-4).

[41] *Ibid.* II, v 7-14 (p. 491, l. 411 sq.; p. 492, l. 438 sq.); II, vi 3-5 (p. 496, l. 124 sq.).

[42] *Ibid.* I, iv 1-7 (p. 472, l. 189 sq.; voir *infra* et n. 48); II, iv 11-13 (p. 478, l. 410-16); II, v 5 (p. 485, l. 214-16); II, vii 8-13 (p. 515, l. 404 sq.).

[43] Cf. *In Sophoniam*, i 10-11 (p. 667, l. 421-31).

[44] *In Michaeam* I, i 16 (p. 438, l. 532 sq.); I, ii 1-5 (p. 440, l. 55-76); I, ii 11-13 (p. 451, l. 404-7).

[45] *Ibid.* I, iii 9-12 (p. 462, l. 197-202). Voir de même I, iii 1-4 (p. 457, l. 15-18); I, iii 9-12 (p. 461, l. 172-p. 462, l. 174). Cf. *In Sophoniam*, i 15-16 (p. 673, l. 658 sq.).

[46] *Ibid.* I, iv 1-7 (p. 467, l. 41-55).

[47] *Ibid.* I, iv 1-7 (p. 467, l. 117-29).

[48] *Ibid.* I, iv 1-7 (p. 472, l. 189-209).

[49] *Ibid.* (l. 209-14).

Il ne sera plus question qu'une seule fois de la seconde captivité, dans le deuxième livre, au moment où Jérôme en arrive à l'oracle sur la naissance du Messie à Bethléem.[50] En revanche, lorsque, en iv 11-13, le prophète évoque les Nations qui s'assemblent contre Sion, Jérôme ne fait état que de la captivité à Babylone, et il refuse avec véhémence — et rapidité — l'interprétation juive selon laquelle l'Empire romain, "qu'ils dévouvrent en Édom" — pourtant non nommé dans le texte de Michée —, sera broyé et écrasé par les cornes de fer.[51] Selon Jérôme,[52] cette dernière promesse est pour "plus tard", tandis que, maintenant, Israël, captif, est puni pour ce qu'il a fait au Christ,[53] en attendant qu'il se convertisse, selon les espoirs de saint Paul, lorsque la multitude des Nations sera entrée dans l'Église.[54]

Loin d'être un oracle isolé,[55] l'annonce de la naissance de Jésus à Bethléem, de son règne de paix et de puissance, s'intègre en ce plan divin; à ceci près qu'on ne voit plus très bien si nous sommes là devant la réalisation historique de la prophétie ou devant l'interprétation spirituelle du texte. En des Commentaires plus tardifs, Jérôme ne manquerait pas de préciser ce point, mais peut-être aussi de mieux distinguer les deux perspectives.[56] Il se contente ici de rejeter les interprétations matérielles des Juifs:[57] l'histoire ne montre aucune réalisation passée de ces annonces de restauration; l'état actuel d'Israël ne permet pas d'appliquer à ce peuple l'oracle du prophète.[58]

---

[50] *Ibid.* II, v 1 (p. 480, l. 25-34).

[51] *Ibid.* II, iv 11-13 (p. 478, l. 398-416).

[52] *Ibid.* II, v 1 (p. 479, l. 6-13).

[53] *Ibid.* (p. 480, l. 17-22).

[54] *Ibid.* II, v 3 (p. 483, l. 141-9).

[55] C'est à ce traitement que l'on voit la différence avec un Justin (*Dialogue avec Tryphon*, 78), un Cyprien (*Test. ad Quirinum*, 2, 12) ou même avec le simple dossier du *Peri Archôn*, 4, 1, 5. La discussion avec les Juifs (Irénée, *Démonstration*, 63; *Adu. Haereses*, 4, 33, 11; Tertullien, *Adu. Iudaeos*, 13, 1-2) apparaît également chez Origène (*Contre Celse*, 1, 52), que Jérôme suit ici (II, v 2-p.482, l. 109-p. 483, l. 118), d'après le parallèle qu'offre l'*Ep.* 70 d'Ambroise. On notera également que l'insistance sur la préexistence de Jésus pouvait se prévaloir de ce qui était dit de la préexistence du Messie en Targ. Michée v 1. Quant à la connaissance du plan divin par les prophètes, elle est une affirmation fondamentale d'Origène. Voir A. Orbe, "La excelencia de los profetas según Orígenes", *Estudios Biblicos* 7 (1955), pp. 191-221, étude importante pour comprendre les Commentaires sur les Prophètes ... de Jérôme.

[56] En 406, Jérôme précise plusieurs fois les plans successifs de la prophétie, simultanés pour le prophète: *In Malachiam*, i 11-13 (p. 912, l. 350-1); *In Osee* I, i 3-4 (p. 10, l. 148-52); *In Amos* III, vii 1-3) et il sera par la suite plus attentif à cette distinction. Voir mon Introduction à l'*In Ionam*: IIe partie, n. 295. En 393, dans l'*In Sophoniam*, i 10-11 (p. 667, l. 421-31), dans une discussion avec un tiers, Jérôme tient à ce que la première captivité soit au moins le type de la seconde.

[57] *In Michaeam* II, v 5 (p. 485, l. 214-16); II, v 7-14 (p. 491, l. 411 sq.).

[58] *Ibid.* (p. 492, l. 438 sq.).

Avec la fin de cette promesse de restauration, nous en arrivons, sans que Jérôme le marque nettement, au deuxième mouvement du Livre, et, tout d'abord, à (un nouveau) procès de Dieu contre Israël. Le contexte historique ne se précise que lentement, d'une péricope à l'autre, de vi 1-2 à vii 1-7: Israël, Samarie et Juda.

L'interprétation juive n'a pas été signalée au long de cette première partie. Elle l'est au contraire dès que commence la deuxième partie qui laisse entrevoir des temps meilleurs. "Ne te réjouis pas de ma chute. ô mon ennemie..." (vii 8...). "Il me semble que, selon la lettre, c'est Jérusalem qui parle contre Babylone et les autres nations qui l'avaient insultée..."[59] Ces "autres Nations" sont peut-être une allusion voilée à la deuxième captivité, car Jérôme ne tarde pas à faire état de l'interprétation juive, selon laquelle, non seulement Jérusalem sera rebâtie, mais la Loi sera aussi retirée des mains des chrétiens pour être rendue aux Juifs.[60] C'est là la dernière mention des Juifs dans ce Commentaire. La péricope suivante (vii 14-17) s'adresse au Fils, selon Jérôme, et nous avons dit plus haut qu'elle était expliquée selon la seule traduction du grec.[61] Quant à l'exclamation finale (vii 18-20), elle est le fait du prophète qui admire la profondeur du dessein divin et qui contemple le salut, à la fois, des Nations païennes *et* d'Israël, à la fin du monde.[62]

Ainsi s'achève, selon Jérôme, cette prophétie qui, de la menace assyrienne ou chaldéenne s'étend, après la naissance du Christ à Bethléem et la conversion des Nations par l'Évangile, jusqu'à la fin de l'histoire humaine et à la rentrée d'Israël dans l'Église. Une telle lecture "historique" et prophétique n'a, semble-t-il, pu être faite que parce que Matthieu avait invoqué le témoignage de Michée. Jérôme note d'ailleurs aussi que le Christ a annoncé qu'il était venu séparer l'homme d'avec son père, la fille d'avec sa mère, la belle-fille d'avec sa belle-mère, en des termes qui rappellent ceux de Michée.[63] Cette lecture suppose la connaissance de l'époque de Michée — réelle ou erronnée — que les Juifs ont procurée à Jérôme, et prend en compte la visée néo-testamentaire que ne peut qu'avoir un prophète, *a fortiori* lorsqu'il annonce avec tant de précision la naissance de Jésus à Bethléem. Mais cette annonce ne peut être isolée. Elle n'est, selon Jérôme, qu'*un* élément du plan divin de salut. Il en interprète l'ensemble à la lumière de ce foyer lumineux, sans rencontrer ici de zone d'ombre. Nous verrons que l'*In Ioelem* posera explicitement le problème.

[59] *Ibid.* II, vii 8-13 (p. 515, l. 377-9).

[60] *Ibid.* (p. 515, l. 404-10).

[61] *Ibid.* II, vii 14-17 (pp. 519-22). Voir *supra*, p. 115 et n. 32.

[62] *Ibid.* II, vii 18-20 (p. 522, l. 668-95).

[63] *Ibid.* II, vii 5-7 (p. 513, l. 329-37). Voir aussi II, v 6-7 (p. 487, l. 260-1); II, vii 5-7 (p. 509, l. 185-7).

A ce discours "historique" s'en juxtapose un autre, qui ne tient pas moins de place, bien au contraire, dans le commentaire de Jérôme. Nous n'aurons pas de peine à déceler son origine. Ses axes sont indiqués dès l'explication du titre de la prophétie: puisque celle-ci concerne Samarie et Juda, "la parole divine parle des doctrines perverses (de l'hérésie) et de l'Église lorsque celle-ci vient à commettre des fautes, et elle compose toute la suite du volume".[64] De fait, on peut, sans trop de difficultés, suivre d'un bout à l'autre du Commentaire ce double enseignement, selon que Michée parle, selon Jérôme, de Samarie, l'hérésie, ou de l'Église qu'est Juda.

Reconnaître que la vie même de l'Église est sujette à bien des défaillances, même chez ses membres les plus élevés, n'était pas au delà des forces d'un satirique. Même s'il prend parfois quelques précautions,[65] nous avons là des propos parallèles à ceux qu'il tient, la même année, dans la Lettre 52, à Népotien, le neveu de son ami Héliodore, qui lui avait demandé une sorte de charte de la vie cléricale. On en trouverait également bien des éléments dans les écrits authentiques d'Origène dont Jérôme doit plus d'une fois emboîter le pas, à en juger par ses Homélies. Il est cependant une thèse d'Origène que Jérôme ne mentionne qu'avec réserve — puisqu'il en laisse la paternité à un *quidam* — à deux reprises, ce qui est à la fois suffisant pour qu'on la reconnaisse, mais trop peu précis pour que l'on puisse en restituer ici tout le développement: il s'agit de la Jérusalem céleste et de l'histoire de sa chute, évoquée à deux reprises au moins.[66]

Un second élément de la théorie d'Origène pouvait être débarrassé de ses connotations hétérodoxes. Il est question une fois, en même temps que de la chute de la Jérusalem céleste, de celle d'Adam. Il ne fait pas de doute que dans ce texte, et dans la pensée d'Origène, il s'agit de la chute de l'âme: "O âme humaine..." est-il dit...[67] Cette âme "dédaigne la Jérusalem céleste", déclare bien à un autre endroit Jérôme, qui ajoute aussitôt "et méprise sa mère-Église";[68] il n'en reste pas moins que la préexistence des âmes et la théorie de leur chute dans les corps n'ont pas laissé grandes traces dans cet *In Michaeam*. Il était facile, en effet, pour Jérôme d'appliquer à la vie spirituelle, au combat de l'âme contre le

---

64 *Ibid.* I, i 1 (p. 422, l. 14-19). La suite justifie cette assimilation. Elle sera reprise dans l'*In Osee* et l'*In Amos*. Elle est commune chez Origène.

65 *Ibid.* (p. 510, l. 228-36). Voir *In Michaeam* I, ii 9-10 (p. 448, l. 328-32).

66 *In Michaeam* I, i 16 (p. 438, l. 540-50) et II, iv 8-9 (p. 476, l. 325-32). On peut y ajouter un développement sur le mal et le non-être, I, ii 9-10-p. 450, 379-87). Cf. Origène, *In Iohannem*, 2, 97 sq.; Ambroise, *De fuga*, 4, 24.

67 *In Michaeam* I, i 16 (p. 438, l. 543).

68 *Ibid.* II, vii 5-7 (p. 513, l. 301 sq.).

monde et le mal, ce qui était dit du statut de l'âme dans le corps et de sa punition. A côté de la figure de l'Église ou de celle de l'Hérésie, ou, parfois à sa place, elle sera l'objet, tout au long du Commentaire,[69] d'une grande attention.

Le Livre de Michée se trouve ainsi tracer, à la fois, l'itinéraire de l'âme ou du chrétien tombé dans le péché, qui subit le châtiment de Dieu, l'excommunication de l'Église, puis revient d'exil en réintégrant la communauté, et le portrait de l'âme pacifiée par Dieu.[70] Ce portrait nous est garanti par une longue lettre de saint Ambroise, souvent parallèle à une bonne partie du Commentaire spirituel de Jérôme et qui, à n'en pas douter, exploite, comme celui-ci, l'oeuvre correspondante d'Origène.[71]

Ambroise a dû filtrer comme Jérôme l'oeuvre de l'Alexandrin, mais s'en tenir à une seule "ligne"; il la morcelle moins que Jérôme. Il peut donc servir à détecter dans le texte de Jérôme des emprunts à Origène et garantir que le puzzle que l'on essaie de reconstruire n'est pas pur produit de l'imagination. Je ne prendrai qu'un seul exemple qui permettra de nous interroger sur l'évolution de Jérôme en cette année 393. Au début de la dernière "partie" du livre, Jérusalem s'adresse à son ennemie, en lui demandant de ne pas se réjouir de sa chute. "Je suis tombée, mais je me relèverai... Je dois supporter la colère de Dieu jusqu'à ce qu'il me juge..." (Michée vii 8-9). Pour Ambroise, comme pour Jérôme, l'âme s'adresse à la puissance contraire, le Diable, qui l'a trompée; mais elle est sûre que la miséricorde viendra après le châtiment et qu'elle sera sauvée.[72] Plus qu'Ambroise, Jérôme s'intéresse aux démons et à leur chef. Il décrit en particulier leurs luttes intestines, qu'il découvre en Michée vii 12 LXX. Mais leur défaite finale est considérée comme un début dans la vertu, et non comme une destruction ou un châtiment sans fin.[73] L'origine d'une telle opinion ne laisse aucun doute.

On peut de fait trouver de multiples traces de la démonologie, de l'angélologie ou de l'anthropologie d'Origène dans ce Commentaire; on peut trouver aussi bien d'autres thèmes moins discutables. Par la manière dont tous s'intègrent à l'interprétation de Jérôme, on peut avoir l'assurance que celui-ci n'est pas allé les quérir dans quelque homélie, où

[69] A partir du moins de *In Michaeam* I, i 16 qui a fait mention de l'opinion d'Origène.

[70] On trouvera en particulier dans cet *In Michaeam* plusieurs thèmes de la doctrine d'Origène sur la pénitence, telle qu'on la trouve développée, en particulier, dans les Homélies sur le Lévitique.

[71] Ambroise, *Ep.* 70 (*PL* 16, c. 1234-41). O. Faller (*CSEL* 82,1, pp. 128-37) a multiplié les parallèles indiqués par les Mauristes. On peut les augmenter encore.

[72] Ambroise, *Ep.* 70, 21 (*PL* 16, c. 1239 C); Jérôme, *In Michaeam* II, vii 8-13 (p. 516, l. 437 sq.).

[73] *In Michaeam* II, vii 8-13 (p. 518, l. 494-5): "...poenarum finis, bonorum exordium est..."

nous sommes aujourd'hui réduits à les rencontrer, mais qu'il les a bien trouvés, pour l'essentiel, dans le Commentaire sur Michée d'Origène. Lui-même nous le laisse entendre: la Préface du deuxième livre de l'*In Michaeam* répond aux griefs de ceux qui l'accusent de "contaminer" — c'est-à-dire de plagier Origène — dans ses Commentaires des prophètes. Loin de rejeter l'accusation, Jérôme se fait gloire d'imiter un tel esprit.[74] On ne doit donc pas s'attendre à ce qu'il ait été beaucoup moins fidèle à ce modèle dans cet *In Michaeam* que dans les Commentaires des mois précédents. Que l'on compare, en revanche, la manière dont il parle de ses prédécesseurs — les *ueteres* — dans la Préface de l'*In Ionam*,[75] reprise de son activité en 396. J'ai montré ailleurs que la thèse qu'y soutient Jérôme venait très probablement d'Origène, bien que celui-ci soit plusieurs fois pris à parti au long de ce Commentaire pour des interprétations qui concernent la chute de l'âme, le salut du Diable ou la théologie trinitaire. Je n'y reviens pas davantage ici.[76]

III. Après le déclenchement de la querelle origéniste: L'In Abdiam de 396

Il est un second Commentaire de 396, dont la Préface n'est pas moins intéressante: l'*In Abdiam*. Jérôme y fournit des renseignements qu'il ne faut réduire trop vite à l'autobiographie: un visiteur a fait l'éloge du premier Commentaire que Jérôme avait écrit sur *Abdias*, au temps de son séjour à Antioche. Or, celui-ci était allégorique, parce que, nous est-il dit, Jérôme ignorait à ce moment l'histoire.[77] Attendons-nous donc à trouver cette histoire dans ce nouvel *In Abdiam*. Mais demandons-nous également pourquoi Jérôme espère le pardon à la façon du fils prodigue.[78]

Abdias ne serait autre, selon les Hébreux, qu'Obadyahu, le Maître du Palais d'Achab, devenu prophète pour avoir protégé des prophètes contre les entreprises de Jézabel.[79] Nous serions donc entre 875 et 850. Que cet homme du Nord s'intéresse à Édom et aux rapports d'Édom avec le royaume de Juda n'arrête pas Jérôme. Toute la partie "historique" du Commentaire est conduite en relation avec le siège de Jérusalem

---

[74] *In Michaeam* II, *Praefatio* (p. 473, l. 226-38).

[75] *In Ionam*, *Praefatio* (p. 377, l. 15 sq.).

[76] Voir, outre les livres et articles cités, mon annotation à l'*In Ionam*, ii 7b, iii 6-9, iv 10-11.

[77] *In Abdiam*, *Praefatio* (p. 349, l. 9-10; p. 350, l. 29 sq.).

[78] *Ibid.* (l. 38 sq.): Jérôme doit se faire pardonner d'avoir proposé des interprétations aujourd'hui scabreuses. Voir p. 124 et n. 99.

[79] *In Abdiam*, 1 (p. 352, l. 1-4): 1 Reg. xviii 4. La datation est celle de la Chronique d'Eusèbe-Jérôme.

de 587 et les oracles de Jérémie contre Édom.[80] Loin de le gêner, un tel parallélisme confirme Jérôme dans son analyse historique. Les menaces contre Édom se réaliseront aux lendemains de la prise de Jérusalem, dont s'est réjoui le frère jaloux. Elles auront pour auteur les Assyriens,[81] puisque l'envoi d'une "ambassade" aux Nations, au début de la page, a été compris de l'annonce de la prédication aux païens.[82] Les alliés d'Édom du *v.* 7 l'abandonnent pour se joindre à Nabuchodonosor, et provoquer sa ruine complète.[83] En définitive, la sentence contre Édom est rangée au nombre des Oracles contre les Nations où Jérémie montre Yahweh faisant boire tous les peuples au calice de sa colère et se servant des Babyloniens et des Assyriens pour réaliser son jugement.[84] Cette domination universelle des Assyriens, attestée, nous dit Jérôme, par Hérodote, les historiens grecs et barbares,[85] permet d'y inclure, semble-t-il, Édom, dont il n'est pas question immédiatement après la prise de Jérusalem. Au contraire, Édom avait-il profité de la ruine de Juda pour faire entrer dans son orbite le sud de la Judée. D'où l'extension merveilleuse promise à Sion, dans la deuxième partie du texte prophétique.

Avant d'en venir à cet avenir lumineux et à l'époque de sa réalisation, il importe de signaler une deuxième "lignée" juive, que Jérôme assure avoir recueillie auprès de l'Hébreu qui l'a initié aux Écritures.[86] Mention en est faite à trois reprises au cours de ce bref Commentaire. Au premier verset, il signale que les "Juifs", en changeant le *daleth* en *resh*, transforment *Duma* en *Roma* et font de cet oracle d'Abdias, comme de celui d'Isaïe xxi, une menace contre Rome et son Empire: celui-ci sera détruit, tandis qu'avec la venue du Messie, le royaume d'Israël sera rétabli, selon la promesse de la seconde partie de la prophétie.[87] L'attention plus

[80] Jérôme remarque en effet la parenté entre les versets 1b-2 d'Abdias et l'oracle de Jérémie contre Édom (xlix 7-22), en particulier les *v.* 1c//Jer. xlix 14; 2-4//Jer. xlix 15-16; 5-6//Jer. xlix 9-10; 7//Jer. xlix 19-22, pour lesquels le commentateur cite parfois, dès le lemme, le texte de Jérémie, à côté des deux traductions d'Abdias sur l'hébreu et sur le grec.

[81] *In Abdiam*, 5-6 (p. 360, l. 261 sq.), 10-11 (p. 363, l. 375-81), 12-13 (p. 364, l. 420-31), 14 (p. 365, l. 459-69)...

[82] *Ibid.*, 1c (p. 356, l. 130 sq.). Jérôme passe immédiatement au sens spirituel.

[83] *Ibid.*, 7 (p. 361, l. 311 sq.); 8-9 (p. 362, l. 337—52).

[84] *Ibid.* 15-16 (p. 366, l. 497-504).

[85] *Ibid.* (l. 505-10).

[86] *Ibid.* 20-21 (p. 372, l. 709-13).

[87] *Ibid.* 1 (p. 355, l. 120-5). Outre le texte cité n. 86, on trouvera une troisième mention de cette opinion juive dans le commentaire des *v.* 17-18 (p. 369, l. 606 sq.). Cette espérance peut être datée; d'une part, le "maître hébreu" de Jérôme identifie le Sépharad du *v.* 20 avec le Bosphore où Hadrien a déporté des Juifs (p. 372, l. 709-13); d'autre part, le Talmud de Jérusalem rapporte l'opinion de R. Meïr qui, à propos d'Isaïe xxi 11, identifiait Édom et Rome (J. Taanith 1, 1-Trad. M. Schwab, VI, p. 144 — Voir L. Ginzberg, "Die Haggada bei den Kirchenvätern. VI. Der Kommentar des Hieronymus zu Jesaya", *Jewish Studies in Memory of George A. Kohut* (New-York, 1935), p. 288. Voir de

grande que marque l'*In Abdiam* pour les espérances juives s'explique peut-être en partie par les difficultés qui s'accentuent pour l'Empire romain avec la mort de Théodose, en janvier 395.[88]

De telles espérances sont inconcevables pour Jérôme. En 396, plus encore qu'en 410 ou les années suivantes.[89] A vrai dire cependant, même si la distinction n'est pas clairement énoncée, un rétablissement du peuple juif n'est pas tant impossible parce que Rome et son Empire seraient inébranlables que parce que la promesse du Christ à l'Église interdit toute restauration matérielle et charnelle d'Israël:[90] l'Église a définitivement supplanté Israël. Dès l'énoncé des menaces contre Édom pour avoir comploté contre son frère Jacob, Jérôme a reconnu dans les adversaires de Jacob les Juifs et les hérétiques, deux groupes acharnés contre l'Église.[91] Il les suit, de manière plus ou moins régulière, au long de cette malédiction, leur joignant, plus épisodiquement, un autre couple, celui de la chair et de l'esprit, dont la rivalité est plusieurs fois évoquée.[92] Il est remarquable que tous ces "niveaux" soient rappelés avec précision au moment où Jérôme entame la deuxième partie de la prophétie.[93]

Celle-ci annonce le retour (?) de rescapés en Sion, associe la maison de Joseph au bonheur de la maison de Jacob et leur promet une extension considérable, au détriment d'Édom en particulier. Quelle échéance donner à ces prédictions? Des Juifs, Jérôme ne mentionne que l'opinion selon laquelle Édom figure l'Empire Romain, comme nous l'avons vu plus haut. Mais il n'est pas impossible qu'il y en ait une autre. Car, Jérôme note tout aussitôt que, "*selon l'histoire*, cette prophétie s'est déjà réalisée sous Zorobabel — avec le retour d'exil —, ou que *selon la prophétie*

---

même *Pesiq* 67b au sujet de Joël iii 3; R. Levi (c. 300), au nom de R. Chama ben Chanina (c. 260): L'Égypte, premier asservisseur des Juifs, Édom/Rome, le dernier). Jérôme signale cette opinion dès 393 dans l'*In Michaeam* II, iv 11 (p. 478, l. 410 sq.) et l'*In Sophoniam*, ii 8-11 (pp. 684-688) où il en tente une réfutation. On la retrouve, en 406, dans l'*In Malachiam*, i 2-5 (p. 905, l. 104-6) et l'*In Ioelem*, iii 19 (p. 208, l. 380-8), en 408, dans l'*In Isaïam* V, xxi 11-12 (*CC* 73, p. 207, l. 40-5).

[88] Dans l'été 395, Jérôme a failli devoir s'enfuir de Palestine devant un raid de Huns déferlant du Caucase vers Antioche. Sa Lettre 60, 16, de 396, trace un tableau apocalyptique des malheurs de l'Empire depuis vingt ans. Cette actualité ne peut manquer d'influencer la lecture de Jérôme.

[89] J'ai étudié l'évolution de Jérôme sur ce point entre 410 et 415 dans "Les métamorphoses de l'historiographie aux IVe et Ve siècles: Renaissance, fin ou permanence de l'Empire romain", Congrès de la F.I.E.C., Budapest, 1979.

[90] Voir l'*In Ioelem*, iii 20-21 (p. 209). Pour Jérôme, la destruction du Temple est définitive. Voir *In Isaïam* I, i 12 ou IX, xxix 1 (*CC* 73, p. 17, l. 14-16; p. 371, l. 90); *In Ezechielem* II, vii 8 (*CC* 75, p. 75, l. 698-708).

[91] *In Abdiam*, 1 (p. 355, l. 96-106).

[92] *Ibid.* (p. 355, l. 116-20).

[93] *Ibid.*, 17-18 (p. 368, l. 557, Peuple juif; l. 581, la chair; p. 369, l. 614—15: Église, âme; p. 370, l. 623, hérétiques). Nous reviendrons plus loin sur ces pages qui sont plus complexes encore.

ET *l'interprétation mystique*, elle s'accomplit chaque jour dans l'Église et se réalise en chacun dans l'empire de l'âme sur la chair''.[94] Il se pose à nouveau la question à propos du verset 19 qui décrit l'accaparement des régions voisines par les exilés de retour: ''Hoc utrum factum sit, Deus uiderit'', déclare-t-il, avant de poursuivre: ''Il est possible que cela se soit accompli *en partie* durant les cinq cents ans avant l'avènement du Christ. Ce que je sais, en tout cas, comme absolument certain, c'est que cela s'accomplit chaque jour et que cela s'avère confirmé dans le royaume de l'Église.''[95] Et de décrire cette géographie spirituelle de la Palestine, où les disciples du Christ l'emportent sur les Juifs, les hérétiques, mais aussi les Païens.[96] La dernière péricope au contraire est toute consacrée à la conversion des Juifs et au triomphe de l'Église.[97]

Aucune mention ici des hérétiques, et moins encore de l'âme. J'ai dit plus haut que cette interprétation ''morale'' de la vie spirituelle n'apparaissait que de loin en loin: en 5 péricopes exactement, sur les 13 entre lesquelles Jérôme a divisé les 21 versets d'Abdias. Si on examine ces mentions, on n'y trouvera rien qui ne soit parfaitement compatible avec l'orthodoxie la plus stricte, mais rien non plus qui s'éloigne des schémas les plus ordinaires d'Origène.[98] Jérôme les a simplement amputés de leurs prolongements les plus discutables. Cette prudence est encore plus sensible pour ce qui concerne le Diable ou les Démons: ils n'apparaissent guère en notre Commentaire, contrairement à l'ordinaire. On ne dira pas trop vite qu'ils n'avaient pas à intervenir; car, en 384, à Rome,[99] Jérôme avait appliqué au Diable l'un des premiers versets d'Abdias, dans tout un dossier scripturaire que le commentateur continuera d'appliquer à Satan vingt et trente ans plus tard,[100] en y incluant parfois ce verset 4 d'Abdias. Il a évité d'en parler ici, à cause même de l'actualité.

Il serait trop ''court'', en effet, d'expliquer simplement cette réserve par la rapidité du travail de Jérôme. Certes, celui-ci déclare avoir dicté ces 25 pages de commentaire en deux veillées; mais il déclare également à

---

[94] *Ibid.*, 17-18 (p. 369, l. 604-15).

[95] *Ibid.*, 19 (p. 371, l. 655-8). Cf. *In Sophoniam*, ii 5-7 (p. 681, l. 163 sq.). Sur ''en partie'' après le retour de captivité, cf., v.g., *In Zachariam* III, xii 9-10 (p. 867, l. 270-3).

[96] *Ibid.* (p. 371, l. 662 sq.).

[97] *Ibid.*, 20-21 (p. 373, l. 729-p. 374, l. 770).

[98] *Ibid.*, 2-4 (p. 359, l. 228-36), 10-11 (p. 363, l. 397-407): sur ces portes ou ces fenêtres des sens, v. *In Nahum*, iii 13-17, p. 570, l. 552 sq.; *In Sophoniam*, i 8-9, p. 666, l. 403 sq.; *In Ioelem*, ii 1-11, p. 181, l. 197 sq.: thème origénien, à partir de Jer., ix 20: v.g. Origène, *In Canticum h.* 2, 12), 12-13 (p. 364, l. 437-p. 365, l. 449).

[99] *Ep.* 22, 4 (*CUF* 1, p. 114, l. 12-15).

[100] *In Isaiam* VI, xiv 13-14 (*CC* 73, p. 242). L'explication du πυροφόρον/πυρφόρον du *v.* 18 LXX d'Abdias fait de même intervenir Satan et l'Antichrist (p. 370, l. 619-25); mais Jérôme ne s'arrête pas.

Pammachius qu'il a surtout suivi l'*hebraica expositio*,[101] ce qui marque bien sa volonté de restreindre la part de la tropologie dans tous ses "étages" et en particulier les plus controversés. En 396, il ne peut plus se permettre d'évoquer le salut du Diable. Il ne serait pourtant pas difficile, en comparant la fin de l'*In Abdiam* à celles de l'*In Aggaeum*, de l'*In Sophoniam* ou de l'*In Nahum* de 393, de montrer que le jugement annoncé d'Esaü et l'instauration du règne du Seigneur pourraient, ici comme là, s'étendre jusqu'au monde céleste. Jérôme s'en est bien gardé ici.

IV. Le Commentaire sur Joël en 406

Repris en 396 par Jonas et Abdias, le commentaire des petits prophètes est aussitôt interrompu par les rebondissements de la querelle origéniste. Ce n'est qu'en 406 que Jérôme pourra commenter Zacharie et Malachie, puis Osée, Joël et Amos. Ce groupe de Commentaires a des points communs qu'il ne serait pas difficile de mettre en lumière: problèmes nouveaux, maturité et information plus riches. Mais ces Commentaires sont également la suite des précédents, en ce qui concerne la méthode, comme les intérêts majeurs. Avec l'*In Ioelem*, je voudrais faire apparaître l'espèce de clivage qui existe, dans le texte même, entre une interprétation historique et prophétique, surtout préoccupée de la réalisation de *tout* le Livre de Joël à l'époque du Christ, et une interprétation spirituelle, tout d'abord très développée, et qui disparaît ou se transforme soudain, sans qu'on nous en dise la raison.

Les Modernes s'accordent à dater Joël de l'époque post-exilique. Contrairement à ses habitudes, Jérôme ne dit rien de la date dans sa Préface, où il se contente de considérations sur l'ordre des prophètes et le sens de leurs noms. Ce n'est qu'au moment où il entame le Commentaire à proprement parler qu'il remarque que Joël, le second des Douze, s'adresse à Juda, comme Osée, le premier des Douze, s'adressait aux Dix tribus. Cette correspondance s'étend, selon lui, aux dates: celles d'Osée et Joël doivent être les mêmes![102] Jérôme est cependant gêné plusieurs fois par l'absence de date précise au cours du livre.

De même a-t-il du mal à se prononcer sur la réalité de l'invasion des sauterelles et autres prédateurs qui ouvre le livre. Il penche cependant pour l'emploi d'une métaphore et, plusieurs fois, identifie ces ennemis avec les Chaldéens,[103] en reconnaissant même, dans la fin subite du fléau, la destruction de l'armée de Sennachérib.[104] Mais il existe chez

---

[101] *In Abdiam*, 20-21 (p. 374, l. 770-2).
[102] *In Ioelem*, i 1 (p. 161, l. 27-37). Cf. *In Amos* I, i 1 (p. 212, l. 4-15).
[103] *Ibid.*, ii 1-11 (p. 177, l. 54 sq.).
[104] *Ibid.*, ii 18-20 (p. 187, l. 421-5).

Jérôme une autre hésitation, qui concerne l'identité des ennemis figurés par ces sauterelles diverses. A la suite des "Hébreux", Jérôme reconnaît dans ces quatre fléaux, en relation avec Zacharie, les quatre empires auxquels Israël a été successivement soumis: Assyriens, Perses, Séleucides et Romains.[105] Il penche d'abord pour les premiers,[106] et, pendant longtemps, ne parlera que d'eux.[107] Mais il est tiraillé par deux autres échéances qui lui sont suggérées, l'une par les Juifs encore, l'autre par la réalisation de la prophétie de Joël lors de la Pentecôte.

A deux reprises, Jérôme fait état de l'opinion des Juifs, qui reconnaît, soit dans la menace d'invasion,[108] soit dans les nations convoquées dans la vallée de Josaphat, Gog et Magog, les envahisseurs de la Fin, qui doivent subjuguer Israël jusqu'à la venue du Messie.[109] De même signale-t-il que, dans l'Égypte et Édom, auxquels Joël promet le châtiment en iii 19, les Juifs reconnaissent, non seulement les Égyptiens, oppresseurs du temps de Moïse, mais aussi les Romains, qui ont conquis la Palestine.[110] L'identification d'Édom avec Rome ne nous surprend plus. Elle ne devrait pas étonner Jérôme qui, en 406, ne semble plus en connaître la raison, tandis qu'il la formule à nouveau dans son *In Isaïam* de 408-410.[111] Pour les raisons profondes qui ont été énoncées, mais ici pour des raisons particulières qu'il tire du contexte,[112] Jérôme ne peut accepter de voir les Romains mêlés à cette prophétie. Ce qui ne l'a pas empêché, quelques pages plus haut, à propos du châtiment de Tyr et Sidon, évoqué de la même façon par Joël iii 4, de pencher pour l'époque de la conquête romaine, à la suite des Juifs une fois encore, mais aussi du Nouveau Testament. En effet, bien qu'il relève lui-même que l'histoire raconte ces événements lors du pillage de Jérusalem par les Chaldéens, il adopte l'opinion juive selon laquelle ce châtiment concernera Tyr et Sidon au Jour du Seigneur, c'est-à-dire, selon les Apôtres, après la Résurrection du Christ — et non pas au Jour du Jugement comme le voudraient les Juifs.[113] Il faut donc rapporter ces faits à la prise de Jérusalem par Titus, et non pas à celle de 587.

En réalité, cet appel à l'autorité des Apôtres ne peut étonner le lecteur des pages précédentes du Commentaire, auxquelles il convient beaucoup

---

[105] *In Ioelem*, i 4 (p. 163, l. 96-124). Cf. *In Zachariam* I, vi 1-8 (p. 792, l. 38-p. 793, l. 77).

[106] *Ibid.*, i 6-7 (p. 167, l. 236-44).

[107] *Ibid.*, ii 1-11 (p. 177, l. 54 sq.), 12-14 (p. 182, l. 235-41), 18-20 (p. 186, l. 393 sq.; p. 187, l. 401-4).

[108] *Ibid.*, ii 15-17 (p. 185, l. 358-61).

[109] *Ibid.*, iii 12-13 (p. 204, l. 251-7). Voir encore ii 14-15 (p. 205, l. 271-4); ii 16-17 (p. 206, l. 313-18) pour la suite de cette interprétation juive.

[110] *Ibid.*, iii 19 (p. 208, l. 381-9).

[111] Voir *supra*, pp. 122-3 — n. 86-7.

[112] *In Ioelem*, iii 19 (p. 208, l. 389-95). Cf. *In Sophoniam*, ii 8-11 (p. 685, l. 336-46).

[113] *In Ioelem*, iii 4-6 (pp. 200, l. 92-p.201, l. 113).

mieux. En effet, lorsqu'il en est arrivé à l'annonce de l'effusion de l'Esprit annoncée par le prophète, Jérôme non seulement a déclaré que cette promesse s'était réalisée lors de la Pentecôte, comme Pierre le proclame dans les Actes, mais il se demande aussi, puisque ce point a trouvé alors sa réalisation, comment tout le reste du livre — ce qui précède et ce qui suit — s'applique également au temps qui a suivi la résurrection du Christ.[114] Et de formuler ce principe de cohérence qui est à la base de ses Commentaires: "il ne faut pas que, sous un seul et même texte continu, on voie poindre une explication incohérente et divergente par rapport à elle-même".[115] Il essaie, de fait, de reprendre l'ensemble de ce qu'il a déjà expliqué en un discours unifié, qui va des menaces à un peuple pécheur jusqu'à une promesse de grandeur, pénitence faite.[116] L'application de ce principe ne va toutefois pas sans difficulté, comme Jérôme le reconnaît aussitôt.[117] Il avance alors deux opinions de tiers, qu'il ne nomme pas, concernant la méthode des Apôtres.[118] Selon la première, par exemple, les Apôtres ont voulu montrer que les promesses finales commençaient dès maintenant à s'accomplir. Ces opinions diverses témoignent, en tout cas, des discussions toujours en cours sur l'interprétation des prophètes. Elles rappellent celles que l'on trouve dans l'*In Ionam* sur l'extension du type: dans l'histoire de Jonas, qu'est-ce qui doit ou peut être appliqué au Christ?[119] L'ensemble de son histoire ou son simple engloutissement par le monstre durant trois jours? Dans le cas présent, au nom de la *consequentia*, Jérôme affirme que tout le livre de Joël est à référer à la réalisation de la Pentecôte,[120] celle-ci ne marquât-elle qu'un début.

Réalisation au temps du Christ ou à la fin du monde? Comme il arrive plus d'une fois, Jérôme est tout d'abord scrupuleusement fidèle au principe qu'il a posé, fût-il d'application difficile. C'est ainsi qu'il entend Joël ii 32b, de l'époque qui a suivi la Résurrection du Christ; car, dit-il, il est impossible que le début concerne la Passion et la suite le Jugement dernier.[121] Il est déjà moins ferme pour les versets suivants qu'il envisage,

---

[114] *Ibid.*, ii 28-32 (p. 192, l. 615-35).
[115] *Ibid.* (p. 193, l. 634-5).
[116] *Ibid.* (p. 193, l. 635-54).
[117] *Ibid.* (p. 193, l. 654-6).
[118] *Ibid.* (p. 193, l. 656-p. 194, l. 674). L'allusion à Porphyre ne situe pas forcément ces discussions après le *Contre les Chrétiens*.
[119] *In Ionam*, *Praefatio* et i 3 (p. 379, l. 63-71; p. 383, l. 124-60). Voir mon Introduction des *Sources Chrétiennes*.
[120] Ce texte de Joël avait, bien entendu, tout un passé dans les dossiers de *testimonia*. Mais il était également le texte par excellence des Montanistes, ce qui en rendait l'utilisation délicate. Voir, chez Jérôme lui-même, l'*Ep.* 41 de 384.
[121] *In Ioelem*, ii 32b (p. 197, l. 797-p. 198, l. 807).

s'il le peut, d'appliquer également au Jour du jugement;[122] ce qu'il fait un peu plus loin.[123] Nous sommes partis naguère de Joël iii 4-6, où nous avions relevé l'appel conjoint aux *Hebraei*, qui situaient l'accomplissement de la prophétie à la fin du monde, et aux Apôtres, qui la voyaient réalisée après le Jour du Seigneur qu'est la Résurrection du Christ, avec une préférence pour cette époque.[124] La dichotomie s'estompe un peu par la suite, dans la mesure où les oracles concernent, pour Jérôme, non la Jérusalem restaurée à la fin des temps dont rêvent les Juifs, mais l'Église, qui peut être aussi bien celle de tous les jours que celle qui aura à lutter à la fin des temps contre l'Antichrist.[125] Mais en iii 19, à propos de l'Égypte et de l'Idumée, où nous avons vu les Juifs reconnaître leurs oppresseurs d'antan et d'aujourd'hui, Jérôme déclare: "Disons pour notre part qu'au temps de la résurrection du Christ ou au jour du Jugement — car nous acceptons l'un et l'autre —, l'Égypte et l'Idumée, en tant qu'Égypte — c'est-à-dire la persécution — et qu'Idumée — c'est-à-dire le monde cruel et terrestre —, seront détruites..."[126] Quant à la dernière péricope qui dit que "la Judée sera habitée pour toujours et Jérusalem de génération en génération", s'il refuse de l'entendre, comme les Juifs, au sens matériel, Jérôme reste dans une certaine imprécision concernant l'identité de la Jérusalem. Il s'agit assurément de l'Église, qui rassemble en son sein les deux générations des Juifs et des Païens, désormais purifiées de tout péché, mais son modèle faisait sans doute allusion à la restauration — plus qu'à l'instauration — de la Jérusalem céleste, désormais habitée par Dieu à tout jamais.[127]

On notera, en effet, qu'à côté de cette "indécision" entre les deux époques de la réalisation de la prophétie en existe une seconde, qui donne à la deuxième partie du Commentaire une apparence différente de la première. En celle-ci, en effet, de i 4 à ii 21-27, Jérôme ne manquait guère d'appliquer à l'âme tout ce qui concerne Juda. On pourrait s'attendre à ce que cette application continue avec la promesse de l'effusion de l'Esprit (ii 28-32). En réalité, il ne sera plus question de l'âme à proprement parler dans la seconde partie. Peut-être par crainte du montanisme? Peut-être parce qu'il s'agit d'une prophétie et que, dit ailleurs Jérôme, il ne faut pas énerver par l'allégorie ce qui est une prophétie manifeste.[128] Certains versets se prêtaient pourtant à des développe-

---

[122] *Ibid.*, iii 1-3 (p. 198, l. 15-18): "...si poterimus...".
[123] *Ibid.* (p. 199, l. 57-75).
[124] V. *supra*, n. 113.
[125] *In Ioelem*, iii 7-8 (p. 202, l. 171 sq.), 9-11 (p. 204, l. 219-23).
[126] *Ibid.*, iii 19 (p. 208, l. 395-400).
[127] *Ibid.*, iii 20-21 (p. 209).
[128] Cf. *In Abdiam*, 1b (p. 353, l. 57-8).

ments.[129] Or, on constate que Jérôme en limite l'application à l'Église, soit d'aujourd'hui, soit de la fin du monde. Le Jugement personnel disparaît d'ailleurs de toutes ces pages, sans que la raison en soit donnée. De même, si la lutte contre les démons est rappelée de ci de là, sous-jacente sans doute partout, Jérôme ne s'intéresse guère à ces puissances adverses pour elles-mêmes. On aimerait connaître la mesure de son "filtrage".

Le Commentaire tel qu'il se présente, la documentation parallèle dont nous disposons, tout permet en effet d'assurer, une fois encore, que l'essentiel de l'interprétation spirituelle vient d'Origène. Une lettre d'Ambroise développe sur le début de Joël un enseignement analogue à celui de Jérôme.[130] Or, quelques fragments d'un Papyrus d'Oxyrhynchos viennent montrer qu'Ambroise comme Jérôme exploitent très directement le Commentaire de l'Alexandrin.[131] Une vérification analogue est possible pour de nombreux autres développements de notre *In Ioelem.*[132]

On ne s'en étonnera pas trop et on ne criera pas non plus au scandale: Jérôme n'a jamais renoncé à utiliser Origène. Lorsque celui-ci ne lui fournissait pas d'esquisse ou de canevas, il était heureux de trouver l'oeuvre de Didyme, comme il le fait en 406 pour Osée et Zacharie. La découverte de l'*In Zachariam* de Didyme a un peu vite fait parler de "copie conforme" pour l'*In Zachariam* de Jérôme.[133] L'indépendance du Latin ne se manifeste pas seulement dans l'*hebraica ueritas* qui trouve peu d'attention chez ses prédécesseurs;[134] elle est dans la manière dont il trie leur doctrine spirituelle. Cette opération a dû commencer avec les premiers Commentaires de 393, qui ne sont jamais une simple traduction continue. Mais on aura vu qu'il faut tenir compte de la date des différents Commentaires et du tournant que constitue l'éclatement de la querelle origénienne durant l'année 393.

Cette opération de "filtrage", et l'abandon pur et simple d'un certain nombre d'éléments des prédécesseurs, rend difficile parfois la reconstitu-

---

[129] *In Ioelem*, iii 9-11, 12-13. Jérôme s'y sépare de ceux qui interprètent ces versets "en bien", des saints et des parfaits, pour appliquer ces textes aux démons ou aux ennemis de l'Église.

[130] Ambroise, *Ep.* 31 (*PL* 16, c. 1065-8 = *CSEL* 82, 1, pp. 100-7: *Ep.* 13).

[131] R. Reitzenstein, "Origenes und Hieronymus", *ZNTW* 20 (1921), pp. 90-3.

[132] Par exemple, pour ii 21-27 (p. 190, l. 538 sq.), sur les puissances de droite et les puissances de gauche, voir Origène, *In Epist. ad Romanos*, i 14 (*PG* 14, c. 860 C-D) qui cite ce passage de Joël; pour ii 28-32 (p. 196, l. 736 sq.), voir *Ibid.* viii 3 (c. 1164-5): même façon de rapprocher Joël ii 30 de Rom. x, 12-15, etc.

[133] Didyme l'Aveugle, *Sur Zacharie*, I, Éd. L. Doutreleau, coll. *Sources Chrétiennes* 83, pp. 129 sq.

[134] *Ibid.*, p. 135 *in fine.*

tion des différentes interprétations qui se trouvent ainsi brisées et démembrées. On ajoutera à l'existence de ces ruptures, de ces "blancs", ou des "silences" subits de telle ou telle "voix" de notre "polyphonie", l'utilisation, parfois, de plusieurs modèles, dont les opinions peuvent être confrontées de façon plus ou moins continue,[135] selon les règles du Commentaire antique ou judaïque, qui compile les opinions des érudits ou des rabbins sur les différents textes. L'unité de chaque livre prophétique n'est cependant pas un simple postulat. Dans une page trop peu connue, Jérôme parle de l'activité des différents prophètes. Il compare les douze (petits) prophètes, qui ne tiennent qu'en un livre, et les grands qui, chacun pour leur part, accomplissent, dit-il, le même travail que les douze. Tous, ajoute-t-il, sont des médecins des âmes. Or, voici comment est décrite leur tâche: "Dans les douze prophètes, est décrite l'âme, malade en quelque sorte, qui, par sa faute, n'a pas voulu être soignée et qui en vient jusqu'à la mort (spirituelle). On raconte ensuite comment, après sa mort, elle est soignée par le Christ, le vrai médecin. Ce que les douze prophètes accomplissent donc par partie et ne font eux-mêmes qu'indiquer brièvement, les grand prophètes l'on fait d'ordinaire en très grand."[136] L'assimilation des prophètes à des médecins des âmes se trouve dans l'Homélie 14, 1, d'Origène sur Jérémie. Il est bien probable que l'idée tout entière exprimée ici par Jérôme vienne de l'Alexandrin, à en juger par ce que nous dit de son côté Ambroise[137] et ce que nous avons entendu de Jérôme, soit de l'ordre des prophètes,[138] soit de l'attitude du pénitent,[139] ou de l'homme devant le "monde" qu'est Ninive.[140] Il est donc possible que le Commentaire d'Origène ait, quant à lui, en suivant l'ordre des Septante, présenté d'un bout à l'autre cette "cure" de l'âme. En modifiant l'ordre dans lequel il a expliqué les prophètes, en tenant compte de l'ordre du canon hébreu, en recourant beaucoup plus qu'Origène à l'histoire, fondée sur le texte hébreu, Jérôme a sans doute profondément désorganisé l'oeuvre de son prédécesseur.

Mais, en s'appliquant à mieux cerner les circonstances historiques, Jérôme ne cherche pas moins à mettre en lumière l'unité de chaque livre. Qui plus est, il met cette unité mieux établie au service de la prophétie.

---

[135] Voir, par ex., l'*In Ioelem* iii 9-11 ou iii 12-13, où plusieurs opinions sont confrontées. Le travail est relativement facile à faire pour l'*In Zachariam*, dont nous possédons maintenant l'une des sources.

[136] Jérôme, *In Isaïam adbreviatio* (*CC* 73 A, p. 803, l. 1-3).

[137] Ambroise, *Ep.* 70, 1.

[138] Michée, troisième selon le canon grec, sixième selon le canon hébreu, "placé au coeur du volume, doit contenir des mystères profonds" (p. 421, l. 1-7).

[139] Voir *supra*, p. 120.

[140] Voir ce qui a été dit de l'*In Nahum, supra*, pp. 112-13. Il est possible que l'histoire de l'âme à laquelle fait allusion l'*In Ionam* recevait chez Origène un développement plus important que celui que lui a laissé Jérôme. Voir le *Livre de Jonas*, pp. 609-13.

Nous l'avons vu plusieurs fois, Jérôme ne se contente pas de la méthode des *testimonia.* La cohérence de chaque livre, la *consequentia* du récit impose ses règles. Elle permet — tant bien que mal — d'interpréter l'ensemble d'un livre à partir d'*une* "prophétie messianique" ou d'*un* texte invoqué par le Nouveau Testament.

Les Commentaires de Jérôme sont donc une oeuvre complexe et, par bien des côtés, imparfaite ou insuffisamment unifiée. Ces disparates tiennent à l'étalement dans le temps, avec tous ses aléas, au "filtrage" dont j'ai parlé, à la juxtaposition et compénétration d'entreprises qui reposent sur deux textes différents au moins.

Je voudrais suggérer pour finir que l'exégèse juive ne constitue pourtant pas un "hors d'oeuvre" dans l'exégèse de Jérôme, ni dans l'exégèse chrétienne où elle a subi, en réalité, une métamorphose. Celle-ci n'a pu se développer qu'en dialoguant avec l'exégèse rabbinique. La remarque vaut non seulement pour l'attente messianique au sens étroit du terme, mais pour tout ce qui concerne l'actualisation de l'Écriture. La prise de Jérusalem par Pompée, la ruine du Temple en 70, la seconde guerre juive sous Hadrien, ont amené les Juifs à relire la Bible avec de nouveaux yeux, comme ils l'avaient fait après la captivité de Babylone ou à l'époque des Machabées. L'exégèse juive que charrient de manière diverse les Commentaires de Jérôme est née au second et au troisième siècle, plus qu'au quatrième — ce qui ne veut pas dire qu'elle n'ait plus cours au moment où Jérôme écrit. Mais, inversement, elle prolonge une exégèse antérieure, aux courants multiples, aux relations complexes avec l'exégèse philosophique ou littéraire profane. Vouloir isoler ces courants au IVe et même au IIIe siècle, vouloir en privilégier tel ou tel, est, me semble-t-il, illusoire; la symbiose est trop profonde. Dans la mesure où l'exégèse chrétienne appliquait à la Communauté ce qui avait été dit au Peuple de Dieu, aux évêques et aux prêtres, ce qui avait été dit des chefs ou des prêtres d'Israël, elle ne faisait que prolonger l'exégèse juive, mais aussi celle du Nouveau Testament. On peut en dire autant de l'application à l'âme elle-même qui, chez Origène, doit plus à saint Paul qu'à Platon. Le point le plus contestable, et sur lequel, en tout cas, nous voyons Jérôme se séparer le plus nettement d'Origène, concerne le domaine angélique, eût-il ici encore la garantie paulinienne et son arrière-plan juif. En tout cas, vouloir réduire à l'histoire du peuple juif, avant ou après la captivité de Babylone, le rôle des prophètes-écrivains était alors une aberration, que même un Théodore de Mopsueste n'ose pas soutenir intégralement. La tendance sera longtemps inverse et assurément exagérée; mais le problème de cette "actualisation" reste toujours posé: c'est celui de la valeur, pour les chrétiens, de l'Ancien Testament tout entier, et pas seulement des prophètes ou des seules "prophéties messianiques".

DER REALITÄTSBEZUG ALTTESTAMENTLICHER EXEGESE

VON

ERHARD S. GERSTENBERGER

Giessen

Wem ist der Exeget zu vergleichen? Er ist weder Holzfäller, noch Schulmeister, noch Ingenieur, wenn er auch gelegentlich gewisse Affinitäten zu diesen Berufen verspüren mag. Eher schon sollten wir ihn beim Gärtner, Komponisten oder Raumfahrer ansiedeln. Oder gehört er gar in die Nähe des Kleinen Prinzen, der ja ein ganz besonderes Verhältnis zur Wirklichkeit hat?[1] Der Ausleger der Schrift liest und liest und liest,[2] teilt das, was er verstanden zu haben meint, anderen Menschen mit und begibt sich so mitten hinein in die fortgehende Wirklichkeitsgestaltung. Andererseits wird er von seiner Umgebung geprägt. Seine Exegese verrät ihn ohne Fehl als Kind seiner Zeit und seines gesellschaftlichen Ortes. Daß also Exeget und Exegese einerseits und geschichtlich gewordene wie aktuelle Wirklichkeit andererseits in einer Wechselbeziehung stehen, ist kein Geheimnis und bedarf keines besonderen Nachweises.[3] Jeder Exeget hat seinen "Sitz im Leben" die brennende Frage ist nur, wie die Lebenswirklichkeit, die ihn hervorgebracht hat und von der er selbst ein lebendes Stück ist, seine Sicht- und Denkweise bestimmt, in welchem Maße die exegetischen Aussagen vom zeitbedingten Umfeld des Auslegers eingeengt werden und in welcher Richtung wir sie in der gemeinsamen Auslegungsarbeit zu korrigieren, extrapolieren oder weiterzuentwickeln haben. Als Herr Professor Alonso Schökel mich im Jahre 1981 fragte, ob ich einen Vortrag auf dem Weltkongreß übernehmen könne, da lebte und arbeitete ich noch in Südbrasilien. Er wollte mit dieser Einladung die für den Alttestamentler vielleicht relevante Wirklichkeitserfahrung

---

[1] A. de Saint-Exupéry, *Le petit prince* (Paris, 1946).

[2] G. von Rad stellt in meisterhafter Konzentration seine Lebensaufgabe dar als "lesen zu lernen und lesen zu lehren" (H. W. Wolff [Hg.], *Probleme biblischer Theologie* [München, 1971], S. 659).

[3] Alle forschungsgeschichtlichen Studien lassen das ahnen, selbst wenn ihre Verfasser diesen Zusammenhang nicht offen aussprechen, vgl. z.B. H. J. Kraus, *Geschichte der historisch-kritischen Erforschung des Alten Testaments* (Neukirchen, 1956); H. F. Hahn, *The Old Testament in Modern Research* (Philadelphia/London, 1954); G. F. Hasel, *Old Testament Theology: Basic Issues in the Current Debate* (Grand Rapids, 1972, ²1975); J. H. Hayes [Hg.], *Old Testament Form Criticism* (San Antonio, 1974).

des lateinamerikanischen Kontinents in Salamanca stärker ins Spiel bringen. Denn tragischerweise sind die Exegeten der "Dritten" und "Vierten" Welt in der Regel nicht in der Lage, an internationalen Konferenzen teilzunehmen. Und auf Seiten der Fachkollegen aus der "1. und 2. Welt" besteht kein übergroßes Bedürfnis, mit ihnen ins Gespräch zu kommen. So gut ich es nach einer sechsjährigen Lehrtätigkeit in Brasilien vermag, will ich darum die verschiedenen Wirklichkeitsbezüge, wie sie für die alttestamentliche Wissenschaft in den Industrienationen und in ihren ehemaligen Kolonien charakteristisch sind, untersuchen. Vielleicht kann ich so ein klein wenig dazu beitragen, die Fronten zwischen den Welthälften durchlässiger zu machen. Ein internationaler Alttestamentlerkongreß darf ja um seines Gegenstandes willen (vgl. Dtn. xv 4 und viele andere Stellen) nicht das Treffen der Selbsterwählten sein, die unbekümmert an reich gedeckten Tischen gastronomisch und geistig schwelgen, und gelegentlich dem armen Lazarus einen Bissen Brot zuwerfen.

1. *Was ist Wirklichkeit?*

Das Bemühen, ausgerechnet die Realität in die exegetische Diskussion einzubeziehen, droht allerdings schon im Ansatz zu scheitern. Was ist denn das überhaupt: Wirklichkeit? Welches der tausend Modelle von Wirklichkeitsbetrachtung soll für uns verbindlich sein? Vor uns tut sich die mehr als zweitausendjährige, verworrene Geschichte eines philosophischen und theologischen Grundproblems auf. Das abendländische Erkenntnisstreben läßt sich in der Frage nach dem wahren Sein, dem tiefsten Wesen der Dinge und ihrem letzten Sinn zusammenfassen. Bis ins hohe Mittelalter hinein lebten und webten die Denker innerhalb einer übermächtigen, aber doch zuhandenen, integralen Wirklichkeit. Mit den naturwissenschaftlichen und geographischen Entdeckungen machten sie sich in halsbrecherischen Kraftakten von den alten Bindungen los. Die geistige Klarheit der Rennaissance, die Überschwenglichkeit des Barock, der Fortschrittsglaube des technischen Zeitalters sind Beispiele für die veränderte Weltbeziehung des Menschen.[4] *Des* Menschen? Sagen wir genauer: Eine schmale, gebildete und begüterte Schicht erlebte Wirklichkeit nun als manipulierbares Gegenüber und schuf so die Voraussetzungen für eine planmäßige Umgestaltung der Welt, wie wir sie heute erleben. Literarische Gestalten wie Peter Schlemihl, Doktor Faustus, Homo

[4] Auch in den Humanwissenschaften muß heute die Frage diskutiert werden, ob der Mensch die von ihm eroberte Position überhaupt aushalten und ausfüllen kann, vgl. A. Plack, *Die Gesellschaft und das Böse* (München, 1967); H. E. Richter, *Der Gotteskomplex* (Hamburg, 1979).

Faber thematisieren das moderne, titanenhafte Selbstbewußtsein; Don Quixote ist bereits ein wirksamer Anti-Held, wie auf einer anderen Ebene der spätere Asterix unter den Supermännern. Aber: So faszinierend die große Kulturgeschichte des Abendlandes mit ihren vielfachen Antworten auf die Frage nach der Realität auch ist, kann sie überhaupt dem Exegeten des Alten Testaments eine brauchbare Definition dessen liefern, was er als Wirklichkeit anzuerkennen hat? Sicher, der in einer Industrienation lebende Bibelwissenschaftler wird sich auch als Glied einer titanenhaften und selbstzerstörerischen Gesellschaft erkennen müssen. Verbindliche Wirklichkeit jedoch kann sie für ihn nicht sein, davor warnen schon Gen. iii und xi. Der Grund, warum das Alte Testament nicht auf den selbstmächtigen, individualistisch isolierten, herrschsüchtigen Menschen abendländischer Träume bezogen werden darf, ist weniger die vielumstrittene Verschiedenartigkeit der geistigen Strukturen Israels und des Griechentums,[5] als vielmehr ganz einfach folgende Tatsache: Das moderne Wirklichkeitsverständnis, welches die Herrschaft über andere notwendig mit einschließt, ist das Privileg jeweils einer dünnen Oberschicht. Der "normale" Mensch lebt bis heute überwiegend in seiner privaten Sphäre.[6] Wenn es sich so verhält, dann ist uns die vorrangige Projektion des Alten Testaments auf die höhere Ebene staatlicher, gesamtgesellschaftlicher Wirklichkeit in doppelter Hinsicht untersagt. Einmal befindet sich die Mehrheit der Menschen, denen wir letztendlich die Botschaft der Schrift auslegen, überhaupt nicht in jenen abstrakten Hallen begrifflicher Allgemeinwahrheiten, sondern in den Häusern und Hütten der angeblich "niederen", alltäglichen Existenz. Zum anderen war das Alte Testament nie in erster Linie für die Denker und Herrscher bestimmt, sondern für das gemeine Volk bei seinen Festen und Gottesdiensten, in Familien- und Dorfgemeinschaft. Erst wenn diese sozialen Bezugspunkte der alttestamentlichen Texte genügend geklärt sind, können wir — vielleicht wird dem auch James Barr zustimmen — über unterschiedliche Denkweisen reden.

Das Alte Testament handelt also in seinem vielschichtigen und weitgespannten Glaubenszeugnis zuerst und vor allem vom menschlichen *Le-*

[5] Vgl. T. Boman, *Das hebräische Denken im Vergleich mit dem Griechischen* (Göttingen, ^{2}1954); J. Barr, *The Semantics of Biblical Language* (Oxford, 1961).

[6] Das zeigen deutlich alle möglichen Umfrageergebnisse, Meinungsforschungen und sozialwissenschaftlichen Spezialuntersuchungen. Die Kleingruppenforschung ist in den letzten Jahren aufgeblüht, vgl. z.B. R. Battegay, *Der Mensch in der Gruppe* (Bern/Stuttgart/Wien, 1974). Auffällig ist auch die Betonung von Praxisnähe und Alltagsbezug in der soziologischen Forschung, vgl. K. Hammerich und M. Klein (Hg.), *Materialen zur Soziologie des Alltags* (Opladen, 1978). Auch die über die Elementargruppe hinausgehenden Organisationsformen kommen in den Blick, vgl. R. König, *Grundformen der Gesellschaft: Die Gemeinde* (Hamburg, 1958).

ben, wie es sich in elementarer Form auf den primären Organisationsstufen gesellschaftlicher Entwicklung, d.h. in Familie, Sippe, Nachbarschaft, Gemeinde, abspielt.[7] Nationale Geschichtsschreibung, priesterliche, zentrale Gesetzgebung, weisheitlich-kosmologische Spekulation, Hypostasierungen des erwählten Volkes — für uns Fixpunkte alttestamentlicher Exegese und Theologie — sind sekundäre Erscheinungen. Sie haben z.T. erst in der Retrospektive originäre Glaubensaussagen der Kleingruppe überdeckt.[8] Im Mittelpunkt des Alten Testaments steht das ständig bedrohte und zu gewinnende, immer wieder verliehene und gerettete *Leben*, das natürlich auch zu seiner Zeit übergreifende Institutionen hervorbringt und von ihnen umfaßt ist. Aber diese Institutionen, und seien es Israel, das Königtum, der Tempel, sind nicht die fundamentale Wirklichkeit. Sie bleiben Hilfskonstruktionen, Sammelbecken für das Leid und die Freude, für Kult und Recht des Einzelmenschen in seiner Gruppe. Nicht die übergeordnete Organisation ist das Primäre, sondern das echte, alltägliche *Leben*. Der Blick der alttestamentlichen Theologen geht in der Regel von unten nach oben. Im Kern hat also Gerhard Ebeling Recht, wenn er Henri Perrin zitiert: Die Theologie steht heute vor der "Notwendigkeit, immer tiefer in das Leben einzudringen, wo es am ärmsten und gewöhnlichsten ist."[9] Ebeling will die Wirklichkeit ernstnehmen, weil er sehr wohl weiß, wie wenig sie in der deutschen Theologie gilt. Hier sind uns die lateinamerikanischen Theologen eindeutig voraus. Sie fangen bei der Realität, im Leben, an zu reflektieren. Nicht bei einer beliebigen Wirklichkeit! Sie gehen von dem neuen Leben aus, das sich in der nachkonziliaren Kirche und darüberhinaus gerade in der ärmsten Basisgemeinden entfaltet hat. Sie gehen von "Gottes Wirken in der Geschichte" aus, würden wir in unserer Sprache sagen, wenn wir den Mut und die Phantasie hätten, das Tun Gottes in unserer Zeit anzuerkennen. Carlos Mesters leitet z.B. seine Auslegung der Gottesknechtslieder mit der Geschichte der Teresinha ein. Die junge Frau, arbeits- und mittellos, will in Rio de Janeiro ihren todkranken Säugling

[7] Die Primärgruppen sind nicht von ungefähr auch in der alttestamentlichen Wissenschaft erst in jüngster Zeit wiederentdeckt worden, vgl. R. Albertz, *Persönliche Frömmigkeit und offizielle Religion* (Stuttgart, 1978); M. Rose, *Der Ausschließlichkeitsanspruch Jahwes* (Stuttgart, 1975); E. S. Gerstenberger, *Der bittende Mensch* (Neukirchen-Vluyn, 1980); J. W. Rogerson, *Anthropology and the Old Testament* (Oxford, 1978).

[8] Die großen sammelnden und bearbeitenden Werke des Alten Testaments wie der Jahwist, das deuteronomistische Geschichtswerk, die Priesterschrift, das chronistische Werk verarbeiten sämtlich älteres Material, das z.T. aus ganz anderen Schichten stammt als die Verfasser, vgl. etwa W. H. Schmidt, *Einführung in das Alte Testament* (Berlin, [2]1982); R. Rendtorff, *Das Alte Testament* (Neukirchen-Vluyn, 1983). In den Psalmen ist ebenfalls die Assimilation früher, z.T. kanaanäischer Texte zu beobachten.

[9] E. Ebeling, "Hauptprobleme der protestantischen Theologie in der Gegenwart", *ZTK* 58 (1961), S. 136.

behandeln lassen. Kein Arzt, kein Krankenhaus nimmt sie auf, weil sie weder zahlen kann noch einen Versicherungsschein hat. Am Abend fährt sie mit dem Bus in ihre favela zurück. Da stirbt ihr Kind auf ihrem Schoß. Eine Momentaufnahme aus der Leidensgeschichte der Kontinents, die durch die Deutung gültige Wirklichkeit wird. Viel später sagt nämlich Teresinha zu einer Gemeindeschwester: "Wir sind arm, wir wissen nichts. Das einzige, was für uns übrigbleibt in dieser Welt, ist leiden... Eines Tages wird sich das ändern! Gott hilft Leuten wie uns!"[10] Das unbeschreibliche Leiden und die unerklärliche Hoffnung der ärmsten Bevölkerung sind für die lateinamerikanischen Befreiungstheologen der Ausgangspunkt für jede theologische Arbeit.[11] Hier ist für sie die Wirklichkeit, die auch der Exeget alttestamentlicher Schriften kennen muß, auf die er sich zu beziehen hat, wenn er dem biblischen Zeugnis gerecht werden will. Wir vermuten und wollen vorläufig festhalten: Jeder Exeget geht bei seiner Auslegungsarbeit von einer textfremden Wirklichkeit aus. Auf der Nordhalbkugel ist es bevorzugt ein übergreifendes System, auf der Südhalbkugel das geschundene und doch hoffnungsvolle Leben.

2. *Das theologische Süd- Nordgefälle*

Verallgemeinerungen sind gefährlich, denn zu jeder Aussage lassen sich Gegenbehauptungen aufstellen. Ereignisse und Gedanken sind ambivalent. Dennoch möchte ich ruhigen Gewissens behaupten, daß auf der nördlichen Hemissphäre überwiegend vom Allgemeinen zum Besonderen, vom eigenen System nach außen, von oben nach untern argumentiert und geurteilt wird. Die alttestamentliche Exegese hat trotz vielfacher Bekenntnisse zur historisch-kritischen Methode Anteil an dieser deduktiven Verfahrensweise. Ob der Denkhorizont eines beliebigen Exegeten als platonisch, aristotelisch, existentialistisch, linguistisch, strukturalistisch, soziologisch oder sonstwie zu klassifizieren sein mag, macht keinen großen Unterschied. Die Ausleger des Nordens gehen bewußt oder unbewußt von vorgegebenen, machmal verabsolutierten, tabuisierten

---

[10] C. Mesters, *Die Botschaft des leidenden Volkes* (Neukirchen-Vluyn, 1982), S. 20 (orig. portugiesisch: *Missão do povo que sofre* [Petrópolis, 1981]). Eine einzige Leidensgeschichte dieser Art ist genug, um die ganze menschliche Gesellschaft in Frage zu stellen. Ähnliches geschieht aber ständig millionenfach.

[11] Befreiungstheologen wie G. Guttierrez, M. Bonino, L. Boff, H. Assmann, J. de Santa Ana betonen mit großem Nachdruck und praktizieren selbst das Zusammenleben mit der armen Bevölkerung. Vgl. exemplarisch C. Mesters, *Sechs Tage in den Kellern der Menschheit* (Neukirchen-Vluyn, 1982), orig. portugiesisch: *Seis dias nos porões da humanidade* (Petrópolis, 1977); B. Mondin, *Os teólogos da libertação* (São Paulo, 1980), orig. italienisch: *I teologi della liberazione* (Roma, 1977).

Wirklichkeitsvorstellungen aus. Sie suchen und finden in den alttestamentlichen Texten das, was ihrer Sichtweise entspricht, und haben wenig Freiraum zur Entdeckung der eigentlichen Realität.

Für mein Empfinden sind, wie gesagt, die lateinamerikanischen Exegeten sehr viel näher bei der wahren Wirklichkeit. Aber auch sie arbeiten selbstverständlich mit Gedankenrastern, Zielvorstellungen, systematischen Entwürfen. Wie könnte es anders sein, wenn der Erkenntnisprozeß in sich die Begutachtung und Aufnahme von Neuartigem in schon bestehende Erfahrung bedeutet?[12] So finden sich bei den lateinamerikanischen Kollegen auch die bekannten Modelle der biblischen Heilsgeschichte, Bundestheologie und Christologie.[13] Zwei Unterschiede aber sind wesentlich: In der lateinamerikanischen Exegese sind die Allgemeinbegriffe und Gedankenraster ganz anders gefüllt. Das liegt offenbar an der größeren Lebensnähe und der tieferen Verankerung der gesamten biblischen Bewegung in den Gemeinden. Zweitens: Unsere Kollegen in Lateinamerika sind in einem erstaunlichen Maße bereit, ihre exegetischen Erkenntnisse mit der gelebten Wirklichkeit zu konfrontieren und von den Laien zu lernen.

Lassen Sie uns diese Unterschiede an einigen wichtigen Punkten skizzieren. Wir wollen allerdings auf Einzelnachweise verzichten.

a. Wer mit Texten umgeht, muß sich wohl oder übel damit befassen, woher diese Texte kommen, welche menschliche Wirklichkeit dahintersteht. Zwar gibt es außer in evangelikalen Gruppen auch sonst genügend Tendenzen, den biblischen Text theologisch zu verselbständigen oder traditions- und redaktionsgeschichtlich zu verflüchtigen. Doch auch der abstrakteste Theologe stößt bei der Auslegungsarbeit unweigerlich einmal auf wirkliche Personen, die maßgeblich an der Entstehung des Textes beteiligt gewesen sind. In solchen Fällen tritt die prägende Kraft gewohnter Wirklichkeit mächtig in Erscheinung. Da müßte Micha eigentlich den Jesaja, Hosea den Amos gekannt haben, so wie Kollege X den Kollegen Y zur Kenntnis nimmt. Da sollen biblische Redaktoren am Werk sein nach Art eines Theologieprofessors, der seine Fahnenkorrek-

---

[12] Daß ein großenteils gesellschaftlich vorgegebenes und von jedem Menschen in seiner Gruppe zu erlernendes (Sozialisation!) Koordinaten- und Wertsystem die Voraussetzung für jeden Erkenntnisvorgang ist, gehört zu den Grundeinsichten der Psychologie und Anthropologie; vgl. auch P. Berger, *The Social Construction of Reality* (Garden City, New York, 1966; London, 1967).

[13] Erstaunlich, mit welcher Unbefangenheit z.T. Denkmodelle aus der sogenannten 1. und 2. Welt übernommen werden. Vgl. J. S. Croatto, *História de la Salvación* (Buenos Aires, ³1968); C. Mesters, *Deus, onde estás?* (Belo Horizonte, ⁵1976); G. Gutierrez, *La fuerza histórica de los pobres* (Lima, 1979), Kapitel I. Ein zaghafter Versuch einer eigenen, sozialwissenschaftlich begründeten Systematik; J. V. Pixley, *Pluralismo de tradiciones en la religion biblica* (Buenos Aires, 1971).

turen liest. Da arbeiten Psalmisten und levitische Prediger, Weisheitslehrer und Gesetzgeber voll ausgestattet mit dem Handwerkszeug einer mittleren theologischen Seminarbibliothek oder zumindest mit den Begriffsanalysen eines guten theologischen Wörterbuches. Kurz, die Erfahrungen des heutigen Exegeten, die er selbst bei der Komposition von Texten macht, die individualistische, zweckrationale, kompetitive Produktion von Literatur für Gebildete, trägt er in seine Beurteilung der antiken Autoren und Tradentengruppen mit ein. Selten und mühsam nur werden Versuche unternommen, die eigenartigen und vielschichtigen Entstehungsbedingungen alttestamentlicher Texte zu begreifen.

Auch die lateinamerikanischen Exegeten stehen unter dem Einfluß ihrer eigenen Erfahrungen, und es kommt darum auch bei ihnen zu manchen Verzeichnungen der antiken Wirklichkeit. Aber sie sind nicht in akademisch-wissenschaftlichen Ritualen befangen. Sie erleben auf der Straße möglicherweise den Balladendichter, der seine Zuhörer spontan mit Versen zu Tagesereignissen erfreut. Sie kennen indianische Mythensammlungen und Rituale. Sie arbeiten zumeist teilzeitlich in der praktischen Gemeindearbeit. Und sie erleben vor allem den lebendigen Umgang mit biblischen Traditionen in den Basisgemeinden. Für sie löst sich die Autoren- und Tradentenfrage darum ganz anders. Wesentlicher Agent des gesamten Entstehungs-, Überlieferungs- und Interpretationsprozesses biblischer Texte ist das Volk. Einzelverfasser sind ebenfalls nur im Gegenüber zu und im Zusammenleben mit der israelitischen Gemeindegruppe denkbar. Armut und Leiden sind damals wie heute Grunderfahrungen der Gemeinde.[14]

b. Von lateinamerikanischen Theologen hört man immer wieder den Vorwurf, die Exegeten der Nordhalbkugel benutzten bei der Auswahl behandlungswürdiger alttestamentlicher Themen eine elitäre Brille. In der Tat werden die für Lateinamerika brennenden Probleme wie "Unterdrückung", "Armut", "Entfremdung", "Leiden", "Befreiung", "Freude", "Dank", "Leben" in unseren Breiten recht selten thematisiert. Die schwerpunktmäßige Streuung der Aufsatzthemen in der *ZAW* seit 1965 scheint bezeichnend zu sein. Mit "Befreiung" und "Rettung" beschäftigen sich vier Hauptartikel, obwohl doch dem "Rettungshandeln Jahwes" (C. Westermann) im Alten Testament hervorragende Bedeutung zukommt. Die Leidensthematik steht in drei Aufsätzen im Vor-

[14] Die starke Betonung von Praxis und Lebensbezug hat tiefe Wurzeln in der katholischen Tradition. Protestanten müssen sich jedoch fragen lassen, ob nicht gerade eine richtig verstandene Offenbarungs- und Worttheologie eines Kriteriums in der wahren Wirklichkeit bedarf; vgl. S. Galilea, *La teologia de la liberación después de Puebla* (-?-, 1979); L. Boff und C. Boff, *Da libertação* (Petrópolis, 1979); M. Bonino, *La fé en busca de eficacia* (Salamanca, 1977); R. Alves, *Tomorrow's Child* (New York, 1972).

dergrund. "Armut" und "Marginalisierung" behandelt ein Beitrag, und das auch in der Wohlstandsgesellschaft — wenn auch unter anderem Vorzeichen — heiße Thema "Revolution" wird in einem weiteren Essay untersucht. Dagegen stehen die Beiträge, welche sich mit Aspekten der "Macht", "Herrschaft" oder mit Führergestalten Israels auseinandersetzen. Es sind 42 an der Zahl; hinzu kommen 26 speziell dem Königtum oder einzelnen Königen gewidmete Aufsätze. Den großen Jahwekult und seine Stätten behandeln 22 Hauptartikel; Fragen von Gesetz, Recht und Ordnung 22; das Heil, die Erwählung, den Besitz weitere 6. Selbst wenn diese Erhebung nur annähernd zutrifft, muß die starke Konzentration auf Probleme der gesellschaftlichen Oberschicht auffallen. Eine Durchsicht von Dissertationsthemen, Monographienreihen, Stichwortregistern in Standardwerken alttestamentlicher Wissenschaft würde ein ähnliches Ergebnis erbringen.[15] Wo liegt denn nun in Wahrheit der thematische Schwerpunkt der alttestamentlichen Schriften? Lateinamerikaner, manche Afrikaner und Asiaten und ganz wenige Amerikaner und Europäer antworten: Das Alte Testament spiegelt vor allem die Geschichte des unterdrückten und befreiten Volkes und — sofern die endgültige Befreiung jeweils aussteht — der kommenden Gottesgerechtigkeit. Andere Forscher, z.B. Walter Brueggemann,[16] sehen zwei parallele Linien sich durch das ganze Alte Testament hinziehen, den revolutionären Kampf um Befreiung und die dynastischen und priesterlichen Bestrebungen, das Bestehende zu bewahren. Und viele Alttestamentler unserer Hemissphäre wollen überhaupt nicht mit den Themen Armut und Unterdrückung konfrontiert werden. Ist das eine instinktive Abwehrreaktion? Wo befindet sich die wahre Wirklichkeit?

c. In den Disziplinen "Geschichte Israels" und "Theologie des Alten Testaments" ist derselbe Gegensatz zwischen südlicher und nördlicher Interpretationsweise unverkennbar. Zwar halten lateinamerikanische Theologen wohl aus Respekt vor den Mutterkulturen formal an manchen heilsgeschichtlichen und dogmatischen Entwürfen fest. Aber sie geben den Gedankengerüsten ein anderes Fundament und einen anderen Inhalt. Die alttestamentlichen Begriffe werden aus der Wirklichkeitserfahrung aufgefüllt. "Unterdrückung" signalisiert jede Herrschaft von Menschen über Menschen, besonders die wirtschaftliche Abhängigkeit und Ausbeutung. "Bund" bedeutet die vorrangige oder ausschließliche Solidarisierung Gottes mit den Armen dieser Erde. "Gerechtigkeit" ist

---

[15] Dissertationen und Monographien, die sich dem Unterdrückten und seinen Erfahrungen zuwenden, stammen oft noch von Doktoranden aus der "Dritten Welt", vgl. M. Schwantes, *Das Recht des Armen* (Frankfurt, 1977).

[16] "Trajectories in Old Testament Literature and the Sociology of Ancient Israel", *JBL* 98 (1979), S. 161-85.

ein Attribut der Gottesherrschaft und diese wiederum ist kongruent mit der wahrhaft humanen Gesellschaft. "Befreiung" meint den aktiven Kampf gegen die nationalen und internationalen Oberschichten, die sich rücksichtslos an den Armen bereichern. "Heil" ist das verheißene Leben, in dem Gewalt und Herrschaft überwunden sind und Freude und Liebe frei walten können. Wahrhaftig, eine imposante, von der Wirklichkeit der sogenannten Entwicklungsländer und vielen alttestamentlichen Aussagen her legitimierte Geschichtsbetrachtung.

Auf der anderen Seite bemerken wir in den meisten nördlichen Entwürfen zur Geschichte Israels und zur Theologie des Alten Testaments eine gefährliche Tendenz, den eigenen theologischen Plan zu verabsolutieren und mit der Wirklichkeit gleichzusetzen. Ist-Aussagen über abstrakte Größen wie "Israel", "das Alte Testament", "das Wort Gottes" sind dafür bezeichnend. Aber es gibt inzwischen schwerwiegende Bedenken gegen die gängigen, vom Triumphalismus inspirierten heilsgeschichtlichen Konstruktionen der israelitischen Glaubenserfahrung. "Bund", "Ausschließlichkeitsanspruch Jahwes", "erstes Gebot", "Wort Gottes" und ähnliche Begriffe können nicht mehr unbesehen als zeitlose Grundlage der geschichtlichen Texte angesehen werden.[17] Die endlos wiederholten Feststellungen, Jahwe sei Subjekt entscheidender verbaler Aussagen und praktisch der Alleinhandelnde in der Geschichte (vgl. Jes. vii 4, xxx 15; 2 Chron. xx 20-22) sind als ethische Anweisungen absurd und beruhen wohl auf einer Fehlenschätzung der relevanten Texte wie der heutigen Wirklichkeit. Das vorherrschende Bild eines autoritären, von der Gehorsamsforderung lebenden Gottes ist mindestens von der Psalmensprache her fragwürdig.[18] Die unkritische Übernahme patriarchalischer Vorstellungen wird zu Recht von feministischen Theologinnen angegriffen.[19] Wir sehen: Die wahre Wirklichkeit meldet sich auch innerhalb traditioneller Theologien zu Wort und erschüttert etablierte Gedankengebäude.

3. *Exegese und Macht*

Wir müssen jetzt nach der Funktion der konstruierten und dann auch der wahren Wirklichkeit fragen. Das Gedankengebäude, das wir uns auf-

---

[17] Vgl. L. Perlitt, *Bundestheologie im Alten Testament* (Neukirchen-Vluyn, 1969); B. Lang (Hg.), *Der einzige Gott* (München, 1981).

[18] Gott gehört ursprünglich mit zur Sippe, vgl. Rogerson, S. 86ff.; E. S. Gerstenberger, *Der bittende Mensch* (Neukirchen-Vluyn, 1980). Für die Befreiungstheologen ist die befreiende Tat Jahwes erstrangig wichtig, vgl. E. S. Gerstenberger, "Deus libertador", in: idem (Hg.), *Deus no Antigo Testamento* (São Paulo, 1981), S. 9-29.

[19] Am schärfsten M. Daly, *Beyond God the Father* (Boston, Mass., 1973); vgl. E. S. Gerstenberger, W. Schrage, *Frau und Mann* (Stuttgart, 1980).

grund unserer begrenzten Wirklichkeitserkenntnis zusammenbauen, hat zuerst einen noetischen Sinn. Ohne ein derartiges Modell dessen, was wir für Wirklichkeit halten, sind Erkenntnis und Kommunikation unmöglich. So weit, so gut. Aber unser Verstand leistet mehr, wenn er ein System entwirft. Die *ratio*, so Rubem Alves,[20] filtert aus der unübersehbaren Menge von Eindrücken die für uns brauchbaren Elemente heraus, verbaut sie in dem subjektiven Weltmodell und unterdrückt gleichzeitig störende Emotionen und fremde Elemente, die dem eigenen Gebäude schaden könnten. Jeder systematische Entwurf, auch der für die alttestamentliche Exegese notwendige, wirkt also nach innen beruhigend und stabilisierend. Er fingiert Wirklichkeit. Nach außen aber muß er sich abweisend, ja aggressiv geben, damit alles, was nicht integrationsfähig ist, draußenbleibt. Das erklärt die manchmal so beliebten Fußnotenschlachten in wissenschaftlichen Veröffentlichungen.

Was vom einzelnen Exegeten gilt, trifft auch auf Gruppen und Schulen von Fachkollegen zu. Das gemeinsame geistige Haus ist heilig zu halten und gegen die Angriffe von außen zu verteidigen. Schließlich herrschen ähnliche Verhaltensmuster auch im globalen Nord-Süd-Verhältnis, nur ist auf dieser Ebene alles wegen mangelnder Kontakte und fehlender gemeinsamer Lebenserfahrung verdeckter und böswilliger. Die Exegeten aus den Industrieländern rümpfen oft die Nase über die Naivität, Unwissenschaftlichkeit und theologische Verantwortungslosigkeit der Kollegen "dort unten". Umgekehrt rebellieren diese gegen die Bevormundung aus dem Norden. Sie sehen in uns manchmal die Nutznießer und Befürworter einer entmenschlichenden Wirtschaftsordnung oder überhebliche Liberale, die aus unangreifbarer Machtposition ein zynisches *laisser-faire* propagieren.

Wieder tut es gut, sich einen Moment auf die Seite derer zu stellen, die unser System "von außen" erleben. Wenn bei unserer Auslegung des Alten Testaments Macht und Ordnung, Gehorsam und politische Abstinenz ungebührlich in den Vordergrund treten, wenn wir unterschwellig eine *theologia gloriae* zwecks eigener Existenzsicherung treiben, dann kann in der Tat der Stützungseffekt für das bei uns herrschende Wirtschaftssystem, unter dem die sogenannten Entwicklungsländer zugrundegehen, nicht ausbleiben. Denken wir nur an die Rolle, die das Alte Testament bei der Ausbildung der kapitalistischen Wirtschaftsethik gespielt hat.[21]

---

[20] *Protestantismo e repressão* (São Paulo, 1979), S. 84ff.

[21] Bei M. Weber, *Gesammelte Studien zur Religionssoziologie*, Bd I und Bd III, wird das nicht unmittelbar deutlich, weil er die Juden als Pariavolk ansieht. Vgl. A. H. J. Gunneweg, *Vom Verstehen des Alten Testaments* (Göttingen, 1977), S. 92ff.; G. Fohrer, *Theologische Grundstrukturen des AT* (Berlin, 1972), S. 206-60.

Eine kritische Rückfrage wird unausweichlich: Wie halten es die alttestamentlichen Zeugen mit Macht und Herrschaft? Lassen wir extreme Antworten beiseite und beschäftigen wir uns mit der gängigen Meinung, das Alte Testament sei eben in sich widersprüchlich. Es verordne einerseits Herrschaft — als Herrschaft Gottes oder Herrschaft von Königen, Männern, Priestern — und stelle andererseits eben diese autoritäre Struktur wieder in Frage. Das "sowohl — als auch" dieser Antwort wird uns gerade zum Vorwurf gemacht, weil der Verdacht auf Selbstrechtfertigung besteht. Ist die doppelte Antwort über die historisch-kritische Bestandsaufnahme hinaus haltbar? Ich glaube nicht. Zwar gibt es zweifellos im Alten Testament Texte, welche göttliches und menschliches Herrschen positiv bewerten.[22] Aber welchen sozialen und politischen Konstellationen entstammen sie? Sind die Herrschaftsvorstellungen auf unsere heutige Situation übertragbar? Und jene andere Linie alttestamentlichen Zeugnisses, nach der sich Gott mit den Entrechteten und Ausgebeuteten solidarisiert,[23] ist sie nicht weit kräftiger gezeichnet? Es imponiert nicht nur die Masse der Belegstellen, sondern die menschlicher Natur entgegenlaufende Tendenz und die oftmals betonte theologische Begründung. Dennoch bleiben im Alten Testament beide Stränge, Befürwortung und Ablehnung von Herrschaft von Menschen über Menschen, sichtbar.

In dieser exegetisch-theologischen Sackgasse kann nur die aktuelle Wirklichkeitsanalyse eine Entscheidung bringen. Bewußt oder unbewußt ist eine Vorstellung von der Wirklichkeit, auf die hin ausgelegt wird, bei jedem Interpretationsprozeß ohnehin mit gesetzt. Jetzt soll diese Vorstellung, das fordern unsere lateinamerikanischen Kollegen, offengelegt und reflektiert werden. Sind die alttestamentlichen Herrschaftsstrukturen in irgendeiner Form für uns verwendbar? Nach allem, was wir im Licht der gesamten Schrift aus der jüdischen und christlichen ethischen Tradition lernen können, nach allem, was uns an aktuellen Informationen zur Verfügung steht, können wir m.E. die gegenwärtige Weltlage nur so beurteilen: Die traditionellen Herrschafts- und Wirtschaftsstrukturen haben bereits die Endkatastrophe — in Gestalt von Massenverelendung, Umweltzerstörung, Sexismus, Rassismus, Wettrüsten, Kriegen, Genoziden — herbeigeführt. Sie haben sich damit als gott- und menschenfeindlich erwiesen und können darum als Auslegungsparameter nicht mehr in Frage kommen. So wie das Königtum in Israel vor der Katastrophe von 587 v. Chr. noch glaubwürdig sein konnte (vgl. Jer. xxii 13), nachher aber in Bausch und Bogen abgelehnt wurde (vgl. 2 Kön. xvii 7ff., xxiii 26f.), so

[22] Vgl. z.B. Gen. i 28; 2 Sam. vii; Ps. ii; Jes. xlix 22f.; Ez. xxxiv.

[23] Vgl. Gen. iv 15; Ex. iii 16f.; Lev. xix 14, xxv 43; Dtn. xv 4, 11; Amos ii 6-8, v 11-12; Ps. x, xxxvii; Jes. v. 8; Jer. xxii 13; Jes. lviii 6-9; Neh. v; Prov. xiv 31 usw.

müssen wir wohl nach Lage der Dinge die uns bekannten Systeme wirtschaftlicher und politischer Dominanz theologisch als untauglich und bis ins Mark sündhaft abschreiben.

An diesem Beispiel wird die entscheidende Bedeutung der wahren Wirklichkeit erkennbar. Carlos Mesters pflegt in seinen Vorlesungen die drei Faktoren "Schriftzeugnis", "Gott", "Wirklichkeit" in einem Dreieck an die Tafel zu malen. Die Schrift erhellt die Wirklichkeit, und im Licht der Wirklichkeit lesen wir die Schrift. In beiden Polen aber wirkt Gott.[24] Herrschaft des Menschen über den Menschen ist nach der leidvollen Erfahrung der Menschen in der "Dritten" und "Vierten" Welt — hunderte von Millionen sind zugrundegegangen wie das Kind der Teresinha — zur Sünde schlechthin geworden.

4. *Bibelauslegung nach der Katastrophe*

Wie können wir heute, im nachapokalyptischen Zeitalter, alttestamentliche Exegese und Theologie treiben? Einige, wenige Thesen sollen unsere Überlegungen vorläufig abschließen.

a. Es gibt viele Wirklichkeitsmodelle. Die Auslegungsarbeit wird durch die bestehende Wirklichkeit motiviert, in der sich der Exeget vorfindet. Sie zielt auf die Erneuerung der todverfallenen Welt, d.h. auf die befreiende Wirklichkeit Gottes.

b. Diese echte, gottes- und menschenwürdige Wirklichkeit ist auch hinter den alttestamentlichen Texten zu spüren. An ihr müssen sich also Ausleger und Text messen lassen.

c. "Wirklichkeit" muß heute im Gegensatz zur Frühzeit Israels ein unversaler Begriff sein. Er beinhaltet "Heil" und "Leben" (Gerechtigkeit, Frieden, Liebe, Hoffnung usw.) für alle Menschen.

d. Zur Analyse der Weltlage bedient sich der Exeget aller wissenschaftlichen Untersuchungsergebnisse, deren er habhaft werden kann. Er mißt und beurteilt sie anhand von Schrift und Tradition.

e. Die schon im Alten Testament verheißene, z.T. verwirklichte und mit Nachdruck geforderte Solidäritat mit den Schwachen öffnet uns die Augen für das Schicksal von 2/3 der Menschheit, die im gegenwärtig praktizierten Wirtschaftssystem zum Tode verurteilt sind.

f. Das unvorstellbare Leiden der Mehrheit aller Menschen, welches einer Minderheit einen weit überdurchschnittlichen Wohlstand garantiert (und deshalb unter den geltenden Bedingungen nicht abgestellt wer-

---

[24] Vgl. C. Mester, *Por trás das palavras* (Petrópolis, 1974); idem, *Um vento começa a soprar. Um estudo sobre o uso da Bíblia na Igreja* (handabgezogene Unterrichtsblätter, ohne Ort, ohne Jahr), S. 6f.

den kann), bringt geistlich gesehen die Erkenntnisse und Erfahrungen hervor, die zur Transformation dieser Welt in eine menschliche Welt unerläßlich sind.

g. Der Exeget muß sich seines eigenen Wirklichkeitsverständnisses bewußt werden und die wahre Wirklichkeit hinter den Texten und in seiner eigenen Umwelt zu erkennen suchen. Seine Lebenserfahrung und seine Glaubenspraxis sind in hohem Maße entscheidend für das Verhältnis, das er zur befreienden Wirklichkeit Gottes gewinnen wird.

"SOLOMON WHO IS GREATER THAN DAVID"

SOLOMON'S SUCCESSION IN 1 KINGS I-II IN THE LIGHT OF THE INSCRIPTION OF KILAMUWA, KING OF Y'DY-ŚAM'AL[1]

BY

TOMOO ISHIDA

Tsukuba, Japan

In a previous study on the "Succession Narrative" (2 Sam. ii[?]-xx; 1 Kings i-ii), I have suggested that this literary complex as a whole was composed from a certain political standpoint, i.e., the defence of Solomon against the old regime of David.[2] From this point of view, the "Succession Narrative" can be summarized in the following fashion: a) Solomon, one of the younger sons of David, gained his designation as David's successor by a court intrigue; b) the legitimacy of Solomon's accession is defended by a claim that the irregular procedure involved was unavoidable under abnormal circumstances; c) the regime which Solomon challenged was supported by the administration whose nominal ruler was the aging David and whose strong-man was the commander-in-chief Joab; d) the description of David's shortcomings in the narrative reflects the political standpoint of Solomon's historiographer; e) Solomon's purge of his opponents is regarded by this historiographer as an initial achievement of his monarch in a matter left unfinished by David.

On the basis of these observations, I shall try to show in the present article that the concluding section of the "Succession Narrative", i.e., 1 Kings i-ii, is an apologetic composition from the early days of Solomon, aiming at legitimatizing not only his irregular succession but also his execution of his brother, high officials of the old regime and a leader of the Saulides.[3] I shall attempt to explain the substance of the Solomonic

---

[1] I am grateful to Professors J. C. Greenfield and H. Tadmor for having read the manuscript and for their valuable comments.

[2] T. Ishida, "Solomon's Succession to the Throne of David — A Political Analysis", in T. Ishida (ed.), *Studies in the Period of David and Solomon and Other Essays* (Tokyo, 1982), pp. 175-87.

[3] For a select bibliography of the "Succession Narrative" up to 1978 see ibid, p. 175, nn. 1-2. Among the literature which appeared since that date, the thesis that regards 1 Kings i-ii as the Solomonic legitimation from his time is held by S. Zalewski, *Solomon's Ascension to the Throne: Studies in the Books of Kings and Chronicles* (Jerusalem, 1981) (Hebrew); and P. K. McCarter, "Plots, True or False: The Succession Narrative as

legitimation by analysing the pertinent biblical texts and by referring to relevant extra-biblical material. The latter may provide us with a much needed analogy for the narrative of Solomon's succession and the events it relates.

I believe that the Solomonic legitimation consists of two conflicting elements: an apology for his legitimacy and a defence for his deeds. Both elements are skilfully blended in the congratulation offered to David by Benaiah (1 Kings i 37) and by similar words of David's servants (i 47) on the occasion of Solomon's accession: "May your God make the name of Solomon more famous than yours, and make his throne greater than your throne."[4] The implication of the words is twofold: on the one hand, an explicit congratulation to David on having a successor, on the other, an implicit wish that the reign of this successor may surpass that of David.[5] This congratulation must have originated in the Solomonic scribal circle, since the canonical view in the biblical traditions regards Solomon as inferior to David in every respect.[6]

We come now to the extra-biblical parallel to the Solomonic succession, which augments the biblical narrative by providing a point of departure for historiographical and historical analysis. The comparative

---

Court Apologetic", *Interpretation* 35 (1981), pp. 355-67. While the former finds a unity of these chapters with 2 Sam. ix-xx, the latter proposes that materials in 2 Samuel, which had been composed originally for the Davidic apology, were attached to 1 Kings i-ii as a preface. An opposite view is suggested by J. Van Seters, "Histories and Historians of the Ancient Near East: The Israelites", *Orientalia*, N.S. 50 (1981), pp. 156-67. According to his suggestion, the Court History (2 Sam. ix-xx; 1 Kings i-ii) was added to the stories of Saul and David as an anti-legitimation story in the post-exilic period (p. 166). A "relative" unity of 2 Sam. ix-xx and 1 Kings i-ii is confirmed by "stylistic and structural analyses" or "literary-structural analysis"; see J. P. Fokkelman, *Narrative Art and Poetry in the Books of Samuel* I: *King David* (Assen, 1981); K. K. Sacon, "A Study of the Literary Structure of 'The Succession Narrative'", in Ishida (ed.), *Studies in the Period of David and Solomon and Other Essays* (Tokyo, 1982), pp. 27-54. Both studies propose the title "(A Story of) King David" for the work (Fokkelman, p. 427; Sacon, p. 54) by assuming Solomon's succession as one of the themes of the composition. A question is raised about the legitimacy of separating a "succession narrative" from the rest of Samuel-Kings by P. R. Ackroyd, "The Succession Narrative (so-called)", *Interpretation* 35 (1981), pp. 383-96. A text reconstructed by a redaction-critical study is suggested by F. Langlamet, "David, fils de Jessé. Une édition prédeutéronomique de l'histoire de la succession", *RB* 89 (1982), pp. 5-47.

[4] See Ishida, "Solomon's Succession", in *Studies*, p. 181; cf. also T. Ishida, *The Royal Dynasties in Ancient Israel* (*BZAW* 142; Berlin-New York, 1977), pp. 105-6.

[5] For the second implication, compare the following text of Esarhaddon, king of Assyria: "*ēnu* ^{d}*Aššur ... eli šarrāni ... šarrūtī ušarriḫma ušarbâ zikri šumija*. When Aššur made my royal power more famous and my fame greater than (that of all) kings", R. Borger, *Die Inschriften Asarhaddons Königs von Assyrien* (*AfO Beiheft* 9, 1956), p. 98, line 32; cf. *CAD* Z, p. 116a.

[6] For David's loyalty to Yahweh in contrast to Solomon's apostasy, see 1 Kings xi 4, 6, 12-13, 33-36.

analogue we are looking for comes from the inscription of Kilamuwa, king of *y'dy*-Śam'al, an Aramaean king in North Syria in the latter half of the ninth century B.C.[7] Both archaeological and epigraphical evidence shows that Kilamuwa reigned about a century after the inception of the Aramaean monarchy in Śam'al.[8] Accordingly, we may suppose that with Kilamuwa, as with Solomon, we have the last generation of the early monarchy in his kingdom.

The introduction of the Kilamuwa inscription reads: "I am Kilamuwa, the son of Hayya. Gabbar became king over *y'dy*, but he did nothing. There was[9] *bmh*, but he did nothing. And there was my father Hayya, but he did nothing. And there was my[10] brother *š'l*, but he did nothing. But I am Kilamuwa, the son of *tm*-[11]. What I have done my predecessors[12] did not do" (lines 1-5).

We have here the names of five successive rulers of Śam'al in the ninth century B.C. The series of names gives us an impression that all the five kings belonged to the same dynasty founded by Gabbar. And indeed, Hayya is called "Haianu/ni, the son of Gabbari" in a ninth-century Assyrian source.[13] Yet, since the Assyrians used to call the land after the name of king who reigned there when they first became aquainted with it, it does not necessarily imply that Hayya was actually Gabbar's son. Nor is

---

[7] *KAI* 24; *ANET*, pp. 654-5; J. C. L. Gibson, *Textbook of Syrian Semitic Inscriptions* III (Oxford, 1982), no. 13.

[8] F. von Luschan et al., *Ausgrabungen in Sendschirli* I-IV (Königliche Museen zu Berlin: Mittheilungen aus den orientalischen Sammlungen XI-XIV; Berlin, 1893-1911); B. Landsberger, *Sam'al* (Ankara, 1948), p. 37; D. Ussishkin, "'Der alte Bau' in Zincirli", *BASOR* 189 (1968), pp. 50-3; N. Na'aman, "Śam'al", in *Encyclopaedia Biblica* VIII (Jerusalem, 1982), cols. 308-16 (Hebrew).

[9] The implication of the verb *kn* here is obviously *mlk*, "he became king" or "he ruled". M. O'Connor suggests that the term *kn* here functions as a marker of a Verb Phrases deletion transformation, "The Rhetoric of the Kilamuwa Inscription", *BASOR* 226 (1977), p. 20; cf. also C.-F. Jean and J. Hoftijzer, *Dictionnaire des inscriptions sémitiques de l'ouest* (Leiden, 1960), p. 117.

[10] There is no possibility of rendering *'ḥ* here by "his brother", making *š'l* Kilamuwa's uncle, from the orthographical as well as morphological point of view, against W. Röllig, *KAI* II, p. 32; T. Collins, "The Kilamuwa Inscription — A Phoenician Poem", *WO* 6 (1971), p. 184. It must be read as *'ḥi*, "my brother", see F. M. Cross and D. N. Freedman, *Early Hebrew Orthography* (New Haven, 1952), p. 16; O'Connor, *BASOR* 226, p. 20; Gibson, *Textbook* III, p. 36.

[11] A letter is missing after *tm*. I am sceptical about the reading *tm*, "perfection", against Collins, *WO* 6, pp. 184f.; Landsberger has suggested a possibility that "Bartumm" may be regarded as the Aramaic translation of the Anatolian name Kilamuwa, *Sam'al*, p. 45, n. 112, p. 56 n. 139. For my interpretation see below.

[12] There is a difficulty with the second *h* of *hlpnyhm*. Still, the rendering "my predecessors" is most suitable for the context, see Cross and Freedman, *Early Hebrew Orthography*, pp. 16f.; O'Connor, *BASOR* 226, pp. 20f. The rendering "their predecessors", making the reference to the kings preceding to Gabbar, is untenable, against Gibson, *Textbook* III, p. 36.

[13] *mḪa-ia-(a)-nu/ni mār Ga(b)-ba-ri*, II*R* 7-8, col. II 24, 83; cf. I 42, 53 (Shalmaneser III).

it absolutely clear that Hayya was a member of Gabbar's House. We should rather look for a clue to the relations among these kings in the curse formula in the end of the inscription (lines 15-16). Kilamuwa invokes here three deities with their titles one after the other: "Baal-Ṣemed who belongs to Gabbar", "Baal-Ḥammon who belongs to *bmh*", and "Rakkabel, lord of the dynasty (*bʿl bt*)". If these three divine names stand for the three tutelary deities of Gabbar, of *bmh* and of the other three kings, respectively, we may assume that there were dynastic changes from Gabbar to *bmh*, and from *bmh* to Hayya, the latter being the founder of the ruling dynasty to which Kilamuwa belonged.[14]

If this reconstruction, suggested first by B. Landsberger, is tenable, we can find here a remarkable parallel to the pattern of the royal succession in early Israel. Both Gabbar of Śam'al and Saul of Israel were the first kings who introduced the monarchial regime into their countries, but each failed to found a lasting dynasty. As for the second set of kings, there is some difference. While *bmh* of Śam'al was a usurper, Ishbaal of Israel was a legitimate successor to the throne. Yet, despite this difference, they played the similar role of representing a transitional stage between the establishment of the monarchy and its consolidation by another dynasty. The third set of kings, Hayya and David, succeeded at last in founding the stable dynasties. They bequeathed the throne to their sons, but the succession in both kingdoms was not achieved without trouble. The position of *š'l*, the fourth king of Śam'al, corresponds to that of Adonijah in Israel, though again there is a difference between them, i.e., while the former became king, the latter failed to seize the throne. But both had a common fate as losers, defeated by their half-brothers in the struggle for the kingship.[15] Finally, the kingship was firmly established by Kilamuwa and Solomon, respectively, the fifth candidate for the throne in both kingdoms.

In this context, it seems possible to expect the name of Kilamuwa's mother in *tm-*, a defective word after *klmw.br* in line 4. The queen-mother's involvement in the problems of royal succession was a

---

[14] Landsberger, *Sam'al*, pp. 46f. He has also pointed out that there is no filiation between Gabbar, *bmh* and Hayya (p. 47, n. 118); cf. also W. Röllig, *KAI* II, p. 34. The dynastic groupings are perceived also from the rhetorical structure of the inscription, in which the introductory section and the curse formula "are linked together by their references to the rulers of Ya'diya", O'Connor, *BASOR* 226, p. 24. For the tutelary deities of dynasties see Ishida, *The Royal Dynasties*, pp. 113f.

[15] It is unlikely that Kilamuwa succeeded *š'l* by a normal procedure. He maintains, "I sat upon my father's throne" (line 9), but not "brother's throne"; cf. Landsberger, *Sam'al*, pp. 51, 56f. In the monarchies of Israel and Judah, the succession from brother to brother took place only in irregular situations, see Ishida, *The Royal Dynasties*, pp. 151f.

phenomenon common to the "Western courts".[16] We may suggest that Kilamuwa's mother's intervention in the struggle for the kingship, like that of Bathsheba, may have been the reason for the special mention of her name in the inscription.

The characterization of the five kings in both kingdoms is summarized as follows:

	Śam'al	Israel
1. Founder of monarchy	Gabbar	Saul
2. Transitional king	*bmh*	Ishbaal
3. Founder of dynasty	Hayya	David
4. Loser in the struggle for the kingship	*š'l*	Adonijah
5. King who established his kingship	Kilamuwa	Solomon

One of the most striking features of the Kilamuwa inscription is a bold statement accompanying each of his four predecessors in the introduction: "but he did nothing (*wbl. pʿl*)" (lines 2-4). This negative evaluation of the former kings is put in a sharp contrast to Kilamuwa's own achievements: "What I have done my predecessors did not do" (lines 4-5). The same is emphasized in conjunction with his social reform, contrasted with the days of the former kings (lines 9-10). The theme of the inscription is what we may call Kilamuwa's propaganda which claims that he is the sole, just king after a series of the ineffective rulers who preceded him.

Recently the Kilamuwa inscription has been subjected to a critical analysis by F. M. Fales, who pointed out the propagandistic and literary typological features of the text.[17] Of the special significance is the literary motif called "heroic priority" or "priority on the predecessors" expressed there. This is one of the recurrent motifs in the historiographical literature of Mesopotamian kings, i.e., a reigning monarch claims that he is the first to perform successfully a task or tasks which none of his predecessors has done.[18] A typical eclectic text would read: "(I accomplished) what no one among the kings who preceded me had done (*ša*

[16] See ibid., pp. 155-7; H. Tadmor, "Autobiographical Apology in the Royal Assyrian Literature", in H. Tadmor and M. Weinfeld (ed.), *History, Historiography and Interpretation: Studies in Biblical and Cuneiform Literature* (Jerusalem, 1983), pp. 54, 57; cf. also N.-E. A. Andreasen, "The Role of the Queen Mother in Israelite Society", *CBQ* 45 (1983), pp. 179-94.

[17] F. M. Fales, "Kilamuwa and the Foreign Kings: Propaganda vs. Power", *WO* 10 (1979), pp. 6-22.

[18] See M. Liverani, "The Ideology of the Assyrian Empire", in M. T. Larsen (ed.), *Power and Propaganda - A Symposium on Ancient Empires* (Copenhagen, 1979), pp. 308f. A dissertation on this theme: R. Gelio, *ša ina šarrāni abbēya mamman lā ēpušu ... Il motivo della*

ina šarrāni ālikūt maḫrīya mamman lā ēpušū)''.[19] In this pattern the events are presented as moving from ''negative past'' to ''positive present'', i.e., against the shortcomings of the predecessors, the present king is not only a more successful ruler but also the just king and the ''restorer of order''.[20]

It is to be stressed, however, that there is also a significant difference between Kilamuwa's assertion and the stereotyped statement of the ''priority on the predecessors''. While former kings in the latter texts are always generalized and their names are no longer important, the four predecessors of Kilamuwa are mentioned by their names and their ineffective rule is clearly remembered in his time.[21]

So far the introduction of the Kilamuwa inscription. The major part of the inscription is devoted to his own personal achievements (in contrast to the lack of achievement on the part of his predecessors). First, he tells how he liberated Śam'al from the oppression of the Danunian king (lines 5-8). Then, he relates his achievement in the sphere of domestic administration, i.e., how he made the *mškbm* happy and prosperous (lines 9-13). It is generally held that the word *mškbm* (lines 10, 14, 15) refers to the conquered Anatolian population, whereas the word *bʿrrm* (line 14) stands for the Aramaean ruling class.[22] Evidently, there had been conflicts between these two elements with the *bʿrrm* ultimately prevailing over the *mškbm*. Then, it was Kilamuwa who put an end to the futile struggle between them and restored the social justice in Śam'al.[23]

---

priorità eroica nelle iscrizioni reali assire (Università di Roma, 1976), was not available to me. This is a frequent theme particularly in the commemorative inscriptions, see K. Grayson, ''Histories and Historians of the Ancient Near East: Assyria and Babylonia'', *Orientalia*, N.S. 49 (1980), p. 191; cf. also H. Tadmor, ''History and Ideology in the Assyrian Royal Inscriptions'', in F. M. Fales (ed.), *Assyrian Royal Inscriptions: New Horizons in Literary, Ideological, and Historical Analysis* (Roma, 1981), pp. 13-25.

[19] Liverani, ''The Ideology'', in *Power*, p. 309; cf. *CAD* M/1, p. 200.

[20] For the pattern of the ''restorer of order'' see M. Liverani, ''Memorandum on the Approach to Historiographic Texts'', *Orientalia*, N.S. 42 (1973), pp. 186-8. For the ideological explanation of the motif of the ''priority on the predecessors'' by the pattern of the ''restorer of order'' see Fales, *WO* 10, pp. 7-9.

[21] Fales has also noted that in the Kilamuwa inscription ''this opposition between the age before the king and the age of the king is charged with more definite connotations'', *WO* 10, p. 7. Because of the lack of the real names of the predecessors, neither the inscriptions of Kapara, ruler of Guzana (*AfO* Beiheft 1 [1933], p. 72-9) nor that of Azitiwadda from Karatepe (*KAI* 26, I 18-19) can be regarded as compositions belonging to the same category with the Kilamuwa inscription.

[22] See M. Lidzbarski, *Ephemeris für semitische Epigraphik* 3 (Giessen, 1915), pp. 233-6; Rosenthal, *ANET*, p. 654; Röllig, *KAI* II, pp. 33f.; Jean and Hoftijzer, *Dictionnaire*, pp. 40, 170; Gibson, *Textbook* III, pp. 37f. But Landsberger has held that the *mškbm* and the *bʿrrm* were two classes of ''Ministerialen'', *Sam'al*, p. 56, n. 140.

[23] It has been suggested that Kilamuwa was the new Anatolian name which he took upon his accession for appeasing his Anatolian subjects; see Gibson, *Textbook* III, pp. 31, 35; Na'aman, *Encyclopaedia Biblica* VIII, col. 309 (Hebrew).

It is clear that this is the central motif of the text. Kilamuwa appears to be the just king, provider for the poor, and restorer of the good order who brings peace and security to his realm. The parallel to Solomon immediately comes to mind. Under his just rule (cf. 1 Kings iii) the people of Israel enjoyed peace and prosperity (v 5). We shall return to this motif somewhat later.

The analogy to Solomon is more explicit in the relationship between Kilamuwa and his two immediate predecessors, his father Hayya and his brother *š'l*, Kilamuwa clearly maintains that not only is he the son of Hayya (lines 1, 9; cf. *KAI* 25, line 3) but also he succeeded to his father's kingship (line 9). Needless to say, the throne of Hayya is mentioned here as the foundation of Kilamuwa's legitimacy. When he won the royal throne in struggle with his brother, he could not but legitimatize his kingship by his royal descent.[24] Yet, at the same time, he did not hesitate to announce that he would not continue the policies of his father and brother. This seems to be the implication of the negative evaluation attached to Hayya and *š'l*.

Before making a comparison between Kilamuwa's propaganda and the Solomonic legitimation, we cannot fail to observe that there are also some differences between them. An important difference is found in the situations in which they inaugurated the kingship. While Kilamuwa, as it seems, dethroned his brother and established his kingship for himself, Solomon was designated co-regent by David and reigned with him, though he resorted to a court intrigue. Evidently, the formal designation and co-regency prevented Solomon from expressing a negative criticism of David as explicitly as Kilamuwa criticized his predecessors. There was also no need for Solomon's historiographer to deal with Adonijah as if he were equal in rank to Solomon. Adonijah was stigmatized as a second Absalom, a rebel.

These differences aside, the Kilamuwa inscription offers close parallel to the Solomonic legitimation, especially in the following three items: a) the emphasis on the father's throne as the foundation of the legitimate kingship;[25] b) the negative evaluation to his father (Solomon's

[24] Strikingly, reference to Kilamuwa's election by the gods is entirely lacking from the text. According to the royal ideology in the ancient Near East, the royal authority was normally legitimatized by royal lineage and divine election. Since Kilamuwa was doubtless a worshiper of Rakkabel (line 16; *KAI* 25), his silence about his divine election must be regarded as intentional. It could be assumed, therefore, that he avoided mentioning any deity belonging to any class or national element as a god who chose him, in order to establish his kingship as the neutral authority over the mixed population.

[25] For Kilamuwa see above pp. 149-50 and n. 24; for Solomon see Ishida, "Solomon's Succession", in *Studies*, pp. 179f.

historiographer made it in the description of David's shortcomings[26] as well as in the wish of David's servants that Solomon's kingship may be superior to that of David);[27] c) the establishment of the kingship based on the restoration of social justice or order. As for this last point, we should note that Solomon's purge of his adversaries was different in nature from Kilamuwa's appeasement policy. But both the political actions brought about a common effect: the restoration of social order. As a result, "the kingdom was established in the hand of Solomon" (1 Kings ii 46b).

Before closing the present inquiry, I should like to suggest in brief my provisional view of the historical circumstances under which Kilamuwa's propaganda and the Solomonic legitimation were composed. Recently, H. A. Hoffner for the Hittite texts[28] and H. Tadmor for the Neo-Assyrian sources[29] have assumed that royal historiographies of an apologetic nature in the ancient Near East were composed with specific aims in the present and future. Accordingly, we may suppose that one of the strongest motivations for writing this sort of royal historiography arose from the necessity of general support for the new enterprise undertaken by the king who had just overcome a crisis. For Kilamuwa, it is likely that the crisis was the struggle against the domination of the *bᶜrrm* supported by the followers of *š'l*, his brother; and the new enterprise was the building of his palace.[30] For Solomon, the crisis was the struggle with the leading members of the regime of David when he became the sole sovereign after his father's demise;[31] and the new enterprise was the

---

[26] See *ibid.*, pp. 181-5.

[27] If we accept B. Mazar's suggestion that Ps. lxxii originated in the days of co-regency of David and Solomon ("The Phoenicians and the Eastern Shore of the Mediterranean Sea", [1965], in *Cities and Districts in Eretz-Israel* [Jerusalem, 1975], p. 262 [Hebrew]), we may find in the psalm a development of the theme of the congratulation offered to David by his servants, especially compare *v.* 17, "May his name endure for ever, his fame continue as long as the sun", with 1 Kings i 47, "May your God make the name of Solomon more famous than yours".

[28] H. A. Hoffner, "Propaganda and Political Justifications in Hittite Historiography", in H. Goedicke and J. J. M. Roberts (ed.), *Unity and Diversity*: *Essays in the History, Literature, and Religion of the Ancient Near East* (Baltimore and London, 1975), pp. 49-62; idem, "Histories and Historians of the Ancient Near East: The Hittites", *Orientalia*, N.S. 49 (1980), pp. 325-7.

[29] H. Tadmor, "Autobiographical Apology", in *History*, pp. 36-57.

[30] Although there is no reference to building operations in the text, it is likely that the inscription was composed on the occasion of the dedication of the palace, since it was found on an orthostat at the entrance to a vestibule leading into the palace, see von Luschan, *Ausgrabungen in Sendschirli* IV, p. 374 and Taf. IL; cf. Rosenthal, *ANET*, p. 654; Gibson, *Textbook* III, p. 30.

[31] E. Ball has laid emphasis on the fact that Solomon became "co-regent with his father David in the full sense", "The Co-Regency of David and Solomon (1 Kings i)", *VT* 27 (1977), p. 270. He seems to overlook, however, the fact that Solomon did not, or perhaps could not, purge any adversary in David's lifetime. In the period of his co-regency with

building of his palace and the Temple in Jerusalem (cf. a prediction about the builder of the Temple in Nathan's prophecy [2 Sam. vii 13a]).[32].

Admittedly, the details of the historical reconstruction of the early monarchies in Śam'al remain hypothetical. Still, it is the best means conceivable to regard both the texts of 1 Kings i-ii and the Kilamuwa inscription as compositions belonging to the category of royal historiographies of apologetic nature. And the pattern of transfer of the royal throne in Israel and Śam'al indicates that there were common features in the political development in the early—inexperienced—monarchies in the national kingdoms of Syro-Palestine at the beginning of the first millennium B.C.

David, Solomon was actually a young boy under the protection of David and Bathsheba. The purpose of Solomon's co-regency was to confirm David's designation of him and its announcement, see Ishida, *The Royal Dynasties*, p. 170; cf. also K. W. Whitelam, *The Just King: Monarchical Judicial Authority in Ancient Israel* (Sheffield, 1979), pp. 149-55.

[32] See Ishida, *The Royal Dynasties*, p. 97; idem, "Solomon's Succession", in *Studies*, p. 187.

THE LITERARY AND THEOLOGICAL FUNCTION OF DIVINE SPEECH IN THE PENTATEUCH

BY

CASPER J. LABUSCHAGNE

Groningen

Since the publication of the first results of my study on divine speech in the Pentateuch[1] closer examination enabled me to make a few adjustments in the Synopsis of the divine speech formulas and to adduce further evidence for the patterns I discovered.[2] When I was invited to read a paper at the Salamanca meeting of the I.O.S.O.T., I decided to present to this audience the results of my further investigation of this fascinating subject. On the basis of my discovery of the literary function of the formulas denoting divine speech in the Pentateuch, where they are arranged in such a way that they form distinct patterns and give structure to the material, I made a closer study of divine speech itself by examining the form of the divine *oratio recta*.

Throughout the Pentateuch, the words reportedly spoken by God are consistently ushered in by introductory formulas containing *verba dicendi*, or, when these are lacking, by *lēʾmōr*. The literary form of "performative speech", also known as "interior monologue" (in German "die erlebte Rede"—a better term would be "subjective speech") where a thought is expressed from the viewpoint of the subject in question without any introductory formula, does occur in the Pentateuch (e.g. in Gen. xxvi 7,9, xxxii 31, xli 51,52), but is only once employed with regard to God (Deut. xxxii 32-35), where the divine speech is easily recognizable.[3] On the

[1] "The pattern of the divine speech formulas in the Pentateuch", *VT* 32 (1982), pp. 268-96.

[2] "Additional remarks on the pattern of the divine speech formulas in the Pentateuch", *VT* 34 (1984), pp. 91-5. Since I completed this article I have realized, as a result of a remark by one of my students, Mr H. Nobel, that the conversation of the two angels with Lot in the Sodom story should be included in the divine speeches of the Pentateuch. When these four divine speech formulas in Gen. xix 2, 12, 17 and 21 are included, the pattern in Genesis is: 7+4 + 7+4 + 7+4 + 4+7 + 4+7 + 4+7 + 4+7 + 7+4 + 7+4 + 7+4.

[3] M. Weiss, "Einiges über die Bauformen des Erzählens in der Bibel", *VT* 13 (1963), pp. 456-75, especially pp. 460ff., focused my attention on this literary form. See also R. Gordis, "Quotations as a literary Usage in Biblical, Oriental and Rabbinical Literature", *HUCA* 22 (1949), pp. 157-219. For Deut. xxxii 32-5, see C. J. Labuschagne, "The Song of Moses: Its Framework and Structure", *De Fructu Oris Sui, Essays in Honour of Adrianus van Selms* (Leiden, 1971), pp. 85-98.

whole, it is relatively easy to determine and to delimit precisely the words to be regarded as divine speech. So far I have come across two problems in this respect: first, the question whether the poetic utterances in Gen. viii 22 and ix 6 should be regarded as belonging to God's speech or not, and, second, the problem whether the ethnographic notices in Deut. ii 10-12 and 20-23 should be considered part of the divine speech.

The quotation in Gen. viii 22, which C. Westermann, for example, considers to be part of the divine speech, seems to me to be so detached from the divine speech, seeing its form, its position in the context and its contents, that it can better be regarded as a concluding remark by the narrator. I do not consider it part of the preceding divine speech. The utterance in ix 6 is different; being enveloped by other words spoken by God (in vs. 5 and in vs. 7), it cannot be separated from the rest of the divine speech. It should therefore be regarded as an integral part of the divine speech. The fact that God speaks here about himself in the 3rd person, is not exceptional: it occurs many times in the Pentateuch.[4] As a matter of fact, the majority of the divine speeches in the book of Leviticus are phrased in 3rd person singular, and so is a large section of the Decalogue (Deut. v 11-16), which nobody would consider a later addition. As for the ethnographic notices in Deut. ii, I consider them part of the divine speech, first, because they are completely enveloped by other divine words (as in Gen. ix 6) and, second, for a number of other reasons which I put forward in my paper read at the Louvain conference on Deuteronomy.

When it comes to the precise determination of the introductory divine speech formulas, there are no problems in the great majority of cases, where we have stereotyped phrases, but in some instances it is not immediately clear what the exact scope of the introductory formula is, e.g. Gen. i 22 *wayᵉbārek ʾōtām ʾᵉlōhîm lēʾmōr*—should the whole phrase or only *lēʾmōr* be regarded as the introductory formula? Or Gen. xv 1 *ʾaḥar haddᵉbārîm hāʾēlleh hāyāh dᵉbar-yhwh ʾel-ʾabrām bammaḥᵃzeh lēʾmōr.* The whole sentence has the function of introducing the divine speech that follows; do we here have an exceptionally long introductory formula or is it only: *hāyāh dᵉbar yhwh* ... *lēʾmōr*, or only *lēʾmōr*?

The divine speeches in the Pentateuch have either the form of the dialogue or that of the monologue. Since indirect speech, used in connec-

---

[4] E.g. Gen. ix 16, xvi 11, xviii 19, xix 13f., xxi 17; Ex. iii 12, iv 5, xix 21f., 24, xx 7, 10-2, xxiv 1, xxx 11-6, 34-8, xxxi 15, xxxiv 10, 14, 23f., 26; *passim* in Lev.; Deut. i 8, 36, ii 12, 21, v 11-6. In Deut. xxxii the references to YHWH between the divine speeches are part of the comment by the poet. The divine speeches are vss. 20-7, 32-5; 37-42; the poet's comments are in vss. 28-31 and 36. See the author's article referred to in the previous note.

tion with God, has not yet been studied systematically, I confined myself to studying direct speech only. So far as I am aware, very little research has been carried out up till now on the literary form of the *oratio recta* in general in the Old Testament, let alone more specifically on the divine *oratio recta.*[5] The divine monologue, however, has been the subject of studies by R. A. F. MacKenzie, who restricted himself to the book of Genesis, and by R. Lapointe.[6]

My own research on divine speech brought to light that there are altogether eleven divine monologues: seven in the primeval story (Gen. i 26, ii 18, iii 22, vi 3, vi 7, viii 21, xi 6f.), and four in the rest of the Pentateuch (Gen. xviii 17ff.; Ex. iii 17, xiii 17 and Deut. xxxii 20-27).[7] This is another example of the 7 + 4 pattern among many others, to some of which I have already referred in the two articles in *Vetus Testamentum.* That these eleven instances are not due to coincidence, but were deliberately constructed in this way to form a structural unity, will be demonstrated presently.

Fresh evidence for the existence of the 7 + 4 pattern, and support for the 7 + 7 pattern I discovered in Exodus-Numbers, came from an unexpected corner: by employing the method of logotechnical analysis, advanced by the Austrian scholar Claus Schedl.[8] This method involves the counting of the smallest syntactical units and assessing their number in the main-, and subordinate clauses, sentences, pericopes and larger literary units. I myself had been sceptical towards this method until I discovered that the divine speech formulas in the Pentateuch were given a careful structure and that the words constituting them were meticulously counted by the author(s) in order to fit them into fixed patterns. The weight of the evidence forced me to accept, and to regard as a fact, that word-counting was an essential part of the composition technique employed by the biblical writers. The fact dawned upon me that in ancient times texts, whether poetic or prose, were not composed in an off-

---

[5] Cf. O. Eissfeldt, *Einleitung in das Alte Testament* (3rd edn, Tübingen, 1964), par. 3; E. Sellin-G. Fohrer, *Einleitung in das Alte Testament* (Heidelberg, 1965), pp. 87f.; and N. P. Bratsiotis, "Der Monolog im Alten Testament", *ZAW* 73 (1961), pp. 30-70.

[6] R. A. F. MacKenzie, "The Divine Soliloquies in Genesis", *CBQ* 17 (1955), pp. 277--86; R. Lapointe, "The Divine Monologue as a Channel of Revelation", *CBQ* 32 (1970), pp. 161-81.

[7] I agree with Lapointe (p. 177), against MacKenzie, that Gen. i 26 should be included; further that the eighth monologue is Gen. xviii 17-9 (vss. 20f. are not part of the monologue, but the disclosure to Abraham in dialogue form). Lapointe does not mention Ex. iii 17 and xiii 17 and writes that in Deuteronomy YHWH always speaks in dialogue form—however, this is certainly not true of Deut. xxxii 20-7, which is a monologue (vss. 32-5, the second divine speech, are not a monologue, but a proclamation, and so is the third speech in vss. 37-42, where the people are addressed—cf. vs. 38).

[8] *Baupläne des Wortes, Einführung in die biblische Logotechnik* (Wien, 1974).

hand way, but were carefully constructed according to the rules of the established composition techniques of those days. Remarkably enough, biblical scholars readily accept this with regard to poetic texts, but when it comes to prose texts, they seem to be reluctant to face the facts. Historical-critical scholarship should accept and make use of this important new insight. It should become part and parcel of all serious methods of literary analysis. Having been born and bred myself in the historical-critical method, I have now accepted the principle of wordcounting and I consider it an essential tool, not only for literary analysis, but for all aspects of biblical study.

One of the many important insights, that emerged from the logotechnical analysis of biblical texts, is that certain numbers (not all) play an important role in the composition technique of biblical times. Since it is impossible to go into any details here, it must suffice to remind you of the frequent use of the number 7 in the Pentateuch,[9] and to focus attention upon two numbers that figure very prominently in connection with divine speech: 17 and 26. The significance of these numbers was completely unknown to me (and I think to most non-Jewish biblical scholars) until recently when I learned that these numbers symbolically represent the divine name YHWH: 26 is the sum of the numerical value of the four letters (10 + 5 + 6 + 5) and 17 seems to be the sum of the digits (1 + 5 + 6 + 5).[10]

---

[9] Cf. O. Goldberg, *Die fünf Bücher Mosis, ein Zahlengebäude* (Berlin, 1908), pp. 30-43.

[10] Cf. Schedl, p. 46. See Goldberg's work, who gives many examples of the addition of digits. The whole question of the origin of these numbers and the problem of the earliest use of the numerical value of letters is a subject for future study. I am not sure whether the numbers 17 and 26 only represent the divine name YHWH. In my opinion the biblical writers also had in mind the glory of YHWH, for both belong together: see Ex. xxxiii 17ff., where it is told that Moses asks to be shown God's Glory, whereupon God proclaims to him his Name (cf. e.g. also Isa. lxix 19). What is more, the numerical values of the word *kābōd* (*scriptio defectiva*) correspond exactly to those of the name YHWH:

scr. def.: Letter value: k = 20 + b = 2 + d = 4 = 26
Alphabet value: k = 11 + b = 2 + d = 4 = 17

The other form of the word, *kābôd* (*scr. plena*) has the following values:

scr. plena: Letter value: k = 20 + b = 2 + w = 6 + d = 4 = 32
Alphabet value: k = 11 + b = 2 + w = 6 + d = 4 = 23

The numbers 32 and 23 are the two basic numbers for the composition of a great number of texts, as Schedl has demonstrated convincingly in his works. They are the numbers of the *Tetraktys*, which has its origin in Babylonia. The Hebrews adopted this model, but, in my opinion, they subjected these numbers to their own symbolism: 32 and 23 are sacred numbers representing the glory of God. There is every reason to believe that the two divine numbers 17 and 26 were also associated with the *kābōd* symbolism. This means that all four sacred numbers, 17, 26, 23 and 32, which figure prominently in the composition technique of biblical times, represent the glory of God. Further study may prove whether this is correct. It is significant that the sum of the digits of both values in the *scr. def.* is 8, a number that figures prominently in Deuteronomy. Incidentally, 8 = 1 + 7 *and* 2 + 6. See

Having taken upon myself the laborious task of meticulously counting all the words constituting the divine monologues, I was amazed at the ultimate result: the total number of words in the introductory formulas (henceforth DSF) is 26 and the grand total of the words spoken by God (henceforth DS) during eleven self-consultations is 289, i.e. 17 × 17.[11]

The following synopsis shows the count and its results:

			DSF	DS
Genesis i 26	*wayyōʾmer*[1] *ʾᵉlōhîm*[2]	I	2	17
Genesis ii 18	*wayyōʾmer*[3] *yhwh*[4] *ʾᵉlōhîm*[5]	II	3	9
Genesis iii 22	*wayyōʾmer*[6] *yhwh*[7] *ʾᵉlōhîm*[8]	III	3	19
Genesis vi 3	*wayyōʾmer*[9] *yhwh*[10]	IV	2	13
Genesis vi 7	*wayyōʾmer*[11] *yhwh*[12]	V	2	20
Genesis viii 21	*wayyōʾmer*[13] *yhwh*[14] *ʾel-*[15] *libbô*[16]	VI	4	23
Genesis xi 6f.	*wayyōʾmer*[17] *yhwh*[18]	VII	2	28
Gen. xviii 17-19	*wᵉyhwh*[19] *ʾāmar*[20]	I	2	42
Exodus iii 17	*wāʾōmar*[21]	II	1	17
Exodus xiii 17	*kî*[22] *ʾāmar*[23] *ʾᵉlōhîm*[24]	III	3	7
Deut. xxxii 20-27	*wayyōʾmer*[25]	IV	1	
	first part (vss. 20-25)			74
	ʾāmartî[26]		1	
	second part (vss. 26-27)			20
			DSF 26	DS 289 (17 × 17)

This means that not only the phrasing of the introductory divine speech formulas, but also the number of words in the divine speeches were dictated by the number symbolism of the two divine numbers. At the same time, the number of words proves that the monologues in the Pentateuch were constructed as a structural unity. It is not yet the time to discuss the consequences of this discovery for our study of the growth of the Pentateuch, but the implications are enormous, to say the least. At the moment we are still at the very first stage of our investigation, i.e. that of discovering how these sections of the Pentateuch are constructed and what techniques were employed.

Let us explore some of the evidence about the use of this type of number symbolism in the texts where the divine speeches occur. We start with a few examples which can easily be checked and controlled by the reader. In Gen. xvi 11-12 the promise given by the angel to Hagar con-

Goldberg, pp. 10, 15, 28ff. He also gives an impressive survey of the Gematria in Gen. x 21-32 (pp. 1-10) and Ex. xvii 8-16 (pp. 11-28), two passages full to the brim with the numbers 17 and 26.

[11] I acknowledge the critical remarks I received from C. Schedl in this respect, and thank him for his encouragement and inspiration. I am indebted to Eep Talstra and Ferenc Postma of the "Werkgroep Informatika" at the Vrije Universiteit in Amsterdam, who kindly placed at my disposal the computer text of Exodus and Deuteronomy to check my counting.

cerning the child she was bearing is formulated in 26 words (= 12 + 14). This might be a mere coincidence, but in chapter xxi 17-18 the author uses once again 26 words to phrase the promise, and this time 14 + 12. In Gen. xxv 23 and xxvi 2-5 the oracle delivered to Rebekah contains 13 words and that to Jacob 55, together 68 (4 × 17). In Gen. xxviii 13-15, where God is said to speak to Jacob in a dream, the oracle consists of exactly 52 words (2 × 26). In Gen. xxxi 3, 11-13, where the story is told that God communicated with Jacob in Mesopotamia to tell him to return to Canaan, we count 51 (= 3 × 17) words spoken by God (7 + 1 + 20 + 23), and the rest of the divine speech addressed to Jacob in chapter xxxi amounts to 17 words (9 in vs. 24, and 8 in vs. 29), and, finally, when Jacob refers in his prayer (Gen. xxxii 10-13) to God's command and his promise, he quotes what God has spoken to him and uses 17 words (5 in vs. 10, and 12 in vs. 13). The total number of words spoken by God to Jacob in Mesopotamia amounts to 68 (= 4 × 17). The two other oracles given to Jacob are reported in Gen. xxxv 10-13 and in xlvi 3-4, and both are phrased in 26 words, in the ratio 13 + 13 (in xxxv 11 the promise of offspring: 13 words, in vs. 12 the promise of land: 13 words; in xlvi 3 the introduction and the promise of progeny in Egypt: 13 words, in vs. 4 God's promise "I will go down with you to Egypt, and I will also bring you up again; and Joseph's hand shall close your eyes": 13 words). In Gen. xlviii 4, where Jacob tells Joseph about God's promise, he quotes 14 divine words. This brings the total number of words spoken by God in the Joseph story to 42 (2 + 26 in chapter xlvi, and 14 here). Is it mere coincidence that the words in the introductory formulas amount to 9, bringing the total number of words in the DSFs and in the DS up to 51 (= 3 × 17)? In my opinion it is not, nor can the other examples given above simply be brushed aside as a matter of coincidence. On the contrary, at this stage of our investigation these examples alone warrant the conclusion that the divine numbers 17 and 26 (and their multiples) were a dominant factor in certain sections of the divine speeches in the book of Genesis.

It would be easy to multiply examples such as these from the whole Pentateuch, e.g. by looking at Gen. i 26 where God's self-consultation concerning the creation of man is formulated in 17 words, and by remarking that the total number of words in the introductory formulas up to this self-consultation is once again 17, and by drawing attention to the fact that in Ex. iii 16 the words God commanded Moses to speak to the elders number 17, and that the divine resolution in vs. 17 with regard to the fulfilment of the promise of land to the Israelites contains 17 words; further, that Ex. xix 3-8 teems with the divine number 17: vss. 3 and 5 and 8 each contain 17 words and the words spoken by God total 51

(= 3 × 17); moreover, that the third commandment is formulated in 17 words in both versions of the Decalogue (Ex. xx 7 and Deut. v 11), and that the sabbath-commandment in Deut. v 14 has 26 words,[12] while the Exodus version (Ex. xx 11) uses 26 words in the phrasing of the motivation of the commandment. There is an abundance of evidence to show that the profuse use of the divine numbers and their multiples is not restricted to the book of Genesis; they occur throughout the Pentateuch, and, as we shall see presently, especially in certain sections of it.

In order to explore the evidence further we shall now examine a few sections which can be checked easily. The first example is that of Ex. xv 25b-26, a section which many commentators assign to the Deuteronomists; it contains 34 words grouped as follows:

Narrative (vs. 25b)		7
DSF (vs. 26)		1
DS (vs. 26)		26
	Total	34 (= 17 + 17).

I have chosen this example deliberately, because we shall learn presently that the two divine numbers, 17 and 26, and their multiples turn up very frequently in certain sections of the Tetrateuch, and of course in Deuteronomy itself. The other example is Lev. xvii 10-14, one of the five passages in the book of Leviticus where the divine speech has a very personal tone, to which we shall return later. It contains 102 words (= 6 × 17) grouped as follows:

Prohibition (vs. 10)	22					
Motivation (vs. 11	18					
Introductory Formula (vs. 12a)			5	17		
Quotation of DS (vs. 12b)			12			
Instruction (vs. 13)	21					
Motivation (vs. 14a)	7					
Introductory Formula (vs. 14b)			3	17		
Quotation of DS (vs. 14cde)			14			
	68	+	34		=	102
	(4 × 17)	+	(2 × 17)		=	(6 × 17)

Total number of words in the DSFs	(5 + 3 = 8)
Total number of words in the DSs	(12 + 14 = 26)

These examples illustrate very clearly how the divine numbers were used as a composition technique to give structure to a passage and to delimit it

[12] In Deut. v 14 Schedl has discovered a very interesting structure, the "menorah-structure": 5 + 4 + 3 + 2 + 4 + 3 + 5 (p. 172). There are more examples of this structure in Deuteronomy, which I hope to publish in my forthcoming commentary on Deuteronomy.

as a separate unity within its context. We shall have occasion later on to focus closer attention upon this skilful literary device, which occurs very often in the Pentateuch, and which has, so far as I know, up till now escaped our notice.

I shall now proceed to give a survey of the use of the divine numbers (and their multiples) in the DSFs and the DSs in the book of Genesis. We start with the Primeval story, Gen. i-xi.

A count of the DSFs gives the following picture of the number of words:

Gen. i 1-25:	DSFs in the 1-7 cluster (including *qārāʾ*) (26)	
Gen. i 1-ii 25:	DSFs with *ʾāmar* in the 1-7 & 1-4 cluster	26
Gen. iii:	DSFs in the whole chapter (26)	
Gen. iii-iv:	DSFs in the whole section (1-7 & 1-4)	38
Gen. vi-ix:	DSFs in the Flood-story (36)	
Gen. vi-xi:	DSFs in the whole section (1-7 & 1-4)	38
Total number of	DFSs introducing DS	
	in the 7 + 4 + 7 + 4 + 7 + 4 pattern[13]	102
		(6 × 17)

When we count the number of words occurring in the seven phrases employing the verb *qārāʾ* with God as subject in Gen. i-xi we get 17. This means that the total number of words in the introductory formulas and in the *qārāʾ* phrases is 102 + 17 = 119 (7 × 17).

Counting the words of the DSs in the Primeval story, we get the following result:

Gen. i 1-25:	DS in the 7 cluster	84		
Gen. i 26-ii 25:	DS in the 4 cluster	104	(4 × 26)	
Gen. iii:	DS in the whole chapter	142	208	(8 × 26)
Gen. iv:	DS in the 4 cluster	66		
Gen. vi 1-ix 7:	DS in the 7 cluster	366		
Gen. ix 8-xi 9:	DS in the 4 cluster 128 + 28 =	156	(6 × 26)	
Total number DS in the Flood story 366 + 128 =			(494)	(19 × 26)
Total number DS in the Primeval story		918		

Total DSF and DS in the Primeval story	102	+	918	=	1020
	(6 × 17)	+	(54 × 17)	=	(60 × 17)

Turning now to the next major section of the book of Genesis, the Abraham cycle, the *tôlᵉdōt teraḥ* (Gen. xi 27-xxv 18), I refrain from giving all the details and restrict my survey to the most significant facts.[14]

---

13 The count includes *lēʾmōr* in i 22 and ii 16. The *lēʾmōr* in iii 17, however, is part of the DS, and must be excluded.

14 A full synopsis of the DSFs and DSs in the Pentateuch will be published in my book *Divine Speech in the Pentateuch*, at the moment in preparation.

In Gen. xii and xiii the words in the four introductory formulas of the 4 cluster add up to 17. In Gen. xviii the eleven DSFs in this 4 + 7 cluster have 17 words. The divine speeches in the 7 cluster in Gen. xx-xxi consist of 104 (4 × 26) words. The DSFs in the last 7 cluster of the Abraham cycle, Gen. xxii, and the three DSFs in Gen. xxiv right at the end of the *tôl*ᵉ*dōt teraḥ* have 13 words each, i.e. together 26. And finally, the total number of words spoken by God in the Abraham cycle is 901 (53 × 17).[15]

Coming to the Jacob cycle the *tôl*ᵉ*dōt yiṣḥāq*, Gen. xxv 19-xxxv 29, we can note only that the number of words spoken by God in the 4 cluster in Gen. xxv-xxviii is 136 (8 × 17), further that the seven DSFs in xxxi-xxxii make a total of 26 words, and that the words assigned to God in this section mount up to 85 (5 × 17). So far as I can see at the moment, there are no further examples of the use of the divine numbers in the Jacob cycle. The total number of divine words in this section, 300, is not a multiple of 17, contrary to what we found in the Primeval story as well as in the Abraham cycle. It is probable that the total number of words in the DSs and the DSFs is a multiple of 17, but it is very difficult to determine the DSFs precisely.

The Joseph cycle, the *tôl*ᵉ*dōt yaʿaqōb*, Gen. xxxvii 1-l 26, contains the last cluster of 4 DSFs.[16] The formulas yield 9 words, and together with the 42 divine words make a total of 51 (3 × 17).

The grand total of words spoken by God in the book of Genesis as a whole is: 918 + 901 + 300 + 42 = 2161, which is not a multiple of 17.

Our survey of divine speech in the book of Exodus will confirm what we found in Genesis. As a matter of fact the outcome of the count of the words spoken by God, and their introductory formulas, is even more striking. Here again I shall confine myself to the main results:

Ex. iii 4-22 with its nine(!)[17] introductory formulas has 17 words in the DSFs and 272 (16 × 17) words are spoken by God.[18] Together they give the perfect sum of 289 (17 × 17).

---

[15] The totals of the four 4 + 7 clusters are: 212 + 273 + 130 + 186 = 801. The 7 cluster at the end of the Abraham cycle, Gen. xxii 1-19, yields 95 words, and the DS in xxiv 7 another 5 words, which brings the total to 801 + 100 = 901. Because of the difficulty of knowing how to determine the precise scope of the DSFs, I refrain from giving a count of their number of words. Future study must reveal whether their number is a multiple of 17, as in the Primeval story, where the counting is relatively easy.

[16] The 7 + 4 cluster connects the Jacob cycle to the Joseph cycle, just as the Abraham cycle is joined to the Jacob cycle by the 7 + 4 cluster in Gen. xxii-xxviii.

[17] See the Synopsis in my article, cited in n. 1 above. The fact that a cluster of seven DSFs is "disturbed" by an eighth or ninth in one and the same pericope or section proves, in my opinion, that there an editorial hand added something to the text covered by the 7 cluster. I labelled these "D", for the DSs there teem with Deuteronomistic phrases and themes. See n. 36 below for a list of these "D-passages".

[18] The DSF *wāʾōmar* in Ex. iii 17 introduces God's resolution with regard to the exodus and the land giving, and is therefore a separate DSF, but, since it is also part of the DS, it

Ex. iv 1-17, where we have the second cluster of seven DSFs, is an amazingly skilful composition. The seven DSFs have 17 words,[19] the number of words spoken by God is 153 (9 × 17, which is also the sum of the numbers 1-17, a number well known from the New Testament: John xxi 11). Adding the words of the DSFs to the divine words, we get 170 (10 × 17). Moreover, God's reprimand to Moses (vs. 11) has 17 words, and his promise of guidance to Moses (vs. 12) has 9: together 17 + 9 = 26 —a good example of the combination of the two divine numbers, which occurs many times in the Pentateuch.[20]

Coming now to the next section of the book, iv 18-xxi 51, I can report that the number of words in the DSFs and in the DSs corroborates the 7 + 7 + 7 + 7 structure I proposed in the Synopsis of the DSFs:[21] the first part, the introduction, iv 18-vi 12, with its first cluster of seven DSFs consists of 234 words (DSF 45 + DS 189 = 234 = 9 × 26).[22]

The Exodus story itself starts in vi 13 with the second cluster of seven DSFs in vi 13,29-vii 29,[23] the third cluster in viii 1-ix 35 and the fourth cluster in x 1-xii 51. The total number of words in the introductory DSFs

---

is also counted as a word spoken by God. Double counting is not unknown (cf. Math. i 1-16, where there are three series of 14, but in the third Jeconiah, already mentioned in the second, is counted again), but still exceptional, and suspect. In Deut. xxxii 26 and 40 the two occurrences of *ʾāmartî* belong, in my opinion, to the DSs and are not again counted among the DSFs. The problem can be solved by reading (with the LXX) in Ex. iii 12 *wayyōʾmer ʾ^{e}lōhîm* (MT has only *wayyōʾmer*); then we get exactly 17 words in the seven DSFs in iii 4-14 without having to count *wāʾōmar* double. At the same time two other problems can be solved: first, the seventh (missing) instance of *ʾ^{e}lōhîm* in the DSFs in the book of Exodus is found (there are six others: iii 4, 14, iii 15, vi 2, xiii 17, xx 1); second, the 7 + 4 pattern of ELOHIM in the DSFs in Exodus-Numbers (the other four are all in Numb. xxii—see my Synopsis) can be completed. Since ELOHIM in Exodus and Numbers occurs in passages which are obviously Deuteronomistic, we must conclude that ELOHIM was introduced in Exodus-Numbers (at least in the DSFs) by the Deuteronomists. If our supposition is correct, then they were also responsible for the 7 + 4 pattern, particularly in Genesis, but also in the larger series of DSFs in the whole Pentateuch.

[19] This passage is a good example of how the principle of seven DSFs overruled the number of DSFs really needed in the context. The divine speech in vs. 4 is interrupted by the narrative in 4b, but it continues in vs. 5 without an introductory formula. The same happens in the DSs in vss. 7 and 8. The context needed nine DSFs, but the author used only seven, being bound to that number. There are many examples of extra DSFs being used in order to get seven in a particular context (e.g. Gen. ix 12,17, xv 5; Ex. iii 6, vi 2, xxxiii 20f., xxxiv 1, etc.).

[20] Other combinations are 26 + 8 = 34; 26 + 17 = 43. The way in which the numbers 26 and 34 are split is: 12 + 14 and 13 + 13; 17 + 17 and 15 + 19. The latter combination is very typical of the "land" texts in Deuteronomy.

[21] See the Synopsis in my article cited in n. 1, pp. 286f.

[22] The 45 words of the DSFs include the 17 words of the phrases in iv 28, 30, v 1.

[23] This section is interrupted by the genealogy in vi 14-27 and the editorial connecting phrase in vs. 28. These verses, 14-28, have a total number of 182 words, a multiple of 26 (7 × 26). In my opinion, this is not a priestly passage, but a "D-passage". See n. 36.

and the DSs in the three 7 clusters of the Exodus story amounts to 1300 (50 × 26): DSF 34 + 30 + 42 = 106 and DS 249 + 320 + 625 = 1194. The Exodus story with its introduction consists of 234 + 1300 = 1534 words (59 × 26).

We now turn to the next cluster (the seventh in Exodus) of seven DSFs in xiv 1-xvii 7, a section enveloped by two "D-passages", viz. xiii 1-19 and xvii 8-16. This section also contains the short "D-passage", xv 25b-26, to which I have referred above, and which should be excluded from the count. The outcome of the counting of the words in the DSFs is as follows: DSFs 34 (2 × 17) and DSs 238 (14 × 17) together 272 (16 × 17). It is important to note that not only the short "D-passage" in xv 25b-26, with its total of 34 words (2 × 17) including the narrative part, but also the "D-passage" at the end of the whole section, viz. xvii 8-16, with its total of 119 words (7 × 17) again including the narrative, is dominated by the divine number 17. Even more striking is the fact that the story of the call of Moses in iii 4-iv 17 and the desert story (xiv-xvii) are dominated by the divine number 17, whereas in the whole Exodus story (with its introduction) 26 is the dominant number. Because of this the Exodus story can be delimited precisely.

The next series of seven clusters of seven DSFs start in chapter xix and end in chapter xl, including the two Sinai-sections, in my view the most complicated part of the whole book of Exodus. In the present context it is impossible to discuss any details, but I can report that my study of the DSFs and of the DSs sheds new light on the problems we encounter here. Let us first survey the results of the count and give some initial comments and draw a few preliminary conclusions.

In the first Sinai section, Ex. xix-xxiv, I have counted all the words (including the narrative parts) and this is the result:

xix 1-25	375 (*sic*: N.B. 374 = 22 × 17)[24]
xx 1-26	312 (12 × 26)
xxi 1-xxiv 18	1462 (86 × 17).

This seems to be an indication of the unity of chapters (xix ? and) xxi-xxiv on the basis of the fact that the grand total of words is a multiple of 17. The whole chapter xx has in its total number of words a multiple of 26. This implies that the Decalogue and its immediate continuation could be

[24] It is indeed remarkable that the number of words in chapter xix is just one above the multiple of 17. In view of the frequent occurrence of multiples of 17, this is suspect. Is there a word too many in the MT? If so, the total number of words in the whole book would not change, on condition that our supposition that the word ELOHIM is missing in iii 12 (see n. 18) is correct. To prove that this is so, one has to probe deeper into the logotechnical aspects of the book.

secondary to chapter xix and xxi-xxiv, which supports E. W. Nicholson's view that the Decalogue and its related verses were incorporated into the Sinai narrative at a relatively late time.[25] The number of introductory DSFs in xix-xxiv (8 or even 9 if we consider the *lēʾmōr* in xix 3 as the first DSF)[26] might produce additional evidence for the secondary character of the Decalogue chapter: two of the nine DSFs in the cluster must belong to a later addition. On the basis of the evidence that the whole Decalogue chapter (with a multiple of 26 in its total number of words) is the exception in its context (having a multiple of 17), we can argue that the two DSFs in vs. 1 and vs. 22 are secondary. In that case the original cluster of seven DSFs in xix-xxiv must be redefined: 1 = xix 3a, 2 = xix 9, 3 = xix 10, 4 = xix 21, 5 = xix 24, 6 = xxiv 1, and 7 = xxiv 12.

We cannot pursue this matter any further here, for we must continue our survey of the results of the count of the DSFs and the DSs in xix-xxiv.

xix 3-8	DSF 1		DS 51	total 52 (D?)
xix 9-xx 21	DSF 22	} 26	DS 232	total 254
xx 22-26	DSF 4		DS 69	total 73
xxi 1-xxiii 33	— —		DS 1210	total 1210
xxiv 1-14	DSF 7		DS 27	total 34 (D?)
Grand total	DSF 34		DS 1589	total 1623

Further study must reveal whether we can draw any conclusions from this information, and, if so, what. At first glance one can see that the "D-passage" xix 3-8 has a multiple of 26 or 17 in the total number of words in the DSF and the DS.[27] One can also observe that the DSFs in xix 9-xx 26 yield 26 words, and that the grand total of DSFs in xix-xxiv amounts to 34. This is no coincidence, in my opinion, but it shows that whatever was added to the more original text was very carefully integrated in accordance with the number of words dictated by the number symbolism in the divine numbers.

With regard to the first Tabernacle section in Ex. xxv-xxxi, it is interesting to note that the total number of words in the seven DSFs is 34. This is a fine example of how the divine number dictates variation in stereotyped formulas: seven 5-word formulas would yield 35 words, but, in order to get 34, one of the stereotyped *lēʾmōr*s was omitted in one of the

[25] "The Decalogue as the direct address of God", *VT* 27 (1977), pp. 422-33.

[26] This is the only instance in the Pentateuch of *wayyiqrāʾ* followed by *lēʾmōr* introducing a DS. The introductory formula proper is, however, *lēʾmōr.* I overlooked this when I prepared the Synopsis, but it must be corrected: *lēʾmōr* is the first DSF in the 7 cluster. See further below.

[27] This goes for xxiv 1-14 too, which contains a "D-passage", vss. 3-8. The DSFs in vss. 1 and 2 yield 7 words, and the two DSs 27 words, giving a total of 34 DSF/DS.

phrases, in xxx 34.[28] The number of words assigned to God in this section (3073) is not a multiple of one of the divine numbers.

As to the second Tabernacle section, Ex. xxxv-xl, I can report that the last chapter is teeming with the divine numbers: 17 words are used to describe how Moses put the testimony in the ark (vs. 20); again, 17 words are used for a description of how Moses put the golden altar in the tent of meeting and burned incense upon it (vss. 26f.); in 34 words it is told that Moses installed the water basin (vss. 30-32); the whole passage containing the seven stereotyped, refrain-like references to God's command (vss. 17-33) has 208 words (8 × 26); and, last but not least, the very last passage in Exodus (vss. 34-38) has 60 words, of which 26 are used to describe that the cloud and the glory filled the tent (vss. 34-35) and 34 to tell what the function of the cloud and the fire was with regard to the desert journey of the Israelites (vss. 36-38).[29]

Returning to the second Sinai section, Ex. xxxii-xxxiv, we find that in the first part, xxxii 1-xxxiii 11 (delimited by the first cluster of seven DSFs) the two DSs in xxxii 7-10 have 31 + 20 = 51 words (3 × 17); the two quotations of DS by Moses in xxxii 13 and 27 yield 14 + 20 = 34 words (2 × 17); the two DSs in xxxiii 1-3 and 5 have 47 + 21 = 68 words.

When we look at the second part of this Sinai section, xxxiii 12-xxxiv 35, we see that the whole passage is teeming with the divine number 17: The first two DSs in xxxiii 14 and 17 expressing God's intention to let his Presence accompany Moses have 17 words. In vs. 21, where God speaks about the place in the rock were Moses can hide, the DS is made up of 26 words; the next DS in xxxiv 1-3, where God commands Moses to go up the mountain with the two stone tablets, has 51 words (3 × 17).

The passage that follows, xxxiv 5-26, contains two DSs, one introduced by *wayyiqrāʾ* (vss. 6-7) and the other by *wayyōʾmer* (vss. 10-26): the latter is made up of 238 words (14 × 17), the former has 32 words, but together with the two DSFs the total amounts to 272 (16 × 17). This seems to suggest that vss. 5-26 is a separate literary unit (a "D-passage"?), the more so because the narrative about the two stone tablets, that was interrupted in xxxiv 4, clearly continues in vss. 27ff.,

---

[28] Another clear example is the second series of seven stereotyped five-word DSFs *wayᵉdabbēr yhwh ʾel-mōšeh lēʾmōr* in Ex. xxx 11, 17, 22; xxxi 1, xxxii 7, xxxiii 1, xl 1, where *lēʾmōr* was obviously left out in xxxiii 1 to obtain 34 words. The first series of this phrase, however, has 35 words (vi 10, 13, 29, xiii 1, xiv 1, xvi 11, xxv 1)—see the Synopsis for these 14 instances of this phrase in the book of Exodus. There are altogether 14 instances of *lēʾmōr* in the DSFs in Exodus (see my article cited in n. 2).

[29] This passage is a fine specimen of literary composition technique. To mention just one peculiarity: the chiastic construction in the number of references to the "cloud", the "glory", the "tent" and the idea of *(m)škn*, 5 + 2 + 2 + 5; both combinations add up to 7; moreover, the roots *ʿlh* (3 ×) and *nsʿ* (4 ×) together occur 7 times.

where it is said that Moses was commanded by God to write down the Ten Words on the new tablets. If 5-26 is excluded, then the seventh DSF in this cluster, which I formerly held to be in xxxiv 10 (see the Synopsis, p. 289, which must now be corrected), must be the one in vs. 27. Consequently, the number of words in the seven DSFs amounts to exactly 17. The whole passage xxxiii 12-xxxiv 29 (excluding the "D-passage" in xxxiv 5-26 containing the two extra DSFs) yields 23 words in the introductory DSFs (including the two formulas introducing the two quotations at the beginning) and 147 in the DSs, which amounts to 170 (10 × 17). This suggests that the original text was xxxiv 1-4, 27-29, which forms a coherent unity, and it shows that vss. 5-26 were added later in such a way that a new creation was produced.

Turning now to the book of Leviticus, we must restrict ourselves and focus attention upon only five passages, which are characterized by the use of the first person singular and by the fact that the divine speech they contain has a very personal quality. They can easily be detected in their context because of these typical characteristics. In contradistinction to the rest of the book, these passages exhibit a syntactical relationship with the introductory DSFs:[30] God addresses Moses (or Moses and Aaron) and refers to the Israelites either in the third person plural, or in the second person plural. We are concerned with the following passages: xi 44-45, xiv 33-35, xvi 1ff., xvii 10-14, and chapters xviii-xxvi.

Having subjected them to a superficial, but nevertheless accurate, logotechnical analysis, I found that they are all, unlike their context, dominated by the divine number 17, in the following way:

Lev. xi 44-45, containing the motivation for the dietary laws, is made up of exactly 34 words. It reads:

> Because I, YHWH, am your God, you shall make yourselves holy and keep yourselves holy, for I am holy. You shall not defile yourselves with any teeming creature that creeps on the ground. Because I, YHWH, am the one who brought you up from the land of Egypt to become your God, you shall keep yourselves holy, for I am holy.

In Lev. xiv 33-35, where the rule is given that, in case of an infection, the owner of the infected house shall report it to the priest, we again count 34 words (the rest of the chapter is devoted to the actions to be taken by the priest):

> YHWH spoke to Moses and Aaron: When you have entered the land of Canaan which I give you to occupy, if I inflict an infection upon a house in the

[30] See D. W. Baker, "Division markers and the structure of Leviticus 1-7", *Studia Biblica 1978* I (Sheffield, 1979), pp. 9-15.

land you have occupied, its owner shall come and report to the priest that there appears to him to be a patch of infection in his house.

Chapter xvi contains the ritual of atonement. It opens with a long DSF, phrased in general terms (vs. 1), followed immediately by a more specific introductory DSF, which ushers in God's warning to Aaron not to enter the sanctuary except at the appointed time. Taken together, the two DSFs are made up of 17 words. It reads:

> YHWH spoke to Moses after the death of Aaron's two sons, who died when they drew near before YHWH. And YHWH said to Moses: Tell your brother Aaron that he must not enter the sanctuary within the Veil, in front of the cover over the Ark, at all times, lest he die, for I appear in the cloud above the cover.

In the rest of the passage it strikes one that certain parts of the ritual are made up of 17 words: vs. 11 dealing with the slaughtering of the bull; vs. 12 where it is prescribed that Aaron shall prepare the incense; vs. 13 containing the prescription to burn the incense; vs. 14 dealing with the sprinkling of the bull's blood; vs. 16 containing the prescription concerning the making of expiation by Aaron for the sanctuary and the tent; and vs. 33, dealing with the act of expiation by the legitimate priest.

Chapter xvii 10-14, the passage to which I have referred earlier, has 102 words (6 × 17) of which 68 (4 × 17) constitute the prohibitions with regard to the eating of blood, and 34 (2 × 17) are used in the two sections where God quotes himself (vss. 12 and 14).

Finally, my count of the words in the Holiness Code itself, chapters xviii-xxvi,[31] gives the following result: the total number of words in the DSFs (in xviii 1 together with the two clusters of seven DSFs in xix-xxvi) add up to 81. The words spoken by God amount to 3948, bringing the total number of words in the Holiness Code to 4029, which is a multiple of 17 (237 × 17).

The results of our preliminary study of these five passages warrant the conclusion that they were composed as a structural unity. The first four, up to chapter xvii, serve as a prelude to the Holiness Code, which is itself a literary unit.

With regard to divine speech in the book of Numbers I must restrict myself to a few remarks illustrating the continuous use of the divine numbers as a technique for composing in this book too. Since I have not yet completed my logotechnical analysis, what I offer here is nothing more than an impression.

---

[31] In my opinion, Lev. xvii is not an integral part of the Holiness Code, but belongs to the prelude.

The very first, exceptionally long DSF in i 1 is made up of 17 words. The phrasing of God's command to number the whole community in i 2 does not seem to have been influenced by the divine number 17, but in xxvi 2 God's command to conduct the census is made up of precisely 17 words, and God's instructions concerning the apportioning of the land (vss. 52-56) are made up of 34 words: 17 words for the general instruction (vss. 53f.), and once again 17 words for the instruction to use the lot (vss. 55f.).

In the passage about the death of Aaron, Numb. xx 22-29, the DS consists of 43 words (17 + 26).[32] In the introduction to the Balaam story, xxi 32-xxii 1, the narrative telling how Moses sent men to explore the city of Jazer has 26 words, and the DS in which God promises Moses the victory consists of exactly 26 words. It is certainly not a mere coincidence that the total number of words in the last seven DSs in the book of Numbers, which deal mainly with the land, together with their introductory DSFs, amounts to a multiple of 17 (907 + 45 = 952 i.e. 56 × 17).[33] The passages in the book of Deuteronomy dealing with the sending of explorers to the land and with the land itself are literally teeming with the divine numbers.[34]

We conclude this short survey of the book of Numbers by referring to the two passages I ventured to label "Deuteronomistic" on the basis of the structure of the DSFs (see my Synopsis, pp. 293f.). Both have a multiple of the divine number in the number of words. The first one, the narrative about Balaam's ass in Numb. xxii 22-35, is made up of 238 words (14 × 17); and the second, the passage in xxvii 12-23, where it is told how God announced to Moses his death and commanded him to instal Joshua, consists of 130 words (5 × 26): the first part (vss. 12-14) has 43 words (17 + 26),[35] and the concluding narrative about Joshua's installation (vss. 22f.) is made up of 26 words.

The great majority of all the "D-passages"[36] we have noticed from Ex. iii to Numb. xxvii have one thing in common: their total number of

---

[32] Together with the DSF the number of words used in connection with divine speech is 56. The narrative part, vss. 22, 27-9, has exactly the same number of words.

[33] This number depends upon the decision to consider the words of Numb. xxxiv 29 part of the DS with regard to the list of the chiefs who were to assign the territories.

[34] Cf., e.g., Deut. i 24f. (9 + 17 = 26); i 35f. (15 + 19 = 34); i 38f. (15 + 19 = 34); likewise iii 35f., vii 5f., 25f.; see also ii 14, 16-9, 20-3, 26-30, iii 8, 12b-13a, 16, 21, and the DS in iii 26b-27, etc.

[35] I.e. DSF 4 + DS 33 + geographical remark 6 = 43. The DS together with the geographical remark yields 39 words, a number that occurs very frequently in Deuteronomy; no wonder, for it is the letter value of *yhwh ᵓeḥād*. For the many instances, see my forthcoming commentary.

[36] These passages are: Ex. iii 15-7; iv 14-28; xiii 1-19, xv 25b-26, xvii 8-16, xix 3-8, xx 1-26, xxiv 3-8, xxxiv 5-26; Lev. xi 44f., xiv 33-5, xvi 1ff., xvii 10-4, xviii-xxvi; Numb. xxii

words is a multiple of either 17 or 26, which renders them recognizable in their context. Deeper probing must show whether they form a structural unity and what their relationship is with Deuteronomy. This is a subject for future study.

Lack of time and space forbids me to go into further detail with regard to divine speech in the Tetrateuch. We must leave it at that, and turn to the book of Deuteronomy to complete our survey. I restrict myself here to giving only the outcome of the count, and refer the reader to the paper that I read at the Louvain conference on Deuteronomy.[37]

There are 30 different divine speeches in Deuteronomy altogether,[38] spread over the book as follows:

i-iii	10 DSs	DSF 31	+ DS 463	= 494	(19 × 26)
		52			
iv-xi	10 { 8 DSs	DSF 21	+ DS 358	= 379	442 (17 × 26)
xii-xxvi	2 DSs	DSF 6	+ DS 57	= 63	
		(58)		936	(36 × 26)
xxvii-xxxiv	10 DSs	DSF 26	+ DS 465	= 491	
	Total:	DSF 84	+ DS 1343	= 1427	
			DS 1343 (79 × 17).		

These numbers speak for themselves. The total number of words in the "historical prologue" (i-iii) is a multiple of 26, and so is it in the "introduction to the law" (iv-xi) and in the "law" itself (xii-xxvi); here, however, it is the perfect number 17 × 26. The total number of words spoken by God in the whole book is a multiple of the other divine number 79 × 17.[39]

22-35; xxvii 12-23. This does not mean that the list is complete. The D-redaction of the Tetrateuch has to be restudied on the basis of this evidence.

[37] "Divine Speech in Deuteronomy", *Bibliotheca Ephemeridum Theologicarum Lovaniensium* 61 (1984).

[38] This includes the only example of divine "performative" or "subjective" speech in the Pentateuch (see n. 3), Deut. xxxii 32-5, without any introductory formula. I did not count the two *ʾāmartî* in vss. 26 and 40, for they belong to the DSs.

[39] It is worth while to focus attention upon the following: a) The only two DSs in the "law section", xii-xxvi, together with their DSFs yield a total of 63 words. This is no coincidence, for 63 is typical of the law (the opening passage of the "law section" in Deuteronomy, xii 1-3, and the concluding passage, xxvi 16-9, both consist of 63 words; and it is known that the Mishnah and Talmud have 63 tractates); see Schedl, p. 50. b) The first two series of 10 speeches have 31 + 27 = 58 words in the introductory DSFs. This number is the sum of the letter value of *k^{e}bôd yhwh* (32 + 26). The third series have 26 words in the introductory DSFs. c) The total number of words in all the introductory DSFs is 84, i.e. one short of 85 (5 × 17), in which case the total would have been: DSF 85 + DS 1343 = 1428 = 84 × 17. But instead of having chosen for the number symbolism in the grand total, the writers have chosen for the symbolism in the sub-sections of the book — one cannot have both.

The evidence gleaned from the counting of the words seems to support my judgement that the "ethnographic" sections in ii 10-12, 20-23 should be considered part of the DSs in which they are included, and that the "3rd person" sections (e.g. in i 8,36) cannot be excluded.[40] In addition to this, the fact that the total number of words reportedly spoken by God (1343) is a multiple of 17 testifies to the unity of the book.

Having concluded the survey of the logotechnical form of the DSFs and the DSs in the Pentateuch, I shall now draw my main conclusions:

1. Evaluating the evidence at this stage of my investigation, I cannot escape the impression that the use of the divine numbers 17 and 26 was a technique employed specifically by the Deuteronomists, and, consequently, that there was a radical redaction by the Deuteronomists of the Tetrateuch at the time when the book of Deuteronomy was fused with it to form the literary unity now known as the Pentateuch.

2. It has now been established beyond any doubt that these authors employed certain symbolic numbers as a composition technique, and that this involves meticulous counting of words. For biblical scholars this has as a necessary consequence that we must take this counting seriously, for, if we do not, we shall never really understand their writings. Word counting is one of the most objective criteria to use in the literary analysis of biblical texts.

3. The weight of the evidence adduced proves conclusively that the Jewish Cabbala and more particularly Gematria have their roots unmistakably in the biblical text. In fact, the writers of the Pentateuch were familiar with them and made use of them. The later development of both literary devices, which brought them into the speculative sphere, should not deter us from taking genuine biblical symbolism, including number symbolism, seriously. A proper evaluation of number symbolism will guard us against rationalizing symbolical numbers in the Bible.[41]

---

[40] Deut. xxxii is a different case; see nn. 3 and 4.

[41] A typical example of western rationalizing of symbolic numbers in the Bible is the literal interpretation of the high life spans of biblical figures. All these numbers are symbolic. For the explanation of the life spans of the antediluvian fathers, see now C. Schedl, ""Der brennende Dornbusch", der Kosmos als Erscheinungsbild Gottes", *Kosmopathie, Imago Mundi* 8 (Innsbruck, 1981), pp. 677-711, 697-700. As to the life spans of the patriarchs, I discovered that they all derive from the divine number 17:

Abraham	$175 = 7 \times 5 \times 5$	and	$7 + 5 + 5 = 17$
Isaac	$180 = 5 \times 6 \times 6$	and	$5 + 6 + 6 = 17$
Jacob	$147 = 3 \times 7 \times 7$	and	$3 + 7 + 7 = 17$
Joseph	$110 = 1 \times 25 + 36 + 49$	and	$1 + 17 + 17 + 17 = 52 = 2 \times 26$.

Moreover, the letter values of Isaac, Jacob and Joseph are multiples of 26:

4. The fact that the divine number 17 and 26 are so frequently, though not exclusively, used in connection with divine speech in the Pentateuch, bears witness to the extreme care with which the authors surrounded their writing about God's speaking.[42] It also attests the theological function they gave to these numbers, which were meant to symbolize the presence of God through his "name" and his "glory", not only in his speaking to men and in the events described in the text, but also in the written text itself. It was a literary device to let the divine presence manifest itself. I call this process latent theology.

5. The way in which the Torah was constructed, its intricate patterns and its ingenious structures, which have now become visible again to us, was certainly not common knowledge in biblical times. The esoteric character of this kind of knowledge implies that it was reserved for the circle of the initiated, i.e. the priests responsible for the construction of the Pentateuch (and other writings). They employed this device for theological reasons, for the benefit of God, so to speak, not for the benefit of the common people.

In my opinion, the difficult text in Deut. xxix 28 should be interpreted in this light:

> *hannistārōt l^e^yhwh ʾ^e^lōhênû w^e^hanniglōt lānû ûl^e^bānênû*
> *ʿad ʿôlām laʿ^a^śôt ʾet-kol-dibrê hattôrāh hazzōʾt*
> The hidden things are for YHWH our God,
> the revealed things are for us and our children for ever,
> that we may do all the words of this law.

In Codex Leningrad B19A there are 10 *puncta extraordinaria* above the words *lānû ûl^e^bānênû* and in the massora it is noted that *hannistārōt* and *w^e^hanniglōt* are written defectively. The precise significance of the points is still unknown, so far as I am aware, but I noticed that the sum of the digits of the letter value of these letters is exactly the same as the sum of

---

Isaac	10 + 90 + 8 + 100	= 208 (8 × 26)
Jacob	10 + 70 + 100 + 2	= 182 (7 × 26)
Joseph	10 + 6 + 60 + 80	= 156 (6 × 26).

I have prepared an article on this subject, in which I take the arguments of Stanley Gevirtz and James G. Williams (see *JBL* 96 [1977], pp. 570-1; 98 [1979], pp. 86-7) a step further. See C. J. Labuschagne, "Number Symbolism in the Life Spans of the Patriarchs". A good specimen of number symbolism in the lives of the patriarchs can be found in Gen. xlvii 28, where it is told in 17 words that "Jacob stayed in Egypt for 17 years and lived to be 147 years old". If one rationalizes this, one misses the whole point.

[42] The insight that they meticulously weighed and counted their words, sheds new light on the injunction in Deut. iv 2 and xiii 1 not to add to or detract from "the word I command you". The real purpose of the so-called "canonical formula" was to preserve the intricate structures of the text.

the digits of the value according to their position in the alphabet: both are 42.

As to the two defectively written words, it is striking to note that here also both numbers of both words are exactly the same: 26.

Sum of the digits of the letter value:
$h = 5 + n = 50 + s = 60 + t = 400 + r = 200 + t = 400 \quad = 26$
$w = 6 + h = 5 + n = 50 + g = 3 + l = 30 + t = 400 \quad = 26$

Sum of the digits according to alphabet value:
$h = 5 + n = 14 + s = 15 + t = 22 + r = 20 + t = 22 \quad = 26$
$w = 6 + h = 5 + n = 14 + g = 3 + l = 12 + t = 22 \quad = 26$

This is probably the reason why attention was drawn to these words: they were considered extremely sacred, for they contain the key to the coded message. Their concealed meaning is now plain.[43] The code is broken, the message understood.

It does not mean, however, that the last word has been said about the hidden things and the revealed things in the Pentateuch.

---

[43] Significantly enough this verse contains the very last instance of the phrase *yhwh ʾelōhênû*, which occurs 23 times in Deuteronomy (see n. 10 for the explanation of the significance of the number 23 as the numerical representation of the *kebôd yhwh*). The phrase has been carefully distributed over the book:

i-iii 10 ×; iv-vi 10 ×; xxix 3 ×.

Moreover, the 17th instance is precisely in the central confession of faith in vi 4: *šemaʿ yiśrāʾēl yhwh ʾelōhênû yhwh ʾeḥād*. There is an exact parallel to this literary device in the 23 occurrences of the verb *qārāʾ* with YHWH as subject: the 17th instance is in Ex. xxxiii 19, where God proclaims to Moses his Name, when Moses asks to be shown his Glory: *weqārātî bešēm yhwh lepāneka*, "I shall proclaim the YHWH name to you". This is no coincidence, neither is the fact that the term *qārāʾ bešēm yhwh*, "to invoke YHWH by name" occurs 17 times—see *THAT* II, col. 673. The study of number symbolism in connection with *šēm* and *kābōd* is a subject for a separate monograph.

MESSIANISM AND SEPTUAGINT

BY

JOHAN LUST

Leuven

In his book on Royal Messianism, J. Coppens ascertains that the Septuagint shows signs of a developing messianism. He refers to Isa. vii 14, ix 1-5; Ps. xc 3.[1] Many others seem to share this conviction.[2] The list collecting the passages adduced in favour of the messianizing tendencies in the LXX is impressive: Gen. iii 15, xlix 10; Num. xxiv 7,17; 2 Sam. vii 16; Isa. vii 14, ix 5-6, xi 4, xiv 29-32; Ez. xxi 30-32, xliii 3; Dan. vii 13; Hos. viii 10; Amos iv 13; Zech. ix 10; Ps. cx 3.[3] To this list one could add two verses which are often overlooked in the debate although they played an important role in the early Christian literature: Lam. iv 20 and Ez. xvii 23.[4]

There appear to be a considerable number of stray references to a messianic exegesis in the LXX. However, as far as I know, a critical com-

[1] *Le messianisme royal* (Paris, 1968), p. 119. According to the author, a comparison between the Hebrew and the Greek texts shows an evolution towards a more personal, supernatural, transcendent messianism. In *Le messianisme et sa relève prophétique* (Gembloux, 1974), p. 149, his thesis remains more vague: "The analysis of the Greek version of the Septuagint displays numerous traces of a continuous development."

[2] I. L. Seeligmann, *The Septuagint Version of Isaiah. A discussion of Its Problems* (Leiden, 1948), pp. 118-20, underlines the Hellenistic overtones of the messianic interpretation of the LXX in Isa. vii 14, ix 5-6, xi 4; S. Mowinckel, *He that Cometh* (Oxford, 1956), pp. 303-4; G. Bertram, "Preparatio evangelica", *VT* 7 (1957), pp. 225-49, esp. p. 232; J. Coste, "La première expérience de traduction biblique: la Septante", *Maison Dieu* 14 (1958), pp. 56-88, esp. p. 75, refers not only to the classical *loci* such as Gen. iii 15 and Is. vii 14 but also to Isa. xiv 29-32; R. Tournay, "Le psaume CX", *RB* 67 (1960) pp. 5-41, esp. p. 15-16, not only refers to Ps. cx but also to Ps. lxxii; R. A. Martin, "The Earliest Messianic Interpretation of Gen. 3 15", *JBL* 84 (1965), pp. 425-7; J. Schreiner, "Hermeneutische Leitlinien in der Septuaginta", *Die Hermeneutische Frage in der Theologie* (Wien, Freiburg, 1968), pp. 361-94, esp. p. 375. U. Kellermann, *Messias und Gesetz* (Neukirchen, 1971), pp. 53-4, refers to Gen. xlix 10; Num. xxiv 7,17; Isa. ix 5; Amos iv 13; Zech. ix 10; A. S. van der Woude, *TWNT* 9 (Stuttgart, 1973), pp. 501-2, adds several texts to the dossier, esp. Hos. viii 10; J. Becker, *Messiaserwartung im AT* (Stuttgart, 1977), p. 85, refers to Martin and Kellerman; L. Monsengwo-Pasinya, "Deux textes messianiques de la Septante: Gn 49, 10 et Ez 21,32", *Biblica* 61 (1980), pp. 357-76; D. Barthélemy, *Critique textuelle de l'AT* I (Fribourg, Göttingen, 1982), p. 246, finds a "processus de messianisation" in the LXX of 2 Sam. vii 16.

[3] For Dan. vii 13 see W. Bousset, *Die Religion des Judentums* (2nd edn, Berlin, 1906), p. 303-4. For the other references see n. 2 above.

[4] See also Ez. xvi 4 in LXX A-544 and Cant. i 7 in LXX S.

prehensive study of this theme has not yet appeared.[5] It is my intention here to give, first, some preliminary methodological remarks on such a study, and, second, to engage you in the analysis of one proof text: Ez. xxi 30-32.

Before we begin our critical investigation it may be useful to provide a tentative definition of messianism.[6] Messianism is the expectation of an individual human and yet transcendent saviour. He is to come in a final eschatological period and will establish God's Kingdom on earth. In a more strict sense, messianism is the expectation of a royal Davidic saviour at the end time.

A. General Preliminary Remarks

1. *Systematic Approach.*

When trying to defend the thesis of the "messianizing" character of the LXX, one should avoid arbitrary selections of proof texts. One should not overlook the many passages in the Greek version where a "messianizing" translation might have been expected but where it is not given.[7] Indeed, many Hebrew texts receiving a messianic interpretation in the Targumim[8] are translated literally by the LXX without any added messianic exegesis. Neither should one overlook those texts in which the messianic connotation has been weakened or given a different nuance by the LXX. Among the latter, several series can be distinguished.

---

[5] This is the more amazing when one notices that the thesis of the more outspoken messianic character of the LXX is not new at all. It was already implied in the repeated accusations of early Christian authors against their Jewish antagonists. According to the Christians, the Jews tampered with the sacred text, removing or altering the passages in which the coming of the messiah was announced. The accusation is most explicit in Justin's Dialogue with Trypho. For the Christians, the sacred text was identified with the Greek translation of the LXX used in the Church. The Jewish used the Hebrew text or their own more literal translations. The superiority of the LXX was still defended by Vossius in his *De Septuaginta* (Amsterdam, 1685), p. 18. R. Simon opposes Vossius saying that Jews merely wished to present the original text of the Bible. In favour of the early Christian authors such as Justin, Simon calls to mind that for them the LXX was the only official text they knew of, since they could not read the Hebrew original (*Histoire Critique* [Amsterdam, 1685], pp. 101-6).

[6] See Coppens, *Le messianisme royal*, pp. 11-15. Other possible definitions are not excluded. However, for the clarity of the argument it is better to have a clear-cut definition. Cp. S. H. Levey, *The Messiah. An Aramaic Interpretation* (Cincinnati, 1974), pp. xviii f.

[7] Compare with the debate concerning the anthropomorphisms in the LXX and H. M. Orlinsky's remarks on the topic. See J. Lust, "The Demonic Character of Jahweh in the Septuagint of Isaiah", *Bijdragen* 40 (1979), pp. 2-14, esp. 2-3, n. 4.

[8] Handy lists of messianic passages in the Targumim can be found in Elias Levita, *Lexicon Chaldaicum* (Isnae, 1541), and in J. Buxtorf, *Lexicon Chaldaicum, Talmudicum et Rabbinicum* (reprinted Leipzig, 1865). See also Levey.

The first series is characterized by a "collectivizing" interpretation. Isa. xlii 1 offers a good example.[9] The Hebrew original allows or even suggests the identification of the Servant-Messiah as an individual: "Behold my servant whom I uphold, my chosen, in whom my soul delights" (*RSV*). The LXX definitely opts in favour of a collective interpretation: "Jacob is my servant, I will help him; Israel is my chosen, my soul has accepted him". A similar "collectivizing" tendency may be discovered in Isa. iv 2, xlix 1-6. Mic. v 2; Ps. lxxxix 4.[10] It converges with a trend traceable in some post-exilic Hebrew texts.[11]

The second series, partly coinciding with the first, shows another remarkable shift in the accents. Where the Hebrew accentuates the role of the royal saviour, the LXX draws attention to God as the one who sends the saviour. The best example here is Isa. ix 5-6 (ix 6-7 *RSV*). The Hebrew begins as follows "For to us a child is born" and a little further bestows on him royal titles: "and his name is called: Wonderful Counsellor, Mighty God, Everlasting Father, Prince of Peace". The LXX opens the same way: "For to us a child is born", but proceeds differently: "and his name is called the messenger of great counsel, for I will bring peace upon the princes and health to him". The reason for the change probably lies in the special character of the royal names given to the child. Most likely the translator understood these as divine epithets and therefore altered the text by dropping some of them and ascribing others to God. The result is that God comes to the fore as the saviour whereas the royal child's role is reduced to that of a messenger.[12] A similar shift in the accents may be found in Mic. v 3 (v 4 *RSV*) and in Isa. iv 2.[13]

---

[9] See recently P. Grelot, *Les poèmes du Serviteur. De la lecture critique à l'herméneutique* (Paris, 1981), p. 87.

[10] In Isa. iv 2 the LXX does not give a messianic interpretation to the *ṣemaḥ* (branch) of the MT. It rather draws attention to the remnant of Israel. In Isa. xlix 5 the MT seems to distinguish between an individual Servant-Messiah and the community of Israel. In the LXX this distinction dissappears; see Grelot, pp. 89-91. In Ps. lxxxix 4 "my chosen one" (*bḥyry*) is rendered by τοῖς ἐκλεκτοῖς "the chosen ones" by the LXX; see Schreiner, p. 375, n. 58; Schrenk, *TWNT* 4, pp. 174, 188. In Mic. v 2 (v 3 *RSV*), "the rest of his brethren" is in the Greek translation rendered by "the rest of their (αὐτῶν) brethren". Cp. further the MT and LXX in Isa. xli 25. Whereas the MT refers to Cyrus, the LXX refers to Israel. See J. C. M. das Neves, *A Teologia da Traduçâo Grega dos Setenta no Livro de Isaías* (*Cap. 24 de Isaías*) (Lisboa, 1973), p. 70, 71; Seeligmann, p. 117.

[11] See Becker, p. 63-73.

[12] This is also noted by Kellerman, p. 54, and by Schreiner, p. 376. In a similar way, the Targum applies the epithets to God, but adds the name "Messiah" for the newborn child. Levey, pp. 45-6, neglects the question of the divine epithets and draws the attention to the added term "Messiah".

[13] Mic. v 3 (v 4 *RSV*) according to the MT: "And he [the coming ruler] shall stand and feed his flock in the strength of the LORD"; the LXX has: 'and the Lord shall stand and see, and feed his flock with power", in the majority of the best manuscripts. Only W and

Third, in some passages in the LXX, the eschatological outlook is replaced by an actualizing tendency. Dan. ix 25-26 may serve as an example here. In *v.* 26 of the LXX, it is suggested that the anointed one is the contemporaneous high priest Onias III, murdered in 171 BC. The emphasis here is on the present and not on the remote messianic future as it is in the Hebrew.[14] This is not to say that there are no texts at all in which the LXX heightens the eschatological and transcendent dimension of messianism and of the Messiah.[15]

We may conclude this first section as follows: one cannot say that the LXX as a whole displays a messianic exegesis. Most often the translation is literal, without any messianic bias. In other cases it shows a shift in accentuation, thereby weakening the royal messianic character of the text.

2. *Textual and Literary Criticism*

When texts are adduced in favour of a heightened (or perhaps of a weakened) messianic awareness in the LXX, the argumentation is often based on questionable decisions in the field of textual and of literary criticism, both of the Hebrew and of the Greek text. Amos iv 13a is often brought to the fore as an illustration of the messianic tendencies in the LXX. It merits special mention for its text-critical implications. The *RSV* translates: "For lo, he who forms the mountains and creates the wind, and declares to man what is his thought". The LXX translation can be rendered as follows: "For lo, I am he that strengthens the thunder and creates the wind, and proclaims to men his Christ". The clause "what is his thought" in the *RSV*, translates Hebrew *ma-śśēḥô*, whereas the Greek τὸν χριστὸν αὐτοῦ, "his Christ", obviously renders Hebrew *měšîḥô*. The main question here is whether the Greek translator deliberately or un-

some Lucianic mss follow the Hebrew, reading ἐν ἰσχύι κυρίου instead of ἐν ἰσχύι κύριος. The Qumran scroll of the Twelve Prophets has ἐν ἰσχύι t[etr]; cp. D. Barthélemy, *Les devanciers d'Aquila* (*SVT* 10; Leiden, 1963), p. 172. In Isa. vi 2 *ṣmḥ* is not considered as a substantive by the translator but as a verb meaning "to shine forth". Through this interpretation, the messianic *ṣemaḥ* disappears and God becomes the subject of the sentence. Cp. Seeligmann, p. 116, and das Neves, pp. 150-2.

[14] See R. T. Beckwith, "Daniel 9...", *Rev Qum* 40 (1981), pp. 521-42, esp. pp. 525, 228. The reference is to the LXX and not to the so called Theodotionic version. The LXX translation of 2 Sam. vii 16 displays similar historicizing tendencies. It definitely applies the dynastic promise to Solomon. Therefore it is difficult to agree with Barthélemy; see n. 5 above.

[15] Num. xxiv 7 LXX has the eschatological figure Gog instead of the historical king Agag who is attested by the MT. In Isa. vii 14 the LXX translates the Hebrew adjective *hrh* by a future tense, ἐν γαστρὶ λήψεται, whereas elsewhere it has a present tense, ἐν γαστρὶ ἔχει(ς): Gen. xvi 11, xxxviii 24 (, 25); Judg. xiii 5, 7. For the transcendent character of the Messiah in the LXX we may refer to Lam. iv 20 and perhaps also to Ps. cx (cix) 3 and Dan. vii 13.

consciously changed the Hebrew text, giving it a messianic interpretation, or whether he worked with a *Vorlage* differing from our MT and attesting *mĕšîḥô* instead of the Massoretic *mā-śśēḥô*. At this stage of the research it is impossible to give a decisive answer to this question. However, it cautions us against hasty conclusions. The messianic interpretation in the LXX is not necessarily due to the Greek translator. It may have been a characteristic of his Hebrew *Vorlage*.

The third and fourth oracles of Balaam in Num. xxiv 7,17 offer a good example of a text where the literary critical or exegetical problems prevail. In particular, the occurrence of ἄνθρωπος both in *v.* 7 and in *v.* 17 of the Greek version is puzzling. For clarity's sake we focus attention on *v.* 17. The Hebrew reads: "There shall come forth a star out of Jacob and a sceptre shall rise out of Israel". The LXX has: "There shall come forth a star out of Jacob and a man (ἄνθρωπος) shall rise out of Israel". According to G. Vermes,[16] the LXX gives a messianizing interpretation. It replaces the symbol "sceptre" by the symbolized ἄνθρωπος or Messiah, ἄνθρωπος being a messianic title. In doing so the LXX is in agreement with the Targumim and the Peshiṭta. It is true that the Targumim interpret "sceptre" symbolically, referring to the royal Messiah. However, it is not so certain that the same reasoning applies to the LXX. Indeed, it is doubtful whether ἄνθρωπος has ever been a messianic title. The instances adduced by Vermes are not convincing and rather refer to the term ἄνηρ.[17] If, for argument's sake, we might admit a vague messianic connotation of ἄνθρωπος, then the use of this term in Num. xxiv 17 would still appear to omit the royal characteristics implied in the term "sceptre". This may explain why Philo quoted precisely this text and no other messianic prophecies. Philo avoided references to a royal Messiah. In his understanding, Num. xxiv in its LXX version did not imply an overt mention of a royal Messiah.[18] If this interpretation is correct it does not question the fact that the LXX adds to the eschatological dimension of the oracle replacing the name of the historical king Agag in *v.* 7 by that of the apocalyptic figure Gog.

---

[16] *Scripture and Tradition in Judaism* (Leiden, 1961), pp. 56-60, 159-60, 165-6; see also W. H. Brownlee "The Servant of the Lord in the Qumran Scrolls II", *BASOR* 135 (1954), pp. 36-7, n. 30.

[17] According to Vermes, "man" is also used as a messianic title in 2 Sam. xxiii 1; Zech. vi 12, xiii 7. One should notice that in these texts the LXX does not render "man" (*gbr*, *ʾyš*) by ἄνθρωπος but by ἄνηρ. Cp. A. S. van der Woude, *Die messianischen Vorstellungen der Gemeinde von Qumran* (Assen, 1957), pp. 90-6.

[18] See Annie Jaubert, *La notion d'alliance dans le Judaisme aux abords de l'ère chrétienne* (Paris, 1963), p. 383.

Most of the other messianic or so-called messianic texts in question are equally well known for their text-critical and literary critical problems.[19]

3. *Background*

The most pronounced messianic interpretation in the Greek text is probably due to Christian influence. It is to be found in Lam. iv 20. There the Hebrew text reads *měšîaḥ yhwh*, "The Lord's anointed", and refers to Jerusalem's captured king. The Greek version has: χριστὸς κύριος "anointed Lord" or "Christ Lord". In J. Ziegler's critical edition this majority reading has been relegated to the footnotes and superseded by χριστὸς κυρίου, a variant with no support in any Greek manuscript.[20] The reading χριστὸς κύριος can hardly be Jewish.[21] It is indeed difficult to imagine a Jewish translator identifying the Messiah with the Lord. Moreover, we know by now that early Jewish manuscripts representing recensions of the LXX did not translate the Tetragrammaton. They simply copied or transliterated it,[22] and did not have to decide upon its case. Christian copyists and authors had no problems with the expression χριστὸς κύριος and readily applied it to Jesus Christ.

The Christian milieu in which the LXX was transmitted favoured a messianic interpretation of several passages. However, it is less likely that the Jewish milieu in which the LXX originated, did so. In Israel, because of the political situation after 332 and especially after 167-164, the royal character of the expected messiah was probably put in a low key, at least by some Jewish factions.[23] The Egyptian political situation, which is

[19] In addition to the bibliography given in n. 2 and as a counterbalance see, for Gen. iii 15: H. P. Rüger, "On Some Versions of Genesis 3.15, Ancient and Modern", *The Bible Translator* 27 (1976), p. 107; E. Lipiński, "Etudes sur des textes 'messianiques' de l'AT", *Semitica* 20 (1970), pp. 47-8; for Isa. vii 14: A. M. Dubarle, "La conception virginale et la citation d'Is., VII, 14 dans l'Evangile de Matthieu", *RB* 85 (1978), pp. 362-80; for Dan. vii 13: J. Lust, "Daniel 7, 13 and the Septuagint" *ETL* 54 (1978), pp. 62-9; for Zech. ix 10: P. Lamarche, *Zacharie ix-xiv* (Paris, 1961), p. 44; for Ps. cx 3: D. M. Hay, *Glory at the Right Hand, Psalm 110 in Early Christianity* (Nashville and New York, 1973), pp. 21-2. The author ignores J. Coppens, "La portée messianique du Psaume CX", *ETL* 32 (1956), pp. 5-23.

[20] So also A. Rahlfs, *Septuaginta* (Stuttgart, 1935). R. Hanhart drew my attention to this phenomenon in a letter dated 10 January 1983.

[21] About the use of the term κύριος as an equivalent of the Hebrew name of God *ʾădōnāy*, see R. Hanhart, *Drei Studien zum Judentum* (München, 1967), pp. 59-60; P. W. Skehan, "The Divine Name at Qumran, in the Massada Scroll, and in the Septuagint", *Bulletin IOSCS* 13 (1980), pp. 14-44.

[22] See e.g. Hanhart, p. 59-60.

[23] An interesting case is to be found in Ez. xvii 22-23. The end of *v.* 22 in the MT can be rendered as follows: "... upon a mountain, high and lofty". *V.* 23 begins a new clause: "on the mountain height of Israel..." The last word of *v.* 22, "lofty", translates the Hebrew *hapax legomenon tālûl.* The LXX regards it as a verb meaning "to hang" (*tālâ*) and connects it with *v.* 23: The result is as follows: "... upon a mountain high" (*v.* 23), "and I

usually seen as the background of the origin of the LXX, may have strengthened such developments. Philo's behaviour confirms this.[24] He lived and worked in this milieu. He tried to introduce the gentiles into the substance of Jewish faith. In his voluminous work he keeps almost completely silent as far as messianism is concerned. When he does touch upon the theme, which happens only once, he avoids its royal dimension.

It is by no means certain that all the books of the LXX originated in one and the same milieu. The difference in the origin of the respective books may be reflected in a diversification of their attitude towards messianism. We shall see that the LXX version of Ez. xxi 30-32 corresponds with, or prepares for, the messianic ideas *en vogue* at Qumran and in some of the intertestamental literature. However, other books of the LXX do not seem to follow this trend. The Hebrew text of Zech. vi 13 is more in line with Qumran's messianism than its Greek version. The Hebrew text of Jer. xxxi 17 ff. which stands close to the Qumran writings is omitted in the LXX.

After having given some general assertions, I shall now proceed with an analysis of one text in detail, comparing the Hebrew original with its Greek version, especially in as far as its messianic message is concerned. Ez. xxi 30-32 is our test case.

B. "Until he comes": Ez. xxi 30-32

In Ez. xxi 23 ff. (*RSV* xxi 18 ff.) the prophet is told to perform a symbolic act. He is to trace on the sand a road junction. The interpretation in *vv.* 26-28 informs us that the king of Babylon, Nebuchadnezzar, stands at a crossroad. With the help of divination he chooses which way to go. The lot falls to Jerusalem, to which he will bring his sword, the instrument of God's justice. Connected with this symbolic act follows a divine saying divided into three sections. The first and shortest of these addresses the people of Jerusalem (*v.* 29), the second threatens the "prince of Israel" (*vv.* 30-32), the third and longest one concerns the Ammonites and their city, the alternative target of Nebuchadnezzar (*vv.* 33-37).

The second part of the saying is of special interest for us. In an introductory sentence (*v.* 30), the prophet turns to the prince in a menacing

---

will hang it/him (αὐτὸν) on a mountain height of Israel..." (*v.* 23). The object of the verb "to hang" is the "sprig" or choice branch of the cedar, a term with messianic connotations. In its Greek translation, the passage, which already had a messianic ring in the Hebrew original, could easily be applied by Christians to the crucifixion or "hanging" of the messiah "on a mountain height of Israel". It should be noticed that the royal character of the Messiah is no longer prominent in this application. According to W. Zimmerli, *Ezechiel* (Neukirchen, 1969), p. 376, the LXX misunderstood the Hebrew.

[24] See Jaubert, p. 382-3.

way. The following lines (*vv.* 31-32) announce his judgement, prefaced by the messenger formula. The conclusion of the oracle is enigmatic: "Until he comes to whom the *mišpāṭ* is and to him I will give it". Its language is reminiscent of the announcement of a ruler or Messiah of Judah in Gen. xlix 10: "Until he comes to whom it belongs and to him shall be the obedience of the peoples". Who is the expected one in Ezekiel's oracle? According to the context he may be either Nebuchadnezzar with his punishing judgement or a new Judaean King-Messiah bringing justice. In the first case, rather surprisingly, Ezekiel appears to have made the promise of Gen. xlix 10 the vehicle of a message of total judgement. In the second case he seems to have reinforced the ancient promise. The interpretation of the clause largely depends on the options of the exegete faced with the problems of textual and literary criticism in this verse and in the oracle as a whole.[25] This is true for both the MT and the LXX.

1. *The Massoretic Text*

Textual Criticism

The Hebrew text of *v.* 31 has four verb forms which are probably to be parsed as third person singular *hifʿil* perfects: *hēsîr*, *hērîm*, *higbēah*, *hišpîl*: "he removed (the diadem)", "he took off (the crown)", "he exalted (the lowly) and brought down (the lofty)". However, this plausible reading, supported indirectly by the Targum,[26] is not accepted by the Massoretes. Their punctuation suggests that we should read the first two verbs and the fourth as infinitive constructs. This hardly makes any sense in the context and conflicts with the punctuation of the third verb as an infinitive absolute. W. Zimmerli and the majority of commentators propose to read the infinitive absolute throughout.[27] This implies erasing the

---

[25] For a survey of recent solutions see B. Lang, *Ezechiel* (Darmstadt, 1981), p. 119, with reference on the one hand to W. Zimmerli, pp. 494-6, and R. Criado, "Teorias nuevas en autores antiguos. Ez. 21,32 y Gén. 49,10", *Archivo Teol. Granadino* 26 (1963), pp. 203-21, and "Messianismo en Ezequiel 21,32?", *XXX Semana biblica Española* (Madrid, 1973), pp. 263-317; and on the other hand to H. Cazelles, *Le Messie de la Bible* (Paris, 1978), pp. 129-36; "Shiloh, the Customary Laws and the Return of the Ancient Kings", *Proclamation and Presence: OT Essays in Honour of G. H. Davies* (London, 1970) pp. 239-51, and Monsengwo-Pasinya, art. cit. in n. 2. Lang's reference to Monsengwo-Pasinya is not entirely to the point since the latter follows Zimmerli as far as the MT is concerned. He finds a messianic interpretation of Ez. xxi 30-32 only in the LXX. Lang himself opts for Zimmerli's solution: see *Kein Aufstand in Jerusalem* (Stuttgart, 1978), p. 120.

[26] The support is indirect: the Targum reads first person sing. imp. *paʿel* forms: "I will remove (*ʾăʿeddî*). I will take off (*ʾăbaṭṭēl*)". The translator may have confused *he* and *ʾalef* in the prefixes.

[27] For the erasing of the *yod*, Zimmerli, p. 483, finds support in some late mss Kenn.; see also e.g. G. A. Cooke, *The Book of Ezekiel* (Edinburgh, 1936), p. 239, with reference to Ges.-K. § 113 *bb*.

yod in three of the four verbs, (following some late manuscripts), or accepting an odd form of the infinitive absolute. The major reason behind this proposal is the translation of the LXX. The critical edition by J. Ziegler reads imperatives, which offer a rather accurate rendering of the Hebrew infinitive absolute (Ges.-K. 113 *bb*). However, we shall see that Ziegler's option is not above suspicion.

In *v*. 32 the line *gam-zōʾt lōʾ hāyâ* is often emended. The reason is that the feminine form of the subject *zōʾt* does not correspond with the masculine verb form *hāyâ*. Following W. L. Moran, Zimmerli suggests that *hyh* may have been abbreviated from an original *thyh*[28] through virtual haplography. However, the conflict is avoided in a more elegant way when one, with H. Cazelles, connects *gam-zōʾt* with the preceding verb *ʾăśîmennâ* and translates: "Overturning, overturning, it is that which I will establish, even that". *lōʾ hāyâ* then introduces a new clause. Its subject is the subject implied in the expression which follows: "There will not have been (one to whom the *mišpāṭ* belongs) until he comes whose right the *mišpāṭ* is..."[29]

Literary Criticism

V. 31 tells the public about the past. It reminds them of what Nebuchadnezzar did to Jerusalem on the occasion of his first invasion: "He removed the turban and took off the crown". In its literal use in the OT, the term *miṣnepet* is confined to the headdress of the high priest.[30] The crown or *ʿăṭārâ* is rather a sign of royal power. Both terms also have a figurative use.[31] This appears to be the case in Isa. lxii 3. There the crown and the turban[32] are parallel notions applied to Jerusalem denoting its worth for God: "You shall be a crown of beauty in the hand of the Lord, and a royal turban in the hand of your God". The only other

---

[28] If one wishes to postulate a haplography, it may be better to presuppose the following original text: *gam-zōʾt lōʾ zōʾt lōʾ hāyâ* ... The original text offered a parallel with *zōʾt lōʾ-zōʾt* in *v*. 31. The eye of the scribe wandered from the first *lōʾ* to the second *lōʾ* in *v*. 32. According to W. L. Moran, "Gen. 49,10 and its use in Ez. 21,32", *Biblica* 39 (1958), p. 422, "*ʾaleph* and *tau* could be confused either in the Phoenician or in the Aramaic square script, and hence the possibility of a virtual haplography in the sequence *lʾ thyh*"; Zimmerli, p. 483. Both authors rightly refuse other emendations such as the one suggested by J. A. Bewer in *JBL* 72 (1953), p. 62, *gm ʾwt lʾ yhyh*, or the one proposed by C. Cornill, *Das Buch des Propheten Ezechiel* (Leipzig, 1886), p. 309, *ʾwy lh kzʾt thyh*, based on a variant reading in the LXX.

[29] Cazelles, art. cit., p. 247, referring to Josh. x 14; 2 Kings xx 15; Jer. lii 20; Ez. ix 14.

[30] Ex. xxviii 4,37,39, xxix 6, xxxix 28,31; Lev. viii 9, xvi 4; see also Zech. iii 5 (*ṣānîp*).

[31] 2 Sam. xii 30 // 1 Chron. xx 2; Jer. xiii 18; Ps. xxi 4.

[32] *Qerê*: *ûṣĕnîp*. There is no doubt that here both terms ("crown" and "turban") are synonyms. This is also the case in Ez. xxi 31 where the verbs *hēsîr* and *hērîm* are parallels: cp. Ez. xlv 9, where the same verbs are used as parallels.

text in which both terms are used as synonyms is Ez. xxi 31. There too they probably have a figurative meaning indicating Jerusalem's glorious élite. Nebuchadnezzar abased the city taking into exile the élite of the town. The sentence can be compared with Ez. xvii 12-13 and its context which deals with the same events. The king is not singled out. He is a member of the upper class taken into exile. The last line of *v.* 31 should be understood in the same light. "He exalted the lowly and abased the lofty."[33] The reference is to the situation in Jerusalem after Nebuchadnezzar's first attack. Everything is turned upside down. More specifically, the élite have been humbled while the lower-class people have been given power. The feminine indicative pronouns in the immediately foregoing expression: *zōʾt lōʾ-zōʾt* probably also point to the town: "She is not the same any more".

If the foregoing interpretation is correct, *v.* 31 makes abstraction of *v.* 30 in which the king is addressed, and continues the line of thought of the preceding section dealing with Jerusalem. This conclusion invites us to have a closer look at *v.* 30. The address in *v.* 30 is unusual for Ezekiel. Seldom in this book with its stereotype expressions and compositions is the guilty person addressed named in the second person immediately before the messenger formula. When it happens, the context appears to reveal the hand of a later redactor.[34] Such seems to be the case here. The terminology in *v.* 30 is almost identical with that of *v.* 34 which may have been a source of inspiration to the redactor. The noun *ḥālāl* meaning "slain", "wounded" fits better in *v.* 34 then in *v.* 30.[35] *V.* 30 was probably inserted by someone who wished to suggest that the following verses 31 and 32 were not to be applied to Jerusalem as a whole but more specifically to its king. He has to take off his crown and to remove his turban. No longer do the feminine pronouns in *zōʾt lōʾ-zōʾt* automatically

---

[33] *hgbh* is a masculine form, suggesting that *hšplh* should also be read as a masculine form (with *he paragogicum*). The word pair *gbh* and *špl* more often refers to "lord" and "slave". See 2 Sam. vi 22; Ps. cxxxviii 6; Qoh. v 7, and B. Lang, *Kein Aufstand*, p. 116. The Massoretic punctuation intends to recommend the masculine form as the more correct, cp. Bauer-Leander § 62 y.

[34] The pronoun *wĕʾattâ*, "and you", is in Ezekiel most often followed by *ben ʾādām* and refers to the prophet: ii 6,8, iii 25, iv 1, vii 2, xii 3, xiii 17, etc. Only three times is the person addressed in an oracle named in the 2nd person immediately before the messenger formula: xx 39 (plural), xxi 30 (singular), xxxv 17 (plural). The analysis of F. Hossfeld, *Untersuchungen zu Komposition und Theologie des Ezechielbuches* (Würzburg, 1977), pp. 36, 282-5, 333, leads to the conclusion that the passages in question are redactional.

[35] In Ez. xxi 30 the term *ḥālāl* receives a connotation which is unusual in Ezekiel and in the Bible as a whole. The term normally means "slain", "wounded" (by the sword); see e.g. Ez. xxi 19, xxxi 17, 18, xxxii 20, 21, 22, 23, 24, 25, 28, 29, 30, 32, 32, and not "profane". Although Ez. xxi 34 is rather obscure the meaning "wounded" seems to fit better there than in *v.* 30 where *ḥālāl* is confused with *ḥôl*. Cp. the LXX translation τραυματίας in *v.* 34 but βέβηλος in *v.* 31.

refer to the town the mention of which now lies at a distance. They are considered as neuter forms, the expression meaning that "nothing will be the same any more". The redactor responsible for the insertion of *v.* 30 is most likely to be identified with the one who, according to B. Lang,[36] replaced Jerusalem by Ammon in the next section. He could not accept the idea of a total and final destruction of the holy town.

In contrast with *v.* 31, *v.* 32 is oriented towards the future: "A ruin, a ruin, a ruin I will make her". This first clause elaborates upon the prophet's symbolic act announcing Nebuchadnezzar's new and final assault against Jerusalem. It indicates the deeper dimension of this event, showing that Nabuchadnezzar is nothing but a human instrument of God's punishing intervention against Jerusalem. Whatever may be the exact meaning of *ʿawwâ*, translated here and in the *RSV* by "ruin", it certainly implies some form of distortion and destruction.[37] The suffix of the feminine personal pronoun added to the verb *ʾăśîmennâ*: "I will make her" again points to the town of Jerusalem. *gam-zōʾt*, immediately connected with it, underlines this. It reminds the hearer of the fact that Nebuchadnezzar chose the road to Jerusalem and not the one leading to Ammon. At a later stage, when *v.* 30 was inserted, the pronouns may have been understood in a neuter way. The reference to the town became less explicit. But the general meaning of distortion and desolation remained.

The final line of *v.* 32 is most intricate. If one accepts Cazelles's hypothesis, it opens with a short introductory sentence, *lōʾ hāyâ*, and proceeds with a longer subordinate clause *ʿad-bōʾ ʾăšer-lô hammišpāṭ* (*ûnĕtattîw*), "until he comes to whom the *mišpāṭ* is". Who is the one to come? Among the possible answers two major options come to the fore. According to the first, the coming one is the king of Babylon. He is about to bring the destruction announced by the prophet. In this case the introductory *lōʾ hāyâ* refers to the disaster saying either that "it has not happened (yet)" or that something like this "had never happened" until the coming of this king. According to the second group, the expected one is a saviour king or Messiah. He may be expected in either the near future or in the remote eschatological times. In this option the introductory sentence *lōʾ hāyâ*, when not emended, is probably to be translated along the lines suggested by Cazelles (see nn. 25 and 29). The subject of *lōʾ hāyâ*

---

[36] *Kein Aufstand*, pp. 120-5. In support of Lang's interesting thesis one may add that the expressions "seeing false visions" and "divine lies", which are attested in *v.* 34, are always used in oracles concerning Israel: xiii 6-7, 9, 23, xxii 28.

[37] A comparison with Isa. xxiv 1 confirms this: "Behold the Lord will lay waste the earth and make it desolate and he will twist (*ʿiwwâ*) its surface and scatter its inhabitants". See Moran, p. 420.

is to be identified with the subject of the following subordinate clause: "There will not have been (a saviour) until he comes to whom the *mišpāṭ* is".

In recent literature on the topic (see n. 25), the choice between the two possible answers largely depends upon the interpretation of the term *mišpāṭ*. When *mišpāṭ* means "judgement-punishment", then the expected one must obviously be the king of Babylon. He will execute all the threats which were announced by the prophet. However, if *mišpāṭ* is understood as "right", "justice", then the coming one must be a saviour. He will bring justice. How are we to decide? The problem is hard to solve because of the lack of good parallels for this particular use of the term in the book of Ezekiel. Ezekiel often mentions the plural *mišpāṭîm*, meaning "rules", "laws", "directives"; or the singular without the article meaning "justice", as a synonym of *ṣĕdāqâ*. In most, if not all, of these cases the term *mišpāṭ* has a positive connotation.[38] Does this also apply to Ez. xxi 32 where *mišpāṭ* occurs in the singular preceded by the article and followed by a *lamed* indicating to whom "it" belongs? The answer to this question may be facilitated through a comparison with the use of the term in the other biblical books. The concordances reveal that the best parallel text is to be found in Dt. i 17. The verse has *mišpāṭ* preceded by the article and followed by a *lamed*. The full expression reads as follows: *kî hammišpāṭ lĕyhwh*, "The *mišpāṭ* belongs to the Lord". The context indicates that *mišpāṭ* here means "juridical power", "judgement". This judgement may entail either vindication or condemnation. The same is probably true in Ez. xxi 32, which means that, after all, the term *mišpāṭ* in this verse does not tell us whether the coming one will be a saviour for Jerusalem or a destroyer. The allusion to Gen. xlix 10 does not help us either. First, the reference is less clear than is often taken for granted.[39] Second, it may imply a reversal of the meaning of Gen. xlix 10.[40]

---

[38] There may be some doubt concerning Ez. xxiii 24, a text which led Zimmerli to accept the position of Moran according to whom *mišpāṭ* has an unfavourable meaning. See, however, Cazelles, pp. 244-5. Notice, moreover, that in this passage, *mišpāṭ* is not defined by the article. According to Criado, pp. 268-70, Ez. xxxix 21 offers a close parallel to Ez. xxi 32 as far as the use is concerned of *mišpāṭ* with an unfavourable meaning. We have to admit that here *mišpāṭ* is defined, not by the article, but by the personal pronoun. However, it is not at all certain that *ʿāśâ ʾet-mišpāṭî* means "to execute judgement". The parallel expression *śîm yād* is a *hapax legomenon* and does not shed much light on the problem. Both expressions may very well refer to God's positive intervention in favour of Israel described in the foregoing verses and resulting in the setting of God's "glory among the nations" (*v.* 21a).

[39] According to Moran, there can be little doubt about the fact that the prophet alludes to Gen. xlix 10 (pp. 416-17), with reference to the context in Ezekiel, esp. to ch. xix. According to Lang, *Kein Aufstand*, p. 119, n. 13, the allusion cannot be proven. For a survey and personal view, see Criado, pp. 307 ff.

[40] See esp. Zimmerli, pp. 495-6.

On rereading the Hebrew text of Ezekiel's oracle in the light of our analysis a feeling of uncertainty and hesitation remains. Nevertheless, I suggest the following tentative conclusions. In a first draft the oracle was directly connected with Ezekiel's symbolic act announcing Nebuchadnezzar's destroying intervention against Jerusalem. Seen in this context, the coming one in *v.* 32 is to be identified with Nebuchadnezzar. The *mišpāṭ* given to him by the Lord brings Jerusalem's condemnation and destruction. A later reworking of the oracle caused a shift in the accents. With the insertion of *v.* 30 the oracle was more or less disconnected from the preceding symbolic act. The one addressed was no longer the town but its wicked king. In this new context the coming one of *v.* 32 was automatically understood as standing in contrast to the condemned king. It was suggested that the expected one would be a just king and not an unhallowed wicked one. He would be a saviour fulfilling the promise of Gen. xlix 10.

A similar process of reinterpretation may be traced in Ez. xvii.[41] The more original level or this oracle deals with the disloyal behaviour of Jerusalem and its king Zedekiah towards Nebuchadnezzar. They broke their vassal-oath and were to be punished. The events are comparable to those treated in Ez. xxi 23 ff. A later editor added an oracle of salvation announcing the coming of a saviour. He partly used the terminology of Ez. xxi 31: "I the Lord abase and exalt..."[42] In doing so he was the first to suggest a messianic exegesis of Ez. xxi 31-32.

2. *The Septuagint version*

How did the Greek translator(s) understand Ezekiel's oracle? Before trying to formulate an answer to this question, we have to give a general appreciation of the LXX of Ezekiel. In non-problematic passages, the LXX proves to be rather faithful to the Hebrew original, giving a close to literal translation.[43] In the scholarly world, towards the turn of the century, this led to an attitude of confidence in the Greek text. In chapters in which the MT tends to be obscure or even corrupt—and chapter xxi hap-

[41] On the history of the redaction of Ez. xvii see Hossfeld, pp. 59-98.

[42] See Hossfeld, p. 88. The antithetic parallel use of the expressions "to abase the lofty" and "to exalt the lowly" occurs only in Ez. xvii 24 and xxi 31. Since the author of Ez. xvii 22-24 appears to have combined several other passages it is most likely that he used xxi 31 as a source of inspiration and not vice versa.

[43] Cp. E. Tov, *The Text-critical Use of the Septuagint* (Jerusalem, 1981), p. 63. The literalness is relative. It is not consistent in the sense that it renders all occurrences of a given Hebrew root or construction by the same Greek equivalent. See J. Ziegler, "Zur Textgestaltung der Ezechiel-Septuaginta", *Biblica* 34 (1953), p. 440.

pens to be reckoned among them[44]—commentators and translators often had recourse to the LXX, hoping to find there a good rendering of the original text.[45]

After this general observation, we return to our initial question. Did the LXX interpret Ez. xxi 30-32 in a messianic sense? Again the answer depends on decisions of textual and of literary critical character.

Textual Criticism

Apart from the verb ἔσται, the verbs in *v.* 31 (26) are to be parsed as second person singular aorists indicatives: ἀφείλου, "you took off"; ἐπέθου, "you put on"; ἐταπείνωσας, "you abased"; ὑψώσας, "you exalted". In his critical edition of the text J. Ziegler preferred imperatives to indicatives in the first two instances: ἀφελοῦ and ἀπόθου. The witnesses supporting this reading are basically Lucianic.[46] However, the great majority of the manuscripts, among which the oldest and most trustworthy ones such as B and papyrus 967, attest the indicative forms. We shall see that the literary analysis of the verse confirms this reading. Against the same majority and with the same Lucianic minority Ziegler preferred the prefix ἀπο- to ἐπι- in the second verb, reading ἀπόθου and not ἐπέθου. In the latter case Ziegler's choice was probably influenced by the MT and in the first by its emendation.[47]

In *v.* 32 (27) some manuscripts insert τὸ κρίμα after καθήκει as a translation of the Hebrew term *mišpāṭ*. At a first look, the better witnesses might seem to have overlooked this term. However, a further investigation reveals that the expression *mišpāṭ* + *l* can be rendered by the verb καθήκω.[48]

---

[44] See G. Fohrer, *Hauptprobleme des Buches Ezechiel* (*BZAW* 72; Berlin, 1952), p. 53, n. 1; Zimmerli, *Ezechiel*, p. 116.

[45] A. Merx, "Der Werth der Septuaginta für die Textkritik des alten Testaments, an Ezechiel aufgezeigt", *Jahrb. prot. Theol.* 9 (1983), pp. 65-77; G. Jahn, *Das Buch Ezechiel auf Grund der Septuaginta hergestellt* (Leipzig, 1905); C. H. Cornill, *Das Buch des Propheten Ezechiel* (Leipzig, 1886).

[46] Ziegler refers to L'$^{-449}$ 410 Tht. for ἀφελοῦ and to L-V-46 410 Tht. for ἀπόθου (p. 185). Monsengwo-Pasinya follows Ziegler without any critical doubts or questioning. In Rahlfs's edition the majority reading is given: ἀφείλου and ἐπέθου (p. 806).

[47] Cp. above, p. 182. It is possible that the LXX had a *Vorlage* allowing it to read 2nd person sing.imperat. It is more likely that the translator introduced these forms of the verb in order to adapt *v.* 31 better to *v.* 30. About *Personenwechsel* in the LXX of Ezekiel, see J. Ziegler, "Zur Textgestaltung der Ezechiel-Septuaginta", *Biblica* 34 (1953), p. 438.

[48] See Deut. xxi 17: *lô mišpaṭ habbĕkōrâ*: καὶ τοῦτο καθήκει τά πρωτοτοκεῖα, cp. Lev. v 10, ix 16. It should be noticed that in Deut. xxi 17 *mišpāṭ* is used without the article.

Literary Criticism

Beginning with *v.* 30 (25), the oracle addresses an ἀφηγούμενος or leader of Israel. He is βέβηλος.[49] This qualification may give us a hint concerning his identity. In the LXX, the term is reserved for cultic matters. In the deutero-canonical books it is applied to a person, but only once, and then in a cultic context. The person is Antiochus IV who "took the holy vessels with his poluted (βεβήλοις) hands" (2 Macc. iv 16). These few data suggest that the ἀφηγούμενος in Ez. xxi 30 (25) was also connected with a cultic situation.

V. 31 (26) is undoubtedly presented as the immediate continuation of *v.* 30 (25). The wicked prince is further addressed in the second person singular. He is accused of having removed his priestly turban, puting on a royal crown. The contrast between the two verbs ἀφείλου and ἐπέθου, "you took off" and "you put on", is remarkable. It indicates that, according to the translator, the respective objects of these verbs were not synonyms. And indeed, when not used figuratively, as in the MT, the κίδαρις, standing for Hebrew *miṣnepet*, normally refers to the priestly headband, whereas the στέφανος, rendering Hebrew *ʿăṭārâ*, is a wordly sign of distinction.[50] The use of the latter term is rare in the OT. Only in the later strands of the Bible, especially in the deutero-canonical or apocryphal books, is it more common. It is significant that the Maccabean high priest Jonathan received a στέφανος out of the hands of Alexander Balas (1 Macc. x 20). He thus received royal authority, not as an independent king, but as a vassal of his Seleucid Lord.[51]

Jonathan may not have been the first high priest to covet royal power and honour. He certainly was not the last. A culminating point must have been reached when the Hasmoneans took the royal title. Some were

---

[49] Only here does the LXX translate Hebrew *ḥālāl* by βέβηλος. The normal translation is τραυματίας (26 ×) or τετραυματισμένος (4 ×) or τραῦμα (1 ×).

[50] The Targum distinguishes between the priestly turban of the high priest Seraiah and the royal crown of Zedekiah, the king.

[51] See Grundmann, στέφανος *TWNT* 7 (Stuttgart, 1964), pp. 623-5; R. Delbrück, "Antiquarisches zu den Verspottungen Jesu", *ZNW* 41 (1942), pp. 124-45, esp. pp. 134-5, 138-40. About the κίδαρις (*miṣnepet*) see above p. 182. The term στέφανος is rare in the more ancient strata of the OT. In 2 Sam. xii 30 it refers to the golden crown of an Ammonite vassal king; in Ps. xxi 4 (xx 4) to the golden crown of the king of Israel and a gift of Yhwh (in the LXX translation it is a crown with precious stones). See also Jer. xiii 18; Zech. vi 11, 14; Est. viii 15. See Delbrück, p. 125. Only in the later strata of the OT is the word more common, esp. in the Apocrypha or Deutero-canonical Books: see e.g. 1 Macc. x 20, xiii 37, 39; 2 Macc. xiv 4; Sir. xl 4, xlv 12. The LXX inserts it in Isa. xxii 18, 21. In all the above references the golden wreath or στέφανος appears to be the headdress of a vassal or vassal-king. See Delbrück, p. 125. For the use of the term in other contexts see Grundmann, pp. 624-5.

enthusiastic about this evolution. Jesus Sirach appears to have been among them, in the period before the Maccabees. He is most exuberant in his praises of Aaron, the archetype of the high priest. It is remarkable that he attributes to Aaron a golden crown (στέφανος) upon his priestly turban (κίδαρις), which suggests that he joined the priestly and the royal powers.[52]

Not everyone was happy with this state of affairs. Especially under the Hasmoneans the opposition grew. Josephus (Ant. xiv 40-41) and Diodorus[53] explicitly refer to it. The Testament of Levi also insists on the necessary separation between royal and priestly functions.[54] The community of Qumran must have played a major role in the opposition.[55] For them, the high-priest-king in Jerusalem was "the wicked priest".[56] They promoted the expectation of a priest-Messiah along with a king-Messiah.

Most probably, the Greek translator of Ez. xxi 31 was also among the objectors. According to him, the high priest defiled his priestly turban, preferring the στέφανος. His following remarks must be understood along the same lines: "She shall no longer be the same αὕτη οὐ τοιαύτη ἔσται". Notice the use of the feminine personal pronoun which according to the context most likely refers to the κίδαρις or priestly turban.[57] The next line describes the consequences of the high priest's behaviour: "You have abased that which was high, and exalted that which was low". He underestimated the value of his priesthood.

---

[52] Sir. xlv 12; cp. xlv 24b-25a which should be read as follows: "that he [Phinehas the high priest] and his descendants should have the dignity of the priesthood for ever and His covenant with David, the son of Jesse, of the tribe of Judah": see P. C. Beentjes, *Jesus Sirach en Tenach* (Nieuwegein, 1981), p. 190.

[53] *Bibliothèque Historique* xl 2, referred to by A. Hultgård, *L'eschatologie des Testaments des douze Patriarches* I (Uppsala, 1977), p. 61.

[54] See esp. Test. of Judah xxi 1-5 and xxiv 1-4; cp. Hultgård, pp. 60ff.; cp. J. Becker, *Untersuchungen zur Entstehungsgeschichte der Testamente der Zwölf Patriarchen*, (Leiden, 1970), pp. 315 ff.

[55] See A. S. van der Woude, *Die messianischen Vorstellungen der Gemeinde von Qumrân* (Assen, 1957), pp. 225 ff.

[56] See esp. van der Woude, pp. 233-5, who identifies the wicked priest with Alexander Jannaeus (103-76), and G. and P. Vermes, *The Dead Sea Scrolls. Qumran in Perspective*, (London, 1977), p. 150-6, who identify him with Jonathan (160-143). For a survey of other possible identifications and bibliography see G. and P. Vermes, pp. 161-2, R. T. Beckwith, "The Pre-History and Relationships of the Pharisees, Sadducees and Essenes", *Rev Qum* 11 (1982) pp. 44ff. Recently, van der Woude suggested that the term "wicked priest" may have been used for a succession of Jerusalem high priests; see his "Wicked Priest or Wicked Priests?", *JJS* 33 (1982), pp. 349-59.

[57] Notice the contrast with the MT. There the reference is either to the "town" or to a neuter "everything". The special accentuation in the LXX is brought to the fore by Monsengwo-Pasinya, pp. 369-70.

A similar rejection of the "wicked high priest" may be found in Ez. xxviii 11-19 in its LXX version. More than the MT, the Greek translation suggests that the "prince of Tyre" is to be identified with the prince-high priest in Jerusalem.[58] In a cryptic language the translator confers on him the στέφανος and the αποσφράγισμα (seal) which are signs of royal power. The jewels of his vestments are identical with those of the high priest described in Ex. xxviii 17-20. His proudness and his greed are the causes of his fall. The accusation sounds very similar to the one brought up against the "wicked priest" in 1Qp Hab viii 10-11: "His heart became proud, and he forsook God and betrayed the precepts for the sake of riches."

After this brief excursion into Ez. xxviii we return to Ez. xxi. The indictment in *v.* 31 is followed by the announcement of the verdict in *v.* 32: ἀδίκίαν ἀδίκίαν ἀδικίαν θήσομαι αὐτήν. Again the feminine object of the sentence must be the κίδαρις. God himself will further defile the priestly turban. It will no longer be the same until the coming of someone to whom it really belongs. This final clause announces the advent of a priestly Messiah who will restore the high priesthood and who will be worthy to receive the headdress of the high priest.

Is the LXX version of Ez. xxi 30-32 more messianic than the original Hebrew text? The answer largely depends on the options taken in the course of the text critical and literary critical analysis of the text. The above investigation suggests the following conclusions:

1. The first draft of the Hebrew text had no messianic connotation. It announced doom for Jerusalem.

2. On a later redactional level the oracle was reinterpreted. The new message foretold punishment for the reigning king and the coming of a messianic saviour.

3. According to the LXX version, the oracle reacts against the unification of the royal and the priestly functions. It condemns the high priests who prefer the royal powers over the priestly ones and announces the coming of a new high priest who will be worthy of the priestly turban. One could call this a priestly messianic expectation as opposed to a royal Davidic messianic expectation.

---

[58] Compare with P. M. Bogaert, "Montagne sainte, jardin d'Eden et Sanctuaire (hiérosolymitain) dans un oracle d'Ezéchiel contre le prince de Tyr (Ez. 28,11-19)", a paper read at the *Colloque interuniversitaire. Le Mythe, Son Langage et son Message*, Liège, Louvain-la-Neuve, 18-19 Nov. 1981, to be published in the series *Homo Religiosus*. In the following short note on Ez. xxviii, 11-19 we refer only to some of the more relevant differences between the MT and the LXX. For further details see the interesting article of Bogaert.

Both our general survey and the analysis of one sample text show that in questions of theology such as messianism, one cannot treat the LXX as a unified entity. Each relevant text should be studied on its own. At the present stage of the investigation we may conclude that the LXX certainly does not display a uniform picture of a developing royal messianism.

ISAÏE XIX 16-25 ET UNIVERSALISME DANS LA LXX

PAR

L. MONSENGWO-PASINYA

Kisangani

L'universalisme n'est pas un concept étranger à l'Ancien Testament en général ni inconnu du livre d'Isaïe en particulier (cf. Isa. ii 2-4, lvi 5-8, lx 3,11-14). Cependant aucun texte comme le nôtre ne pousse cette note au point de faire aussi clairement de l'Assyrie, et surtout de l'Egypte, l'anti-salut par antonomase (Dt. xxviii 68), une partie intégrante du projet salvifique de Dieu.

Il existe, certes, dans l'Ancien Testament nombre de textes favorables à l'Egypte, pays hospitalier, organisé du point de vue politique et administratif, terre d'abondance (Gen. xv 13, xlii-xlvii), terre d'asile (Jer. xxvi 21), où l'on trouve des craignant-Dieu (Ex. i 19-21, viii 15), des gens bons et compatissants comme la fille de Pharaon (Ex. ii 5-10).[1] Il reste cependant que l'Ancien Testament parle généralement de l'Egypte en termes d'invectives et de menaces, comme en témoigne le texte d'Isa. xix 1-15, au contraire de notre péricope. Aussi les commentateurs relèvent-ils à juste raison l'opposition existant entre ces deux textes.

Ce traitement réservé d'habitude à l'Egypte dans l'Ancien Testament accentue encore davantage le caractère universaliste de notre péricope parsemée d'affirmations impressionnantes sur le salut que Dieu prépare pour l'Egypte.

A priori on est fondé à croire qu'un universalisme aussi large devait intéresser les milieux de la Diaspora, d'autant que pour les prosélytes notamment le texte d'Isa. xix 16-25 pouvait représenter un argument de poids dans la revendication de leurs droits cultuels et la définition de leur situation au sein de la religion hébraïque. Les prosélytes n'étaient-ils pas en quelque sorte une actuation en même temps qu'une illustration de ce texte d'Isaïe?

C'est pourquoi l'interprétation qu'en donne la version des Septante, réalisée précisément en milieu égyptien, doit pouvoir être de grand intérêt. Aussi nous proposons-nous, dans la présente étude, d'analyser les faits littéraires susceptibles de révéler l'intention et la pensée du traducteur alexandrin du texte d'Isa. xix 16-25.

---

[1] Cf. L. Alonso Schökel, *Il triplice Esodo* (Notes de cours, Rome), pp. 27-8.

Pour ce faire, nous passerons d'abord en revue le texte massorétique, afin d'en dégager le message. Ensuite nous procéderons à l'examen du texte grec avec l'hébreu en regard.

Pour une exégèse détaillée du texte, nous renvoyons le lecteur aux commentaires et études publiés sur notre péricope.[2] En ce qui nous concerne, nous épinglerons surtout les faits littéraires qui soulignent de manière particulière l'intégration totale de l'Egypte dans le projet salvifique de Dieu.

1. *Isa. xix 16-25 (TM)*

1.1. L'idée générale de cette péricope est claire: un jour viendra où le salut de Dieu sera étendu à l'Egypte et à l'Assyrie, ennemis traditionnels et par excellence d'Israël. A l'instar du peuple élu et avec lui, la grande puissance orientale (Assyrie) et celle de l'Occident (Egypte) confesseront le nom de Yahweh, l'Unique et Vrai Dieu. Certains mots-clés soulignent spécialement cette note universaliste et illustrent les différents aspects de cette insertion totale de l'Egypte dans le plan de salut divin.

1.2. *bayyôm hahûʾ* — Cette incise scande notre texte (*vv.* 16, 18, 19, 23, 24), et, jointe au temps futur des verbes, elle indique que, du point de vue du rédacteur, les faits relatés et notamment l'insertion totale de l'Egypte dans le salut de Dieu sont considérés comme appartenant à la sphère du futur: ils se vérifieront aux temps eschatologiques. Ce sera le jour de la manifestation de Dieu à l'Egypte: le Seigneur viendra à l'Egypte, non plus en juge qui condamne (cf. Isa. xix 1), mais en sauveur (*v.* 22).

1.3. *wᵉḥārad* (*v.* 16) — Le champ sémantique du verbe *ḥārad* s'étend à des frémissements ou tremblements divers, provoqués soit par un danger (1 Sam. xxviii 5) ou un fait inattendu et contrariant (Gen. xxvii 33), soit le plus souvent par la perception d'une intervention divine favorable (1 Sam. xiv 15) ou défavorable (Isa. x 29, xxxii 11, xli 5),[3] soit enfin par une théophanie (Ex. xix 16,18). Une telle intervention de Dieu est accompagnée de hauts-faits, ou d'actions punitives ou de phénomènes naturels.

Du point de vue grammatical, rien ne s'oppose à ce que *miṣrayim* (*v.* 16) désigne les Egyptiens (peuple) plutôt que l'Egypte (terre), l'accord

---

[2] Pour les commentaires, voir notamment J. Bright, "Isaiah I", in *Peake's Commentary on the Bible* (Londres, 1962), pp. 502-3; A. Penna, "Isaiah", in *A New Catholic Commentary on Holy Scripture* (Londres, 1969), pp. 581-2; O. Kaiser, *Der Prophet Jesaja Kapitel 13-39* (Göttingen, 1973), pp. 85-91; et surtout H. Wildberger, *Jesaja* 2 (Neukirchen-Vluyn, 1978), pp. 727-46. Outre Alonso Schökel, l'étude suivante a retenu notre attention: A. Feuillet, "Un sommet religieux de l'Ancien Testament. L'oracle d'Isaïe, xix (vv. 16-25) sur la conversion de l'Egypte", *Recherches de science religieuse* 39 (1951-2), pp. 65-87.

[3] Gen. xlii 28; Ez. xxvi 16, xxxii 10.

d'un sujet au pluriel avec un verbe au singulier (*yihyeh*) étant monnaie courante. Mais dans un tel cas, l'auteur aurait pu mettre au pluriel les deux verbes (*ḥārad* et *pāḥad*) qui suivent le nom (*miṣrayim*).[4] Le pluriel reste cependant facultatif. Néanmoins le maintien du verbe *ḥārad* au singulier a pour effet de rapprocher Isa. xix 16 de Ex. xix 16,18, où le Sinaï tremble à la manifestation de Yahweh. Cette parenté littéraire donne à penser qu'en Isa. xix 16, la terre d'Egypte elle aussi tremble à l'instar du Mont Sinaï, car elle devient lieu de théophanie. Le jeu de mots introduit par le maintien du singulier est sans doute intentionnel.

En ce contexte de théophanie, le tremblement (*ḥārad*) et l'effroi (*pāḥad*) des Egyptiens paraissent signifier la peur révérentielle du pécheur face à Yahweh qui vient juger les impies (cf. Isa. xxxiii 10,14-16). Le salut que Yahweh accordera aux Egyptiens présuppose donc la conscience de leur péché, la conversion et la reconnaissance de Yahweh comme leur Dieu. Ainsi le *v.* 16 rejoint et annonce déjà le *v.* 21.

1.4. Isa. xix 16-25 affirme à maintes reprises que Yahweh sera connu et vénéré par les Egyptiens. Tout d'abord, non seulement la langue de Canaan — très probablement l'hébreu resté langue du culte (Feuillet, p. 69) — sera parlée en Egypte, mais de plus il se trouvera dans ce pays des personnes qui adhéreront à Yahweh au point de se lier à lui par serment (*nišbaᶜ lᵉ*) (*v.* 18) (Wildberger, p. 728).

1.5. Ensuite il y aura un autel dédié à Yahweh au coeur même du pays (*bᵉtôk ʾereṣ*) de l'Egypte. Le culte de Dieu n'est donc plus limité à Jérusalem: il s'étend en terre païenne, de surcroît à l'Egypte (*v.* 19a). L'autel est un premier signe de la présence de Yahweh au pays de Pharaon.

1.6. Nous verrions dans la stèle (*maṣṣēbāh*) un deuxième signe de la présence de Dieu (Gen. xxxii 28,18; Ex. xxxiv 13) en même temps que le témoin d'une alliance entre Yahweh et l'Egypte et d'un engagement des Egyptiens vis-à-vis de Yahweh; un peu comme en Jos. xxiv 26 et surtout Ex. xxiv 4-8, où nous trouvons aussi un autel et douze stèles.[5] Faut-il croire qu'au contraire de Ex. xxiv 4, Isa. xix 19 ne parle que d'une stèle, parce que celle-ci ne représente que le seul peuple égyptien? Quoi qu'il en soit, Isa. xix 19 n'est pas sans accuser une parenté littéraire avec Ex. xxiv 4.

1.7. De ce qui précède il apparaît que le *v.* 19b prépare le *v.* 20, où l'on affirme que l'autel et la stèle constitueront un signe (*'ōt*) et un témoin (*ᶜēd*) pour Yahweh.

Bien que, grammaticalement parlant, *lyhwh* puisse se traduire par: (signe et témoin) de Yahweh, à Yahweh, ou pour Yahweh, nous pensons

---

[4] P. Joüon, *Grammaire de l'hébreu biblique* (Rome, 1947), § 150 *e*.

[5] Cf. R. de Vaux, *Les institutions de l'A.T. II* (Paris, 1960), pp. 109—10.

qu'il faut préférer la dernière traduction (pour), qui est le sens habituel de ces tournures: Ex. xii 13; xiii 9; Nb. xvii 3,25 pour *'ōt* et Isa. lv 4 pour *ᶜēd*.

Comme le montrent les textes cités ci-dessus, les signes sont généralement pour les hommes plutôt que pour Dieu. Un objet n'est habituellement appelé signe pour Dieu qu'en contexte d'alliance. Ainsi en Gen. ix 13 et xvii 11, l'arc-en-ciel et la circoncision sont signes d'alliance respectivement entre (*bên*) Dieu et l'homme d'une part et, d'autre part, entre Dieu et Abraham avec ses descendants. En Ez. xx 12,20, les sabbats sont un signe entre (*bên*) Dieu et Israël (cf. Ex. xxxi 13,17). Dans ces textes, il s'agit de signes qui rappellent à Yahweh et à Israël l'alliance conclue entre eux.

Quant au terme *ᶜēd*, témoin, Gen. xxxi 44 emploie *hāyāh leᶜēd be* dans un contexte d'alliance, tandis que Dt. xxxi 19,21,26 se servent de *leᶜēd lî* pour Yahweh en contexte de punition en cas d'infidélité à l'alliance (Dt. xxxi 20). Dans ces trois textes du Deutéronome la tournure *leᶜēd bibenê yiśrāʾēl*, témoin contre les enfants d'Israël, éclaire le texte d'Isa. xix 20: l'autel et la stèle seront des témoins pour Yahweh contre (*b*) la terre d'Egypte. Cette phrase prépare l'alliance de Dieu avec l'Egypte telle qu'affirmée en Isa. xix 25. L'autel et la stèle rappelleront à Dieu son alliance et ses engagements vis-à-vis de l'Egypte. En même temps ils seront un témoignage contre l'Egypte en cas d'infidélité, tout comme d'autres objets furent des témoins contre Israël (Dt. xxxi 19,21,26). Ici encore l'auteur exprime clairement l'intégration de l'Egypte dans l'Alliance de Dieu.

1.8. Isa. xix 20b reproduit, à n'en pas douter, la situation décrite en Jg. vi 7-9 (Feuillet, p. 75) et en Ex. iii 9-10. On y trouve les mêmes éléments: l'oppression (*lḥṣ*), le cri du peuple opprimé (*ṣᶜq*), l'envoi du libérateur (*šlḥ - hṣl - hwšyᶜ*). Les mêmes idées se retrouvent en Ex. vi 2-8. De la comparaison de ces textes il ressort que, suivant Isa. xix 26, les relations entre Dieu et l'Egypte seront celles-là mêmes que comportait l'alliance conclue entre Yahweh et Israël.[6]

Aussi n'est-ce pas étonnant que l'envoi du libérateur ait pour l'Egypte les mêmes effets salutaires que connut Israël (Feuillet, p. 75): non seulement Yahweh se révélera (*nôdaᶜ*) aux Egyptiens,[7] mais de plus ceux-ci le reconnaîtront comme leur Dieu, au point de lui rendre un culte,[8] par des

---

[6] Feuillet, p. 75; Wildberger, p. 741; Bright, p. 503.

[7] Le verbe *yādaᶜ* est avec *gālāh* et *rāʾāh* l'un des termes utilisés pour parler de la révélation de Dieu (1 Sam. iii 7; Ps. xcviii 2).

[8] Cf. Ex. iv 23, v 1,3,8, xii 31: *ᶜbd* et *zbḥ*.

sacrifices (*zebaḥ*), des offrandes (*minḥāh*) et des voeux (*nēder*), à l'instar d'Israël (*v.* 21).[9]

1.9. Mais en ce *v.* 21, l'affirmation ne porte pas tant sur le fait que Dieu se révèle aux Egyptiens — il le faisait déjà[10] —, mais plutôt sur le fait que ceux-ci saisissent cette révélation et se convertissent à Yahweh. Ainsi Isa. xix 21 prend le contre-pied de Ex. v 2, où Pharaon rejette Yahweh en disant: "Qui est Yahweh pour que j'écoute sa voix...? Je ne connais point Yahweh (*lōʾ yādaᶜtî yhwh*)." Aussi préférerions-nous considérer *weᵉnôdaᶜ yhwh... weᵉyādeᶜû* (*v.* 21a) comme une proposition conditionnelle (Joüon § 167 b), symétrique au *v.* 22.

1.10. Au *v.* 22, grâce à la tournure hébraïque de l'infinitif absolu postposé suivi d'un second infinitif absolu (Joüon § 123 *l*), l'auteur exprime avec élégance comment en ce jour-là l'Egypte sera totalement intégrée dans le projet salvifique de Dieu. Alors que, pendant l'Exode, Dieu frappait l'Egypte (*ngp*, *maggēpāh*) pour sauver Israël (Ex. xii 13,23,27; Jos. xxiv 5), dans notre texte, par contre, si Dieu frappe les Egyptiens, c'est pour aussitôt les guérir (quasi-simultanéité). Il s'agit avant tout de peines médicinales, telles qu'Israël en a connu au fil de son histoire, et qui auront pour effet la conversion des Egyptiens (*weᵉšābû ᶜad yhwh*). Compte tenu de ce qui vient d'être dit, il s'agit en fait de la conversion qui signifie résipiscence, et non plus de la première conversion ou adoption du yahwisme déjà opérée au *v.* 21.[11] Une telle conversion fera que Dieu exaucera (*nᶜtr*) la prière des Egyptiens. Ici l'auteur se sert du verbe typique de l'intercession (cf. Ex. viii 26) (Alonso Schökel, pp. 32-3).

On notera qu'aux *vv.* 21-22, en plus des contacts littéraires, un rappel de l'Exode *a contrario* est contenu dans le fait que Yahweh ne traite plus les Egyptiens comme au temps où Israël sortit de l'Egypte.

1.11. Le verset 23 annonce qu'il y aura une route (*mᵉsillāh*) allant de l'Egypte à l'Assyrie et inversement. Sans doute cette phrase annonce-t-elle une ère de paix entre les deux nations ainsi que la fin de leur rivalité traditionnelle. Mais le texte recèle une connotation particulière. En effet, sur un total de 8 autres emplois dans le livre d'Isaïe — 26 dans tout l'Ancien Testament — le terme *mᵉsillāh* est utilisé 4 fois en contexte de second Exode, pour désigner la grand-route qu'empruntera le peuple sauvé et racheté ou Reste d'Israël (xi 16, xl 3, xlix 11, lxii 10). Le contexte est similaire en Isa. xix 23: Assur et l'Egypte sont considérées

---

[9] Cf. Lev. xxvii 2 ss.; Nb. vi 2: *hiplîʾ neder*; xxi 2, xxx 3,4: *nādar neder.*

[10] Cf. Ex. vii 5,17, viii 18-19 et xi 7, xii 30-32. Voir notre étude sur "Révélation-dans-l'histoire", dans *Christianisme et identité africaine* (Kinshasa-Aachen, 1980), pp. 160-3.

[11] Cf. Feuillet, p. 76; contre Wildberger, p. 742.

comme des peuples rachetés et sauvés à l'instar d'Israël (cf. *v.* 20). Aussi tous les trois vont-ils de concert rendre un culte (*ᶜbd*) à Yahweh: ce n'est plus à Israël que revient l'exclusivité du culte de Yahweh. Le culte qu'Assur et l'Egypte rachetées rendront à Dieu n'est pas sans rappeler celui qu'Israël (re)commença à lui rendre après la libération d'Egypte (Ex. iii 12, iv 23, x 26, xiii 5).

1.12. Nous croyons que le *v.* 24 est une allusion à la situation historique pendant laquelle l'Egypte et l'Assyrie se disputaient la domination du monde aux dépens d'Israël placé entre les deux. Mais cette situation va changer: Israël n'est plus "troisième" en tant que nation intermédiaire au sens purement topographique, mais comme médiateur de bénédiction et de salut pour l'Egypte et l'Assyrie, conformément à Gen. xii 3 et parallèles. Israël joue donc pleinement le rôle que Dieu lui a confié dans l'histoire du salut.

Mais parler d'Israël comme bénédiction pour l'Egypte ne va pas sans évoquer la requête de Pharaon à Moïse: "Allez rendre un culte à Yahweh ainsi que vous l'avez demandé... et appelez la bénédiction sur moi aussi (*ûbēraktem gam ʾōtî*)" (Ex. xii 31-32). La requête a été exaucée par Dieu.

1.13. L'actuation et la réalisation effective du rôle médiateur d'Israël dans le salut que Dieu accorde à tous les peuples signifie que le Seigneur fait *exemplariter* pour le peuple élu ce qu'il fait ou entend faire à tous les peuples. De fait, le *v.* 25, point culminant de cette péricope, place l'Egypte et Assur sur le même pied qu'Israël. En effet nous voyons appliquer à ces deux peuples les attributs les plus exclusifs d'Israël. L'Egypte est appelée *ᶜammî*, mon peuple. Cette appellation revient trois fois dans la Genèse pour désigner le peuple d'un roi (xxiii 11, xli 40) ou celui dont quelqu'un est originaire (xlix 29).

Aucun autre livre du Pentateuque n'utilise l'expression, hormis l'Exode. Dans le cycle de l'Exode, *ᶜammî*, ou *ᶜammî bᵉnê yiśrāʾēl*, mon peuple les enfants d'Israël (iii 7, v 1, vii 16, viii 19, — iii 10, vii 4,26, viii 1,23) est employé pour désigner Israël, peuple de Dieu, par opposition à l'Egypte que seul Pharaon appelle *ᶜammî* alors que Dieu l'appelle *ᶜammeka*, ton peuple (cf. viii 19, xii 31).

Dans le livre d'Isaïe *ᶜammî* désigne Israël (i 3, iii 12, v 13...) tantôt opposé à Assur (x 24) tantôt opposé à tous les autres peuples qui sont sur le point d'être punis par Dieu (xxvi 20). Le caractère prégnant de notre verset ressort d'une comparaison de Isa. xix 25 avec li 16, où *ᶜammî-ʾattāh* désigne Sion.

Quant à l'attribut *maᶜăśēh yādāy*, "oeuvre de mes mains", "ma création", appliqué ici à Assur, il est réservé à Israël en Isa. lx 21 et lxiv 7;

tandis qu'en xlvii 6, *naḥălātî*, mon héritage, lui est appliqué en parallélisme avec *ᶜammî*.

De ce qui précède, rien ne semble confirmer l'opinion qui veut que le *v.* 25 réserve à Israël une place privilégiée dans la nouvelle situation décrite en Isa. xix 16-25. Bien au contraire ce verset est le point culminant de l'universalisme affirmé dans toute cette péricope: l'Egypte et l'Assyrie sont désormais membres à part entière de l'Alliance réservée jusqu'alors au peuple élu.

Conclusion

Si d'emblée le texte d'Isa. xix 16-25 frappe par son universalisme, les analyses que nous venons de faire viennent confirmer cette impression d'ensemble. Le jour viendra donc, où les prérogatives spirituelles d'Israël, fondées sur l'Alliance conclue avec Yahweh, ne seront plus l'apanage du peuple élu, mais seront étendues à ceux-là mêmes qui incarnaient l'opposition à la réalisation du plan salvifique de Dieu.

Mais ce qui impressione dans cette péricope, c'est le grand nombre de liens littéraires entre notre texte et le cycle de l'Exode. Pour dépeindre le salut que Dieu accordera à l'Egypte, le rédacteur utilise le vocabulaire qui décrivait le salut et la libération même d'Israël au temps de la sortie d'Egypte. Ce fait littéraire rend plus marquante la note universaliste de cette péricope: l'Egypte vivra l'expérience même de salut qu'a connue Israël. Ce recours au vocabulaire de l'Exode n'est que normal, si l'on sait que le vocabulaire du cycle de l'Exode constitue dans la Bible le moule littéraire du salut de Dieu.

Le temps est venu d'examiner le traitement que la Version alexandrine (LXX) a réservé au texte d'Isa. xix 16-25.

2. *Isa. xix 16-25 (LXX)*

2.1. Il va sans dire que l'étude de notre péricope dans la LXX ne vise pas à retrouver dans la Version alexandrine toutes les analyses du texte faites ci-dessus ou encore celles des commentateurs contemporains. Il s'agit avant tout de montrer comment le traducteur a compris le texte et d'expliquer pourquoi il l'a ainsi compris. Mais ce but ne peut être atteint sans que soient explorées au préalable les différentes lectures possibles sinon probables du texte original. Celles-ci, en effet, permettent bien souvent d'élucider les options du traducteur. C'est dire que la lecture de la LXX avec le texte hébreu en regard doit être complétée par une lecture autonome du texte grec.

2.2. Comme remarque générale pour notre péricope, il faut reconnaître que, dans l'ensemble, mis à part les faits que nous signalerons ci-après, la Version des LXX suit de très près l'original hébreu. Aussi nous arrêterons-nous seulement à des écarts de traduction ou à d'autres éléments dignes d'attention.

2.3. Au *v.* 16, la LXX rend les verbes *w*[e]*ḥārad ûpāḥad* par deux substantifs ἐν φόβῳ καὶ ἐν τρόμῳ déterminant le verbe ἔσονται. Le sens est le même, mais la traduction grecque est plus élégante.

Quant à la locution *mipp*[e]*nê*, la LXX la traduit littéralement par ἀπὸ προσώπου au *v.* 16, alors qu'au verset suivant, elle est rendue normalement par la préposition διά. On trouve ailleurs la tournure ἀπὸ προσώπου comme pendant grec de *mipp*[e]*nê*, tant au sens causal — à cause de — (Isa. ii 10,19,21, lvii 1) qu'au sens local — devant — (Isa. vii 16, xvii 9, xix 1, xxxi 8). Au sens causal, la LXX ne paraît pas faire de distinction entre les deux traductions de *mipp*[e]*nê* (διά et ἀπὸ προσώπου).

2.4. Quand il signifie "agiter, brandir", ἐπιβάλλειν (*v.* 16) se rencontre comme correspondant grec de *hēnîp* en Ex. xx 25; Isa. xi 15, xix 16, même si cette équation ne revient que 6 fois sur 51 emplois dans la LXX.

2.5. Au *v.* 17 le traducteur alexandrin distingue, comme il se doit, le sujet du verbe *yazkîr* (ὀνομάσῃ) de celui de *yipḥad* (φοβηθήσονται). L'équivoque est évitée par la traduction de *miṣrayim* et *ʾēlāw* par Αἰγυπτίοι et αὐτοῖς (au pluriel). Cependant l'anacoluthe reste en grec comme en hébreu. En comparant ce verset avec Jos. xxiii 7, Amos vi 11 et Isa. xxvi 13, où ὀνομάζειν traduit *hizkîr*, il faut comprendre que la cause de l'effroi des Egyptiens n'est rien d'autre que le seul fait de prononcer le nom de Juda. La LXX explicite de façon heureuse le texte original.

2.6. Au même *v.* 17 comparé au *v.* 16, nous trouvons un fait littéraire surprenant: le participe *yôʿēṣ* est traduit par le parfait moyen βεβούλευται, alors qu'au *v.* 16 *mēnîp* était rendu par le *futur* ἐπιβαλεῖ. Mais ces deux traductions du participe sont absolument correctes, du fait de la concordance des temps: ἐπιβαλεῖ par rapport à ἔσονται qui lui est simultané (*v.* 16), et βεβούλευται par rapport à φοβηθήσονται qui lui est postérieur (*v.* 17). Néanmoins, si on lit le texte grec en lui-même, le parfait βεβούλευται et le futur ἐπιβαλεῖ nous semblent se rapporter à l'ensemble des actes punitifs dont il est question aux *vv.* 3-15. Dans la LXX, "ce jour-là" du *v.* 16 signifie le jour où Dieu entrera en Egypte (*v.* 1) et les *vv.* 16-17 sont la conclusion des *vv.* 3-15. Mais ces punitions divines seront le point de départ d'un choc salutaire chez les Egyptiens (*vv.* 18ss.). Signalons que le futur ἐπιβαλεῖ comme le parfait βεβούλευται conserve au participe son aspect duratif que l'hébreu ne pouvait ici rendre autrement.

2.7. L'expression ὀμνύναι τῷ ὀνόματι κυρίου mérite que l'on s'y arrête. Ainsi que nous l'avons dit, l'expression hébraïque *nišbaʿ l*[e], utilisée au *v.*

18, signifie "se lier par serment (à Yahweh)". Il s'agit de voir si la traduction grecque rend correctement l'hébreu.

2.7.1. On le sait, le grec classique construisait le verbe ὀμνύναι avec le datif pour désigner la personne à qui on fait le serment, celle à qui on se lie par le serment, et l'accusatif ou encore κατά avec le génitif pour la personne par qui on jure, c'est-à-dire celle qu'on prend ou invoque comme témoin du serment.

De prime abord, "jurer au nom de Yahweh" semble appartenir à cette dernière catégorie. Mais les options lexicographiques de la LXX ne paraissent pas entièrement aller dans ce sens.

2.7.2. Tout d'abord nous trouvons dans la LXX la construction classique, soit avec le datif et l'accusatif (Gen. xxi 23; Jos. ii 12, ix 18,19), soit avec κατά et le génitif (1 Sam. xxx 15; Soph. i 5). A ces exemples est assimilée l'expression "jurer par sa (main) droite ou bien par sa gloire", qui régit soit l'accusatif (Dt. xxxii 40) soit κατά avec le génitif (Isa. lxii 8). Ce qu'il y a d'intéressant dans cette première catégorie, c'est que l'hébreu construit le verbe *nišbaᶜ* avec les prépositions *lᵉ* et *bᵉ*, pour désigner respectivement la personne à qui on se lie par serment et celle par qui on fait le serment: *hiššābᵉᶜāh lî bēʾlōhîm* (Gen. xxi 23). La LXX traduit: ὄμοσόν μοι τὸν κύριον. Ainsi donc, pour traduire *nišbaᶜ bēʾlōhîm*, la LXX met à l'accusatif la personne par qui l'on jure (Dieu), tandis que celle à qui on jure se trouve au datif.

2.7.3. Or cette même locution (*nišbaᶜ bēʾlōhîm*), qu'elle comporte ou non le datif de la personne à qui on fait le serment (1 Sam. xxiv 22 et 1 R. ii 8 [avec datif]; Jg. xxi 7 [sans datif], est rendue par ἐν κυρίῳ pour indiquer la personne par qui on jure, tandis que, le cas échéant, celle à qui on jure se trouve au datif.

2.7.4. En revanche l'expression "jurer au nom de", *nišbaᶜ bᵉšēm*, est toujours traduite dans la LXX par τῷ ὀνόματι (Dt. x 20; Isa. xlviii 1; Jer. xii 16, li [xliv] 26; Zach. v 4; Mal. iii 5). Que ὄνομα soit déterminé par un nom propre (κυρίου) ou par un pronom (μου, αὐτοῦ), le datif n'est jamais précédé par la préposition ἐν, comme c'est le cas dans la locution précédente, où *byhwh* se traduit par ἐν κυρίῳ. Ceci frappe d'autant plus que cette formule sémitique invitait à l'emploi de la préposition ἐν, comme l'atteste le NT (Mt. v 34-35); surtout que "jurer par la terre (*bāʾāreṣ*)" est traduit en Mt. v 35 par ἐν τῇ γῇ et dans la LXX par ἐπὶ τῆς γῆς (Isa. lxv 16).

En conclusion, l'examen des faits littéraires montre que la LXX met toujours au datif la personne *à qui* on prête le serment, tandis que celle *par qui* on le prête se construit de trois manières différentes: à l'accusatif, avec κατά et le génitif, ou encore avec ἐν et le datif. Par cette dernière construction, la LXX se distingue du grec classique.

2.7.5. C'est pourquoi nous inclinons à croire que, dans l'expression qui nous occupe, le datif τῷ ὀνόματι indique, par une influence de la signification du nom chez les Sémites, la personne *à qui* on fait le serment. Ce datif aurait donc la même fonction que les autres datifs employés dans la LXX pour traduire la locution *nišbaᶜ lᵉ*, "jurer à quelqu'un". De ce fait la traduction adoptée par la Version alexandrine en Isa. xix 18 rend parfaitement l'original hébreu qui dit "se lier par serment *à* Yahweh".

2.8. Pour ce qui est de πόλις ασεδεκ (*v.* 18), l'explication la plus probable est qu'il s'agit d'une simple translittération de l'hébreu *haṣṣedeq*: "Ville de la justice". Une seule difficulté: ce même nom se trouve déjà en Isa. i 26 pour désigner Jérusalem, ville où règne à nouveau la justice, la sainteté, la fidélité à Dieu. Et ici la LXX traduit simplement par πόλις δικαιοσύνης. Sans doute le traducteur a-t-il évité de donner à la ville égyptienne le même attribut qu'à Jérusalem. Cette explication tient, même si l'on admet que πόλις ασεδεκ signifie "ville de la légitimité (du culte du Seigneur en Egypte)", c'est-à-dire Héliopolis.[12]

2.9. Signalons un écart de traduction au verset 20: le texte hébreu affirme que "ce sera un signe et un témoin pour Yahweh", et la LXX traduit: "ce sera pour le Seigneur un signe éternel". L'auteur alexandrin a-t-il simplement lu *ᶜad* au lieu de *ᶜēd* (cf. Job. xix 24)? Il y a plus, nous semble-t-il. Car l'expression ἔσται σημεῖον avec un datif de personne comporte trois acceptions dans la LXX: 1° un signe, une réalité qui rappelle à quelqu'un ses engagements ou liens vis-à-vis d'un autre (cfr. Ex. xiii 16, xxxi 17; Nb. xvii 10 [25]); 2° la preuve, le témoignage d'un fait ou d'une réalité (Isa. xxxvii 30, xxxviii 7; Jer. li [xliv] 29); 3° le symbole, le présage, le signe d'un événement futur (Isa. xx 3; Ez. iv 3). Nous pensons qu'en Isa. xix 20 il s'agit de la deuxième acception (preuve, témoignage). Aussi n'était-il plus nécessaire de traduire le terme *ᶜēd* qui, dans cette acception de σημεῖον, devenait superflu.

2.9.1. Nous trouvons un texte semblable au nôtre en Isa. lv 13. Mais ici la LXX modifie quelque peu le texte hébreu et parle du Seigneur qui sera lui-même un nom et un signe éternels qui ne disparaîtront pas, alors que l'hébreu dit: "ce (= le retour de l'exil) sera pour Yahweh un nom et un signe éternels (des voies insondables de Dieu présent dans son peuple: *vv.* 8-9)".

2.9.2. Signalons au *v.* 19 que la parenté littéraire relevée avec Ex. xxiv 4 n'est plus aussi apparente dans la LXX qui, en ce passage, traduit *maṣṣēbāh* par λίθος, pierre.

2.9.3. Il faut noter que la conséquence des *vv.* 19-20 dans la LXX n'est pas tout à fait identique à celle du texte hébreu, du fait que le tra-

---

[12] *TOB* (Paris, 1976), p. 791, note n.

ducteur alexandrin a rendu par un causatif le *kî* temporel du *v.* 20. La suite logique de ces versets se présente dès lors comme suit: l'autel et la stèle seront à jamais un témoignage pour le Seigneur, puisqu'ils (Egyptiens) crieront vers le Seigneur à cause de leurs oppresseurs et que le Seigneur leur enverra un sauveur... Autrement dit: si tant est que, dans l'avenir, ils crieront vers le Seigneur et qu'il leur enverra un sauveur, c'est parce que la stèle et l'autel constituent un témoignage éternel pour le Seigneur.[13] On le voit, de façon prégnante et plus marquée encore que l'hébreu, cette phrase de la LXX affirme que l'autel et la stèle sont signes de l'alliance et de la fidélité de Dieu et de ce fait un recours sûr pour le peuple égyptien.

2.9.4. Le sujet du verbe "crieront" (κεκράξονται) est moins précis dans la LXX: cela pourrait être les "cinq villes juives" du *v.* 18, comme le montre une comparaison du *v.* 18 (ἐν Αἰγύπτῳ) avec les *vv.* 19 et 20 (ἐν χώρᾳ Αἰγύπτου). Mais cela pourrait aussi signifier les Egyptiens en tant que tels; ce qui s'accorderait mieux avec le τοῖς Αἰγυπτίοις du *v.* 21, qui en serait la suite logique. Nous optons plutôt pour cette deuxième interprétation.

2.9.5. Nous retrouvons dans la LXX les ressemblances du texte hébreu d'Isa. xix 20b avec Ex. iii 9-10 et Jos. vi 7-9 concernant la situation similaire d'Israël et de l'Egypte dans l'oppression, l'appel à Dieu et le salut divin.

2.10. De ce que nous avons dit en 2.9.4 découle que la phrase "le Seigneur sera connu des Egyptiens" (*v.* 21) peut signifier une connaissance qui leur vient soit du fait de la présence d'Israël sur le territoire égyptien, soit d'une révélation communiquée par le ministère du sauveur que leur enverra le Seigneur. Mais en comparant Isa. xix 20 avec le Ps. lxxv 2,4 (LXX), nous devons sans doute affirmer que Dieu sera connu à partir des merveilles qu'il déploiera pour les Egyptiens.

2.10.1. Dans ce même *v.* 21 on notera deux tournures absolument classiques: εὐχὰς εὔχεσθαι[14] ou ἀποδιδόναι: adresser des voeux ou (les) accomplir.

2.11. Au *v.* 22, la phrase principale de l'hébreu (*wᵉšābû wᵉneᶜtar...*) n'est pas rendue dans toutes ses nuances par la LXX qui coordonne simplement tous les verbes de ce verset, les situant pour ainsi dire dans une action successive au *v.* 21. Mais en soi cette traduction peut se justifier du point de vue purement grammatical.

2.12. Le terme ὁδός (Isa. xl 3, xlix 11, lxii 10) tout comme δίοδος (Isa. xi 16) est utilisé aussi dans le cadre du retour de l'esclavage et de l'exil. Cependant, si l'on tient compte de la deuxième partie du *v.* 23 (καὶ

---

[13] Voir l'emploi de ὅτι en Luc viii 47.

[14] Dém. 381,10; Eschn. 4,10; Xén. Mem. 2,2,10.

εἰσελεύσονται...), il ne semble pas que le traducteur l'entende ici en ce sens. Il doit plutôt s'agir d'une route permettant le commerce et même la guerre entre l'Egypte et l'Assyrie, puisque le traducteur affirme que "les Egyptiens serviront les Assyriens". On a l'impression qu'il s'agit d'une déportation des Egyptiens, puisque la LXX traduit "une route ira de l'Egypte à l'Assyrie" (TM) par "le chemin de l'Egypte sera vers les Assyriens" (LXX). Les trois phrases qui suivent ("Et les Assyriens entreront en Egypte et les Egyptiens chez les Assyriens, et les Egyptiens serviront les Assyriens") semblent signifier que les Assyriens asserviront les Egyptiens en les déportant dans leur pays.

Tout cela paraît être une interprétation que le traducteur fait du *v.* 22: "Dieu frappera (πατάξει) les Egyptiens d'un grand malheur (πλήγη) mais il les guérira; et ils se convertiront au Seigneur..." C'est le "pattern" même des peines médicinales infligées par Dieu à Israël, notamment pendant la servitude d'Egypte et l'exil à Babylone. Aussi n'est-il pas étonnant que le traducteur interprète le "malheur" en question comme étant un asservissement de l'Egypte par l'Assyrie, un peu comme le fut l'exil pour Israël. Le traducteur recourt donc à l'expérience d'Israël pour concevoir et exprimer le salut que Dieu donnera à l'Egypte. Grammaticalement cette traduction de la LXX est correcte et le texte s'y prête, mais le traducteur a simplement perdu de vue le sens cultuel de *ʿābad*, λατρεύειν (Ex. iii 12, iv 23, x 26, xiii 5). Notons qu'en ce passage la LXX contient la même lecture que les Targums.[15]

2.13. Les *vv.* 24-25 affirment qu'"en ce jour-là Israël sera (le) troisième béni parmi les Assyriens et les Egyptiens sur la terre que le Seigneur Sabaoth a bénie en disant: Béni soit mon peuple qui est en Egypte et celui qui est en Assyrie et Israël mon héritage."

2.13.1. Au *v.* 24 la lecture des LXX diffère de celle des commentateurs modernes, mais elle est grammaticalement inattaquable: le traducteur lit *beru${}^{}$kāh* plutôt que *berākāh* et en fait un deuxième adjectif de *yiśrāʾēl* à la suite de *šelîšîyāh*; aussi lit-il logiquement au *v.* 25: *ʾăšer bērākāh*, "que le Seigneur a bénie (terre)".

2.13.2. De prime abord, on a l'impression que la Version alexandrine s'éloigne du texte hébreu: le *v.* 24 affirmerait sans plus un séjour d'Israël parmi les Egyptiens et les Assyriens, tandis qu'au *v.* 25 seul Israël serait appelé mon peuple et mon héritage, et bénéficierait dès lors de la bénédiction divine, dont seraient exclues l'Egypte et l'Assyrie.

2.13.3. Mais tout compte fait, la LXX rend parfaitement le texte hébreu. En effet, si le *v.* 24 affirme qu'Israël est (le) troisième béni, c'est

[15] Nous remercions R. Le Déaut de nous avoir fourni ces données du Targum.

qu'il l'est avec deux autres.[16] Ceux-ci sont précisément désignés par l'incise "parmi les Assyriens et les Egyptiens", qui doit donc signifier "avec les Assyriens et les Egyptiens". C'est le sens de τρίτος en pareil cas (Dan. v 7,16,29 Theod.). Le sens qu'il a en Nb. ii 24, où cet adjectif indique la succession, ne convient pas ici. Trois faits littéraires confirment cette interprétation.

Tout d'abord la position de l'incise ἐν τοῖς 'Ασσυρίοις καὶ ἐν τοῖς Αἰγυπτίοις entre τρίτος et εὐλογημένος écarte toute équivoque sur la possibilité d'une bénédiction exclusive à Israël et qu'il recevrait en Egypte ou en Assyrie. Ces deux peuples sont donc bénis, eux aussi, ensemble avec Israël (le troisième).

Ensuite la répétition du pronom personnel au *v.* 25b: ὁ ἐν Αἰγύπτῳ καὶ ὁ ἐν 'Ασσυρίοις distingue deux sujets.

Enfin, cela étant, la structure littéraire des *vv.* 24 et 25b amène à la même conclusion. Ces deux versets sont construits, dans la LXX, en un parallélisme chiastique commandé par le participe εὐλογημένος: *v.* 24 -Ισραηλ (a) (τρίτος) (x) - ἐν 'Ασσυρίοις (b) - ἐν Αἰγυπτίοις (c) - εὐλογημένος (d) *v.* 25b - εὐλογημένος (d') (ὁ λαός μου) (x') - ἐν Αἰγύπτῳ (c') - ἐν 'Ασσυρίοις (b') Ισραηλ (a').

On remarque la position-clé de εὐλογημένος ainsi que l'importance de l'adjectif τρίτος qui, allant avec ce participe, répond à λαός μου. En vertu de cette structure, les parties équivalentes a-a', b-b', c-c' et d-d' doivent signifier la même chose. Dès lors l'incise "mon peuple qui est en Egypte et celui qui est en Assyrie" (*v.* 25) signifie non pas Israël qui garde son titre de "héritage de Dieu", mais bien les Egyptiens et les Assyriens comme au *v.* 24. Il faut donc conclure que le traducteur alexandrin n'exclut pas Egyptiens et Assyriens de la bénédiction divine dont ils sont l'objet dans le texte hébreu.

On pourrait ajouter l'expression ἐν τῇ γῇ, qui n'a cependant pas plus qu'une valeur d'indice. Pour ce qui est de notre propos, notons tout d'abord qu'en Isaïe comme dans le reste de la LXX, le terme γῆ traduit non seulement *ʾădāmāh* (Isa. vi 11, vii 16, xiv 1,2, xxiv 21... xxxii 13: 8 fois) mais aussi et surtout *ʾereṣ* (Isa. i 2,7,19, v 8, vi 3... 147 fois). Le vocable γῆ signifie tantôt toute la terre (Isa. xii 5, xxxvii 11,16,20), tantôt une région, un pays (Isa. xxxii 13: Israël; xxxiv 9: Edom; xxxvii 7: Assyrie) ou encore la terre, séjour des morts (Isa. xxvi 19). Quant aux prépositions, la LXX d'Isaïe donne nettement la préférence à l'expression ἐπὶ τῆς γῆς (28 fois) par rapport à ἐν τῇ γῇ que nous ne rencontrons que neuf fois dont trois dans la tournure "dans une terre aride" (διψώσῃ) (xxxii 2, xxxv 6, liii 2).

[16] Cf. Homère, Od. 20,185: τρίτος ἦλθε, cité par A. Bailly, *Dictionnaire grec-français* (Paris, 1950), p. 1964.

Compte tenu de ces faits, notamment des équations lexicographiques et des acceptions du terme γῆ dans la LXX, on ne peut manquer de constater le soin avec lequel le traducteur évite en Isa. xix 16-25 de traduire *ʾădāmāh* et *ʾereṣ* par γῆ, en dehors du *v.* 24. Il les traduit l'un et l'autre par χώρα (*vv.* 17,19,20), terme qui ailleurs ne revient qu'une fois en Isaïe (i 7) comme pendant grec de *ʾădāmāh* et 18 fois comme celui de *ʾereṣ*, ce qui est minime par rapport aux équations de γῆ pour chacun des deux termes. On peut se demander si dans cette péricope le traducteur ne veut pas opposer γῆ à χώρα (région, pays) et lui donner un sens plus général. D'autant que dans la LXX d'Isaïe, ce *v.* 24 est le seul passage (sur neuf), où ἐν τῇ γῇ traduit *beqereb hāʾāreṣ*: on ne peut donc pas parler d'une expression consacrée. La "terre" (γῆ) ne signifierait donc pas la terre d'Israël, mais aussi l'Egypte et l'Assyrie du *v.* 25.

Il faut donc reconnaître que, loin de trahir l'original hébreu, le traducteur alexandrin, grâce à des retouches rédactionnelles, est parvenu à affirmer la même idée: l'Egypte et l'Assyrie sont intégrées dans la bénédiction réservée à Israël depuis l'élection d'Abraham.

Ces analyses nous donnent la traduction suivante pour les *vv.* 24-25: "Ce jour-là, Israël sera le troisième béni avec les Assyriens et les Egyptiens sur la terre, que le Seigneur Sabaoth a bénie en disant: 'Béni soit mon peuple qui est en Egypte et en Assyrie ainsi qu'Israël mon héritage.'"

Cette lecture repose essentiellement sur deux faits littéraires: 1° le sens classique de la préposition ἐν (dans, au milieu de, parmi), sens que nous retrouvons fréquemment dans la LXX en général et Isaïe en particulier (Isa. v 26, xii 14, lii 5);[17] 2° la répétition du pronom relatif ὁ déterminant le substantif λαός au *v.* 25. En effet, dans la LXX d'Isaïe, le pronom relatif déterminant un substantif n'est pas répété après la conjonction καὶ lorsqu'il s'agit du même sujet (Isa. xi 11, xlii 5, xlv 6,18,19b).[18] Ces deux faits, à leur tour, commandent la structure du texte mentionnée ci-dessus.

Néanmoins, dans la LXX, la préposition ἐν signifie parfois: "entre" (*bên*) (Isa. v 3: *hapax*; Ex. xxxi 13,17). En ce cas, le texte grec d'Isa. xix 24-25 peut se lire comme suit: "Israël sera le troisième entre les Assyriens et les Egyptiens; (il sera) béni sur la terre que le Seigneur Sabaoth a bénie en disant: 'Béni soit mon peuple qui est en Egypte et en Assyrie et Israël mon héritage.'"

Dans cette traduction la bénédiction peut se comprendre comme étant réservée seulement à Israël et aux membres de ce peuple qui se trouvent

---

[17] Isa. liii 12, lv 4, lx 9, lxi 9, lxvi 19.

[18] Isa. xlvi 3, xlviii 1, li 1,15, lx 16, lxi 8, lxv 11.

en Egypte et en Assyrie.[19] Ainsi l'équivoque du texte hébreu au *v.* 24 serait reprise dans le texte grec.

Si l'on adopte cette hypothèse, le traducteur alexandrin a compris le texte en un sens anti-universaliste. Une telle réaction de la part des milieux juifs d'Alexandrie ne serait pas surprenante. Néanmoins toute la teneur du texte et les raisons invoquées ci-dessus pour la première lecture nous portent à préférer l'interprétation universaliste de Isa. xix 24-25 dans la LXX.

Conclusion

Aussi bien dans la LXX que dans l'original hébreu, Isa. xix 16-25 apparaît nettement comme un texte universaliste: le projet salvifique de Dieu va au-delà d'Israël et le salut de celui-ci ne passe plus par le malheur et l'anéantissement des autres peuples.

Au contraire, les Egyptiens connaissent Yahweh qui se manifeste à eux aussi. Cette connaissance les amène à se convertir à Yahweh et à lui rendre un culte, non plus à Jérusalem mais en pleine terre d'Egypte, où un autel et une stèle seront à jamais des signes de la présence de Dieu et des garants de sa fidélité envers les Egyptiens.

Bien plus, l'Egypte et l'Assyrie, ennemis traditionnels et irréductibles du peuple de Dieu, sont bénies au même titre qu'Israël, dont elles partagent désormais les prérogatives et les titres de gloire: elles sont, elles aussi, "peuple de Dieu" (TM + LXX) et "oeuvre de ses mains" (Assyrie: TM). Si l'anti-salut est ainsi intégré dans le projet salvifique de Dieu, on comprend pourquoi les commentateurs appliquent aux autres peuples de la terre cette extension du salut de Dieu à l'Egypte et à l'Assyrie.

L'intégration de l'Egypte (et de l'Assyrie) dans le salut conféré à Israël est donc totale. Aussi voyons-nous le texte hébreu comme la LXX employer, pour concevoir et exprimer ce projet de salut divin, le vocabulaire même utilisé dans l'expérience spirituelle d'Israël, notamment dans le cycle de l'Exode. C'est dire que Dieu fait à Israël ce qu'il entend faire à tous les peuples de la terre.

Le traitement rédactionnel que la LXX a réservé aux *vv.* 24-25 montre que le traducteur alexandrin a bien perçu le message universaliste de

---

[19] Cf. Isa. xxvii 13; mais ici les relatifs ne déterminent pas un même sujet comme en xix 25. Cette bénédiction exclusive à Israël peut évoquer celle dont il est question en Isa. lxi 9 et lxv 23. Signalons en passant que le Targum réserve la bénédiction à Israël.

l'original hébreu et l'a assumé pour son compte. On pouvait s'y attendre eu égard au milieu où la Version des LXX a été effectuée.

Dans la saisie et la maturation progressives de l'idée d'un salut universel de Dieu destiné à tous les hommes, notre péricope constitue certainement un sommet, qui ouvre des perspectives nouvelles et prépare la voie au Nouveau Testament.

ZUM EBLAITISCHEN KONJUGATIONSSYSTEM

VON

HANS-PETER MÜLLER

Münster

Da das Hebraïsche — wie das Altsüdarabische und das Äthiopische — auch in seiner Grammatik viele archaische Elemente aufweist, werden einige Bemerkungen zum eblaitischen Konjugationssystem und dessen semitistischer Relevanz am ehesten auch für die alttestamentliche Wissenschaft fruchtbar sein. Leider muß die eblaitische Konjugationsmorphologie vorwiegend aus konjugierten Elementen in Personennamen erschlossen werden: nur hier liegt allermeist syllabische Schreibung vor; im Kontext dagegen werden auch Konjugationsformen fast ausschließlich sumerographisch wiedergegeben.[1]

1. *Die Afformativkonjugation (AK)*

Das Eblaitische bestätigt die von W. von Soden[2] u.a. am Akkadischen gewonnene Erkenntnis, daß die semitische AK, d.i. das hebraistisch sog. Perfekt, ursprünglich einer tempusneutralen Konjugation von Nomina, vor allem von Adjektiven diente, also im Sinne H. Bauers ein "Nominal" war.[3] Schon im Eblaitischen hat sich dann aber wie im Akkadischen die Konjugation der Nomina von den Adjektiven (eblait. Personennamen wie *ṭa-ba-a-du* "gut ist der Vater") auch auf Substantive ausgedehnt (*a-ba-il* "ein Vater ist Il"[4]), soweit diese beschreibende

---

[1] Die Eblatexte sind mit den jüngeren frühdynastischen Perioden Mesopotamiens gleichzeitig. Dabei vertritt das Eblaitische, soweit wir bis jetzt sehen, eine alte nordsemitische Sprachgruppe (vgl. W. von Soden, "Das Nordsemitische in Babylonien und in Syrien", in L. Cagni [ed.], *La Lingua di Ebla* [Napoli, 1981, = *LdE*], S. 355-61). Geht dann die eblaitisch sprechende Semitenschicht auf eine Gruppierung zurück, die *vor* den Trägern des Reichs von Akkade nach Nordsyrien und Mesopotamien kam?

[2] *Grundriß der akkadischen Grammatik* (Roma, 1952, = *GAG*) § 77a u.ö.

[3] Etwa in *Historische Grammatik der hebräischen Sprache des AT* (Halle, 1922; Hildesheim, 1962) § 42 u.ö.

[4] Wo keine Belegstellen angegeben sind, handelt es sich um Personennamen oder Elemente von Personennamen. Zu deren Nachweis vgl. die Register zu
— G. Pettinato, *Materiali epigrafici di Ebla I* und *II* (Napoli, 1979/80);
— Ders., *Ebla. Un impero inciso nell'argilla* (Milano, 1979);
— D. O. Edzard, *Archivi reali di Ebla. Testi II* (Roma, 1981); und
— A. Archi-M. G. Biga, *Archivi reali di Ebla. Testi III* (Roma, 1982).
Aus Raumgründen können hier nur jeweils ganz wenige Beispiele gegeben werden; voll-

Funktion haben. Das Endmorphem [*-a*] für die 3.P.m.sg. ([*ṭâb-a*], [*ʾab-a*]) ist dabei Prädikativanzeiger und insofern letztlich mit der mimationslosen prädikativen Akkusativendung beim Nomen identisch.[5] Ein Funktionsunterschied zwischen der konjugierten Prädikation in *a-ba-il* und einer deklinierten Prädikation in *a-bù-il* ist nicht erkennbar. Daneben gibt es morphemlose Prädikative, etwa in *a-ḫu-ṭab* "der (göttliche) Bruder ist gut". Bei dreikonsonantigen Adjektiven lassen sich für die 3.P.m.sg. zudem drei Bildungstypen unterscheiden, da eine Tendenz besteht, die Dreisilbenstruktur durch Elision eines [*a*] auf eine Zweisilbenstruktur zu reduzieren: neben dreisilbigem *qá-ra-ba-il* "nahe ist Il" erscheint so eine *qatla*-Bildung wie *wa-at-ra-bù* [*watra-ʾabu*] "hervorragend ist der Vater" und eine *qatal*-Bildung wie *a-dar-li-im* "mächtig ist Lim".[6]

Ist also der Charakter des hebräischen "Perfekts" als einer ursprünglichen Nominalkonjugation durch eine weitere altsemitische Sprache bestätigt, so werden das hebräische "Perfekt" der sog. neutrischen Verben, also *kābēd* und *qāṭōn*, aber auch das Nipḥʿal als alte Nominalkonjugation[7] sowie einzelne Adjektivkonjugationen wie *nāʾwû* "sie sind lieblich" Jes. lii 7 von *nāʾwā* oder *yopyāpîtā* "du bist sehr schön" Ps. xlv 3 von dem Steigerungsadjektiv *ypypyh* morphologisch erst eigentlich ver-

ständigeren Nachweis bietet der Vf. in: "Das eblaitische Verbalsystem nach den bisher veröffentlichten Personennamen", *LdE*, S. 211-33, ferner demnächst in: "Neue Erwägungen zum eblaitischen Verbalsystem", bei L. Cagni (ed.), *Il bilinguismo a Ebla* (Napoli, 1984).

[5] Vgl. zum Prädikativanzeiger [*-a*] im Altakkadischen und Amurritischen I. J. Gelb, "The Origin of the West Semitic *Qatala* Morpheme", *Symbolae Linguisticae in Honorem Georgii Kuryłowicz* (Breslau-Warschau-Krakau, 1965), S. 72-80.

[6] Zur *qatla*-Bildung vgl. akkadisch *parsat* und hebräisch *qāṭᵉlā*, beides freilich für die 3.P.*fem.*sg., zur *qatal*-Bildung akkad. *paris* und hebr. *qāṭal.*

[7] Es handelt sich um diejenigen Stämme, bei denen die 3.P.m.sg. AK als Ausgangsform der Konjugation mit dem "Partizip" als Ausgangsform der betr. Deklination identisch ist. Die Bezeichnung der letzteren Funktion als Partizip ist allerdings wenig sinnvoll, da der Ausdruck für die nomina agentis fientischer Verben vorbehalten bleiben sollte, es sich bei den hier vorliegenden gemeinsamen Ausgangsformen von Deklination und Konjugation allermeist aber um beschreibende Adjektive handelt; entsprechend wird in *GAG* bei den "Zustandsverben" des Akkad. kein Partizip notiert. — Die Differenz der Vokallänge zwischen der 3.P.m.sg. AK *niqṭal* und dem Partizip Nipḥʿal *niqṭāl* fällt dabei nicht ins Gewicht: ersteres entspricht verbalem Standard ohne Tondehnung (*qāṭál*), letzteres nominalem Standard mit Tondehnung (*dābā́r*). Nach J. Blau ("Eine Theorie der Haupttondehnung im Althebraischen", *ZDMG* 133 [1983], S. 24-9, bes. 27/8) war "die Vokaldehnung" im älteren Semitisch "auf offene Haupttonsilben beschränkt"; "zur Zeit dieser Vokaldehnung hatten nur die Absolutformen der Nomina die kurzen Endvokale bewahrt, während die Konstruktformen und Verba sie bereits eingebüßt hatten und geschlossen blieben". Diese Theorie wird nicht nur vom Akkadischen, sondern auch vom Eblaitischen bestätigt: es kennt neben Nomina mit kurzen Endvokalen wie [*ʾab-u*] "Vater" Konjugationsformen ohne Endvokale wie [*ʾadar*] "mächtig ist" und [*ʾakal*] "gefressen hat".

ständlich.[8] Im Maße seiner verbalen Standardisierung wird aus dem konjugierten Adjektiv das sog. Zustandsverb, das genetisch keine eigene Kategorie darstellt.[9]

Schon im Eblaitischen findet sich die AK aber auch von fientischen Verben. Bei den transitiven Verben scheint sich dabei der Wandel von einer älteren Ergativfunktion der AK zu deren Aktivfunktion abzuspielen.[10] War die Eblaitische wie die akkadische AK einmal überhaupt eine nicht-objektbezogene Nominalkonjugation, so ist ihre Ergativfunktion bei der Anwendung auf transitive Verben sozusagen vorprogrammiert. Vermutlich hat die AK transitiver Verben in dieser Ergativfunktion, also etwa akkadisch *paris* "ist entschieden (worden)", einmal überhaupt das Passiv ersetzt. Daß das Passiv keine ursprüngliche Kategorie des Semitischen ist, zeigt schon die Vielzahl seiner Verwirklichungsformen in den semitischen Einzelsprachen. Die Nachwirkung eines alten Agentiv-Kasus mag man in der morphologischen Identität von akkadischem Nominativ und Lokativadverbialis, beide mit dem Endmorphen [*-u(m)*], erkennen, sofern gleiches Phonem vorliegt; auch im Sumerischen scheint die Postposition -e für den Agentiv mit -e für den Lokativ-Terminativ identisch zu sein. Freilich ist das semitische Verbalsystem deshalb noch nicht im ganzen ergativisch.[11] Die Überlagerung eines ergativischen und eines akkusativischen Syntaxsystems kommt auch im Georgischen[12] und

[8] Für weitere Beispiele vgl. Vf., "Die Konjugation von Nomina im Althebräischen", demnächst in *ZAW*.

[9] Eine rein verbale Erklärung der semitischen AK, wie sie etwa noch K. Aartun ("Zur morphologisch-grammatischen Interpretation der sog. neutrischen Verben im Semitischen", *UF* 7 [1975], S. 1-11) vertritt, dürfte also endgültig obsolet sein.

[10] Bekanntlich wird in einem ergativischen Konjugationssystem das Handlungsobjekt einer transitiven Verbalaussage wie das Subjekt einer intransitiven Aussage behandelt: das Handlungsobjekt wird dabei zumindest dann zum Subjekt eines von der betr. Handlung hervorgerufenen Zustands, wenn das Handlungssubjekt in der Aussage unrealisiert bleibt; die syntaktische Kategorie eines direkten Objekts fehlt ebenso wie die morphologische eines Akkusativs.

[11] Gegen I. M. Diakonoff, *Semito-Hamitic Languages* (Moskau, 1965), S. 86ff.

[12] Im Georgischen steht bei transitiven Verben, wenn eine Form des Aoriststamms gewählt wird, das Handlungsobjekt in einem ersten Nominativ, das Handlungssubjekt dagegen in einem zweiten Nominativ (Agentiv). Der erste Nominativ wird aber auch für das Subjekt intransitiver Aussagen gebraucht, gleichgültig ob der Aoriststamm oder der Präsensstamm gewählt wird. Insofern liegt also eine ergativische Struktur vor. — Wird dagegen bei transitiven Verben eine Form des Präsensstamms gewählt, so steht das Handlungssubjekt im ersten Nominativ, das Handlungsobjekt dagegen im Dativ, der nun gleichsam den Akkusativ einer Sprache mit Akkusativstruktur vertritt. Ein eigentliches Passiv mit dem Handlungsobjekt im ersten Nominativ und dem Handlungssubjekt im Dativ wird u.a. mit dem Perfekt gebildet (vgl. dazu auch τοῦτο πέπρακταί μοι). Zum einzelnen F. Zorell, *Grammatik der altgeorgischen Bibelübersetzung* (Roma, 1930) § 19, 1-4, dazu S. 7.

vielleicht im Sumerischen[13] vor; die sog. gespaltene Ergativität ist anscheinend sogar ein verbreitetes Phänomen.[14]

Die AK des G-Stamms (Qal) [*maḫiṟa*] in der eblaitischen Wendung 56 UD:KÙ lú *ma-ḫi-la* é sa-za$_x$^{ki} níg-sa$_x$(NÍNDAxŠE.ZA) udu-nita udu-nita[15] kann dementsprechend sowohl ergativisch, als auch aktivisch erklärt werden. Im ersten Falle würde der Singular [*maḫiṟa*] mit UD:KÙ als sing. Bezeichnung des Gezählten kongruieren; é stände für einen Agentiv, also wie sumerisch *é-e. Die Übersetzung müßte lauten: "56 (Einheiten) Silber, die vom Hause sa-za$_x$^{ki} als Kaufpreis für Widder empfangen *sind*". Gegen diese Deutung spricht, daß der agens bei passivisch gebrauchten Stativen transitiver Verben im benachbarten Akkadischen nicht bezeichnet zu werden pflegt. — Im zweiten Falle würde [*maḫiṟa*] mit é als Bezeichnung des Handlungssubjekts kongruieren; 56 UD:KÙ lú wäre dazu das Akkusativobjekt. Die Übersetzung müßte nun lauten: "56 (Einheiten) Silber, die das Haus sa-za$_x$^{ki} als Kaufpreis für Widder empfangen *hat*". Für die letztere Übersetzung spricht, daß die AK (der Stativ) des G-Stamms vom *maḫāru(m)*, also *maḫir(a)*, auch im Akkadischen seit alter Zeit präterital-aktivisch wie das hebräische "Perfekt" gebraucht wird.[16] Das [-*â*] *in* [*maḫiṟa*] kann übrigens bei beiden Übersetzungen sowohl als Morphem der 3.P.m.sg. wie auch als altes Subordinativmorphem im Relativsatz[17] verstanden werden.

---

[13] Dazu jetzt P. Michalowski, "Sumerian as an Ergative Language, I", *JCS* 32 (1980), S. 68-103.

[14] So hat E. A. Moravcsik ("On the Distribution of Ergative and Accusative Patterns", *Lingua* 45 [1978], S. 233-79, bes. 233) aufgewiesen, "that just like ergative languages have both ergative and accusative patterns, accusative languages, too, have patterns of both major types" (freundlicher Hinweis von Herrn Koll. G. Wilhelm, Hamburg). — Dabei scheint es kein Zufall zu sein, daß sich im Semitischen gerade eine "Perfekt"-Funktion aus der ursprünglich ergativischen AK entwickelt hat: auch im Georgischen und im Sumerischen sind präteritales Tempus und perfektiver Aspekt einem ergativischen System, Präsens-Futur und Imperfektiv einem Akkusativsystem zugeordnet. — Temporale und aspektuale Funktionen brauchen in der Grammatik übrigens ebensowenig voneinander abgeleitet zu werden wie Nebenbedeutungen von sog. Grundbedeutungen in der lexikalischen Semantik; hier wie dort herrscht primäre Komplexität der Funktionen bzw. Bedeutungen.

[15] Text TM.75.G.1782 VII 17-VIII 4; Publikation bei Edzard, *Archivi reali di Ebla. Testi II*, S. 21. — Zu [*maḫiṟa*] vgl. Anm. 34; zur Lesung SA.ZA$_x$^{ki} P. Mander, "Coeva documentazione mesopotamica per il sa-za$_x$^{ki} 'governatorato' di Ebla", *OrAnt* 19 (1980), S. 263 f.

[16] Vgl. M. B. Rowton, "The Use of the Permansive in Classic Babylonian", *JNES* 21 (1962), S. 233-303, bes. 239ff.; zum präterital-aktivischen Gebrauch des Stativ allgemein vgl. ferner die zurückhaltenden Äußerungen von Sodens (*GAG* § 77e).

[17] Zu [-*a*] als Subordinativmorphem im Altakkadischen und Altbabylonischen vgl. D. O. Edzard, "Die Modi beim älteren akkadischen Verbum", *Or.*, N.S. 42 (1973). S. 121-41, bes. 127 mit Anm. 15.

Weniger sicher scheint die präteritale Aktivfunktion der eblaitischen AK in Personennamen wie *ba-na-a-ḫu* "geschaffen hat der (göttliche) Bruder", *da-na-il* "gerichtet hat Il", *qá-na-ab* "erworben/geschaffen hat der (göttliche) Vater" u.a. Zwar verwenden die Beispiele Verbalwurzeln, die auch in anderen eblaitischen Bildungen bezeugt sind;[18] aber die zugrundeliegende Struktur ist nicht wie bei [*maḫiṛa*] und bei akkadischem *paris* das *qatil*, sondern *qatal*, das wir wie später im Hebräischen und Arabischen auf Verbalisierung eines nomen agentis *qatal*[19] zurückführen müssen.

Immerhin scheint die präterital-aktivische AK nicht länger als "westsemitisches" oder "jungsemitisches Perfekt" bezeichnet werden zu können. Schon im Akkadischen sind die Beispiele für präterital-aktivischen Stativ mit Akkusativrektion relativ häufig.[20] Vollends das mit der semitischen AK verwandte ägyptische Pseudopartizip wird gerade in der alten Sprache präterital-aktivisch verwendet,[21] um von der amurritischen und ugaritischen AK zu schweigen.[22] Durch den frühen Übergang der AK transitiver Verben von einer alten Ergativ- zur präteritalen Aktivfunktion wurde im Semitischen denn auch die Bildung eigener Passivformen nötig. So entsteht im Akkadischen der N-Stamm, der im Eblaitischen — abgesehen von einigen vierradikaligen Nomina mit der Präformativsilbe [*na*-], die den Ursprung des N-Stamms (Nipḥᶜals) aus einer Nominalkonjugation bestätigen[23] — noch ebenso zu fehlen scheint wie später im Aramäischen. In den westsemitischen Sprachen aber, in denen die präterital-aktivische Funktion der AK deren Ergativfunktion ganz verdrängt, wird ein inneres Passiv mit der Vokalfolge [*u*] - [*a*] gebildet, wozu das hebräische Puᶜᶜal und Hophᶜal gehören. Weiterhin werden Passivfunktionen

---

[18] Vgl. zu *ba-na-a-ḫu*: *ib-na* + GN "GN schuf" und *ab-na* + GN "ich schuf, o GN", zu *da-na-il*: das Partizip ᵈ*da-i-in*, das ein Verständnis von *da-na-* als konjugiertes Substantiv "Richter ist ..." ausschließt (vgl. Anm. 7), zu *qá-na-ab*: *iq-na-da-mu* "D. erwarb/schuf" und das Hypokoristikon *iq-na-um* u.a.

[19] Vgl. etwa eblaitisch *ba-da-lum* "Händler"; Archi-Biga, *Archivi reali di Ebla. Testi III*, S. 340.

[20] Etwa *šīmam maḫrāku* "den Preis habe ich erhalten" AbB 6 126 II 16; Rowton, S. 245.

[21] Vgl. E. Edel, *Altägyptische Grammatik I* (Roma, 1955) § 590, u.a.

[22] Vgl. Vf., "Wie alt ist das jungsemitische Perfekt?", demnächst in einer Festschrift.

[23] Es handelt sich um die beiden folgenden Gleichsetzungen in lexikalischen Listen:
— GÍ[RX*gunû*] = *na-sar-du-lum*
— a l - k u l = *na-pár-su-um*;
G. Pettinato, *Materiali epigrafici di Ebla IV* (= *MEE*) (Napoli, 1982), Nr. 1129.993b; freundlicher Hinweis Prof. W. von Sodens, vgl. *GAG* § 110. Ein Partizip Nt(n?) zu der in *MEE IV* Nr. 993b bezeugten vierradikaligen Wurzel *pl̥šh* will M. Krebernik ("Zu Syllabar und Orthographie der lexikalischen Texte aus Ebla", *ZA* 72 [1982], S. 178-236; 73 [1983], S. 1-47, bes. 25) in a - b a l = *ma-wu mu-tà-pár-si-ù-tum*[*mutta(p)pal̥šihūtum*]*MEE IV* Nr. 640a finden.

von Stämmen mit [*t*]-Infix und, im Aramäischen, von AKK des Passivpartizips (Verbaladjektivs) *q^eṭîl* verwirklicht.

Nachdem die AK aus einer Nominal- zu einer Verbalkonjugation geworden war, wurde das Morphem [-*a*] für die 3.P.m.sg. völlig redundant: die ohnehin eindeutige Prädikatsfunktion einer verbalen AK brauchte nicht mehr von einer Deklinationsfunktion, etwa des Nominativs einer Akkusativsprache, unterschieden zu werden; so entstehen die westsemitischen *qatal*-Perfekte und die akkadischen *paris*-Stative transitiver Verben, jeweils mit [-ø].

2. *Die Präformativkonjugation (PK)*

Die PK ist in den drei Kurzformen *yiqtul* (<*yaqtul*), *yiqtal* und *yiqtil* (<*yaqtil*) und, freilich viel seltener und darum immer noch nicht ganz sicher, in der Langform *yiqattal/ul* bezeugt. Die Kurzform dominiert in den Personennamen; die Langform scheint auf Kontexte beschränkt, wobei die sumerographische Schreibung der finiten Verben ein Grund für deren schwache Bezeugung sein wird. Bei den Kurzformen der Verba III infirmae ist die morphologische Standardisierung noch unvollkommen: so finden sich Bildungen mit thematischem Stammvokal wie *ab-ra-ḫu* [*'abra-ʾ aḫ-u*] neben Bildungen mit lexikalischem Stammvokal wie *ab-rí-a-ḫu* [*ʾabrī-ʾaḫ-u*], beide von der gleichen Wurzel *brī* "sehen" u.v.a. — Besteht auch in der eblaitischen PK eine Opposition von Kurzform und Langform, so bietet die punktual-präteritale Bedeutung der ersteren insbesondere in den Personennamen ein weiteres Argument für die von J. J. Stamm[24] angenommene präteritale, nicht jussivische Übersetzung der PK auch in den hebräischen Personennamen; sie liefert ferner einen Hintergrund mehr für die präteritale Funktion vieler scheinbarer Jussive besonders in der hebräischen Poesie.[25] Vor allem ist die präteritale Kurzform der historische Hintergrund für das narrative *wayyiqṭōl* des Prosahebräisch. Wie mir Prof. Pettinato freundlicherweise bestätigt, ist die syntaktische Figur /*wa* + (präteritales) Verb + Subjekt/ schon in eblaitischen Erzählungen relativ häufig, etwa in *wa* du_{11}-ga en "da sagte der Herrscher"[26] oder — mit *-ma* statt *wa* — in *ʾà-si-kà-ma* du_{11}-ga *an-tá* "ich ...-te dich und du sagtest".[27] Zwar stellt die Identifikation eines Su-

[24] Jetzt in *Beiträge zur hebräischen und altorientalischen Namenkunde* (Freiburg/Schweiz-Göttingen, 1980), S. 2,62 u.ö.

[25] Vgl. G. Bergsträßer, *Hebräische Grammatik II* (Leipzig, 1929; Hildesheim, 1962) § 3b, 7b.

[26] Text TM.75.G.1444 IV 4-6; Publikation bei Edzard, *Studi Eblaiti* 4 (1981), S. 35-9, bes. 38.

[27] Text TM.75.G.1394 VII 9-VIII 1; Publikation bei Edzard, *Archivi reali di Ebla. Testi II*, S. 84.

merogramms wie d u$_{11}$ - g a u.v.a. als punktual-präteritale Kurzform der PK einen gewissen Unsicherheitsfaktor dar; doch werden gerade punktuale Verben wie d u$_{11}$ (- g) "sagen" im Sumerischen meist präterital, als *ḫamṭu*, verwendet, während für den durativischen Aspekt und das präsentisch-futurische Tempus, also das *marû*, ein eigenes Lexem, nämlich e "reden", zur Verfügung steht.

Offenbar also hat es im ältesten Semitisch eine Opposition von afformativisch konjugierten Adjektiven und präformativisch konjugierten Verben gegeben, wobei einstweilen offen bleiben mag, wie früh die Verbalkonjugation ihrerseits die Opposition von Kurzform und Langform ausbildete. Nachdem nun die Afformativkonjugation auch Verben, ja sogar Transitiva erfaßt hatte, ergab sich eine Komplementarität zwischen der Ergativfunktion der AK und der ursprünglichen Aktivfunktion der PK. Da aber die PK insbesondere bei transitiven Verben wesentlich häufiger verwendet wurde als die AK, überwog das akkusativische Syntaxsystem das ergativische und entschied so über die Akkusativstruktur der semitischen Sprachen. Entsprechend erscheint in den "zweisprachigen" lexikalischen Listen aus Ebla[28] der auf das Handlungssubjekt bezogene Nominativ als die Normalform des eblaitischen Nomens.[29] Als vollends die AK von der Ergativ- zur Aktivfunktion übergegangen war, trat sie zur punktual-präteritalen Kurzform der PK in Konkurrenz; noch im Hebräischen besteht daher ein Nebeneinander von "Perfekt" und "Imperfectum consecutivum", mit einem genetisch begründeten Häufigkeitsbefund bei letzterem.

---

[28] Daß es sich bei den lexikalischen Listen bei Pettinato (*MEE IV*; vgl. Anm. 23) nicht eigentlich um Bilinguen, sondern allermeist um die Gegenüberstellung sumerographischer und semitisch-syllabischer Schreibungen handelt, hat J. Krecher auf dem Convegno internazionale su 'Il bilinguismo a Ebla' 19-22 aprile 1982 Napoli vermutet. Der Tatbestand ergibt sich m.E. auch aus dem Vorkommen phonetischer Komplemente auf "sumerischer" Seite, die nur unter Voraussetzung einer semitischen (eblaitischen) Aussprache sinnvoll sind, etwa: ^{d}BE k a l a m^{tim} = *ṭì-lu ma-tim* (Nr. 795a), d i n g i r k a l a m^{tim} = *be-lu ma-tim* (795b), g a b a^{ru} = *ma-ḫa-lu-um/lum* (947), vielleicht auch in n ì - m ù š^{tù} = *a-nu-tum* (12), u š bzw. u š^{rum} = *ša-ḫa-lum* (1112; zum graphischen Wechsel *r/l* vgl. Anm. 34) und s a g - GAR^{tù} bzw. KA.GAR^{tù} = *sá-gú-la-tum* (1221). Eigentliche sumerische Lexeme stehen dann vielleicht nur hinter den gelegentlich beigegebenen syllabischen (unorthographischen) sumerischen Schreibungen; vgl. das Register bei Pettinato, S. 406/7.

[29] Der Nominativzwang zeigt sich an:

— der gelegentlichen logogrammartigen Verwendung des Nominativs, wo man einen Genitiv erwartet, etwa in einer Gottesbezeichnung wie ^{d}BE *ma-tum* "... des Landes" oder nach Präpositionen wie in *ší-in ma-lik-tum* "für die Königin" (Krecher, "Sumerogramme und syllabische Orthographie in den Texten aus Ebla", *LdE*, S. 135-54, bes. 150/1; Krebernik, *ZA* 73, S.7[29], 36) und an

— der Anfügung der Nominativendung [*-u*(*m*)] sogar an syllabisch geschriebene sumerische Wörter (vgl. Anm. 28) und Zahlwörter (Edzard, "Sumerisch 1 bis 10 in Ebla", *Studi Eblaiti* 3 [1980], S. 121-7).

Man hat den Eindruck, als sei die fundamentale Bedeutung des Nominativs eben erst entdeckt und werde nun plerophorisch verwendet.

3. *Nomina actionis (Infinitive)*

Unter den lexikalischen Eintragungen in G. Pettinato, *Materiali epigrafici di Ebla* (=*MEE*) *IV* (Napoli, 1982), entspricht kú = *a-kà-lu-um* "essen" (Nr. 0191) nicht nur der akkadischen Bildung *akālu(m)*, sondern vor allem dem hebräischen Infinitivus absolutus *ʾākôl*. Doch gibt es neben diesem Infinitiv mit [*a*]-Vokalismus die Bildung mit [*u*] wie *du-bù-ḫu* "opfern", die neben den hebräischen Infinitivus constructus *qeṭōl* zu stellen ist. Ein Infinitiv mit [*i*] liegt in igi-íla = *na-ší-ux* (NI) *a-na-a* "die Augen erheben" (*MEE IV* Nr. 723) vor.

Nomina actionis auf [*-(a)tum*] sind unspezifisch auf die Verbalklassen verteilt; das Morphem begegnet auch bei starken Bildungen wie in zi = *nu-pù-uš-tù-um* "leben" (*MEE IV* Nr. 1050). Offenbar handelt es sich um das arabistisch sog. nomen vicis für die einmalig ausgeführte Handlung (arab. *faʿlatun*), hier also um die Bezeichnung des individuellen Lebens.

Die Gleichsetzung von sumerisch (sumerographisch) al-DU mit *ʾà-a-ku*$_{17}$(TIK)*-um* bzw. *a-a-*GÚM [*haʾ*?*āGum*] "gehen" (*MEE IV* Nr. 984) neben di-di bzw. du-du = *ʾà-la-*GÚM (Nr. 635.1000) weist auf semivokalisches [*l̥*] im Eblaitischen, das zu [ʾ?] wird; [*l̥*] ist der 2.Radikal der Wurzel *hl̥G* "gehen".[30] Das entsprechende nomen vicis scheint in di = *ʾa*$_x$(NI)*-kà-tù-um* bzw. *a-a-kà-tù* und *a-la-ak-*[ ] vorzuliegen (*MEE IV* Nr. 830). Zwei [*L*]-Phoneme, darunter wohl ein semivokalisches, scheint es allerdings auch im präsargonischen Sumerisch gegeben zu haben.[31] Wird darum sumerisch dingir in Ebla u.a. durch din-gi-li wiedergegeben?[32] Liegt also nur der Einfluß eines sumerischen Adstratums vor? Für den semivokalischen Charakter eines altsemitischen [*L*] hat dagegen W. von Soden auf biblisch-aramäisches *yehāk* "er wird gehen" und *mehāk* "gehend" hingewiesen.[33] Auf semitische Herkunft eines semivokalischen [*l̥*], dazu vielleicht eines [*r̥*], deuten ferner nicht nur gewisse Unregelmäßigkeiten der eblaitischen Schreibung dieses Lauts bzw. dieser Laute,[34] sondern auch Erscheinungen der hebräischen Sprache wie

---

[30] Wir verwenden /*G*/, weil zwischen stimmhaften, stimmlosen und emphatischen Lauten graphisch offenbar nicht unterschieden wird; dazu Krebernik, *ZA* 72, S.207, speziell zu *hl̥G* Ders., *ZA* 73, S. 35 f.

[31] Vgl. A. Falkenstein, *Das Sumerische* (Leiden, 1959), S. 24; weitere Lit. bei W. H. Ph. Roemer, *Einführung in die Sumerologie* (Nijmegen, ²1982), S. 38[192].

[32] Vgl. Pettinato, *OrAnt* 18 (1979), S. 333; Krecher, S. 139.

[33] "*n* als Wurzelaugment im Semitischen", *Wiss.Z.Univ.Halle* 17 (1968) G, H.2/3, S. 175-84, bes. 178.

[34] So erscheint gelegentlich:

— *a* statt *la*: die o.g. Schreibungen zur Wurzel *hl̥G*; vgl. auch ù-di = *na-a-um* "schlafen" (*MEE IV*, Nr. 1131; akkad. *nâlu*[*m*]),
— *a* statt *li*: še ú-ri-ga = *a-ga-tum* neben *li-gi-tum* (Nr. 282/3);
— *a* statt *lu*: nu-uš = *a-wa-um* neben *lu-wu-um* (1439) und

— die gelegentliche Differenzierung einer Basis mit [*L*] wie **ʾL* zu verschiedenen Lexemen mit [*l*] :: [*r*] wie *ʾlh* :: *ʾrr*, beides in der Bedeutung "fluchen";
— der Wechsel *l/r* beim gleichen Wort wie *ʾalmân* neben *ʾarmôn* "Palast" oder *mazzālôt* neben *mazzārôt* "Tierkreisbilder"[35] oder
— das Vorliegen von [*L*] in zwei kombinatorischen Varianten im samaritanischen Hebräisch.[36]

4. *Zusammenfassung*

Die systematische Konsistenz des eblaitischen Konjugationssystems scheint einstweilen gering. Eine morphologische Standardisierung fehlt etwa, wenn die 3.P.m.sg. auf drei verschiedene Weisen verwirklicht wird oder wenn in der PK der Verba III infirmae thematische neben lexikalischen Vokalen erscheinen. Verteilt sich also die vorliegende Evidenz auf verschiedene "Dialekte"? Was besagt dieser Terminus auf so früher Sprachstufe? Unvollständig ist auch die Symmetrie des Paradigmas, wenn ein klares Oppositionssystem zwischen den Phonemfolgen der AK und der PK nach dem Barthschen Gesetz noch nicht ausgebildet ist. Unter den Stämmen überwiegt G (Qal); daneben gibt es Gt-, sowie wenige D- und Š- bzw. Št-Bildungen. Auffällig viele nomina actionis werden von Stämmen mit [*t*]-Infix unter Hinzufügung eines weiteren [*t*-] Präformativs gebildet, etwa téš-teš-kú = *tù-uš-tá-kí-lum* (*MEE IV* Nr. 164) neben dem o.g. kú = *a-kà-lu-um* "essen". Vollends scheint eine Mehrzahl syntaktischer Formen promiscue gebraucht, als gäbe es noch keine funktionsspezifischen Satzbautypen. In der Gesamtgeschichte des Semitischen erscheint eine synchrone Systematik offenbar erst am Höhepunkt einer diachronen Entwicklung.[37]

— *um* statt *lum*: še-geštin = *iš$_x$-ga-um* neben *áš-ga-lum* (660).
Vor allem tritt [*l*] oft für [*r̥*] ein, etwa in dem o.g. *ma-ḫi-la* für [*maḫir̥a*], gelegentlich auch am Silbenende, so in der Schreibung des Personennamens *íl-ʾà-aq-da-mu* neben *ìr-ʾà-aq-da-mu* "D. entfernte sich" von der Wurzel *rḥq*. Besonders auffällig ist schließlich das völlige Fehlen einer mit [*l̥*] oder [*r̥*] beginnenden Silbe, etwa in eme-bal = *a-pá/pi$_5$-lu-um* neben *a-pá-um* (179) oder ^{giš}šu-me = *šì-rí-mi-nu* neben *ša-mi-nu* (379). Vgl. Krebernik, *ZA* 72, S.210 f. Auf die nomina agentis (Partizipien) und die Bildungen in den abgeleiteten Stämmen kann hier aus Raumgründen nicht eingegangen werden; vgl. Vf. in "Neue Erwägungen zum eblaitischen Verbalsystem" (dazu Anm. 4) und "Ebla und das althebräische Verbalsystem", *Bibl.* 65 (1984). S. 145-67, bes. 162-4.

[35] Vgl. A. Fitzgerald, "The Interchange of *L*, *N* and *R* in Biblical Hebrew", *JBL* 97 (1978), S. 481-8, wo das Phänomen allerdings nicht erklärt wird.

[36] Vgl. R. Macuch, *Grammatik des samaritanischen Hebräisch* (Berlin, 1969), S. 114.

[37] Sie erscheint offenbar aber auch *nur* an solchen Höhepunkten. Ist dieser einmal erreicht, so scheinen die Sprachen gern zu geringerer Spezifizität und Differenzierung der Formen und zur Asymmetrie von deren System zurückzukehren: schon im Hebräischen werden nicht mehr alle konjugierten Adjektive, wie im Fall von *kābēd* und *qāṭōn*, nach *qatil*

Ich schließe mit einem Dank an Prof. Pettinato, der durch die zügige Veröffentlichung so zahlreicher Texte der Semitistik und den orientalistischen Einzelfächern ein großes neues Arbeitsgebiet erschlossen hat. Möge sich dadurch auch die alttestamentliche Wissenschaft an die philologische bzw. linguistische Basis aller exegetischen Bemühungen erinnern lassen.

---

und *qatul* gebildet, sondern gehen zu *qatal* über (etwa *gādal*, *ḥāzaq*, *ḥākam*); der AK *gādal* steht jetzt gegen das Barthsche Gesetz *yigdal* gegenüber. Nach Überschreiten eines Entwicklungshöhepunktes führt der Zeitablauf, wie es scheint, zur Kontingenzvermehrung und Symmetrieverminderung.

THE SPEAKING PERSON AND HIS VOICE IN 1 SAMUEL

BY

ROBERT POLZIN

Ottawa

It is my intention today to offer an interpretation of 1 Sam. i, using the philosophy of language and literary stylistics of that group of Russian theorists that has come to be known as "the Bakhtin Circle". How this circle came to be and who composed it makes a fascinating story that is only now being told in the West. The central figure of this group was Mikhail Bakhtin, who according to Michael Holquist "is gradually emerging as one of the leading thinkers of the twentieth century".[1] So far as I know, neither Bakhtin nor those associated with him ever applied their literary theories to biblical material; this is the task I have been setting for myself since 1977 when I found that the Deuteronomic History provided exciting material for such an approach. I shall be doing two things in this paper. First, I intend to run through the beginning of 1 Samuel in an attempt to give you a feel for what my literary voice sounds like. What I present here will be to some the beginning of a promised sequel to previous work[2] and to others an introduction to a new way of reading the biblical text. Second, I shall retrace the course of my own reading to lay bare in a confessional mode some of the assumptions and

---

[1] M. Holquist (ed.), *The Dialogic Imagination. Four Essays by M. M. Bakhtin* (Austin and London, 1981), p. xv. This book's last essay, "Discourse in the Novel", was, in its theoretical insights and apt verbal formulations, especially useful to me in the research for and preparation of the present paper. In addition to the works by Bakhtin, Voloshinov, and Uspensky referred to in the Works Cited section of my *Moses and the Deuteronomist* (New York, 1980) I have found the following books and articles helpful in understanding and applying the theoretical insights of Bakhtin and his group: M. M. Baxtin, *Rabelais and his World* (Cambridge, Mass., 1968); M. Bakhtin, "The Problem of the Text (An Essay in Philosophical Analysis)", *Soviet Studies in Literature* (Winter, 1977-78), pp. 3-33; Gary Paul Morson, "The Heresiarch of *Meta*", *PTL: A Journal for Descriptive Poetics and Theory of Literature* 3 (1978), pp. 407-27; Krystyna Pomorska, "Mixail Baxtin and his Verbal Universe", *PTL* 3 (1978), pp. 379-86; I. R. Titunik, "M. M. Baxtin (the Baxtin School) and Soviet Semiotics", *Dispositio* 3 (Ann Arbor, 1976), pp. 327-38; I. R. Titunik, "Bachtin and Soviet Semiotics", *Russian Literature* 10 (1981), pp. 1-16; and V. V. Ivanov, "The Significance of M. M. Bakhtin's Ideas on Sign, Utterance, and Dialogue for Modern Semiotics", in Henryk Baran (ed.), *Semiotics and Structuralism. Readings from the Soviet Union* (White Plains, N.Y., 1974), pp. 310-67.

[2] Robert Polzin, *Moses and the Deuteronomist. A Literary Study of the Deuteronomic History*, Part One (New York, 1980).

points of view that constitute my approach to the text. I have entitled this paper, "The speaking person and his voice in 1 Samuel i", so that the first part of my talk will concentrate on the various voices I hear in chapter i of 1 Samuel; the second and shorter part will centre on the voices you may hear within my interpretation itself.

The story of the birth and consecration of Samuel is a type-scene of annunciation, as Robert Alter would say.[3] At the same time, its location at the start of 1 Samuel gives its meaning added dimensions and it is this "sense of a beginning" that will largely occupy my interest. Clearly, the birth story signals the central role Samuel will play as kingmaker in Israel. However, if the patterning of the Deuteronomic History in previous books is assumed to continue in 1 Samuel, then the story of Samuel's birth must be more than this. Just as the beginning of Joshua gave us a preview of major themes to be worked out through the course of that book, and just as the beginning of the book of Judges was a synopsis of what was to come there, so also we may profitably expect that the story of Samuel's birth contains within its texture threads that extend beyond the life and death of Samuel, well into the lives of Saul and David and, in the case of Saul, even encompass his death. In other words, the opening scene of Samuel's birth ought to be a prospective statement about the entire book. The answers that the book itself provides are answers to a set of questions that are first voiced in chapter i.

Whom do we hear speaking in chapter i? First and foremost, we have an omniscient narrator who not only conveys to us what his characters say out loud but even what they vow or think within their own hearts. Then there are the characters themselves quoted by the narrator; these are only three: Elkanah, his wife Hannah, and old Eli, the priest of Shiloh. No other obvious voices are heard in the story. A simple matter, therefore, to listen to only four voices and puzzle out the function of the story for the rest of the book. However, we have but to look more closely at what each voice says, in itself and in relation to the other voices, to discover that surrounding these obvious voices are a number of others from both within and without this chapter. The utterance of each voice speaking in the story provides a focal point for the intersecting words of others. The point of view represented by a single utterance of a single voice resonates with the words of others either in agreement or in opposition, with either emotive similarity or contrast. Loudly or faintly, we can perceive a cross section of voices even when only a single person speaks in the text.

---

[3] *The Art of Biblical Narrative* (New York, 1981), pp. 81-7.

What is the voice of the narrator like? What does he say and what accents characterize his speech? His words, which at first glance appear to be one-dimensional and ideologically unified, contain a variety of hidden voices and competing viewpoints. Here, as in any example of artfully constructed narrative, there is to be found a profound speech diversity that in fact is the determining factor of its prose style.

The narrator, as one would expect, is omniscient: he knows what has happened in the past and what is happening in the story's "here and now". Moreover, he so understands behaviour that he is able to describe it "from the point of view of the person himself or from the point of view of an omniscient observer who is permitted to penetrate the consciousness of that person".[4] This is narrator's speech which, from a psychological point of view, is internal to the characters he describes for us. For example, the narrator can repeat word for word Hannah's vow to God in *v.* 11, even though we know (from *v.* 13) that "only her lips were moving and her voice was not being heard". Again, the narrator is able to penetrate Elkanah's consciousness because, even though this husband gives many portions to Peninnah but only one portion to Hannah, the narrator is able to tell us that Elkanah nevertheless loved Hannah (*v.* 5).

It is because of the convention of omniscience normally belonging to a narrator's voice that we have the distinction in narration between exposition and the story proper.[5] Exposition gives the reader the background information that is necessary for an adequate understanding of the story itself. Chapter i divides up neatly into *vv.* 1-8 as preparatory exposition and *vv.* 9-28 as story proper. The narrator's voice fundamentally shifts in tone between these two sections: in *vv.* 1-8 that which is habitual over a long period of time is emphasized; in *vv.* 9-28 three main concrete events are described: Hannah's meeting with Eli, Samuel's birth, and finally his consecration at Shiloh. In the expository overview of *vv.* 1-8, information is packed and condensed through the description of repetitious or habitual behaviour indicated by imperfective verb forms: he would give (*w*^{e}*nātan*) *v.* 4; he would give (*yittēn*) *v.* 5; so it went on (*yaᶜ*^{a}*śeh*) *v.* 7; she would provoke her (*takᶜīsennāh*) *v.* 7; she would not eat (*tō'kal*) *v.* 7. so, we are told, these things went on year by year, Peninnah habitually provoking the barren Hannah so that the latter would weep and refuse to eat. And Elkanah would habitually respond to Hannah's behaviour with words of attempted consolation. Year by year Peninnah taunted Hannah, and year by year Elkanah tried to console her.

---

[4] Boris Uspensky, *A Poetics of Composition* (Berkeley, California, 1973), p. 83.

[5] The best work I know of on the function of exposition in narrative is Meir Sternberg, *Expositional Modes and Temporal Ordering in Fiction* (Baltimore, 1978).

Then the narrator's voice shifts to the singular events of the story itself and to signal such a move we encounter once more a piling on of imperfective verb forms, like those encountered earlier but here having a different function: Eli "was sitting (*yōšēb*)" (i 9), "was observing (*šōmēr*)", (i 12); Hannah "was crying (*tibkéh*) (*v.* 10), "was speaking (*m^e^dabbéret*)" (i 13), "only her lips were moving (*nāᶜôt*) and her voice was not being heard (*yiššāmēaᶜ*)" (i 13). It is largely by means of these imperfective verb forms that we are enabled to enter the here and now or synchronic perspective of the story.

So far, we have introduced a number of literary categories that might be said normally and obviously to concern a narrator's omniscience: retrospective versus synchronic perspective, expository versus narrative point of view. These categories are well known and easily applied to the narrator's voice in chapter i of 1 Samuel. But there are a number of voice characteristics that are not so well recognized and it is to some examples of these that we now turn.

A primary function of a narrator is to report to us, his readers, the words of his characters. There are many obvious examples of this in chapter i: the narrator directly quotes Elkanah's words in i 8,23, Hannah's words in i 11,15-16,18,22 and 26, and Eli's words in i 14,17. A little less obvious, but still quite clearly recognized, is the narrator's direct quoting of Hannah's words without the expected introduction: in *v.* 20 "... she called his name Samuel, for (she said) 'I have asked him of the LORD'". The "she said" is not in the Hebrew text but is, for example, in the *RSV* translation because of the context: "I have asked him of the LORD" are the very words of Hannah directly reported to us by the narrator, but not signalled as such in the normal manner.

There are other voices speaking in this chapter, introduced by the narrator in not so obvious a fashion as in the preceding cases. For example, when the narrator tells us in *v.* 6 that Peninnah, Hannah's rival, "used to provoke her sorely, to irritate her, *because the* LORD *had closed her womb*", the question arises whether this characterization of Hannah's barrenness ("the LORD had closed her womb") proceeds in fact from the narrator's convictions, from Peninnah's or Hannah's convictions, or from a combination of both. Again, when the narrator tells us in the preceding verse (i 5) that Elkanah gave Hannah only one portion, for again "the LORD had closed her womb", the same type of question arises: is this the narrator's or Elkanah's view or both? If one contends, as I do, that in these two verses we have reported to us at least the motivation of Elkanah in verse five and of Peninnah in verse six, then we are on safe ground in asserting that we have in the words "for the LORD had closed her womb" the concealed reported speech of Elkanah and Peninnah in response to, and explanation of, Hannah's continued barrenness. The inner speech, as it were, of Elkanah and Peninnah, if not of the Israelite populace generally, is represented by these words, and it remains to be seen whether the narrator as well as the implied author who controls his voice share this view in the same way and with the same emotive accents as do Elkanah and Peninnah. If we were to conclude that the narrator's viewpoint is significantly different from that of his two characters here, then we would have an instance not only of the reporting of concealed speech but also of pseudo-objective motivation, which occurs when (to use Bakhtin's words) "the logic motivating the sentence seems to belong to the [narrator], i.e., he is formally at one with it; but in actual fact, the motivation lies within the subjective belief-system of his characters, or of general opinion" (p. 305). In either case, it is enough to see here how part of *vv.* 5 and 6, apparently in the narrator's own voice, form also the concealed speech of his characters.

Another example of concealed reported speech occurs in *v.* 13 where the narrator tells us that "Eli took [Hannah] to be a drunken woman". Here we can generalize by stating that, whenever the narrator through his omniscience invades the consciousness of one of his characters to reveal in his, the narrator's, own words their thoughts, convictions or the like, or anticipates their words which he is about to quote, he is actually reporting to us the speech of these characters. So that here in *v.* 13 the narrator's words indicate to us that Eli is to have said to himself, or is about to say out loud, something like "This woman is drunk!" just as his direct speech in i 14 indicates.

Another kind of concealed reported speech occurs when the very words of a character, directly quoted by the narrator, show up elsewhere in the same or a similar context as words belonging to the narrator himself. When, for example, the narrator tells us in *v.* 19 that "the LORD *remembered* [Hannah]" through the conception and birth of Samuel, we are meant to recall Hannah's words in verse eleven, "O LORD of hosts... *remember* me ... and give to thy maidservant a son..." Thus the narrator, by using the very speech of a character in his own speech, once more calls attention to that speech. The narrator, in this manner also, conceals in his own speech the speech of another. When we hear the narrator's voice there is concealed within it Hannah's voice.

But the most important aspect of the narrator's voice, as of any voice we encounter in the text, is its ideological perspective. By ideology or ideological perspective I mean, in Bakhtin's words, "a specific point of view on the world, a specific belief-system or form for conceptualizing the world in words, specific world views, each characterized by its own objects, meanings and values" (p. 291). The voices we hear in 1 Samuel do not simply express individual ideologies in relation to one another; they represent social points of view that intersect each other in a variety of ways, forming, in fact, what I call the implied author's story, the meaning (or meanings) of which is certainly a major task of the reader to discover. As Bakhtin writes:

> Behind the narrator's story we read a second story, the author's story; he is the one who tells us how the narrator tells stories, and also tells us about the narrator himself (p. 314).

Up to this point we have made a few observations about the narrator's voice: its omniscience, its retrospective or synchronic emphasis, its expository or narrative tacks, the obvious or concealed ways it reports the speech of others. We can now turn to the reported speech of our characters in order to concentrate primarily on its ideological dimensions. In this way we should be able to begin saying something about what the author's story is about.

The first character to speak directly in the story is Elkanah:

> Hannah, why do you weep? And why do you not eat? And why is your heart sad? Am I not more to you than ten sons? (i 8).

It is certainly correct to emphasize, as Alter does, the unusual prominence given to Hannah's barren bitterness, and to conjecture that it is "a thematically apt introduction to the birth of a lonely leader..." (pp. 85-6). But the intersection of the various characters and their speech in chapter i serves a much more profound and extensive function than this: chapter i is an introduction to the entire book, not just to its first chapters; what the characters say in this opening chapter illumines and foreshadows what will not be finished until Saul is killed in chapter xxxi.

The area occupied by Elkanah's voice is much broader than his "actual" words in this chapter. Following Bakhtin, we can call such an area a "character zone" and will attempt to describe what Elkanah's is like. Listen first to the emotive accents that surround his words. These are words of consolation certainly; after all, the narrator told us above, in verse five, of Elkanah's love for Hannah. But listen again, and you will hear an aggrieved tone, a more gently expressed bitterness than Hannah's but a bitterness nonetheless, in resonance with her own. Is there not also a mild reproach here? For Hannah to be so disconsolate is to exhibit insufficient appreciation of her husband. If Hannah really understood the worth of Elkanah, she would know that ten children could not replace him in her heart. There is present in Elkanah's words to Hannah at least the beginning feelings of being rejected. These words of

Elkanah push him in two directions: he loves Hannah and thus understands her desire to have children; at the same time Hannah's bitterness says something about her attitude toward him. The situation is immediately understandable at the individual level. A woman lacks what her rival has in abundance: children; she desires greatly to receive what she does not have. Her husband has some understanding of her plight, yet cannot help feeling to some degree rejected. Is there some political or ideological significance to this simple familial situation, to this intersection of conflicting emotions? By the end of my discussion I hope to offer the beginning of an answer. For now, the emotional overtones of Elkanah's *character zone* bespeak loving understanding mixed in with feelings of being rejected.

When we turn to the meeting between Hannah and Eli in *vv.* 9-18 and to the direct speech there, we encounter first the inner words of Hannah. What kind of ideological and emotive accents do we hear in them?

Hannah's words in *v.* 11 are spoken silently to the LORD. With an anxious, vexed, insistent voice she promises that in return for a son from the LORD she will return him to the LORD "all the days of his life". Like Jephthah, she wants to make a deal with God to insure success in obtaining her request. At first Eli, who has been observing her, thinks her drunken, but when she corrects his misimpression without divulging what she has been asking for, he responds: "Go in peace; (for) the God of Israel will grant your petition which you have made to him" (or: "may the God of Israel grant...") (i 17). Hannah responds with one of the many word-plays in the chapter, "Let your maidservant (that is, Hannah) find favour (*ḥēn*) in your eyes" (i 18). Eli, without even knowing it, is in favour of or prophesies Hannah's receiving a son. As such, he fits into the same character zone as Hannah's so far as certain emotive and ideological aspects are concerned: sympathy with her vexation at not having a son, joy and peace in contemplation of obtaining one, and a *quid pro quo* belief-system whereby bargaining with the LORD is desirable to achieve one's ends.

We again ask: what does having children or not have to do with the major enterprise that concerns the entire book of 1 Samuel, the establishment of kingship in Israel? What evaluative social accents accompany Hannah's desire to have a child, sanctioned unknowingly or prophetically by Eli, but somewhat opposed by Elkanah who expresses a loving conviction that he is indeed worth more to her than ten sons? Is the implied author of this opening story introducing us solely to Samuel the man or is he in addition giving us a thematic overture to the entire book of 1 Samuel?

The prophetic or supplicatory words of Eli in *v.* 17 echo similar words both inside and outside the chapter, and so provide us with some hints toward an answer. Eli says: "The God of Israel will grant the request you made to him (*šēlātēk* ... *šāʾalt*)" (i 17). Then, when her son is born, Hannah names him, saying "For I requested him (*šeʾiltîw*) from the LORD" (i 20). Hannah, in her meeting with Eli after Samuel's birth, once again refers to "the request I made (*šeʾēlātî* ... *šāʾáltî*) to him" (i 27), and finally Eli later on refers to further progeny as "in place of the request asked of the LORD (*haššeʾēlāh* ... *šāʾal*)" (ii 20). In all these cases Samuel her son personifies the request itself.

There is another request that receives as much prominence in the opening chapters of 1 Samuel, and it is no great step to make a connection between the two. In chapter viii we hear the narrator's voice characterizing the people as those "who were requesting a king from him" (*haššōʾalîm*) (viii 10). Then later in the story Samuel introduces Saul to the people as the king "whom you requested (*šeʾeltém*)" (xii 13) and speaks of the people's wickedness, "in requesting (*lišʾōl*) a king for yourselves" (xii 17). The people respond by referring to this evil as "to ask (*lišʾōl*) for ourselves a king" (xii 19). There are no other specific requests made of the LORD in these chapters, so that there seems some basis in the text for assuming that the story of Hannah's request for a son is intended to introduce, and foreshadow and ideologically to comment upon the story of Israel's request for a king.

Confirmation of this close literary connection is found in Hannah's directly quoted words to Eli that conclude the chapter, "It is for this child I prayed; and the LORD has granted me my petition which I made to him. Therefore I have lent him (?) to the LORD; as long as he lives he is lent to the LORD, that is, he is Saul! (*hûʾ šāʾûl*)" (i 27-28). These words of Hannah's are to be considered together with her concealed speech of i 20, where the narrator has her naming her son Samuel "for I asked him (*šeʾiltîw*) of the LORD". In both these pericopes (i 20,28) commentators have grappled with the word-play whereby Hannah speaks of Samuel, or refers to his name, using a puzzling etymology that appears more appropriately to explain the name of Saul. Is there an accidental or haphazard mixture here of two traditions, a hybrid, a *tébel*, which confusingly "explains" Samuel's name by offering an etymology for Saul's? This historical-critical option may be premature, as is sometimes the case; it certainly casts no light on the story itself and simply causes these verses to stick out like a sore thumb. Can these "confused" etymologies be integrated into the story by taking them at face value?

One such attempt would be to imbue the details of the story of Samuel's birth, a familial story, with socio-political overtones, that is, to assume that the implied author is foreshadowing and putting into context his complex account of the LORD's decision to give Israel a king by prefacing that account with an account of the LORD's decision to give Hannah a son. The birth of Samuel, in all its complex detail, introduces and foreshadows the birth of kingship in Israel.

"The having of sons" is the image chosen by the author to convey the complicated story of how Israel came to have kings. In chapter viii it is Samuel's evil sons who give the elders of Israel a pretext for requesting from him a king "to govern us like all the nations", but Samuel considers this request with displeasure. When he prays to the LORD about it he is told to hearken to the people's request: kingship is a rejection not of Samuel but of Yahweh himself. In chapter i Hannah has no son and Peninnah taunts her about this: both simplistically represent having or not having a son as a sign of God's favour or disfavour. Elkanah, as well as the narrator in places, appear to be neutral on this point: the narrator simply states "Peninnah had children but Hannah had no children" (*v.* 2) and Elkanah, who believes that the LORD had closed (Hannah's) womb, cannot understand why the childless Hannah, having him, would need another. The words of the LORD to Samuel "they have not rejected you, but they have rejected me" (viii 7) are very close in their emotive register and ideological accent to Elkanah's words to Hannah: all one has to do is have God say to Israel what Elkanah says to Hannah:

> Israel, why do you weep? And why do you not
> eat? Any why is your heart sad? Am I not
> worth more to you than ten kings?

In other words, the story in chapter i about how and why God agreed to give Hannah a son, Samuel, is an artistic prefiguring of the larger story of 1 Samuel about how and why God agreed to give Israel a king, specifically Saul. It is in the light of these and other thematic, emotive and ideological connections within the larger story line that the etymology spoken by Hannah makes artistic sense: the story of Samuel's birth *is* the story of Saul's birth as king of Israel. Saul's destiny, like his name, explains Samuel's. When Hannah says "For I asked for him (*šeʾiltîw*) from the LORD", she speaks for Israel about Saul (*hûʾ šāʾûl*).

The belief-systems represented by Hannah, Peninnah and Eli *vis-à-vis* Samuel's birth correspond more or less to the belief-systems of the people and Samuel represented by their words in chapter viii *vis-à-vis* the kingship to be established under Saul: threat, provocation, simplistic rejection or acceptance, the whole covenantal sub-structure of the Mosaic covenant, etc. On the other hand, Elkanah is non-condemnatory: he loves and supports Hannah, and in spite of her put-down of him (at least in his own eyes) co-operates with her in bringing forth Samuel just as the LORD reluctantly co-operates with the people in crowning Saul.

This reading of the Samuel birth story helps to explain finally Elkanah's response to Hannah's plans for bringing Samuel to Shiloh after weaning him:

> Do what seems best to you, wait until you have weaned him; *only may the Lord establish his word* (i 23).

Elkanah's statement, "only may the LORD establish his word" seems anomalous and strangely intrusive, until we put it in the context of the larger story line as we have been developing it: the central problem of the kingship is not whether it is good or evil for Israel. Rather, given Israel's partial rejection of the LORD for a king and given the LORD's reluctant acceptance of their request, why in fact was Saul's kingship aborted soon after it had been established? How can the LORD be seen to have established his word after he has rejected Saul? In Hannah's words, Samuel/Saul is to appear in the presence of the LORD and abide there *for ever* (i 22), "I will give him [Samuel/Saul] to the LORD all the days of his life" (i 11). That Samuel stands for or prefigures Saul is made explicit in Hannah's final words of the chapter, "As long as he lives he is lent (?) to the LORD, he is Saul!" Elkanah's statement in i 23 sets up the central puzzle of the book: once having selected Saul how can the LORD have then rejected him? How can the LORD be seen as establishing his word (*yāqēm dᵉbārô*) when he has Samuel say to Saul "But now your kingdom shall not be established (*lōʾ tāqûm*)" (xiii 14)? And the reason given in xv 11 is that Saul has not established God's word (*dᵉbāray lōʾ hēqîm*). This same dilemma, by the way, is expressed in xv 29, 34 where the LORD or the glory of Israel will not repent (29) yet repented (34) that he made Saul king over Israel. Israel had remained in existence for over 200 years during the period of the judges, even though the people were consistently disobedient to the LORD. Why did Saul's line, indeed Saul's rule itself, not last, given the LORD's choice of him? This is the central problem of 1 Samuel and perhaps its main ideological theme.

Much more could be said about other features of 1 Sam. i that in various ways prepare for later positions about kingship in the book. For example, Hannah's description to Eli of her "standing here (*hanniṣṣébet*) to pray before the LORD" for a child, in i 26, resonates with Samuel's command to the people, "...But you have this day rejected your God ... and you have said, 'No! But set a king over us! Now therefore stand before the LORD (*hityāṣṣᵉbû*)" (x 19); Hannah's words in chapter i resonate also with the narrator's word in x 23 that Saul "took his stand (*wayyityaṣṣēb*) among the people'' to be proclaimed their king, and with Samuel's command to the people, in xii 7, 16, ''Now therefore stand before the LORD, (*hityaṣṣᵉbû*)'' so that he could discuss the matter of kingship with them. Hannah's words also prepare for the narrator's account of how the LORD came ''and took his stand (*wayyityaṣṣab*)'' to condemn Eli's house (iii 10). And finally they sound in our ears when the narrator describes the birth-and-death scene involving Eli's daughter-in-law, where the women who were standing over her (*hanniṣṣābôt*), say ''Fear not for you have borne a son'' (iv 20). All this and more could be developed to further my account of how the voices we hear in 1 Sam. i concerning the birth of Samuel are heard over and over again in the book concerning the matter of the kingship.

I want to conclude my remarks here by reflecting on some of the prominent accents to be found in my own voice as I was speaking about the meaning of 1 Sam. i. First, my talk assumes that much of the speech in 1 Samuel, as in all speech, be it literary or extra-literary, is *concealed*, that is, it is ''someone else's'' speech hidden within ''one's own speech'' whether this latter is understood as implied author's, narrator's or character's speech. Moreover, a good part of this concealed speech was not indicated by formal, linguistic, or syntactic markers. But when it was so indicated, I took some pains to point this out, for example noting shifts from perfective to imperfective verb forms or highlighting similar semantic contexts for certain words or phrases, and the like. This first assumption of mine implies that exegesis, like reading itself, it both a formal and a creative or intuitive process. When either of these aspects is inappropriately ignored or played down, interpretation suffers.

Second, I believe with Bakhtin (pp. 332-3) that literary discourse (such as we find in 1 Samuel) is not simply transmitted or reproduced; it is artistically represented in such a way that it does not have simply an individual but rather a certain social significance. What Elkanah, Hannah, Eli, and Samuel stand for in the narrative are personifications of complex socio-political ideologies in internal dialogue with one another. Their discourse is *always* ideologically saturated, filled with emotive and evaluative accents that speak to or respond to other evaluative positions or points of view within the narrative. Similarly, I believe every voice that comments on or speaks about specific biblical texts is of necessity internally saturated with all kinds of emotive and evaluative positions, no matter how descriptive, objective, scientific or non-normative the interpreter's language appears to be or asserts itself to be. I believe, therefore, that both biblical language and the language of the biblical scholar in Bakhtin's words ''is multi-voiced from top to bottom; it represents the co-existence of socio-ideological contradictions between the present and the past, between differing epochs of the past, between different socio-ideological groups in the present, between tendencies, schools, circles and so forth, all given a bodily form. These [biblical and scholarly] languages intersect each other in a variety of ways forming ever new socially typifying languages'' (p. 291).

Third, the nature of 1 Samuel and of the Bible itself as an ancient text creates a special problem in analysis. To a very real extent, we have lost for ever the background of many of the words and meanings, that is, the ideological background against which the narrative sounded and with which it dialogically interacted (Bakhtin, p. 417). Nevertheless, I assume that a significant portion of the ideological confrontations forming the contemporary background of our story can be recovered from the narrative itself. If all this is understood to be an *apologia* for continued historical-critical research, I assure you that I intend it to be so. Nevertheless, the example of interpretation I have offered here today is a cautious and preliminary attempt to draw out from the text whatever evaluative and ideological perspectives can be gleaned from it, before such necessary historical critical investigation takes over. However much you might be inclined to view my procedures as similar to those of source, form, tradition, or other kinds of historical criticism, I would firmly deny such comparisons. I speak only of an implied author of the text, that is, of my reconstruction of an overarching ideological voice drawn from the text itself, rather than of any ''real'' author or authors of the text who might be constructed using historical-critical and extra-biblical data.

Finally, my voice today is a plea to cease seeing biblical words, phrases, sentences, verses, pericopes, chapters, books, sources, forms, traditions, or redactions as smooth single language unities. Rather, it is a plea to begin uncovering biblical language's ''three dimensionality, its profound speech diversity, that which constitutes the determining factor of its unique and individual style'' (Bakhtin, p. 315).

A ROOT TO LOOK UP?
A STUDY OF THE HEBREW *NŚ*ʾ ʿ*YN*

BY

S. C. REIF

Cambridge

Among those whose earliest introduction to Biblical Hebrew was through the medium of translation into a modern European language, there can be few who do not recall the combined sense of wonder and amusement with which they encountered the fact that God's ancient people so often "lifted their eyes" before they saw. The extensive use and influence of the Authorized Version (= AV) ensured that its literal rendering of the Hebrew *nś*ʾ ʿ*yn* was, as in so many similar cases, slavishly followed for centuries, so that familiarity with its form bred complacency about its meaning. Progress and modernity do, however, ultimately overtake even the most reactionary of teachers and in recent years it has become fashionable to prefer the more idiomatically satisfying translation "look up", or its other European equivalents, on the assumption that it is this physical activity that is being described by the Hebrew phrase under discussion.

For scholars reasonably well acquainted with the post-biblical form of the language any feeling of satisfaction that this modern translation "look up" is a universally accurate as well as an idiomatically pleasing rendering is soon tempered by an awareness that the linguistic evidence from Tannaitic and later Hebrew supports no such blanket assumption. However negligent some previous generations of biblical scholars were about taking due account of the rabbinic sources in their researches into the emergence and development of Biblical Hebrew expressions, there are surely few who would today dare to offer a definition of the semantic range of any such expression without making a critical comparison with the later evolution of the language. Important as cognate languages are for lexicographical work, their use is best complemented by a judicious examination of internal linguistic developments.[1] In the case under discussion such an examination undoubtedly invites a comprehensive

---

[1] See e.g. my remarks about the mediaeval Jewish commentators, and the relevant documentation, on the first page of my article "Ibn Ezra on Psalm i 1-2", *VT* 34 (1984), pp. 232-6.

analysis of past and present translations of the phrase and their degree of reliability.

True as it is to claim, as has been claimed above, that the AV was once the dominant factor in the translation of common Hebrew phrases, it is no less valid to point out that contemporary versions such as the New English Bible (= NEB), the Jerusalem Bible in the English edition (= JB) and the New JPS Translation (= NJPS) both reflect and influence current trends in the translation of Biblical Hebrew.[2] A comparison of their renderings of the phrase *nś꜀ ꜥyn* with those of their earlier counterparts reveals a slight but distinct move away from "lift the eye" towards less literal and more interpretative translations. At the same time, however, there is still a considerable lack of consistency, both within each version and between the versions, in the treatment of the phrase in its various contexts, so that it remains unclear which of the renderings, if any, is truly indicative of the way forward for the accurate translator.

Having dealt with the statistical evidence and established that in the majority of cases today's versions still adopt the rendering "lift the eye" and what are regarded as its more idiomatic equivalents, I shall seek the source of this rendering in the ancient versions and trace its occurrence through the mediaeval Jewish commentators and lexicographers to their modern counterparts. It will then be necessary to examine those sources —modern as well as ancient, classical and mediaeval—that provide evidence of alternative renderings and to reach a conclusion about the extent to which these alternatives are scientifically justifiable. In the light of such a conclusion it will be possible to offer some general guidelines about the types of rendering that are required and to judge whether the tendency of contemporary scholarship and translation is soundly based and should be more consistently applied.

The various forms of the phrase *nś꜀ ꜥyn* occur a total of 50 times in the Hebrew Bible, 18 of them in the Pentateuch, 6 in the Former Prophets, 20 in the Latter Prophets and 6 in the Hagiographa. If these occurrences are divided according to the literary form in which they are to be found, 23 are in classical narrative prose, 18 constitute part of a prophetic or poetic utterance and 9 belong to the introductory phraseology preceding the report of a prophetic revelation.[3] As far as the sense of the phrase in

[2] These translations appeared in Oxford and Cambridge, 1970, London, 1966, and Philadelphia, 1967^{2}, 1978 and 1982 respectively.

[3] The fifty cases are, according to this tripartite classification: a) Gen. xiii 10, 14, xviii 2, xxii 4, 13, xxiv 63, 64, xxxi 10, 12, xxxiii 1, 5, xxxvii 25, xxxix 7, xliii 29; Exod. xiv 10; Deut. iii 27; Josh. v 13; Judg. xix 17; 1 Sam. vi 13; 2 Sam. xiii 34, xviii 24; Job ii 12; 1 Chron. xxi 16; b) Deut. iv 19; 2 Kings xix 22; Isa. xxxvii 23, xl 26, xlix 18, li 6, lx 4; Jer. iii 2, xiii 20; Ezek. viii 5 (first), xviii 6, 12, 15, xxiii 27, xxxiii 25; Zech. v 5; Ps. cxxi 1, cxxiii 1; c) Num. xxiv 2; Ezek. viii 5 (second); Zech. ii 1, 5, v i, v 9, vi 1; Dan. viii 3, x 5.

each of these three contexts is concerned, it appears to describe a visual activity in the narratives, an intellectual and spiritual concentration in the prophecy and poetry, and an ecstatic or apocalyptic vision in prophetic reports. The verb is always in the *qal* conjugation, the noun is consistently plural and the object marker *ʾet* is employed between *nśʾ* and *ʿyn* in 17 out of 50 cases. The preposition *ʾel* follows the whole expression in 8 occurrences and the preposition *ʿal* in 2. To complete these apparently dry but nevertheless important statistics it should be noted, firstly, that of the 39 instances of the perfect and imperfect indicative, 23 are in the third person, 5 in the second and 11 in the first, and, secondly, that of the 11 instances of the imperative, 5 are masculine singular, 3 feminine singular and 3 masculine plural.

If the NEB, JB and NJPS may for the purposes of this examination be taken as typical of modern translations, it will have to be admitted that the traditional rendering of the AV, "lift the eyes" albeit in its more modern, idiomatic garb of "raise the eyes", "look up", remains predominant. There is a growing tendency to adopt some more adventurous translations so that while the JB has 42 out of 50 traditional renderings, the NEB has 40 and the NJPS 32. Nevertheless, these are still very much in the minority and there is no consistency between the three versions or within each of them. Only four such adventurous translations are common to all three versions, viz. Gen. xxxix 7; Deut. iii 27; Ezek. xxiii 27; and Job ii 12, and the first of them is already exceptional in the AV.[4] What must now be determined is the source of this predominant translation and the validity of the alternatives to it.

As in so many similar cases, a close examination of the ancient versions is revealing. On the Semitic side, the Targumim and the Peshiṭta, with minimal exceptions to which reference will later be made, render the Hebrew with literal Aramaic equivalents, *zqp ʿynʾ* in the case of the former and *ʾrym ʿynʾ* in the case of the latter. The Greek and Latin versions demonstrate the same tendency although here too there are a limited number of exceptions to be dealt with further in this analysis. The two standard Greek renderings are ἐπαίρειν τοὺς ὀφθαλμοὺς and ἀναβλέπειν τοῖς ὀφθαλμοῖς while the Latin equivalent is *(e)levare oculos*. What has clearly happened is that these ancient versions have translated the verb in what they regard as its usual sense of "lift" and simply attached the noun

[4] The other "non-traditional" renderings are, in the JB, Gen. xiii 10, 14; Exod. xiv 10; Isa. xlix 18; in the NEB, Gen. xliii 29; Num. xxiv 2; 2 Sam. xviii 24; 2 Kings xix 22; Ezek viii 5 (twice); in the NJPS, Gen. xiii 10, 12, xxxiii 5, xliii 29; Exod. xiv 10; Judg. xix 17; Isa. xlix 18; Ezek. viii 5 (twice); Ps. cxxi 1, cxxiii 1; Dan. viii 3, x 5.

"eyes" as its direct or indirect object.[5] What has been produced neither makes sense of the Hebrew idiom nor reads as authentic Aramaic, Greek or Latin. Consultation of the relevant entries in the standard dictionaries of those ancient languages confirms that "eye-lifting" is no more familar an occupation of the Classical world than it is of the Elizabethan.[6] The tale of slavish literalism clearly begins here.

While the authoritative Onqelos version and the other less standard Targumim adhere to this literalism it would appear not to be represented in the Hebrew literature of the Talmudim and Midrashim; quite the contrary, the evidence from that source is of a different kind and will occupy our attention in a later part of this article. A somewhat similar judgement may be made of some of the classical Jewish commentators of the mediaeval and early modern periods in certain contexts although here a few more detailed comments are required since the position is not quite so clear-cut.

In their summaries and paraphrases of the respective verses in Num. xxiv 2 and Ps. cxxi 1 both the commentary cited in the name of Saadya[7] and that of Ibn Ezra[8] make use of the expression *nśʾ ʿyn* but the general contexts of their remarks provide no clue to the precise linguistic definition they are presupposing for the expression and to cite these uses would simply amount to begging the question. Similarly, David Qimḥi's understanding of the first three words in Isa. xl 26 as "look at the stars" is no indication that he was defining *nśʾ ʿyn* as "look upwards" since the word *mārōm* occurs between the verb and the noun and could carry that directional sense.[9]

In the eighteenth century, however, the Jewish commentator David Altschuler in Poland often used the phrase *hrym ʿyn* to explain the Hebrew expression under discussion.[10] Whether this was ultimately due to the influence of standard Bible translations in European languages, a

[5] For an attempted explanation of other similar phenomena in the LXX see S. Daniel, "Expressions containing the world *rʾš*, *ph*, *lb* in the Septuagint of the Pentateuch" (Hebrew) in M. Bar-Asher, A. Dotan, G. B. Sarfati, and D. Téné (ed.), *Hebrew Language Studies presented to Professor Ze'eb Ben-Ḥayyim* (Hebrew; Jerusalem, 1983), pp. 161-72.

[6] For Greek and Latin see the dictionaries of H. G. Liddell and R. Scott, and C. T. Lewis and C. Short; as fas as Aramaic is concerned, the use of the root *zqp* in this context seems not to tally with earlier linguistic usage, as indicated on p. 239 below.

[7] See the Hebrew translation published by J. Kafiḥ in Jerusalem in 1966 which unfortunately provides no Judaeo-Arabic original for comparison.

[8] As printed in the standard Rabbinic Bible: *mnhg kwl šhwʾ bmṣwr lśʾt ʿynyw ʾwly ybwʾw ʿwzrym lw lhrḥyq hʾwyb.*

[9] As printed in the standard Rabbinic Bible: *hstklw bkwkbym.*

[10] His commentary on the Prophets and Hagiographa, first printed in its entirety at Livorno in 1780-82 by his son, Jeḥiel Hillel, who had completed it, is included in standard editions of the Rabbinic Bible; see his comments on Jer. iii 2; Zech. v 1, 5, vi 1.

knowledge of the ancient versions or an internal intellectual development must be left for discussion on another occasion. What is clear is that Altschuler is offering a slightly more idiomatic form of the literal rendering.

Perhaps he was simply following a lead given by the Hebrew dictionaries available to him by that time since such a rendering is by no means excluded by these. As far as I am aware none of the earliest Hebrew lexicographers or grammarians regarded the phrase *nśʾ ʿyn* as sufficiently controversial or problematic to warrant lengthy comment and this in itself may be indicative that they took the sense that occurs in the Talmudic/Midrashic sources as self-evident. Be that as it may, the dictionaries of Jonah Ibn Janaḥ in 11th century Spain and David Qimḥi in 12th century Provence appear to record what has earlier been referred to as the idiomatic form of the literal rendering. Ibn Janaḥ identifies ten senses of the root *nśʾ*, viz. "carry", "lift", "favour", "donate", "forgive", "consent", "promise", "count", "declaim" and "burn", but he places the phrase *nśʾ ʿyn*, for which he cites three examples together with *nśʾ rgl* and *nśʾ qwl*, strictly in the second sense of "raise", "lift". It would seem that for him, the verb carries no special and noteworthy sense when used with *ʿyn* nor, apparently, is there any distinction to be made between its various occurrences.[11] David Qimḥi takes the matter no further. On the contrary, he simplifies the definition of the root meaning to "carry", "bear", "take" and fits all examples into semantic areas covered by these three senses. Phrases in which the object of the verb *nśʾ* varies from "wine" and "blessing" to "gift" and "vegetation" are listed together with those in which it is the "eye", "leg" or "voice", and only one example of *nśʾ ʿyn* is offered in this context, without specific comment.[12]

The more modern dictionaries of leading Christian Hebraists continued to record the literal rendering. Buxtorf employs the Latin verbs *levare* and *ferre* with sundry prefixes to translate *nśʾ* and takes *nśʾ ʿyn* so for granted as to offer no specific comments.[13] The general definition of the latter phrase in Gesenius-Buhl is "die Augen aufheben"[14] while BDB suggests "lift up eyes".[15] To be fair to these latter two dictionaries, however, it is necessary to stress that they also mention a special applica-

---

[11] W. Bacher (ed.), *Sefer Haschoraschim* (Berlin, 1896), pp. 319-23.

[12] J. H. R. Biesenthal and F. Lebrecht (ed.), *Radicum Liber* (Berlin, 1847), cols. 452-6.

[13] *Lexicon Hebraicum et Chaldaicum* (Basle, 1631^4), p. 487.

[14] F. Buhl (ed.), *Wilhelm Gesenius' Hebräisches und Aramäisches Handwörterbuch über das Alte Testament* (Leipzig, 1915^{16}) p. 523.

[15] F. Brown, S. R. Driver, and C. A. Briggs, *A Hebrew and English Lexicon of the Old Testament* (Oxford, 1907) p. 670.

tion of the term to denote desire or admiration, with particular reference to Potiphar's wife and Ezekiel's condemnations. This special application is, however, limited by them to instances where the object is introduced by the preposition *ᵓel*.

This same combination of a translation "raise the eyes" and a note that such a raising may be in desire or admiration is also to be found in many of the standard commentaries of the last hundred years. C. A. and E. G. Briggs on the Psalms refer to "attentive, patient waiting";[16] A. B. Davidson notes that the lifting of the eyes in the Ezekiel passages is being done "in prayer to the idols, or trust in them, or perhaps generally, in acknowledgement of them";[17] G. A. Cooke on one of the same passages speaks somewhat more loosely of "idolatry", "true worship" and "other senses";[18] J. W. Wevers defines the use in Ps. cxxi 1 as "in the sense of observe and thus seek help from"[19] while A. A. Anderson finds anxious and expectant looking in the two Psalm verses.[20] Among the other comments worthy of attention here are those of J. Skinner[21] and J. A. Montgomery[22] who simply stress the physical nature of the act; H. P. Smith[23] and H. Gunkel[24] who refer to the literary nature of the expression and the context in which it is to be found; K. von Orelli[25] who defines the sense of the verb *nśᵓ* as "aufheben, tragen und wegnehmen" but also points out that *nśᵓ ᶜyn* in the context of a revelation describes a new vision following closely on its predecessor; and M. J. Dahood[26] who cites the inevitable Ugaritic parallel but retains the translation "raise the eyes" in both languages.

A. B. Ehrlich, the Jewish Bible commentator from Poland whose work of some seventy to eighty years ago has not perhaps received the attention it deserves, was one of those who noted the physical act of *nśᵓ ᶜyn* and its context. In his German comments on Gen. xxxix 7 he explains that *nśᵓ ᶜyn ᵓel* does not mean to cast one's eye upon someone but to look up at someone admiringly or imploringly while kneeling before that person. The context may be worship, supplication, or, as in the case of Potiphar's

---

[16] *A Critical and Exegetical Commentary on the Book of Psalms* (Edinburgh, 1906-7) 2, p. 451.

[17] *The Book of the Prophet Ezekiel in the Revised Version with Notes and Introduction*, revised by A. W. Streane (Cambridge, 1916) pp. 137-8.

[18] *A Critical and Exegetical Commentary on the Book of Ezekiel* (Edinburgh, 1936) p. 203.

[19] *Ezekiel* (London, 1969) p. 142.

[20] *The Book of Psalms* (London, 1972) pp. 851-2.

[21] *A Critical and Exegetical Commentary on Genesis* (Edinburgh, 1910), p. 252.

[22] *A Critical and Exegetical Commentary on the Book of Daniel* (Edinburgh, 1927) p. 328.

[23] *A Critical and Exegetical Commentary on the Books of Samuel* (Edinburgh, 1899) pp. 46-8.

[24] *Genesis übersetzt und erklärt* (Göttingen, 1901), p. 330.

[25] *Das Buch Ezechiel und die zwölf kleinen Propheten* (Nordlingen, 1888) pp. 69, 367, 376.

[26] *Psalms* (Garden City, New York, 1966-70) 3, p. 200.

infamous wife, unrequited love.[27] He makes the same points in his Hebrew commentary on the verse but there stresses the contribution made by the presence of the preposition *ʾel* to this idiomatic sense.[28]

It is, however, his comment on the general use of *nśʾ* with parts of the body that is particularly interesting since it is one of a number of comments and definitions by various scholars that have begun to influence the translation of such phrases in recent versions and that must now therefore be detailed.

Commenting on the first occurrences of the expression in the Hebrew Bible in Gen. xiii 10, Ehrlich draws a parallel with the other expressions *nśʾ rgl, nśʾ lb, nśʾ yd, nśʾ kp* and *nśʾ qwl* and argues that the verb is not here being used in the sense of "lifting" such parts of the body but in the idiomatic sense of "affecting" or "activating" them.[29] This interpretation commended itself to E. A. Speiser and he therefore rejected the tendency to understand the word *nśʾ* as equivalent to the adverbial use in English, viz. "loudly" with *qwl* and "upwards" with *ʿyn*, preferring to convey what he referred to as the "ingressive force of the phrase" by the adoption of a different translation. In his own words, "the verb *nśʾ* is used with bodily organs ... not with the sense of 'to lift', to signify the degree or volume, but with the shading of 'to pick up', to focus attention on the activity involved".[30] His renderings stress the *ʿyn* rather than the *nśʾ* and he offers "look about", "glance", "sight", "see", "notice" and "note"[31] without, however, eliminating "look up" and "raise eyes" from all contexts.

Among more contemporary dictionaries than those already cited, it should be noted that, although F. Stolz in the *Theologisches Handwörterbuch zum Alten Testament*[32] appears to take the discussion little further than BDB, the lexicographers E. Ben Yehuda,[33] L. Koehler-W. Baumgartner (first edition),[34] R. Alkalay,[35] A. Even-Shoshan[36] and J. Knaani[37] for their part list, in the respective languages in which they write, the figurative sense of "hope", "desire", "trust", and complement the

---

[27] *Randglossen zur Hebräischen Bibel* (Leipzig, 1908-18) 1, *Genesis und Exodus*, pp. 196-7.

[28] *Mikrâ ki-Pheschutô. Die Schrift nach ihrem Wortlaut* (Berlin, 1899-1901) 1, *Der Pentateuch*, p. 107.

[29] *Randglossen* (n. 27 above), p. 52.

[30] *Genesis* (Garden City, New York, 1964) pp. 155-6.

[31] See his translations of Gen. xiii 10, 14, xxii 4, xxiv 63, 64, xxxi 12.

[32] Ed. E. Jenni and C. Westermann (Munich, 1971 and 1976) 2, p. 112.

[33] *Thesaurus Totius Hebraitatis et Veteris et Recentioris* (Berlin-New York-Jerusalem-Tel-Aviv, 1910-59) 8, p. 3846.

[34] *Lexicon in Veteris Testamenti Libros* (Leiden, 1953), p. 636.

[35] *The Complete Hebrew-English Dictionary* (Tel-Aviv-Jerusalem, 1964-5) 3, p. 1695.

[36] *Hammillōn Heḥādāš* (Jerusalem, 1966-70) 4, p. 1729.

[37] *ʾOṣar Hallāšōn Hāʿibrīth* (Jerusalem-Ramat Gan-Givatayim, 1962-) 11, p. 3838.

usual "raise the eyes" with "see from afar", "glance towards", "look about", "fix one's glance upwards" and "look and see" respectively.

The third volume of the third edition of Koehler-Baumgartner, now edited by J. J. Stamm, has appeared just soon enough to permit a further note. The new entry for *nśʾ ʿynym* expands on the Akkadian evidence as presented in von Soden's *Handwörterbuch* and offers the senses of "raising covetous or friendly eyes" and "selecting" in that language. As far as Biblical Hebrew is concerned, however, the entry seems less helpful than that included in the first edition since all that is offered is "aufblicken zu" ("to look up to" in English) without indication of what precisely this may be said to mean.[38]

In all the modern lexicographical works just mentioned no consensus has yet emerged but what is clear is that all the compilers are aware that "lifting the eyes" in Hebrew is not necessarily to be equated with the English idiom "look up".

A growing awareness of this fact and of wider scholarly evidence soon to be examined has made an impact on the English translations of the last twenty years and produced the kind of adventurous renderings to which reference was earlier made and to which closer attention may now be given.

Since even the AV rejects the otherwise ubiquitous "lift eyes" for the passage in Gen. xxxix that describes the attempted seduction of Joseph and uses the preposition *ʾel* in addition to the phrase under discussion, it is no surprise to find that the JB, NEB and NJPS all offer more linguistically meaningful renderings, viz. "looked desirously at", "took notice of", "cast her eyes upon" respectively, the last-mentioned, interestingly enough, remaining content to follow the precise wording of the AV, something it most certainly avoids doing elsewhere. As earlier noted, there are three other cases in which all these versions depart from any semblance of eye-raising, namely, Deut. iii 27; Ezek. xxiii 27; and Job ii 12. The three respective renderings in each case are, for the first one, "let your eyes turn", "look" and "gaze about"; for the second, "look to", "cast longing eyes" and "long for"; for the third, "saw him from a distance", "looking at him from a distance" and "saw him from a distance". Similar such renderings occur four times more in JB, six times more in NEB and fourteen times more in NJPS.[39] The questions that must be answered in the next part of this analysis are whether these departures from the established tradition earlier traced to the ancient

---

[38] *Hebräisches und Aramäisches Lexikon zum Alten Testament* (3rd edn, Leiden, 1967, 1974 and 1983), Lief. 3, p. 685.

[39] For details see n. 4 above.

versions are justified by the linguistic evidence, to what extent they are adumbrated in earlier sources and in how many other verses of the Hebrew Bible, if any, they may properly be adopted.

The Hebrew root *nś*ʾ and its cognates are not geographically restricted to the north-west branch of the Semitic languages, including Aramaic and Ugaritic, nor chronologically limited to the biblical period. Linguistically equivalent verbs occur in the Arabian languages to the south and the Akkadian to the east and have a sound pedigree long before the earliest possible date of Biblical Hebrew. Bergsträsser could thus include the verb among those that he termed "gemeinsemitische Wörte" and list the perfect forms as *nāśā* in Hebrew and Aramaic, *iššī* in Akkadian and *nš*ʾ in South Arabian and Arabic.[40] Although the sense of "lift" and "carry" is attested, the root has vaguer and less clearly defined meanings such as the transitive "take" and "move" in Akkadian[41] and the intransitive "emerge", "develop" in Arabic.[42] It would appear to have enjoyed a somewhat catholic use until more sharply defined verbs displaced it in specific contexts. With the growing awareness of the root's wide semantic range such scholars as M. H. [Goshen-]Gottstein,[43] L. Kopf[44] and E. A. Speiser[45] devoted articles to indicating the problematic nature of applying the sense of "lift" in a number of Biblical Hebrew expressions, particularly the word *nāśī*ʾ, and offered alternative renderings. Since these particular articles did not concern themselves with the subject of this paper they need not be discussed here at length; the point need only be made that "motion", "activation" and "election" were being suggested as the theme rather than "lifting" and "bearing".

Lest it be argued that the older, more elastic sense of the root *nś*ʾ might not be applicable to a Biblical Hebrew idiom of a later date, it should immediately be noted that, in addition to those senses to which reference has already been made, the Chicago *Assyrian Dictionary* lists the phrase *našû īnu* and defines it as "look intentionally", "look for something" and "covet", "desire". Although a text is also cited in which reference is made to a person who "in his sickness does not raise his eyes" there

---

[40] *Einführung in die Semitischen Sprachen* (Munich, 1928), p. 187.

[41] *The Assyrian Dictionary of the Oriental Institute of the University of Chicago* (Chicago-Glückstadt, 1956-) 11, part 2, p. 80; W. von Soden, *Akkadisches Handwörterbuch* (Wiesbaden, 1965-81) 2, pp. 762-4.

[42] E. W. Lane, *An Arabic-English Lexicon* (London, 1863-93) p. 2790, col. 3; H. Wehr, *A Dictionary of Modern Written Arabic* (Wiesbaden, 1979⁴) p. 1131.

[43] "*nśy*ʾ ʾ*lhym* (Gen. xxiii 6)", *VT* 3 (1953), pp. 298-9.

[44] "Arabische Etymologien und Parallelen zum Bibelwörterbuch", *VT* 8 (1958), p. 186.

[45] "Background and Function of the Biblical *Nāśī*ʾ", *CBQ* 25 (1963), pp. 111-17.

seems to be no reason why the listed definitions of *našû īnu* rather than this more physical description should not be applied there too.[46]

When Speiser, in his comment on the relevant phrase in Gen. xxxix 7, cites an Akkadian parallel describing Ishtar's designs on Gilgamesh, he quickly adds that "a literal rendering would be misleading since the Hebrew phrase can also denote truthfulness (Ezek. xxxiii 25) or prayerful appeal (Ps. cxxiii 1f)".[47] It is not clear whether he was advocating the abandonment of the literal rendering only in Hebrew, or in Akkadian as well as Hebrew; whatever his intention, the evidence from Akkadian usage would certainly support the application of his statement to both languages.

Another piece of relevant evidence may be adduced from Akkadian by reference to the verb *naṭālu* in that language, meaning "to see".[48] It seems reasonable to suppose that the original form here was *naṭālu īnu* and that this became so formulaic and unitary in sense that the *īnu* was eventually lost. Here, too, the original sense of the verb in the phrase was to "employ", "activate" rather than literally to "lift".

There is a precise Aramaic parallel to the Akkadian *naṭālu īnu* in Dan. iv 31, either borrowed directly from the eastern Semitic language or simply a translation of the Biblical Hebrew expression under discussion. Either way it further attests the wide use of the idiom and the occurrence of the word *lšmyʾ* in the phrase permits one to assume that the verb need not have conveyed the upward sense but simply the sense of seeing since *lšmyʾ* provided the directional qualification.

As far as the Ugaritic evidence is concerned, it provides excellent parallels to the Hebrew text, but, as in so many other cases, there is the danger of arguing circularly about the meaning of the phrase. Be that as it may, the verb *nśʾ* occurs with the noun *ʿyn* in both the infinitive construct and the imperfect forms and the phrase refers, in a standard narrative style, to a stage in the act of seeing, without any indication, *pace* the usual translation "lifted up his/her eyes", that such an act was in the upward direction. One text, indeed, has three expressions for "seeing", supporting the assumption that what occurs there is a narrative technique rather that a precise description: *bnšʾi ʿnh . wyphn // yḥd . hrgb* (Aqhat I D [*CTA* 19] iii 120-21).[49]

---

[46] *The Assyrian Dictionary* (n. 41 above) 11, part 2, pp. 85, 104.

[47] *Genesis* (n. 30 above), p. 303.

[48] *The Assyrian Dictionary* (n. 41 above) 11, part 2, p. 121; *Akkadisches Handwörterbuch* (n. 41 above) 2, p. 766.

[49] See also Baʿal and ʿAnat Cycle, texts II AB (*CTA* 4) ii 12 and IV AB (*CTA* 10) ii 13-14, 26-27; for the three texts see J. C. L. Gibson's second edition of G. R. Driver's *Canaanite Myths and Legends* (Edinburgh, 1978), pp. 56, 118, 132.

The internal linguistic and exegetical evidence from the Hebrew Bible permits similar conclusions. Pursuing further the statistical clues that were earlier presented, the researcher will find that the use of the phrase *nś᾽ ʿyn* as a technical term of introduction in both narrative and prophetic contexts covers both the physical and metaphorical senses of "vision" but in no way presupposes that the object of such vision is on a higher level than the observer.

Indeed, there are some cases in which the physical situation is quite to the contrary, and the view most certainly downwards. Moses' view of the Holy Land is from the summit of Mount Pisgah (Deut. iii 27), the old man arriving in Gibeah sights the Levite sitting in the street (Judg. xix 17), while the look-out waiting for news of Absalom's fate is stationed on the roof of the city-gate (2 Sam. xviii 24). In the account of the division of the land of Canaan between Abraham and Lot, both the patriarch and his nephew appear to be on ground high enough to permit them a clear view of the surrounding territory (Gen. xiii 10, 14) while Rebekah's sight of Isaac from the top of a camel is described with the same *nś᾽ ʿyn* as is used for his sight of her. Although no definitive statements may be made about the physical situation in the case of Abraham's arrival on Mount Moriah, the use of the verb *hlk* seems to indicate that his first sight of the place might have been from a distant part at the same height rather than from below (Gen. xxii 3-8). Similarly, in the case of Joseph's confrontation with his brothers, it is unlikely that Pharaoh's viceroy would have been on a lower level than his Canaanite supplicants (Gen. xliii 29).

As far as the remaining cases are concerned, they are, with one exception in Chronicles, neutral as far as the direction of *nś᾽ ʿyn* is concerned, for a number of different reasons. Sometimes, a locative adverb is specifically employed, implying that no assumption may be made from the verb itself; examples are *hšmymh* (Deut. iv 19), *mrwm* (2 Kings xix 22, Isa. xl 26) and *sbyb* (Isa. xlix 18, lx 4). At other times, a prophetic vision is being described and the context is therefore not a physical one, as in the cases of Jacob (Gen. xxxi 10, 12), Balaam (Num. xxiv 2) and Zechariah (e.g. ii 1, v 1, vi 1). In a number of narratives, the visual realization seems to be the important element rather than the relative positions of the subject and what he saw; this is clearly the case with Abraham's sight of the ram (Gen. xxii 13), Jacob's sight of Esau (Gen. xxxiii 1), the Israelites' sight of Pharaoh (Exod. xiv 10), the invitation to Jeremiah to look north (Jer. xiii 20) and Job's friends' sight of him (Job ii 12).

If it is acknowledged that Ehrlich's explanation of the use of the preposition *᾽el* with the phrase *nś᾽ ʿyn* as describing the admiring, upward look of the lowly towards the exalted subject of his or her emotion is nowhere indicated by the Hebrew and begs the very question here being asked, and that the look may just as well be an intensive one relating to a particular object, there remains only one example that stands in the way of the theory that is being propounded about direction. In 1 Chron. xxi 16 David "lifts up his eyes" to see a messenger of God positioned between heaven and earth. This threat to the theory may, however, be rendered harmless by reference to the parallel passage in 2 Sam. xxiv 17. There the simple verb *rʾh* is used and the Chronicler has clearly introduced another narrative technique to embellish the original account rather than to clarify the precise sense. At any rate, the variation between the accounts calls into question the permissibility of drawing conclusions from the linguistic structure of one or the other.

Further linguistic evidence for a sense of *nśʾ* more general than that permitted by the English translation "raise", "lift" is provided by the parallel use of the word with parts of the body other than the eye. When it governs the nouns *qwl, rgl, npš, lb, yd* and *kp*, the sense is more akin to "use", "direct", "activate"; when used with *rʾš* and *pnym* the equivalent would rather be "favour", except in the case of Pharaoh's butler and baker where a pun is made by contrasting this sense with that of "removal". Joseph predicts that Pharaoh will raise the butler's head, i.e. favour him, but raise the baker's head from the rest of his body, i.e. hang him (Gen. xl 13, 19). The very fact that the writer makes use of such a pun is itself an indication that an idiomatic sense existed side by side with a more literal one.

What appears to be happening here is that Hebrew is making good its inability to use a noun directly in a verbal sense by calling upon the services of a nondescript verb and harnessing it to the noun to create the same effect. In more concrete terms, English allows one to "eye" objects, to "voice" opinions and to "face" friends while Hebrew prefers *nśʾ ʿyn, nśʾ qwl* and *nśʾ pnym.*[50]

In an article shortly to be published it has been argued by G. Khan that *ʾet* tends to be omitted before objects that lack salience and distinctiveness from the action of the verb.[51] Since *ʾet* is so often absent between *nśʾ* and *ʿyn*, Khan's argument provides additional support for the theory that the phrase represents the formulaic expression of a unitary concept,

---

[50] M. I. Gruber has recently published a brief study of the expression *nśʾ pnym* in *ZAW* 95 (1983), pp. 252-60, the basic findings of which tally with what I am here suggesting. He argues that the expression is an idiom for making a pleasant face, i.e. favouring, smiling, and suggests the idea of looking up in only a few cases. In my own view even these cases (e.g. Job xxii 26) do not necessarily imply an upward look and may be used to support his more general theory, as well as my own submissions.

[51] "Object markers and agreement pronouns in Semitic languages", scheduled for publication in the *Bulletin of the School of Oriental and African Studies* 47 (1984). I am grateful to my colleague Mr Geoffrey Khan for this reference and other kind assistance.

i.e. "vision" of one sort or another, rather than two distinct concepts, i.e. "lifting" and "eye", and is close to having the status of an intransitive predicate.

To conclude the internal linguistic analysis, one needs to point to the fact that Hebrew has more physical vocabulary, in the shape of the verbs *rwm* and *gbh*, and all their related nominal forms, capable of conveying more precisely than *nśʾ* a sense of height. Those whose eyes are truly uplifted, that is, in the metaphorical application, haughty and superior, are referred to with phrases such as *gbh ʿynym* and *rwm ʿynym* and not the phrase that is the subject of this article.[52] Although the use is always metaphorical in the biblical texts available, one is surely entitled to presuppose a physical original for the figurative derivative.

Although, as has already been established, the ancient versions prefer the literal rendering "raise the eyes" in the vast majority of cases, it should now be noted that there are a few cases in which they demonstrated an awareness of a more general sense of "look" or a specialized meaning of "setting one's sight on". The LXX describes how Potiphar's wife "cast her eyes" on Joseph (Gen. xxxix 7) and twice translates Ezekiel's use of the phrase into the Greek equivalent of "fixing" or "setting" one's eyes (Ezek. xviii 12, 15). In two other cases, however, it renders the Hebrew with the simple verb "to see" (Gen. xxxi 10 and Job ii 12). Similarly, the Latin employs *injecit* in the case of Gen. xxxix 7, *circumfer* for what Moses did on Mount Pisgah (Deut. iii 27), and describes one simple act of vision in two other cases where the Hebrew uses both *nśʾ ʿyn* and *rʾh* (Gen. xxiv 64 and xxxvii 25). As far as the Peshiṭta and the Targumim are concerned, their only departures from the standard rendering are towards the sense of lifting and not away from it. TJ2 offers the more specific phrase *ttlwn ʿynykwn* in Deut. iv 19 and the Peshiṭta uses the same root *rym* for both Hebrew roots *nśʾ* and *rwm* in 2 Kings xix 22 and its parallel Isa. xxxvii 23.

More significantly, the living Hebrew tradition of the Tannaim supports the alternative senses of "looking" and "looking with enthusiasm". In the mishnaic passage dealing with the choice of brides by young Jewish men on the fifteenth of the month of Av, the prospective grooms are invited to "have a good look", or "look carefully" and see the advantages of good breeding over physical beauty: *bḥwr śʾ nʾ ʿynyk wrʾh mh ʾth bwrr lk* (Mishnah, Taʿanith 4.8).

The Babylonian Talmud explains that one of the reasons for not reading the book of Esther on the Sabbath is because the poor "set their sights" on the reading, knowing that it brings with it gifts for them, and

[52] See e.g. Ps. ci 5; Isa. v 15; Ps. cxxxi 1; Prov. vi 17.

such gifts could not be offered on the Sabbath: *mpny šʿynyhm šlʿnyym nśwʾwt bmqrʾ mgylh* (Megillah 4b).

That a strong emotion is associated with the phrase *nśʾ ʿyn* is specifically noted by a midrashic comment on Num. xxvii 12 that contrasts the great joy felt by Abraham when he saw the land promised to him with the deep sadness of Moses when he saw the land denied to him: *bʾbrhm hwʾ ʾwmr śʾ nʾ ʿynyk ... zw hyʾ rʾyyh šlnḥt* (Sifrey on Numbers, § 136).

In one passage the Hebrew *lammārōm* defines the direction in which the Jews will "set their sights" but the phrase itself clearly conveys the sense of an enthusiastic gaze rather than an upward look: *myd nśʾw ʿynyhm lmrwm wʾwmrym ʾth hšm ʾbynw gwʾlnw mʿwlm šmk* (Babylonian Talmud, Šabbath 89b).

That the Tannaitic sense of the phrase continues to occur in the literary, poetic and mundane texts of the mediaeval Jewish world is only to be expected, given the dominant influence of Talmudic Hebrew on the development of the language of the middle ages.[53] What is more noteworthy is the fact that some of the classical Jewish commentaries of the period, if closely examined, reveal definitions of the phrase more in keeping with the authentic evidence already presented than with the literalistic renderings of the ancient and modern versions. Strangely enough such definitions are also offerd by Qimḥi and Altschuler whose views elsewhere appear to indicate, as has already been noted, some degree of support for the literal rendering.

Underlying these comments is the common basic assumption that there is some form of conscious, intellectual decision associated with the element of sight in the phrase *nśʾ ʿyn*. This may take the form of an understanding that arises out of the sight, as implied by Qimḥi on Isa. xl 26 followed by Altschuler on Isa. li 6,[54] or one that precedes and inspires that sight, as well as arising out of it, as explained by Obadya Sforno on Gen. xviii 2 and 4.[55] Alternatively, the intellectual decision may have to do with a sympathetic identification with the object of one's sight such as is presupposed by Rashi on Deut. iv 19,[56] Qimḥi on Ezek. xviii 6 and

[53] To the examples offered by Knaani (n. 37 above) may be added a thirteenth century personal letter in the Genizah collection at Cambridge University Library (T-S 13J20.9) in which a husband exhorts his wife: *śʾy ʿynyk lšmym wʿśy lmʿn yqrwtyk.*

[54] In the standard Rabbinic Bible: *kbr ʾmr lhm šybynw ... ʿth ʾmr lhm šystklw bkwkbym ... wrʾw bdʿtkm my brʾ ʾlh.*

[55] In the standard Rabbinic Bible and ed. Z. (W.) Gottlieb and A. Darom (Jerusalem, 1980) pp. 47 and 56: *htkwwn lhstkl* and *šlṭh bw ʿynw lrʾt.*

[56] In the standard Rabbinic Bible and ed. A. Berliner (Frankfurt-am-Main, 1905), p. 362: *lhstkl bdbr wltt lb*; for the English edition see M. Rosenbaum and A. M. Silbermann (London, 1934) 5, p. 26.

xxxiii 25 and Altschuler on Ezek. xviii 6 and 12, xxiii 27 and xxxiii 25.[57] A third possibility is that it heralds an appeal for assistance as described by Ibn Ezra, followed by Altschuler, on Ps. cxxi 1, and a fourth that it denotes the experience of a spiritual vision, as defined by Ibn Ezra on Zech. ii 1 and 5 and on Dan. x 5.[58] Sometimes the AV reflects these mediaeval commentaries; in this case it chose not to do so and the translations of the modern world have therefore taken that much longer to come into line with the authentic sense of the Hebrew.

The wheel has turned full circle and I have again arrived at the contemporary versions. The evidence presented seems clearly in favour of what I earlier referred to as the adventurous translations and of the marked tendency of the NEB and NJPS, the latter probably inspired by Speiser following Ehrlich,[59] to depart from the AV. It now remains only to summarize what has been found and to suggest some possible translations for consistent application to all fifty Biblical Hebrew instances rather than to a small selection of them.

Neither the literal rendering "lift eyes", originating in the ancient versions, nor its assumed idiomatic equivalent "look up" that have been preferred in some modern translations is justifiable in the light of the evidence of the Hebrew Bible itself, the post-biblical Hebrew usage, the Semitic cognates, and the mediaeval Jewish commentators. As correctly argued by Speiser and Ehrlich and hinted at in some older sources, the idiom *nś*ʾ *ʿyn* carries the basic sense of "activating the eye" i.e. deciding to employ one's visual faculty. There are three Biblical Hebrew contexts in which the idiom occurs, the narrative, the poetic and the revelational, and the translation of the phrase should take account of the context in which it occurs. In the case of narratives and poetry, the simpler rendering would be "look", particularly when the idiom is being used for literary effect rather than to convey a special sense, with the option of "have a (good) look", "take a good look" when a more significant or metaphorical meaning is intended. Where the prepositions *ʾel* and *ʿal* follow the phrase, the emotion involved requires a more active rendering such as "set one's sight (up)on". In the case of a prophetic revelation a more appropriate rendering would be "have a vision". Whichever rendering is ultimately regarded as most suitable in each case, I hope that translators will continue to look up the phrase but that the phrase will no longer translate as "look up".

---

[57] In these comments the root *pnh* is consistently used to denote the sense of *nś*ʾ *ʿyn*.

[58] Ibn Ezra employs the word *mrʾh* to describe the event; see also n. 8 above.

[59] See the preface to the Pentateuch of the NJPS translation and p. vi of Speiser's preface to his volume on Genesis (n. 30 above).

THE USE OF SOCIOLOGY IN OLD TESTAMENT STUDIES

BY

J. W. ROGERSON

Sheffield

It is well known that the word "sociology" was coined by August Comte in 1837 in the fourth volume of his *Cours de philosophie positive.*[1] Because Comte was the first to use the word "sociology", and because he advocated the formulation of methods that would be special to the scientific study of societies, he is usually regarded as the founding father of sociological studies. H.-J. Kraus, in his article "Die Anfänge der religionssoziologischen Forschungen in der alttestamentlichen Wissenschaft",[2] takes his survey of the use of sociology in Old Testament studies back as far as the time of Comte.

However, sociological thought goes back in history much further than the time of Comte, and interpreters of the Old Testament have been using sociological judgements at least since the time of Josephus. Jerzy Szacki, in his recent *History of Sociological Thought,*[3] begins his account with Plato and Aristotle and does not reach Comte until chapter 7. I owe to my colleague, David Clines, the observation that in *Antiquities* V ii 1,7, Josephus states that, after the death of Joshua, the government of Israel was committed to the tribe of Judah. Several paragraphs later, Josephus complains that during the period of the Judges the Israelites "did not ordain themselves a senate, nor any other such magistrates as their laws had formerly required". Clearly, for Josephus, Roman models of government were necessary for any people that was to be properly organized.

Jumping to the 18th century, we can note that J. D. Michaelis's *Mosaisches Recht* (Göttingen, 1770-5) was an investigation of the Old Testament legal system in the context of ancient Israelite society and ecology. Although Michaelis's detailed expositions owed much to earlier

---

[1] For the details see Jerzy Szacki, *History of Sociological Thought* (London, 1979), p. 185. Szacki points out that Comte used the term alternately with others, such as "social philosophy" and "political philosophy".

[2] *Biblisch-theologische Aufsätze* (Neukirchen, 1972), pp. 296-310.

[3] See n. 1. E. E. Evans-Pritchard, *A History of Anthropological Thought* (London, 1981), also begins his survey before Comte.

Jewish and Christian scholarship, the fundamental inspiration for *Mosaisches Recht* came from Montesquieu's pioneering sociological work *De l'esprit des lois* of 1748.[4] Montesquieu saw societies as systems, their laws, social classes, climates and ecologies being parts of the system that related together to form a whole. Michaelis attempted a similar description for the Old Testament, and in so doing he reproduced Montesquieu's cultural relativism in his celebrated phrase

> The Laws of Moses were necessarily regulated by the circumstances of the Israelites, and are not to be introduced among a people in different circumstances.[5]

J. G. Herder, in his *Ideen zur Philosophie der Geschichte der Menschheit* (1784-91), attributed what he saw as the misfortunes of Israel in the post-exilic period to the fact that they lacked a political constitution, as a result of which "their sentiments fluctuated between monarchical and sacerdotal government".[6] Many more examples from the 19th and 20th centuries could be given; but I will content myself with pointing out, in the light of the current fashion of describing Saul and possibly David as chiefs rather than kings, that W. Vatke made a similar point in his *Biblische Theologie* of 1835, on developmentalist grounds.[7]

However, if it is true that the tradition of making sociological observations about the Old Testament is a long one, it is also true that the past ten years have seen an explosion in the number of sociological treatments of the Old Testament. For the moment, I shall deliberately not define the term sociology; but I shall record my welcome for the great increase in interest in sociological approaches to the Old Testament. V. I. Lenin posed the question:

> From where are you to get your conception of society and progress in general when you have not studied a single form of society in particular ... when you have been unable even to approach a serious factual investigation, an objective analysis of social relations of any kind?[8]

---

[4] Charles-Louis de Secondat, Baron de Montesquieu, *De l'esprit des Lois* (Geneva, 1748).

[5] *Mosaisches Recht*, Bk I art. 8. English translation from *Commentaries on the Laws of Moses* (translated by Alexander Smith, London, 1814) I, p. 21.

[6] In B. Suphan (ed.), *Herders Sämmtliche Werke* (Berlin, 1877-1913) 14, p. 62. English translation from *Reflections on the Philosophy of the History of Mankind* (translated by T. O. Churchill, London, 1800), p. 139.

[7] *Die biblische Theologie wissenschaftlich dargestellt* I, *Die Religion des Alten Testaments* (Berlin, 1835), pp. 297-314.

[8] "What the 'Friends of the People' Are and How they Fight against the Social Democrats", in *Selected Works in Two Volumes* (Moscow, 1952) I, pp. 111-2. Quoted in Szacki, p. 384.

I think that we must agree, applying Lenin's point to the Old Testament, that it is ill advised to make sociological observations about what must have been the case in ancient Israel if we ourselves have not attempted to discover how at least one society works. Indeed, it is possible to be left behind by new advances in research even when one's knowledge of societies is quite extensive. For example, no one can accuse Julius Wellhausen of not having made a profound study of the structure and function of Arabian and Israelite society; yet in his *Israelitische and Jüdische Geschichte* he made some influential sociological observations which, in the light of present-day knowledge, are clearly inadequate. For him, the key concept which enables us to understand the unity of the Israelite tribes in the pre-monarchic period is that of "blood":

"Alle *legitime* Gemeinschaft ist Blutsgemeinschaft."

Furthermore, for Wellhausen, the "natural" group, bonded by the tie of "blood" has a common piety and holiness, nourished and reinforced by an intimate relationship with its god who is regarded as a kind of kin relative.[9]

In the light of more recent knowledge we can comment on Wellhausen's position that small groups are not necessarily bonded together by kinship ties, that the mechanisms of their unity do not depend on shared mystical notions about piety and holiness (see below, n. 24), and that the tacitly assumed totemic idea of the relation between a group and its deity has been abandoned by anthropologists.[10] However, Wellhausen's observations have not been quoted so that a cheap point can be made against him because he did not take account of factors that he could not possibly have known about; he has been quoted for two reasons. First, it serves as a reminder that the sociological observations of the giants of 19th century and early 20th century Old Testament scholarship can be, and have been, overtaken by subsequent research. Second, it is interesting to note the form in which Wellhausen's observation is cast. It is not based upon abstract theoretical formulations about the structure and function of societies; rather, it appeals to the readers' imaginations, and invites them to try to think what it must be like to belong to a group which apparently has none of the institutions of government with which we are familiar.

A knowledge of the structure of societies and of the ways in which they function will, then, enable us to break away from "common sense" judgements, and will enable us to base our conclusions upon abstract theorizing that takes account of the great complexities of societies.

---

[9] *Israelitische und Jüdische Geschichte* (Berlin, 1958[9]), pp. 21-2.

[10] See J. W. Rogerson, *Anthropology and the Old Testament* (Oxford, 1978), pp. 24-6.

However, it is not sufficient, in my opinion, for us simply to read anthropological and sociological monographs. We need to know something of the history of sociological thought, to know what schools are to be found within it, and what are the strengths of these various schools. Since this latter point is an important one, I shall now proceed to elaborate it.

Any student of the history of sociological thought will quickly discover that in the United States an important ''school' is the neo-evolutionary school founded by Leslie A. White, of which scholars such as E. R. Service and M. D. Sahlins are representatives. Within the broad context of the historical study of cultures which goes back to Franz Boas, this school is interested in the evolution of culture and society especially as this evolution has been affected by ecological factors.[11] In Britain, the tradition of social anthropology has developed in the broad context of the study of individual societies and their ''collective representations'', a tradition which owes much to E. Durkheim. The work of E. E. Evans-Pritchard, one of the most distinguished British anthropologists, has been particularly concerned with investigating the beliefs and attitudes of members of African societies, with the aim of seeing how those beliefs and attitudes can be understood in the light of the structure and function of the society as a whole.[12]

Unfortunately, anthropologists of differing schools can afford the luxury of disagreeing fundamentally with each other about the rightness of what they are doing. In an article by Sahlins on segmentary lineages, there is criticism of Evans-Pritchard on the grounds that he fails to take proper account of the economic and ecological factors which determine the emergence and subsequent transformation of segmentary lineage systems within the general trend of cultural evolution.[13] Evans-Pritchard's is a ''static'' perspective concerned with the inter-locking features of a society as a whole; Sahlins's perspective is historical and developmentalist, seeking to relate the evolution of political organisation to economic factors. On the other hand Evans-Pritchard, in ''notes and comments'' on the work of Leslie A. White, is deeply dissatisfied by neo-evolutionism, and believes that it generates theories to which many exceptions can be found, and which do not help to explain actual societies (*A History of Anthropological Thought*, pp. 202-4).

---

[11] For a survey of American sociological and anthropological thought see Szacki, pp. 495-8; E. Hatch, *Theories of Man and Culture* (New York, 1973), pp. 37-161.

[12] See Adam Kuper, *Anthropologists and Anthropology. The British School 1922-1972* (London, 1973).

[13] M. D. Sahlins, ''The Segmentary Lineage: An Organization of Predatory Expansion'', *American Anthropologist* 63 (1961), pp. 332-45; reprinted in R. Cohen and J. Middleton (ed.), *Comparative Political Systems. Studies in the Politics of Pre-industrial Societies* (New York, 1967), pp. 89-119.

If anthropologists can afford the luxury of in-fighting, we cannot. While I do not wish to suggest that disagreements among anthropologists are trivial, and that we can learn nothing from them, I want at the same time to urge that, as Old Testament scholars, we must pay attention to the strong points in all the differing schools, and we must not make the mistake of assuming that there is only one type of authentic sociology or anthropology, and that we can happily disregard the rest.

If we consider the range of the uses of anthropology and sociology in recent Old Testament study, we shall discover how many different schools or approaches are being used. The cultural-evolutionary approach of Service and Sahlins can be found in the work of Gottwald and Flanagan on the period of the Judges and the early monarchy respectively;[14] social psychology is invoked by Bernhard Lang and Robert Carroll in their work on prophecy.[15] Lang also uses economic sociology to illumine the *Rentenkapitalismus* of 8th century Israel, as well as the classic work of Durkheim to explore religious piety in Old Testament times.[16] Work according to the tradition of Evans-Pritchard has produced new interpretations of Old Testament sacrifice, magic and rules about purity, while the political anthropology initiated by the celebrated volume *African Political Systems* features in the work of R. R. Wilson and A. Malamat on biblical genealogies and the work of F. Crüsemann on opposition to the kingship.[17] We can mention also that work has been done on the bureaucracy of ancient Israel in the classic tradition of Weber and that P. D. Miller has invoked "sociology of knowledge";[18] and we must not

---

[14] N. K. Gottwald, *The Tribes of Yahweh. A Sociology of the Religion of Liberated Israel, 1250-1050 B.C.E.* (Maryknoll, New York, 1979; London, 1980); J. Flanagan, "Chiefs in Israel", *JSOT* 20 (1981), pp. 47-73.

[15] B. Lang, *Wie wird man Prophet in Israel?* (Düsseldorf, 1980), pp. 11-58; R. P. Carroll, *When Prophecy Failed. Reactions and Responses to Failure in the Old Testament Prophetic Traditions* (London, 1979).

[16] B. Lang, "The Social Organization of Peasant Poverty in Biblical Israel", *JSOT* 24 (1982), pp. 47-63; "Persönliches Gott und Ortsgott. Über Elementarformen der Frömmigkeit im alten Israel" in *Fontes atque pontes. Eine Festgabe für Hellmut Brunner* (Wiesbaden, 1983), pp. 271-301.

[17] M. Fortes and E. E. Evans-Pritchard (ed.), *African Political Systems* (Oxford, 1940). The word "initiated" is important. *African Political Systems* is in some respects now dated. See also R. R. Wilson, *Genealogy and History in the Biblical World* (New Haven, 1977); A. Malamat, "Tribal Societies: Biblical Genealogies and African Lineage Systems", *Archives européennes de sociologie* 14 (1973), pp. 126-36; F. Crüsemann, *Der Widerstand gegen das Königtum* (Neukirchen, 1978). Crüsemann draws heavily on the important work by C. Sigrist, *Regulierte Anarchie. Untersuchungen zum Fehlen und zur Entstehung Politischer Herrschaft in segmentären Gesellschaften Afrikas* (Frankfurt/M., 1979²).

[18] See most recently, with literature, U. Rüterswörden, *Die Beamter der Israelitischen Königszeit*, (Diss., Bochum, 1981); P. D. Miller, "Faith and Ideology in the Old Testament" in F. M. Cross et al. (ed.), *Magnalia Dei. The Mighty Acts of God. Essays on the Bible and Archaeology in Memory of G. Ernest Wright* (New York, 1976), pp. 464-79.

overlook women's studies, which are only just beginning in Old Testament study, and which will undoubtedly contribute much in the future.[19]

When we look back over the range of approaches that have been mentioned, we see that they range from "Positivist" and "Materialist" to "Idealist" and "Holist" approaches, by way of "Behaviourism" and "Functionalism". This is why I have deliberately avoided defining the term "sociology". I agree in principle with W. G. Runciman that it is very difficult to define "sociology" in spite of the existence of departments of Sociology in universities, and that the term can cover social history, anthropology, social psychology and philosophy of history, not to mention economics and politics.[20] In practice we see most of these branches of study represented in sociological approaches to the Old Testament, and in the circumstances, we would be ill advised to concentrate upon only one area as "authentic" sociology to the exclusion of the rest. We need to know all we can about the ecology and the economy in ancient Israel, about collective and individual psychological factors, about religion and symbolic behaviour in the context of laws and institutions. In short, we need a plurality of methods in the sociological sphere.

Given a plurality of approaches, can we say anything further, at the level of method, about how these approaches should be used in Old Testament studies? I now propose to answer this question in the affirmative by attempting to adapt to Old Testament purposes the account of sociological "understanding" contained in the first volume of Runciman's *A Treatise on Social Theory* I *The Methodology of Social Theory* (Cambridge, 1983). Runciman's aim is to provide a methodological framework that will be valid for all the sciences of mankind, especially history, anthropology and sociology, and which will enable the strengths and weaknesses of varying "schools" to be readily appreciated. The scheme is remarkably simple, although Runciman claims that it has never before been proposed in his exact terms. It entails that we distinguish between reportage, explanation, description and evaluation. Reportage involves describing the events, phenomena or attitudes that are to be investigated, in language which is as far as possible value free. Explanation attempts to discover the causes of what has been reported. Description is the attempt to expound what it is like for a person or group of persons to be in a particular society or situation. Evaluation tries to decide whether social phenomena or their effects are good or bad, in the

---

[19] See the issue of *JSOT* 22 (1982) entitled "The Effects of Women's Studies on Biblical Studies".

[20] W. G. Runciman, *Social Science and Political Theory* (Cambridge, 1969²), pp. 1-2. See also the essay by Runciman which provides the title for the collection *Sociology in its Place and Other Essays* (Cambridge, 1970), pp. 1-44.

light of an observer's criteria for making such judgements. Runciman's summary of the four categories is: what happened, why, what is is like, is it good or bad? I shall discuss each category in turn.

1. *Reportage* (see Runciman, pp. 57-144)

There are two particular problems here for Old Testament scholarship. The first is the almost unavoidable factor that where we are dealing with periods of ancient Israel's history for which our sources are scanty, the sociological models that we use to explain what little we know will themselves become part of the reportage. An obvious example is the model or theory of the amphictyony, in which an attempt to explain, among other things, the organization of the tribes under the Judges ends by becoming part of the reportage. The amphictyony moves from being a model to becoming a "fact", and explanation becomes reportage. Now this tendency for explanation to become reportage may be unavoidable, if the alternatives are either to say that we know nothing about pre-monarchic Israel, or to accept the Old Testament uncritically as an authentic piece of reportage. If the collapse of reportage into explanation is unavoidable, then it is vital that we recognize it for what it is, and that we apply the most rigorous testing to explanations, as will be indicated shortly.

The second main problem arises in connection with what Runciman calls "pre-emptive taxonomies". A pre-emptive taxonomy is a term used in the reportage that in fact pre-judges the later operations of explanation, description and evaluation. The point can be well illustrated by the deliberate avoidance of a pre-emptive taxonomy in the *NEB*'s rendering of *ṣāraʿat* where it occurs in the Pentateuch. In place of the familiar English word "leprosy", the *NEB* in the Pentateuch has "malignant skin-disease". This is a value-free translation, whereas "leprosy" is likely to arouse in the minds of readers all sorts of associations not necessarily implied in the Hebrew term. According to Runciman, terms such as "magic", "charismatic", and even "sacrifice" may become pre-emptive taxonomies, depending on how they are used in reportage. It is well known that Weber himself used "charismatic" as a value-free term, indicating a type of authority in which one person was both the source and the agent of power, while at the same time Weber seemed to prefer "charismatic" leadership as indicating something creative and dynamic, as opposed to the static and non-creative situation that obtained after "charisma" had been routinized (Runciman, pp. 51-2). In Old Testament study, the term "magic" used in reportage may well trigger off all sorts of pre-emptive ideas that go back to J. G. Frazer, whereas the phrase "symbolic behaviour" is as value-free as we are likely to get in this area.

At the risk of being in a minority of one, I want to contend that the word "tribe" is an outstanding instance of pre-emptive taxonomy in Old Testament studies.[21] The virtually unexamined opinion that *šᵉbāṭīm* and *maṭṭōt* were "tribes" has led to assumptions such as that the genealogies in the Old Testament are equivalent to those in segmentary lineage tribes, or that because tribal societies evolve into chiefdoms the rise of Saul and David must be explained as an instance of such a development.[22] I believe that it can be argued as a working hypothesis that Israelite *maṭṭōt* and *šᵉbāṭīm* were like the very small chiefdoms classified in the well-known volume *Tribes without Rulers*,[23] and described in further detail in Aylward Shorter's *Chieftainship in Western Tanzania.*[24] These latter very small chiefdoms are clusters of small villages in particular localities, and are led by a chief who is elected, from the chiefly lineage, by elders. They possess genealogies for the chiefly family, but the genealogies are not politically significant in the way that they are in segmentary lineage societies. They live in hilly, wooded areas, just as the Israelites may have lived in the forests of the southern, central and northern hill country of ancient Israel. These small chiefdoms also belong to larger associations of chiefdoms. The point cannot be elaborated here, and I freely admit that to call a *šēbeṭ* a small chiefdom is to use a pre-emptive taxonomy which may turn out on further investigation to be wrong. But I hope that the example has pointed up the dangers of pre-emptive taxonomies.

2. *Explanation* (see Runciman, pp. 145-222)

The value of sociology for explaining, and thus better understanding, Old Testament history and institutions, lies in providing us with conceptual models which will enable us to take fullest possible account of the complexities which make up history and institutions.[25] The familiar observation that the Israelite tribal federation broke down because it was unable to withstand the pressure of the Philistines is little more than a

---

[21] See also my *Anthropology and the Old Testament*, pp. 86-97.

[22] I exempt from this criticism the work of Gottwald (n. 14 above) and C. H. J. de Geus, *The Tribes of Israel* (Assen, 1976).

[23] J. Middleton and D. Tait (ed.), *Tribes without Rulers. Studies in African Segmentary Systems* (London, 1958). See especially the essay "The Mandari of the Southern Sudan" by Jean Buxton, pp. 67-96.

[24] (Oxford, 1972).

[25] I agree here with a good deal of N. K. Gottwald's "Sociological Method in the Study of Ancient Israel", in M. J. Buss (ed.), *Encounter with the Text. Form and History in the Hebrew Bible* (Philadelphia and Missoula, 1979), pp. 69-81.

tautology. To explain why the Philistines almost succeeded in reducing Israel to a subject people, we need to know much more than that the Philistines had a monopoly of iron. Perhaps we shall not be able to explain these events at all satisfactorily in view of the paucity of our information.

Once we have formulated a causal explanation for a set of events, or a model to describe social institutions, it is essential that we test out the explanation and model against other possible explanations and models, as well as against all the relevant factors. It is not sufficient to introduce a single model such as the amphictyony, or segmentary lineage societies, or enclosed nomadism, and then assume that the work of explanation is over because the model plausibly explains the data under consideration. As Runciman points out, such explanations are often selective; and the attempt to present a model plausibly involves an element of bias of which we must be aware. The model for which we should always strive, and which would, in any case, be liable to be superseded by a better model, would need to show how it was superior to other rival models, and how it explained the widest possible set of relevant factors. In Old Testament study it would need to cover such factors as the ecology, and the known distribution of villages and settlements.

Especial caution is necessary where what is being explained is not a particular set of historical circumstances, such as the rise of the monarchy, but the whole sweep of Old Testament history, as in M. Weber's *Ancient Judaism*. The question which Weber posed and attempted to answer was "how did Jewry develop into a pariah people with highly specific peculiarities?"[26] If we leave aside the question how accurate it was to describe "Jewry" in these terms (the word "pariah" is highly pre-emptive and value-loaded), it must be pointed out that any "end" or "telos" which serves as the reference point for an explanation can itself pre-empt the discussion, can prejudice the selection of which are significant factors, and in any case does not absolve a scholar from arguing at every point that the model or explanation adopted is the superior among the possibilities. A teleological approach runs the danger of justifying its explanations in terms of the "telos" or end, as opposed to justifying them in relation to the successive sets of circumstances which make up the whole historical sequence. Runciman, indeed, warns against the fallacy of "affirming the consequent", and requires of evolutionary-type sociological explanations that they do more than "narrate a chosen

---

[26] *Ancient Judaism* (Glencoe, Illinois, 1952; reprinted in New York, 1967), p. 5, translated by H. H. Gerth and D. Martindale from *Gesammelte Aufsätze zur Religionssoziologie* (Tübingen, 1921), p. 3.

sequence of steps assumed without test against possible alternatives to lead inevitably to the end-state''.[27]

3. *Description* (see Runciman, pp. 223-300)

This is an important section, because it covers matters such as attempts to describe what it was like to be a prophet or to be confronted by a prophet, what it was like to engage in sacrifice or to wrestle with the paradoxes inherent in religious belief. In short, it concerns attempts to discover what it meant to live as people who believed in the God of Israel.

It is at this point that I wish to consider briefly the eleventh part of Gottwald's *The Tribes of Yahweh*, entitled ''Biblical Theology or Biblical Sociology?'' (pp. 667-709). This is a most interesting section, in which Gottwald argues that an approach based upon historical cultural materialism will yield a more satisfactory understanding of the premonarchic religion of Israel in its socio-cultural setting, than the ''idealist'' approach of the ''biblical theology movement''. Gottwald carefully builds up a picture of the main characteristics of pre-monarchic Israelite religion, and accounts for these characteristics in terms of his retribalization model. In so doing, he deliberately ''demythologizes'' the chief articles of Israelite faith into socio-economic terms.

I am quite certain that Gottwald has shown that the scholars whom he describes as ''idealists'' have not paid the sort of attention to the relation between religious symbolism and socio-economic factors, that Gottwald's own work will make obligatory for all future studies. However, it seems to me that Gottwald has treated under one heading what the present lecture wishes to distinguish under two headings. As I understand it, Gottwald is trying both to account for the origin of Israel's pre-monarchic faith in historical cultural terms, and to describe what that faith must have been like in socio-economic terms.

Let us assume that Gottwald is correct, that in the period of the Judges Israel became an ''egalitarian intertribal counter-society'' (p. 692), and that this socio-economic movement had a profound influence upon the religious faith of Israel. Let us assume, that is, that Gottwald's explanation can become reportage. The question still remains what it would have been like to believe in the God of Israel, whatever the origins of that belief. That it is possible for people who live in simple economic circumstances in ''tribes'' to articulate their belief in ''idealist'' terms, and that this belief can be systematically interpreted by observers in terms of the society as a whole, is indicated by the classic monographs of

[27] On teleology, see Runciman, pp. 208-14. The sentence quoted is on p. 213.

Evans-Pritchard on the Nuer and the Azande, Lienhardt on the Dinka and Middleton on the Lugbara, to mention only the most obvious examples.[28] It would be strange if pre-monarchic Israel were, in principle, an exception. To deny, in principle, that Israel's pre-monarchic faith could be described in "idealist" terms is to assert that there is only one valid way of doing sociology of religion.

It may be objected that all this is purely academic, since we are unable to consult with pre-monarchic Israelites. However, Runciman makes the important point that at the level of description, literature has a sociological function, and does articulate what it is like to be in a particular situation (pp. 21, 236-42). Now we certainly possess, in the Old Testament, Israelite religious literature, and although the critical problems of determining what, if any, dates from, or accurately reflects, the pre-monarchic period, are very great, there is a potential source here to enable us to describe Israel's pre-monarchic and later faith.

In short, I do not see biblical sociology, as formulated by Gottwald, and biblical theology as mutually exclusive. The former can belong to the category of explanation, the latter to the category of description, provided that biblical theologians take full account of sociological factors.

4. *Evaluation*

An evaluation of an institution, an action, or a person's motives must be grounded in a theory of values that can at least be inspected if not accepted. In Old Testament study, theological evaluations have often been made which have, in effect, prevented any contribution that could be made from the sociological side. For example, prophetic religion has been evaluated as "better" than priestly religion, or "spontaneous" religion has been deemed superior to religion with complex ceremonial rules. The pre-exilic period has been preferred to the post-exilic period. The theory of values upon which such evaluations have been made has usually owed much to Protestant attitudes.

I am not opposed to scholars making value-judgements on explicitly stated grounds. It is unfortunate, however, if a dislike of the ceremonial of expiatory sacrifice, to take one example, prevents scholars from considering what light anthropology can shed on sacrifice, as part of a coherent set of symbols within a specific religious tradition. In other words, value-judgements, if pre-emptive, may restrict our awareness of research and understanding.

---

[28] E. E. Evans-Pritchard, *Witchcraft Oracles and Magic among the Azande*, (Oxford, 1937); *Nuer Religion*, (Oxford, 1956). G. Lienhardt, *Divinity and Experience. The Religion of the Dinka* (Oxford, 1961). J. Middleton, *Lugbara Religion* (Oxford, 1960).

This attempt to adapt Runciman to Old Testament purposes has done scant justice to the analytical power of his book. Some of you may think that Runciman is too demanding, and that life is too short to accept the rigour of his demands. Again, the whole approach is very British, owing much to the analytical tradition of British philosophy. However, Runciman advocates what seems to me to be essential at the present stage of Old Testament study—a readiness to be open to a variety of sociological methods, but a readiness tempered by intellectual and conceptual discipline.

IBN EZRA BETWEEN MEDIEVALISM AND MODERNISM: THE CASE OF ISAIAH XL-LXVI[1]

BY

URIEL SIMON

Ramat Gan

I. Medievalism versus Modernism in Biblical Exegesis

As far as we know, Abraham Ibn Ezra (1089-1164) was the first to attribute the second part of the book of Isaiah to an anonymous prophet who began to prophesy in Babylon on the eve of the Persian conquest. The veiled, enigmatic language in which Ibn Ezra hints at this is evidence of the magnitude of the innovation which this position represented and of the force of the contrast between it and the beliefs and opinions held by his readers. But while Ibn Ezra trusted that "the wise would understand" (Commentary on Isa. xl 1) these hints, his modern readers find it very difficult to decipher them and even more difficult to evaluate them. Ibn Ezra's esoteric statements readily admit of both archaization (obscuration of the daring, innovative dimension for apologetical purposes),[2] and modernization (exaggeration of their critical character out of the common tendency to attribute our own views to our predecessors).[3] We can avoid these opposing pitfalls only if we refuse to content ourselves with the correct understanding of his views, but endeavour also to discover his true motives. Only when we understand why Ibn Ezra felt obliged to deny Isaiah's authorship of chapters xl-lxvi of the book which bears his name, shall we be able to evaluate the commentator's place between medievalism and modernism.

For medieval man, the Bible was the immortal word of God addressed directly to his own generation, just as to any other generation. Even when a prophecy clearly refers to the affairs and needs of the prophet's contemporaries, it was included in Sacred Scripture because of its message to every generation. Despite the general awareness of the great

---

[1] This article was written while its author was a Fellow of the Institute for Advanced Studies, The Hebrew University, Jerusalem.

[2] Cf. M. Friedlaender, *Essays on the Writings of Abraham ibn Ezra* (London, 1877), pp. 60-9, 226, 229, 235.

[3] Cf. B. Spinoza, *The Theologico-Political Treatise* (1670), Chapter viii. Nachman Krochmal, *Works* (1831), edited by S. Rawidowicz (Berlin, 1924²), pp. 114-18 (Hebrew).

differences in style and theme among the writings of the prophets, their common divine origin requires that they be included not only in a unitary theological system, but also in a common prognosis of our future. The absolute veracity of the prophecy enables us, though it does not always require us, to assume that it was actually fulfilled even when the Bible contains no independent historical evidence of its fulfilment. The glory of prophecy lies in the prophet's ability to foresee the distant future, and the fulfilment of short-range prophecies is documented as a guarantee of the utter truth of the vision of the end of days.[4] The medieval commentator never stands alone *vis-à-vis* the text, and, even when he is fully committed to the plain, literal meaning, he views himself as the builder of a bridge between Sacred Scripture and the community of faith.

The primary innovation in the modern approach to the Bible is its keen historical awareness. The changes wrought by time are so great that the discovery of the meaning of Scripture to its original audience must always precede any investigation of its message to later generations. While medieval philological exegesis was guided by the principle that "The Tora speaks the language of men", modern philological-historical interpretation is guided by the fundamental assumption that Sacred Scripture speaks in the language and ideas of men of a specific time. Even the eternal must be garbed in the temporal, for as purposeful speech every biblical text must have been intelligible to its audience and tuned to its needs, problems, and longings. It is thus inconceivable that prophecy should have been either incomprehensible to its original audience or meaningless for it.

In view of this conception of prophecy, the tidings of Cyrus' restoration of the Babylonian exiles is meaningless to the Judeans still living in their own land and battling the Assyrian king Sennacherib, just as the consolations of the imminent rebuilding of the Temple would be meaningless to a generation which knew nothing of the impending destruction of the First Temple. In addition to this common literary-historical outlook, modern biblical scholars feel their primary obligation to scientific truth. The religious scholar shares this sense of obligation since the essentially rationalistic faith in the validity of the scientific method requires him to use it as a reliable tool for gaining true knowledge of the word of God, and because he sees intellectual integrity as a basic religious duty.

In the late eighteenth century, J. G. Eichhorn concluded that the second part of the book of Isaiah was not written by Isaiah the son of Amoz,

---

[4] Cf. The book of ben Sira xlviii 24-25; Josephus Flavius, *The Antiquities of the Jews*, Book xi, 1,2.

but by an anonymous prophet who prophesied in Babylon.[5] He was not aware that in this he had been anticipated in the mid-twelfth century by Ibn Ezra whose hints to this effect aroused no response or comment for over six centuries.[6] Eichhorn's explicit and detailed argument is obviously a logical outcome of the modern approach to the Bible, whereas Ibn Ezra's arguments can be discovered only by a meticulous examination of his method in interpreting the book of Isaiah as a whole. However, we must first discuss the method of his great predecessor, Ibn Chiquitilla in his commentary on Isaiah, for Ibn Ezra frequently contended with him in his own commentary.

II. Ibn Chiquitilla's Historical Approach: The First Breach in the Medieval Attitude

R. Moses Hakkohen Ibn Chiquitilla, biblical commentator, linguist, poet, and translator, was born in Cordoba early in the eleventh century and was active in Saragossa and southern France. His commentaries on the Prophets, like most Jewish biblical commentaries written in Arabic in Spain, have not survived. But in Ibn Ezra's commentaries on Isaiah and the Minor Prophets, it is cited close to eighty times, and some twenty more quotations have been preserved in the works of other authors.[7] Ibn Chiquitilla's modernism finds expression in his great sensitivity to literary form and historical setting. The obvious fact that the psalms have the literary form of prayers and the clearly poetic terminology of their headings prevented his regarding them as prophecies, and therefore he assigned a post-exilic date to the psalms with a Babylonian setting.[8] Also in his interpretation of the words of the prophets he gave maximum consideration to their literary and historical contexts. In the literary field, he strenuously avoided breaking prophecies up into excessively small units; moreover, he sought to discover the common thematic and chronological basis of consecutive passages.[9] In the historical field, his goal was to discover the political events because of which or about which the prophet prophesied by giving clear preference to short-range fulfilment. Thus, for example, he applies both Obadiah's prophecy and Isa. xxxiv to the imminent destruction of Edom by Assyria, which occurred, according to his

---

[5] *Einleitung ins A.T.* iii (Leipzig, 1783), pp. 84-109.

[6] As far as I can see, Kimhi, Nachmanides, Ibn Caspi and Abrabanel simply avoided the entire issue, preferring to ignore rather than refute Ibn Ezra's dangerous views.

[7] S. Poznanski, *Mose B. Samuel Hakkohen Ibn Chiquitilla nebst den Fragmenten seiner Schriften* (Leipzig, 1895), pp. 98-102, 135-49.

[8] Cf. U. Simon, *Four Approaches to the Book of Psalms - From Saadya Gaon to Abraham ibn Ezra* (Ramat-Gan, 1982), pp. 110-19 (Hebrew).

[9] See Ibn Ezra's commentary on Isa. xi 1, xxx 26, xxxiv 2.

conjecture, while Sennacherib marched on Judah during the reign of Hezekiah. Only those prophecies which explicitly mention that they refer to "the latter days" he felt compelled to interpret messianically,[10] just as he refrained from postdating those Psalms specifically attributed to David. Thus, he interprets the prophecy "There shall come forth a shoot from the stump of Jesse" (Isa. xi 1) as referring to Hezekiah, king of Judah, relying *inter alia* uon the similarity between "him shall the nations *seek* [*yidrōšû*]" (xi 10), and the story of the visit to Jerusalem of the envoys of Babylon after Hezekiah's recovery "to *inquire* [*lidrōš*] about the sign that had been done in the land" (2 Chr. xxxii 31).

Ibn Chiquitilla's persistent endeavours to see the prophecies as short-range predictions constrained him to make excessive use of two methods: a. making wild assumptions about supposed historical events for which there is no evidence outside the prophecy itself, a kind of *eventus ex vaticinio*, as, for example, his supposition that there was a restoration to Zion in the reign of Hezekiah, based on Isa. xi 11-12, xxx 3-10;[11] and b. the interpretation of supernatural eschatological promises as mere metaphors in order to adjust them to the natural conditions of the near future; for example, the application of Zechariah's promises to the time of Nehemiah required him to explain the prophesied changes in the natural order metaphorically.[12] Nonetheless, Ibn Chiquitilla did not try to bridge the time span between the eighth-century prophets Isaiah and Micah and their prophecies of consolation which he quite naturally applied to the restoration to Zion in the sixth century. Thus he interprets Micah iv 11 as a prophecy regarding the Second Temple period on the basis of the linguistic similarity between "to be *ruler [môšēl*] in Israel" (Micah v 1) and "shall sit and *rule* [*ûmāšal*] upon his throne" (Zech. vi 13) which obviously refers to Zerubbabel, and on the basis of the similarity between the metaphor which follows in Micah iv 13, "Arise and thresh, O daughter of Zion", and the one following in Zechariah, "What are you, O great mountain? Before Zerubbabel you shall become a plain" (Zech. iv 7).[13] And as he sees no objection to the fact that Micah is comforting his contemporaries with the prophecy of the restoration to Zion from Babylon, he makes the same assumption regarding Isaiah. Apparently, he was not at all bothered by the fundamental requirement that prophecy be intelligible and meaningful to its original audience. Indeed,

---

[10] See Ibn Ezra's commentary on Joel iii 1. This was also his opinion regarding Mal. iii 23, as quoted by Ibn Balᶜam, ad loc. (edited by S. Poznanski, *JQR*, N.S. 15 [1924/5], p. 53).

[11] See Ibn Ezra's commentary on Isa. xi 11, xxxv 3.

[12] See Ibn Ezra's commentary on Zech. ix 9, xiii 1.

[13] See Ibn Ezra's commentary on Micah iv 11.

not only is there not a single expression of this "modern" criterion in the citations from his commentaries, but his identification of the Servant of the Lord in Is. lii 13-liii 12 with Hezekiah[14] is clear evidence that the idea of attributing the chapters of consolation in Isaiah to a late prophet never occurred to him.

The scope of Ibn Chiquitilla's innovational approach is clearly reflected in the accusations levelled against him by his younger contemporary, Ibn Balᶜam. On the one hand, he censures "his misleading, perverse views" expressed in his rationalistic tendency to play down the degree to which miracles violate the laws of nature. On the other hand, he attributes to Ibn Chiquitilla the intent to undermine the belief in the coming redemption expressed in his method of applying nearly every prophecy to historical events which had since occurred rather than to the messianic era.[15] However, from our modern vantage point, Ibn Chiquitilla's historical approach is still anchored in an obviously medieval attitude. He assiduously makes quasi-historical identifications based on stylistic analogy and the uncritical reconstruction of the events from the expounded prophecy itself. And he does not at all take seriously the question of the meaning of the prophecy for its original audience. Indeed, his motives are rationalistic, but, even more than he seeks to understand the prophecy in relation to the needs of the period, he tries to present it in as natural and realistic a way as possible in order to make it more reasonable.

III. Ibn Ezra's Critique of Ibn Chiquitilla

In quite a few of Ibn Ezra's references to his predecessor's interpretations, we detect his admiration for their interpretative virtuosity and innovative qualities. At the same time, he has his reservations about Ibn Chiquitilla's excessive conclusions, although he never rejects his critical suggestions for dogmatic reasons. Ibn Ezra has two main complaints against the drastic reduction in the number of messianic prophecies. First, prophecies which have obviously not yet been fulfilled (such as the splitting of the Mount of Olives in two [Zech. xiv 4]) must refer to the future. Second, although many promises were not fulfilled because they were conditional from the very beginning upon Israel's total responsiveness to the prophetic call (see his Commentary on Joel iv 17, 20; Hagg. ii 9), promises accompanied by the oath of the Lord were not sub-

---

[14] Quoted by Ibn Balᶜam in his Arabic commentary on Isa. lii 13 (*REJ* xxiii [1892], p. 209); Poznanski, pp. 101, 146.

[15] See Ibn Balᶜam's commentary on Josh. x 12-13 (published by S. Poznanski in *A. Berliner's Festschrift* [Frankfurt A.M., 1903], p. 103 (Hebrew section), and his commentary on Zech. ix 9 (quoted by Poznanski, pp. 157-8).

ject to such conditioning. The prophecy acquires absolute validity on the strength of that oath and for this reason we may expect its complete fulfilment with the coming of the messiah (see his Commentary on Isa. lii 1). These arguments were not innovated by Ibn Ezra, since they had already been presented systematically by Saadia in the tenth century (*The Book of Doctrines and Beliefs*, VIII 7-8). We may suppose that Ibn Chiquitilla could have ignored them by resorting to his favourite method—radical interpretation in terms of metaphor, which reduces eschatological promises to natural dimensions and makes it possible to view the oath of the Lord as nothing more than rhetorical emphasis. By contrast, Ibn Ezra took these arguments very seriously, and was guided by them also in his commentary on the prophecies of consolation in the book of Isaiah.

In his elucidation of the heading of the book of Isaiah (i 1), Ibn Ezra says that the first part of the book consists "mostly of his prophecies about the cities of Judah which the king of Assyria had captured, and about Jerusalem which had escaped him". Indeed, in the body of the commentary, he applies most of the prophecies in Isa. i-xxxix to Sennacherib's campaign and his defeat before the walls of Jerusalem.[16] It is obvious that he adopts Ibn Chiquitilla's method of contemporary application, although he considers it unnecessary to note this. On the other hand, Ibn Ezra informs us of an exegetical controversy raging over four prophecies (or sections of prophecies) of salvation: 1. Isa. xi-xii; 2. xxiv-xxvii 6; 3. xxx 19-26 (presumably); 4. xxxiv-xxxv. Ibn Chiquitilla applied all these to the rescue from Sennacherib; "most of the commentators" applied them to the messianic era; while Ibn Ezra does not decide the issue, preferring to offer two parallel interpretations of each prophecy based on these two methods.

In addition to the short-range prophecies (which represent the majority), and the long-range prophecies (only one of which, he says, refers with certainty to the messianic era), Isa. i-xxxix contains three medium-range prophecies which, Ibn Ezra tells us, are also controversial: the destruction of Jerusalem and Tyre by Nebuchadnezzar, king of Babylon (xxii-xxiii), the overthrow of Belshazzar by the Persians and Medes and the restoration of the Babylonian exiles to Zion (xiii 1-xiv 27, xxx 1-10). Not only does Ibn Ezra (and probably Ibn Chiquitilla as well) not see any objection to the fact that Isaiah, who announces the rescue of Jerusalem from Sennacherib, also prophesies, without any attempt at a transition or explanation, the destruction of Jerusalem by the Babylonians, but he even finds obviously prognostic allusions in his prophecies: "and though

---

[16] See e.g. Ibn Ezra's commentary on Isa. i 8, vii 17, 20, viii 8, ix 4-5, x 11, 24, xi 1, xvii 3,5,12, xviii 3-6, xx 1, xxiv 14, xix 4-7, xxx 18, xxxi 3-4, xxxii 15, xxxiii 14.

a tenth remains in it'' (vi 13) shows that ''ten kings will yet reign over Judah before the exile'', and ''an uproar of kingdoms, of nations gathering together'' (xiii 4) shows ''that the king of Persia who is Cyrus, and the king of Media who is Darius, both joined together against Babylon, as is stated explicitly in Daniel (v 28)''. It thus seems that the application of the majority of the prophecies to the immediate future can, in the mind of medieval commentators, be reconciled quite naturally with the foretelling of quite specific information, which in our view can have no real meaning for the prophet's audience.

The remarkable similarity of Ibn Ezra's and Ibn Chiquitilla's opinions on the first part of Isaiah by no means prevails when we come to the second part, as Ibn Ezra states in his elucidation of xl 1:

> *Comfort, Comfort my People*: This chapter has been attached to the preceding one because above it was mentioned that all the treasures of the king, and even his sons, will be exiled to Babylon. Thus, after this prediction should follow the consolations. The first consolations with which the second part of the book begins refer, in the opinion of R. Moses Hakkohen, to the rebuilding of the Second Temple, but, in my opinion, everything refers to the coming redemption from our present exile. There are, it is true, also prophecies concerning the Babylonian exile; they have been included only in order to state that Cyrus released the exiles.[17] In the last section of the book all the prophecies surely refer to a period yet to come, as I shall explain.

This passage is rather obscure, though not intentionally so, for in the widespread controversy over whether the prophesied promises applied to the restoration from Babylon or from the present exile there is nothing that need be concealed. At any rate, Ibn Ezra and his predecessor agree that, as a counterbalance to the bleak end of the first part of the book, the second part begins with consolations. But while Ibn Chiquitilla stresses the close connection between Isaiah's prediction of the exile of the treasures of the king of Judah and his sons *to Babylon* and the consolations of the restoration of the exiles *from Babylon*, Ibn Ezra thinks that the consolation is even greater since the consolations bring tidings primarily of the last and final redemption. However, does Ibn Chiquitilla really apply only ''the *first* consolations from the second part of the book'' to the Second Temple period? It would seem so, since Ibn Balʿam informs us in his Commentary on Isa. lii 13 that Ibn Chiquitilla identified the Servant of the Lord in the prophecy ''Behold, my servant shall prosper'' (lii 13-liii

[17] The obviously faulty text has to be emended through conjecture, as the seven extant MSS and the *editio princeps* (Venice, 1525) offer no better reading. The minimal emendation would be the erasure of the dittographical *š* in *šeššālaḥ* since it creates a meaningless incomplete subordinate clause.

12) with King Hezekiah, that is, he applies this prophecy to the time of the First Temple. Presumably, he did likewise with the chastisements in chapters lvi 10-lix 21, because of their obvious setting in the Land of Israel. On the other hand, we see from Ibn Ezra's controversy with him (which is explicit in his elucidation of lv 2 and covert in his commentary on lxii 8), that Ibn Chiquitilla did interpret the consolations in lv and lxii as applying to the Second Temple period. Presumably, he did likewise with the entire collection of consolations in lx-lxvi. In other words, the expression "first consolations" is not meant to exclude "last consolations", but to say that Ibn Chiquitilla thinks that all the consolations which immediately follow chapter xl apply without exception to the time of the Second Temple, while after lii 12ff. there is no such uniformity. There are some prophecies concerning the First Temple, some concerning the Second Temple, but none concerning the latter days.

Whereas, on the one hand, Ibn Ezra determines that, in his opinion, "everything refers to our present exile", he admits, on the other, that there are prophecies concerning the Babylonian exile. He reconciles this seeming contradiction by explaining that the Babylonian consolations were included in this messianic collection not for their own sake, but "in order to state that Cyrus released the exiles". In order to understand this statement, we must examine how in his commentary on chapters xl-lxvi Ibn Ezra actually solved the problem of the times to which the various prophecies refer.

Ibn Ezra explains all the prophecies in chapters xl-li as consolations addressed to the Babylonian exiles on the eve of the downfall of Belshazzar, the last king of Babylon, at the hands of the Medes and Persians. The early news of Cyrus' victory, including the mention of his name in both xliv 28 and xlv 1 is meant to serve as decisive proof of the divinity of the God of Israel, who makes Cyrus his messiah without the emperor's being aware of his role as redeemer, and whose prophet proclaims future events before they happen.[18] li 1-11 is the first prophecy which Ibn Ezra, in open disagreement with Ibn Chiquitilla (in his com. on lii 1, 11), applies to the messianic era because of the unconditional promise to Zion, which clearly had not been fulfilled in the time of the Second Temple: "for there shall no more come into you the uncircumcised and the unclean" (lii 1). From here till the end of the book he regards all the prophecies as messianic, except those of the section lv 6-lix 21, which he interprets as prophecies of rebuke addressed to the prophet's "contemporaries", of whom he demands that they repent so that their iniquities may not delay both the imminent deliverance and final redemption: "Once you know

[18] See Ibn Ezra's commentary on Isa. xli 4, 23, xlii 1,8.

that you will be delivered from Babylon, and from all the nations a second time, seek the Lord'' (his com. on lv 1 and lvi 1). From this and many other statements, it is obvious that the prophecies on the latter days (continued in lx-lxvi) were addressed to the Babylonian exiles *before* they were released by Cyrus. Just as the prophecy about the latter days in chapter ii was intended for the inhabitants of Jerusalem, who had not yet been rescued from Sennacherib, as he says about ii 1: ''for Zion will now be saved from the hands of Sennacherib, and she will besides be highly distinguished in the future'', so also in the second part of the book are the messianic promises interwoven with the immediate promises.

In other words, when Ibn Ezra writes in his explanation of xl 1 that henceforth ''everything refers to our present exile'', he presumably means to say that for the exiles in Babylon, too, the messianic promises were the heart of the prophet's message. And when he adds that ''There are, it is true, also prophecies concerning the Babylonian exile; they have been included only in order to state that Cyrus released the exiles'', he presumably means to say that the consolations for the time of the Second Temple are subordinate to the messianic promises, since they are cited only for the sake of analogy. As these were fulfilled not long afterwards when Cyrus released the exiles, so, too, will the prophecies regarding ''our present exile'' be fulfilled. As, when the Jews were still in Babylon, the messianic prophecy was meant to impart an added dimension to the topical prophecy, so in the ''present exile'' the prophecy of the deliverance from Babylon, which has meanwhile been fulfilled, is intended to lend additional strength and credibility to the prophecy of the latter days.[19]

To sum up, we found significant differences between the commentaries of Ibn Chiquitilla and Ibn Ezra on the second half of Isaiah, but their disagreements are not fundamental. For both of them, it was enough that the prophecy should have had a loose, general relevancy for the prophet's contemporaries. And as Ibn Chiquitilla sees nothing problematical in Isaiah's consolations regarding the restoration of the exiles from Babylon serving to counter-balance his evil tidings of the exile of Hezekiah's sons and treasures to Babylon, so Ibn Ezra sees nothing strange in assuming that the burden of the message to the exiles in Babylon is not their own restoration to Zion, but the future, final revival of Jerusalem after a future destruction which they cannot even imagine.

---

[19] Cf. Ibn Ezra's commentary on Isa. xliii 9, xlvi 13, xlix 6, l 8, lii 15.

IV. Why Did Ibn Ezra Attribute Chapters XL-LXVI to Another Prophet?

As is well-known, Ibn Ezra was not deterred from concluding that several anachronistic statements in the Pentateuch must be regarded as late interpolations. In his comment on Dt. i 2 he reveals to the wise reader, in carefully veiled, allusive language, that Moses could not have written in the past tense "*at that time* the Canaanites *were* in the land" (Gen. xii 6) or in the present tense "as it is said *to this day*, 'On the mount of the Lord it shall be provided'" (Gen. xxii 14). It is equally unreasonable that, in the body of the Pentateuch, Moses should refer to the Law as completed: "And Moses wrote *this law*, and gave it to the priests" (Dt. xxxi 9). Because of this sensitivity to anachronisms,[20] Ibn Ezra in his comment on Isa. xxxiv 6 rejects the identification of Bozrah with Constantinople: "This is impossible, because, since the foundation of that town, there have not yet elapsed a thousand years; (Bozrah) is a town in Edom." If in Ibn Ezra's opinion it is impossible that Isaiah should have referred to the city of Constantinople by name centuries before its founding, would he not have found it equally absurd that this prophet should have mentioned by name Cyrus, the king of Persia, over a century before his birth? Though this seems a reasonable conclusion, it cannot be accepted for two reasons. First, nowhere does Ibn Ezra indicate that he (nor Ibn Chiquitilla) finds the two references to Cyrus, in Isa. xliv 28 and xlv 1 problematic. Second, as we have seen, Ibn Ezra quite naturally assumes that the words of the prophets also contain detailed prognostic prophecies. Not only does he not see any problem in the fact that the man of God from Judah should prophesy in the reign of Jeroboam the son of Nebat about the future ruler of Judah some three hundred years later ("Behold, a son shall be born to the house of David, Josiah by name" [1 Kings xiii 2]), but in his introduction to his Commentary on Zechariah, he even cites this prophecy as evidence for his assertion that the power of prophecy had declined in Israel (at the time of the First Temple, the man of God saw far with great clarity, while in the time of the Second Temple Zechariah needed an angel to explain the obscure night visions to him). Ibn Ezra's objection to anachronisms does not arise, therefore, from the absurdity inherent in premature information about the future. Rather, only the fact that it is presented as already known and familiar undermines the reasonableness of its style and the clarity of its content. On the other hand, the reference to Cyrus within the framework of a prophecy of consolation describing the future redemp-

---

[20] Cf. Ibn Ezra's commentary on Ex. iii 1,2; Lev. xxii 27; Dt. xxii 8.

tion of Israel from Babylon is no less reasonable than the Man of God's foretelling the name of King Josiah.

Just as their audience could not have comprehended the meaning of the long-range prophecies, so the prophets themselves did not understand everything they uttered. Ibn Ezra's strong objection to computing the date of the final redemption from hints in the Scriptures led him to stress the idea that prognostic prophecy could be fully understood only upon its fulfilment—"...Daniel too did not know the end, for, as he said, 'I heard but I did not understand' (Dan. xii 8), and he also said at last, 'seal the book, until the time of the end' (xii 4). 'But those who are wise shall understand' (xii 10) when the end would come from the words of the angel" (The Long Commentary on Dan. viii 25).

Hence, neither his objection to anachronisms nor any adherence to the principle of meaningfulness led Ibn Ezra to conclude that Isa. xl-lxvi was uttered by another prophet, but purely exegetical considerations. The denial of Isaiah's authorship of the second part of the book required camouflage (lest it shock the naive faith of most of his readers), as well as justification (so that the wise reader should acknowledge its legitimacy). Thus he writes in his comment on Isa. xl 1 (in direct continuation of the paragraph cited above):

> Take note that the statement of the transmitters of the Oral Law, of blessed memory, to the effect that the book of Samuel was written by Samuel, is indeed correct, but only as regards the first part, up to the words "And Samuel died" (1 Sam. xxv 1). This is confirmed by the fact that the book of Chronicles contains the genealogy of the descendants of Zerubbabel for many generations. The evidence (for what I wish to demonstrate) consists in the words "Kings shall see and arise; princes shall prostrate themselves" (Isa. xlix 7). Of course, one may argue that this verse means that they will arise and prostrate themselves when they hear the name of the prophet, even after his death. The wise shall understand.

Despite the fact that the whole book is named after the prophet Samuel, the events following his death were obviously recorded by a later prophet since the historiography of the future is clearly beyond the bounds of biblical prophecy and is inconceivable. In keeping with this approach, Ibn Ezra (in his commentary on Dt. xxxiv 1) attributes the last twelve verses of the law of Moses to Joshua, for it is far more reasonable to assume that the sequence of events narrated here became known to Joshua "through a prophecy" than that Moses wrote in advance about his own death and burial. As there are biblical books which were completed by another prophet, so there are also comprehensive interpolations containing information which is obviously beyond the scope of the rest of the book. Evidence of this is found in the fact that to the books of

Chronicles, which end with Cyrus' proclamation, thereby bringing the chronicles up to Zerubbabel, is added a genealogy of Zerubbabel's descendants for many generations (1 Chr. iii 19-24). The wise reader who thus understands that the content of the biblical books does not always verify the traditional authorship, and that this fact does not detract from their sacredness, will realize that in the second part of the book of Isaiah the Lord promises the prophet (in the present tense) that one of the marvellous expressions of the imminent redemption will be the reversal of the prophet's personal fortunes, from humiliation and persecution to the recognition and respect of kings: "Thus says the Lord, the Redeemer of Israel and his Holy One, to one deeply despised, abhorred by the nations, the servant of rulers: 'Kings shall see and arise; princes shall prostrate themselves; because of the Lord, who is faithful, the Holy One of Israel, who has chosen you'" (xlix 7).

In his commentary on this verse, Ibn Ezra answers the reader who may be troubled by the question how the sixth-century kings and princes of Persia would arise before the eighth-century Isaiah, with these words: "I have already hinted to you this secret in the middle of the book." At the same time he reassures those readers who could not accept his assumption that there was a later prophet, by repeating the answer which he had already offered in his commentary on xl 1, which was intended to reconcile his interpretation with the accepted view. Cyrus and his princes will not arise before the prophet himself, but will honour his memory by arising and prostrating themselves when the prophecies which Isaiah uttered so long before have been fulfilled before their very eyes. After this he once again addresses the wise reader, who refuses to ignore linguistic and stylistic data for the sake of theological convenience, and remarks that the second person singular in "who has chosen you" is "evidence of the correctness of that interpretation". That is to say, it clearly proves that here the Lord is speaking directly to the prophet and not about him.

Ibn Ezra's alertness to changes of speaker in prophetic texts and his literary sensitivity to the continuity of theme between prophecies (or as he calls it, "the cohesiveness of sections") led him to identify the Servant of the Lord with the prophet, and to discover the autobiographical character of the Servant of the Lord prophecies. Moreover, this twofold sensitivity enabled him to see the great affinity between these prophecies and to offer a unitary interpretation of them as reflecting the personal fate of the Servant within the concrete circumstances of the Babylonian exile.[21] To be

[21] Among modern scholars it was B. Duhm (*Das Buch Jesaia* [Göttingen, 1892]) who first pointed out the distinctive character of the "Servant of the Lord Songs"; and S. Mowinckel (*Der Knecht Jahwäs* [Giessen, 1921]) who first identified the Suffering Servant with the prophet himself. Neither of them realized that Ibn Ezra had anticipated them.

sure, Ibn Ezra mentions that "most of the commentators" viewed the Servant as the personification of the righteous ones of Israel (Commentary on Isa. xlii 1, li 12), and he, too, is forced to interpret single verses in this way (xli 8, xliv 1, 21). But, whenever possible, he proposes an individual identity for the Servant, even when it entails a rather forced interpretation (see especially his commentary on xliii 10, xlix 3). In four prophecies (xlii 1-25, xlix 1-13, l 4-11, li 12-16) the Servant-prophet is obviously speaking about himself in his role as the herald to Israel and the nations of the imminent release of the exiles, his persecution by the wicked ones of Israel and the Babylonians, and the honour that he will enjoy when his prophecy is fulfilled. Ibn Ezra consistently and systematically emphasizes the Babylonian setting of these prophecies on the one hand, and their autobiographical form on the other. But, aside from hints in his elucidation of xlix 7-8 (quoted above), he leaves it to the reader to draw the necessary conclusion about the identity of the prophet and his time from the combination of these two features. But when he comes to the Suffering Servant prophecy *par excellence* (lii 13-liii 12), he surprises the reader by resuming the discussion of the identity of the Servant. In his elucidation of lii 13 he rejects out of hand the christological interpretation, both because the description does not fit the fate of Jesus and because the context of the prophecy requires that it be applied to Israel.[22] He refrains from adopting the messianic interpretation, since it leaves many verses without any concrete meaning. He praises Saadia's attempt to identify the Servant-prophet with Jeremiah, but rejects it contending that the sufferings of Jeremiah do not relate in any way to the consolations to the exiles in Babylon. Finally, he comes to the conclusion that the Servant personifies all the servants of the Lord in exile, or the entire Jewish people as a collective servant. In his view, the latter possibility is the most reasonable, and on the basis of it he expounds the entire prophecy in great detail as a most impressive and vivid description of the suffering of Israel in the present exile for the sake of all mankind, and of the reward which awaits the God-fearing at the time of the last redemption.

Especially moving is Ibn Ezra's reliance upon the fact that the personal experience of his readers in the Exile renders commentary superfluous. About the verse "He was oppressed, and he was afflicted, yet he opened not his mouth; like a lamb that is led to the slaughter" (liii 7) he writes, "There is no need to interpret this, for every Jew in exile is in this situation, for when he is afflicted he will not open his mouth to speak ... nor

[22] The fact that Ibn Ezra argues from the context proves that he did not regard the Servant of the Lord prophecies as interpolations.

does he know any prince or great man who will protect him when he is attacked by people.'' Ibn Ezra's comment on the verse ''...So marred was his appearance, unlike that of man, his form, beyond human semblance'' (lii 14) is shockingly forceful: ''It is a well-known fact that there are many gentiles who think that the form of the Jew is different from that of all others, and ask, 'Does the Jew have a mouth or eyes?' This is the case in the land of Ishmael and as well as in the land of Edom.''

Ibn Ezra wrote his Commentary on the book of Isaiah in 1145 in the town of Lucca in northern Italy. Only five years previously he had been forced to flee from Spain because of ''the rage of the oppressors'',[23] and in his commentary and in his poetry he attests the fact that both in Muslim Spain and in Christian Italy he personally suffers the bitter fate of the despised Jew, humiliated and persecuted. A strikingly similar expression of the dehumanization of the Jew, which is the essence of antisemitism, was written four and a half centuries later by William Shakespeare. As Shylock says in *The Merchant of Venice*, Act III, Scene I:

> I am a Jew. Hath not a Jew eyes? Hath not a Jew hands, organs, dimensions, senses, affections, passions? ... If you prick us, do we not bleed? If you tickle us, do we not laugh? If you poison us, do we not die? And if you wrong us, shall we not revenge?

It is indeed a great consolation for Israel in its exile to know that not only are its present sufferings prophesied with amazing accuracy in the Sacred Scriptures, but these sufferings have a noble purpose and glorious end. However, the power of this prophecy as a source of comfort and faith derives both from the collective interpretation of the Servant's identity and from the application of his fate to the condition of Israel in the present and its hope for the future still ahead of us. Yet, surprisingly enough, Ibn Ezra is willing to forfeit all this. At the end of his elucidation he reverts to his individual-historical interpretation, albeit in a very abbreviated form and without any attempt at developing it. According to this interpretation, the Servant was none other than the prophet who lived and prophesied, suffered and was saved in far-away Babylon in the distant past. As Ibn Ezra writes at the end of his elucidation of liii 12:

> I have thus expounded for you the whole passage, but, in my own opinion, ''my servant'' mentioned here (lii 13) is the very same about whom the prophet has said, ''Behold my servant, whom I uphold'' (xlii 1), as well as ''And He said to me, 'You are my servant''' (xlix 3). It is also stated here, ''By his knowledge shall the righteous one, my servant, make righteous'' (liii 11), as it is written above, ''I gave my back to the smiters'' (l 6). The secret is, as I hinted to you, in the middle of the book (xl 1), and thus all these passages are connected with each other.

---

[23] See the introduction to his commentary on Lamentations (written in Rome, 1142).

Despite his profound identification with the collective-topical interpretation, Ibn Ezra is not seeking to evade the exegetical decision by maintaining that this prophecy has two different meanings which find expression in two different layers. To be sure, he does not raise any objection to the collective interpretation, but he does offer his own opinion as a definitive alternative. Any reader who can comprehend the secret which he hints at in his elucidation of xl 1 and is willing to accept the assumption that the prophet of these chapters is post-exilic and the same person as the Servant will admit the obvious exegetical advantage of the individual interpretation which affords a unitary conception of all the Servant prophecies and takes into account the many linkages between them. Ibn Ezra confines himself to mentioning two such linkages and offers only meagre documentation for them. One is linguistic, the title "my servant" which is set in this prophecy (lii 13) and in two earlier Servant prophecies (xlii l, xlix 3); and the second is thematic. Here the suffering of the Servant in the service of prophecy is described (liii 11), and in Isa. l 6 the prophet says about himself, "I gave my back to the smiters, and my cheeks to those who tore out my beard; I hid not my face from shame and spittle."

In his Commentary on the book of Isaiah, Ibn Ezra thus makes two great sacrifices: he forfeits both the traditional unity of the book and the identification of the Suffering Servant with the people of Israel in exile. With due caution, he is willing to take upon himself the twofold responsibility for undermining the integrity of the accepted tradition on the one hand, and the potential weakening of the unmediated effect of the words of the prophet on the community of believers on the other. In the final analysis, he does this solely because of his conviction that this is the correct interpretàtion of Scripture. We may assume that for him it was important, if not essential, that the consolations of the prophets be truly and reliably understood by us, and that, instead of being swept away by our wishful thinking, we should ground our hopes and expectations firmly on irrefutable exegesis. It is also possible that the story of the suffering and the salvation of the Servant of the Lord seemed to Ibn Ezra a powerful enough source of encouragement even if it refers to a prophet who lived and was active in the Babylonian exile. At any rate, it is clear that his prime loyalty to his obligation as a commentator and his devotion to the truth of the Bible render his approach very close to our modern one. Indeed, though his exegetical considerations are essentially medieval, the decisive weight which he gives them is one of the fundamentals of modernism.

INTERPRÉTATION DES NOMS PROPRES DANS LES ORACLES CONTRE LES NATIONS

PAR

ANDRZEJ STRUS

Rome

1. *Remarques préliminaires*

Le fonctionnement des noms propres dans leur contexte littéraire n'est pas un phénomène absent de la linguistique contemporaine. C'est surtout à partir des études de F. de Saussure,[1] qu'on cherche à mieux saisir la nature et la portée herméneutique de ce phénomène ainsi que son importance pour le lecteur. Le facteur provocateur est le nom propre lui-même, qui se définit justement comme le "prince des signifiants"[2] ou comme "une véritable métaphore de l'être individuel".[3] Par-delà ces belles définitions, le nom propre, envisagé du point de vue linguistique, tout en désignant l'individuel, est du même coup dénué de toute signification en lui-même, et en même temps de toute valeur classificatoire dans son usage. D'où le premier sens de la définition de son fonctionnement: le nom propre fonctionne sinon comme index, du moins comme intermédiaire entre le langage et le geste, entre le signifier et le montrer.[4] D'une telle affirmation se déduit une remarque très importante: si le nom propre est vide de toute signification quelconque, cependant il identifie l'être qui le porte. Pour le dire avec L. Morin: "il ne dit rien de l'être, il dit tout l'être d'emblée et d'un seul coup".[5] En d'autres termes, si je prononce le nom d'Abraham dans l'abstrait, je ne dis rien de l'Abraham biblique en un sens, car ce nom en soi ne peut être le point du départ de ma connaissance de la personne d'Abraham, mais en un autre sens, je dis tout d'Abraham, mais à vide. Il faut que ce nom soit employé dans un discours, dans l'ensemble des phrases liées entre elles, pour qu'il acquière du sens. Mais le discours n'explique pas directement le nom propre, sauf dans les cas d'étymologie. Il tend plutôt à remplir le vide de

---

[1] *Cours de la linguistique générale* (Paris, 1965).

[2] C'est la définition de R. Barthes, "Analyse textuelle d'un conte d'E. Poe", dans *Sémiotique narrative et textuelle* (Paris, 1974), p. 34.

[3] Cf. C. Lévi-Strauss, *Mythologiques II, Du miel aux cendres* (Paris, 1968), p. 280.

[4] Voir les remarques dans ce sens en L. Morin, *Sémiotique de la Passion. Topiques et figures* (Paris, 1971), p. 24.

[5] P. 25.

signification du nom propre d'une façon indirecte: en le remplaçant par d'autres mots chargés de signification, ou bien en l'évoquant par d'autres signifiants qui lui ressemblent sur le plan sonore. C'est ce dernier aspect qui nous intéresse.

La sonorité est un phénomène non négligeable dans la création des oeuvres littéraires, car elle détermine d'une certaine façon la sélection des mots sur l'axe de la combinaison syntaxique. Il y a ici une relation étroite entre les sons et le sens. Tandis que la mise au point de cette relation est aujourd'hui à la mode parmi les théoriciens de la linguistique,[6] l'interaction des sons et du sens est bien connue autant dans les oeuvres littéraires contemporaines, que dans les chansons des troubadours du Moyen-Age ou dans les poèmes des prophètes d'Israël.[7] Le phénomène est universel et connu à toutes les époques chez plusieurs peuples. Les mêmes procédés sonores, les mêmes figures stylistiques, les mêmes jongleries phoniques peuvent être trouvés soit dans les poèmes de Baudelaire et de Poe, soit dans les chansons de l'époque carolingienne, soit dans les récits de la Genèse ou dans les oracles prophétiques. Or, dans ce vaste champ de sonorité poétique, le chantier onomastique qui ne cesse d'attirer l'attention des chercheurs se distingue. Là encore, la littérature biblique n'est pas en reste avec sa fantaisie onomastique et sonore. Parmi les recherches entreprises sur la sonorité des noms propres dans l'Ancien Testament, citons les études de L. Alonso Schökel, de I. Zakovitch, la nôtre, et d'autres renvois à ce phénomène dans les commentaires et les monographies bibliques.[8] Ceci pour dire que le sens de l'infrastructure du texte, celui codifié dans la forme sonore des noms propres, n'échappe pas à l'attention des biblistes. On pénètre le niveau significatif sous-

---

[6] Une bonne synthèse des études linguistiques dans ce domaine est offerte par T. Todorov, "Le sens des sons", *Poétique* 1 (1972), pp. 446-59.

[7] En ce qui concerne la sonorité dans les poèmes populaires du Moyen-Age, on trouvera des materiaux abondants dans l'étude de P. Zumthor, *Langue, texte, énigme* (Paris, 1975). Pour les études des procédés stylistiques basés sur les effets sonores dans les textes de l'Ancien Testament, nous renvoyons à l'article de L. Alonso Schökel, "La poésie hébraïque", *SDB* VIII (Paris, 1967), col. 47-90, et à la bibliographie sur le sujet complétée dans A. Strus, *Nomen-Omen. Stylistique des noms propres dans le Pentateuque* (Rome, 1978), p. 202.

[8] L. Alonso Schökel, *Estudios de poética hebrea* (Barcelona, 1963), chap. 11: "El Libro de Emmanuel", pp. 363-404; "Erzählkunst im Buche der Richter", *Bib* 42 (1961) pp. 143-172; L. Alonso Schökel-A. Strus, "Salmo 122: Canto al nombre de Jerusalén", *Bib* 61 (1980), pp. 234-50. L'étude de I. Zakovitch, *šny mdršy šm* (en hébreu) (Jérusalem, 1971) constitue un apport indirect mais très utile pour comprendre l'interprétation des noms propres dans l'Ancien Testament. Outre nos études *Nomen-Omen* et "Etymologies des noms propres dans Gen 29, 32-30, 24: valeurs littéraires et fonctionnelles", *Salesianum* 40 (1978), pp. 57-72, méritent d'être citées: C. Carmichael, "Some Sayings in Genesis 49", *JBL* 88 (1969), pp. 438-44, et R. Tournay, *Quand Dieu parle aux hommes le langage de l'amour* (Paris, 1982).

jacent à la transparence du lexique et de la syntaxe hébraïques, on décèle les couches du sens non exprimé mais dit, on le décodifie pour le mieux comprendre. C'est dans la même ligne de recherche que nous proposons ici la relecture du "langage onomastique" dans des textes particulièrement déterminés par les noms propres, à savoir les oracles prophétiques contre les nations. Avant d'aborder quelques exemples, il nous faut préciser deux remarques importantes qui sont, d'ailleurs, d'une grande portée méthodologique.

a) En premier lieu, la sonorité des noms propres hébraïques. Plusieurs facteurs se rejoignent dans le processus de la création des jeux sonores avec les noms hébraïques, lesquels s'y prêtent beaucoup plus facilement que les noms des langues européennes. Le premier facteur consiste dans le fait que les noms propres bibliques sont souvent des noms communs qui, par l'usage culturel ou par la volonté des hommes, ont accédeé à la dignité de noms propres. Tels sont Sukkot, Mahanayim, Yishaq, Yosep etc., des noms communs promus au rang de noms propres. Ces noms remplissent très facilement le vide de leur signification, car ils contiennent en eux-mêmes des signifiants analysables et réductibles à des noms communs. Leur influence sonore s'exerce avant tout sur le plan morphologique en choisissant des mots semblables selon les procédés dérivatifs usuels. La nature du rapprochement sonore est ici mi-étymologique, mi-fonctionnelle, où les "étyma" renvoient à la fonction et vice versa.[9] Le deuxième facteur repose sur la structure fondamentale trilitère de lexique hébraïque. La plupart des noms propres en hébreu sont réductibles à un groupe phonique de trois consonnes. Là s'ouvre une vaste gamme de possibilités de rapprochements sonores: homophonie de trois consonnes identiques en ordre normal ou inverti (métathèse), rapprochement de deux consonnes identiques avec une troisième semblable et tout cela en ordre normal ou en métathèse, rapprochement de trois consonnes identiques plus un préfixe ou un suffixe, etc. Toutes ces figures appelées paronomases sont bien connues dans la littérature de l'Ancien Testament.[10] Le troisième facteur dérive de la fonction sonore inégale des phonèmes en hébreu. Les consonnes y jouissent de la priorité, et parmi elles il y a encore des préférences, p.ex. la sonorité plus marquée des bilabiales, dentales-apicales et dentales-sifflantes. Les voyelles y sont moins actives et elles appuient plutôt les consonnes en exerçant une certaine influence

---

[9] Cf. Morin, p. 194.

[10] Quant au terme de paronomase, il désigne une figure bien connue dans les textes bibliques étudiée particulièrement par I. M. Casanowicz, *Paronomasia in the Old Testament* (Boston, Mass., 1894), et, en ce qui concerne l'euphonie onomastique, par nous même, *Nomen-Omen*, pp. 48-52.

sonore au sein des syllabes et des diphtongues.[11] Par conséquent il ne faut pas négliger de telles figures rhétoriques comme la consonance, l'allitération, la déclinaison des syllabes, par contre, on peut donner une moindre importance à l'assonance et à la paréchèse.[12]

Face à ces moyens sonores qui concourent dans l'activité linguistique, voire poétique, des noms propres, on peut se demander si leur interprétation sonore objective est encore possible. Car, ayant tant de possibilités de combinaisons phoniques, le lecteur peut voir des procédés sonores partout, et même là, où en réalité ils n'existent pas et n'ont jamais été inventés par l'auteur. Là encore, il y a des critères de contrôle et de vérification qui relèvent de l'ensemble des composants littéraires des textes bibliques. Ces critères sont les suivants: la présence du nom propre lui-même dans le voisinage de groupes phoniques s'en rapprochant, les procédés sonores attestés par les auteurs bibliques dans les explications étymologiques,[13] le renforcement des rapprochements sonores par les mots synonymes dans le même contexte ou ailleurs,[14] les jeux sonores parallèles rencontrés dans les commentaires rabbiniques, les témoignages des anciens "onomastica" chrétiens.[15] Comme tous les critères n'interviennent pas de concert dans chaque cas, et d'autre part, comme les rapprochements sonores ne sont pas évidents au même degré, il faut garder une certaine souplesse dans la qualification de chaque exemple.

b) En second lieu, le côté significatif des effets sonores onomastiques: le premier but de l'activité sonore des noms propres est celui d'indiquer leur signification la plus accessible, et cela se fait souvent par la voie de l'étymologisation. Dans ce cas, la demande sur la signification d'un nom propre renvoie à la recherche de son "étymon" et débouche sur une explication étymologique, qu'elle soit réelle, approximative ou fantaisiste. Ensuite, comme le désir de connaître le plus exhaustivement possible l'être indiqué par son nom ne s'épuise pas dans l'étymologie, on fait

---

[11] Pour la valeur des consonnes et des voyelles en hébreu, voir *Nomen-Omen*, p. 32. Par conséquent nous ne notons pas, dans la transcription de l'hébreu, la longueur et le timbre des voyelles — le *šᵉwa* en constitue une exeption — et par contre, nous signalons la présence de semi-voyelles dans les syllabes ouvertes finales et internes au moyen de l'accent circonflexe, p. ex. *ay* = *ê*, *iy* = *î*, *aw* = *ô*, *ah* = *â*, *eh* = *ê*.

[12] Quant à la définition de ces figures, voir *Nomen-Omen*, pp. 20s., et W. Buehlmann-K. Scherer, *Stilfiguren der Bibel* (Fribourg, 1973).

[13] Ils ont été systématiquement étudiés dans *Nomen-Omen*, pp. 55-89.

[14] Pour les procédés synonymes dans les explications de noms propres bibliques, voir I. Zakovitch, "The Synonymous Word and Synonymous Name in Name-Midrashim" (en hébreu), *Shnaton* 2 (1977), pp. 100-15.

[15] R. Singerman, *Jewish and Hebrew Onomastics: A Bibliography* (New York, 1977), donne des renseignements bibliographiques sur les procédés onomastiques dans le judaïsme; P. de Lagarde, *Onomastica Sacra* (Göttingen, ²1887), offre un utile repértoire des étymologisations anciennes sur les noms bibliques.

de la forme sonore de ce nom une espèce de clé pour le choix d'autres signifants qui puissent donner des informations ultérieures. C'est ainsi qu'on rapproche du nom propre des signifiants variés et par conséquent on le charge progressivement de signification. En vertu de sa sonorité, le nom propre attire autour de lui les différentes étiquettes décrivant l'être qu'il désigne. Sur le plan du discours, il devient, au fur et à mesure de sa "transparence sonore", un facteur fonctionnant comme un condensé de programmes narratifs, anticipant et laissant préfigurer le destin même des personnages qui les portent.[16] En étant générateurs sonores de signifiants, les noms propres inspirent les thèmes où les motifs narratifs, influencent la texture des récits, et même déterminent parfois leur sens final. Il s'agit donc là d'un élément important de la lisibilité du récit.

Il y a encore d'autres conséquences à la sonorité onomastique qui ne sont point indifférentes à l'égard de la compréhension du récit. Elles se placent sur le plan des attitudes subjectives de l'auteur et embrassent des traits narratifs tels que: la désignation burlesque des personnages, l'ironie, l'humour, l'affection de l'auteur envers son héros, la justification des rapports géographiques et politiques donnés.[17]

Découvrir ces éléments et comprendre leur fonction dans la structure du récit c'est précisement la tâche de l'herméneute. Nous ne pouvons la réaliser pleinement dans cet article soit en raison de l'ampleur des textes à étudier, soit par le nombre des noms propres où l'on constate l'effet des jeux sonores. En parcourant rapidement le chantier des oracles contre les nations, nous allons d'abord voir le recueil des paronomases et des autres jeux sonores pour nous centrer ensuite sur la fonction de générateur d'un nom propre envisagé dans l'exemple du nom Sennachérib en Isa. xxxvi-xxxvii.

2. *Les paronymes onomastiques dans les oracles contre les nations*

Un exemple singulier, unique dans les textes analysés, mérite d'être envisagé dès le commencement. C'est le concert des jeux sonores sur 12 noms de villes, que le prophète Michée compose dans la complainte sur les cités du Bas-Pays, i 9-16. Le texte n'est pas bien conservé, il y a même des lacunes,[18] mais, par-delà les incertitudes, on est encore capable de connaître le génie poétique du prophète:

---

[16] Cf. Ph. Hamon, "Pour un statut sémiologique du personnage", dans *Poétique du récit* (Paris, 1977), pp. 147-50.

[17] Ce dernier aspect était traité par S. Gevirtz, "Of Patriarchs and Puns: Joseph at the Fountain, Jacob and the Ford", *HUCA* 4-6 (1975), pp. 33-54.

[18] En ce qui concerne la reconstruction du texte, nous suivons B. Renaud, *La formation du livre de Michée* (Paris, 1977), pp. 21-37, sauf le deuxième stique du *v.* 10, où nous proposons le nom propre Kabbôn, nom d'une cité près de Lakish, cf. Jos. xv 40, et le *v.* 14, où nous proposons, pour motifs de rythme et d'euphonie, l'insertion du mot *m*ᵉ*'orašâ*.

v. 10: *b^e^gat 'al-taggîdu* (GAT-NAGAD); *b^e^kabbon? 'al-tibku* (KABBON-BAKAH) *b^e^bet l^eᶜ^aprâ ᶜapar hitpallaši* (ᶜAPRÂ-ᶜAPAR); *v.* 11: *šapir ᶜeryâ-bošet* (ŠAP-IR = ᶜER-BOŠ-), *lo' yaṣ^e^'â ... ṣa'anan* (ṢA-'A-NAN = YA Ṣe-'Â), *mispad bet ha'eṣel* (BET-ha'EṢL = MIS-PAD); *v.* 12: *marot — yarad raᶜ me'et yhwh* (MA-ROT = YA-RAD RAᶜ ME-'ET), *šaᶜar y^e^rušalayim* comparé à *šaᶜar ᶜammî ... y^e^rušalayim* au *v.* 9 (Ye-RU-ŠA-LAYIM = ŠA-ᶜAR AM-MÏ); *v.* 13 *r^e^tom hammerkabâ larekeš... lakiš* (Re-TOM HAM-MERK-LA-REKEŠ = LA-KIŠ); *v.* 14: *battê 'akzib l^e^'akzab* ('AK-ZIB = 'AK-ZAB), *šilluhim ᶜal m^e^'orašâ? morešet gat* (Me'O-RA-ŠÂ = MO-RE-ŠET); *v.* 15: *hayyoreš ... marešâ* (YO-REŠ = MA-REŠÂ), *ᶜad-ᶜadullam yabo' k^e^bod yiśra'el* (ᶜAD-DULLAM = ᶜAD-BO'-BOD).

Le prophète dresse la liste des villes au rythme des mots qui leur correspondent sur le plan sonore, mais qui déploient en même temps le thème de la complainte: le Seigneur va détruire le Bas-Pays jusqu'aux portes de Jérusalem (2x) et on perçoit dans chaque ville les coups de sa colère, signalés et annoncés par les noms mêmes des villes. La dynamique sonore retentit spontanément en vertu de règles non fixées, abandonnées à l'inventivité du poète, mais contenues dans l'espace de la complainte et de la douleur. Notons que Michée ne reviendra plus, dans ses oracles, aux procédés sonores onomastiques. Il est donc légitime d'en déduire que le prophète a recours à la sonorité des noms propres, non par un goût singulier pour ce procédé, ni grâce à la capacité d'exercer ce genre de créativité poétique, mais parce qu'il y est contraint par une circonstance et par les finalités particulières déterminant son oracle. Il semble que, dans notre cas, ce soit la douleur du prophète, son engagement affectif attesté aux *vv.* 8 et 16, et le devoir de dévoiler à ses contemporains l'approche d'une terrible catastrophe.

Dans les oracles proférés contre les nations païennes, deux noms de pays se distinguent par la fréquence des paronomases: l'Egypte et Babylone. Toutefois leur fonction sonore n'est exploitée que dans les trois prophètes: Isaïe, Jérémie et Ezéchiel.

Le nom Egypte, *miṣryaim* et *maṣor*, exerce une attraction paronymique sur les mots suivants:
en Isaïe — *mizraᶜ*, xix 7; *sor^e^rim*, xxx 1; *ṣel*, xxx 2-3; une paraphrase du nom propre au moyen de la déclinaison des syllabes dans les expressions *ṣarâ w^e^ṣuqâ*, *ᶜayarim*, *'ôṣ^e^rotam*, *yaᶜzoru*, xxx 6-7; *l^eᶜ^ezrâ*, xxxi 1; en Jérémie — *miṣṣarayu*, xlvi 10; *q^e^ḥî ṣorî*, xlvi 11; *qereṣ miṣṣapon*, xlvi 20; *ᶜam ṣapon*, xlvi 24 (le rapprochement est moins évident); en Ezéchiel — *ᶜariṣê goyim*, xxx 11; *meṣal*, *ṣammartô*, xxxi 3; *ṣammartô*, xxxi 10; *zarim ᶜariṣê goyim* et *miṣṣillô*, xxxi 12; *kol-ᶜaṣê-mayim* et *ṣammartam*, xxxi 14. Du point de vue sonore, le rapprochement *miṣrayim —ṣel* et *miṣrayim — miṣṣillô* est sembla-

ble à celui qu'on trouve dans les traditions yahviste et élohiste de l'Exode.[19] Toutefois la plupart des paronymes de *miṣrayim* sont originaux et renvoient le nom Egypte à des signifiés tals que "secours" — *ᶜezrâ*, "plantes" — *mizraᶜ*, "cime (d'un arbre)" — *ṣammeret*, "rebelles" — *sorerim*, "vase de potiers" — *nebel yoṣᵉrim*, "ennemis" — *ṣarim*, ou à des images telles qu'Egypte — génisse visitée par le taon du Nord, Egypte envahie par la plus barbare des nations, ou Egypte vide et néants fréquentés, d'après une belle paraphrase sonore en Isa, xxx, par les Israélites — rebelles.

Le titre royal du souverain d'Egypte, *parᶜô*, est accompagné dans les oracles des trois prophètes par les signifiants dérivés de *rapa'*, ce qui témoigne d'une association assez commune du titre de Pharaon avec les idées de "guérir" et de "remède", Isa. xix 22; Jer. xlvi 11; Ez. xxx 21. Peut-être dans le même champ sémantique faut-il situer un jeu euphonique, répété deux fois en Isa. xxx 2-3, qui rapproche de Pharaon l'idée de "protection": *laᶜoz bᵉmaᶜoz parᶜô*. Plusieurs trouvailles paronomastiques interéssantes sont dues à la fantaisie d'Ezéchiel. La paronomase *zᵉroaᶜ parᶜô*, xxx 21, 22, 24, 25, dresse une image sonore semblable à celle des bas-reliefs égyptiens avec une seule différence, à savoir que Pharaon en Ezéchiel a les bras non croisés, mais brisés par Yahvé. Le rapprochement entre *parᶜô* et *sarᶜappot*, *po'rot*, Ez. xxxi 5-13, fait partie de l'allégorie du cèdre, et le couple *ḥereb parᶜô*, xxxii 31-32, conclut les oracles d'Ezéchiel contre l'Egypte.

En ce qui concerne Babylone, son nom n'inspire que deux prophètes, Isaïe et Jérémie, chacun différemment l'un de l'autre. Isaïe fait uniquement le choix des signifiants qui correspondent au groupe phonique *babel*, tandis que Jérémie s'inspire de trois synonymes de Babylone: *babel*, *kaśdim* et *pᵉqod*; ajoutons encore que les textes du second Isaïe contiennent des allusions tantôt aux synonymes *babel*, *kaśdim*, tantôt au nom de *bel*.

Dans le premier et second Isaïe domine nettement le substantif *leb*, employé sous différentes formes morphologiques. Il associe au nom de *babel* les sentiments intérieurs de l'homme, tels l'orgueil, xiv 13, xlvii 8, 10, le frisson, la peur, xiii 7 et xxi 4, et l'encouragement, xlvi 8, 12. Un autre signifiant, donnant à Babylone une signification tout à fait singulière, est le verbe *napal*: *napalta miššamayim*, xiv 12 et *napᵉlâ*, *napᵉlâ babel*, xxi 9. Les autres groupes sonores rapprochés de ce nom, tels: *tebel*, *ḥabbel*, *bahal*, *ḥabalim*, *bilti sarâ*, *bᵉlî ḥaśak*, *nᵉbalêka*, *lᵉbanayu*, sont concentrés dans les chap. xiii et xiv. Ils associent à Babylone les idées de puissance,

---

[19] Cf. Ex. ii 19, iii 8, 22, xii 36, xviii 4, 8, 9, 10. C'est peut-être à cette paronomase que font allusion les explications anciennes du nom Egypte: σκότος, cf. P. de Lagarde, pp. 99 et 209.

d'orgueil, de cruauté, Isa. xiv, mais aussi ils laissent lire dans ce nom la force et l'étendue de la vengeance de Yahvé, Isa. xiii, ainsi que la joie et l'ironie du prophète devant la chute de Babylone, Isa. xiv, xxi, xlvi et xlvii.

Quant à Jérémie, on perçoit dans ses procédés sonores une tendance à substituer un nom à un autre, jusqu'à recourir à la figure *ᵓatbaš*, comme *leb qamay* au lieu de *kaśdim*, li 1, et *šešak* pour *babel*, li 41. Aucun des prophètes n'est si riche en jeux sonores avec les noms propres que l'auteur des chap. l et li dans Jérémie. Citons quelques exemples:
qešet rapproché tantôt de *babel* tantôt de *kaśdim* l 14, 29, 42, li 3, 56; *paqad* rapproché, dans ses formes dérivées, tantôt de *kaśdim*, tantôt de *pᵉqod*, l 27, 31, li 18, 44, 47, 52, 56;
napal rapproché de *babel*, l 15, li 8, 49 et de *kaśdim*, li 4; *šadᵉdim* — de *kaśdim*, et *šoded*, *qaššᵉtôtam* — de *babel*, li 48, 53, 55, 56.

Il y a aussi de belles paraphrases des noms *babel* et *kaśdim* développées tout au long d'un verset, p.ex. *napᵉlu* ... *ka'ašer ᶜaśᵉtâ ᶜaśu-lah-babel*, l 15-16; *upaqadti ᶜal-bel babel wᵉhoṣe'ti 'et-bilᶜô mippiyu* ... *babel napᵉlâ*, li 44. Les deux chapitres de Jérémie constituent un véritable concert d'euphonie onomastique dépassant, dans la richesse des figures sonores, soit la créativité du même Jérémie dans les oracles contre les nations, soit la fantaisie des autres prophètes dans le même genre d'oracles. L'auteur des chap. l et li est proche, sous certains aspects, tantôt du premier, tantôt du second Isaïe,[20] mais dans la plupart des cas il est indépendant et orginal.

Signalons encore rapidement les exemples les plus significatifs dans les oracles contre d'autres nations:

Edom-Esaü — Les jeux sonores sur ces deux noms, souvent sous-entendus l'un dans l'autre, sont bien connus dans l'Ancien Testament.[21] Quant aux prophètes, en Isaïe et Joël se rencontre la paronomase incomplète *'edom* — *dam*, Isa. xxxiv 3-7 et Jl iv 19, 21; en Jérémie se trouve l'expression *yošᵉbê dᵉdan* — *ki 'ed ᶜeśaw* ... *ᶜet pᵉqadtiyu*, xlix 8, où, à côté du nom d'Esaü, apparaît celui de Dedan qui s'allonge dans les syllabes *'ed*, *ᶜet*, *pᵉ-qad-*; en Ezéchiel il y a un rapprochement paronomastique *'edom* — *'adam*, xxv 13, et une espèce de jonglerie avec *'edom*/*ᶜeśaw* dans l'expression *ᶜaśot 'edom binqom naqam*, xxv 12; et encore le nom d'Edom se voit expliqué en Abdias dans la paronomase *ᵓedom* — *ᵓedô*, *ᵓedam* v. 13, *ᶜeśaw* — *yašaᶜ* (*môšiᶜim*), *v.* 21, où le jeu sonore, de concert avec l'antithèse

[20] Jer. l-li est souvent rapproché d'Isa. xiii qui, d'après le plus grand nombre des commentaires serait daté de la fin de l'empire néo-babylonien, cf. J. Vermeylen, *Du prophète Isaïe à l'Apocalyptique* (Paris, 1977), pp. 288-91. Les procédés onomastiques confirmeraient, indirectement, cette hypothèse.

[21] P. ex. Gen. xxv 23, 25, 30; Dt. ii 5, 12, 22, 29.

syntaxique, met en relief un intéressant rapport politique et géographique entre Edom et Israël.[22]

Moab — On trouve deux exemples en Isaïe, prouvant que le nom de Moab est associé à celui de Lot: *mo'ab — yil^elotah* (2x) et *lipleṭat mo'ab*, xv 8-9. 'Les autres exemples en Isaïe témoignent d'une large invention poétique: *mê dimon mal^e'u dam*, xv 9; *g^e'on-mo'ab gê' m^e'od*, xvi 6; *me^cay l^emo'ab* et *qirbî l^eqir*, xvi 11. En Jérémie notons la paronomase sur Heshbon, *b^eḥešbon ḥaš^ebu*, xlviii 2 et sur le nom du dieu Kamosh, dont la signification est portée par les mots *boš*, *baššobî* et *š^ebut*, xlviii 13, 46, 47.

Philistie — une certaine paraphrase euphonique en Isa. xiv 29 pourraît être considérée comme une métaphore sonore hissée à l'intention des Philistins. En Ezéchiel il y a une paronomase sur Kerétiens, *k^eretim — hikratti*, xxv 15-16, et en Abdias un rapprochement sonore de caractère géographique dans *p^elištim — hašš^epelâ*, *v.* 19. Parmi les noms des villes, on note la paronomase sur Gaza dans Amos i 6, Soph. ii 4 et Jer. xlvii 1-2, sur Ashdod dans Jer. xlvii 4-5 et sur Eqrôn et Ashqelôn dans Soph. ii 4.

Aram — en Isaïe *'aram-'amir*, *ha'amir*, xvii 6, 9 et en Amos *'aram qirâ 'amar yhwh*; 5. Les exploits sonores sur les noms d'Assyrie, de Kush, de Ninive et de Tyr se retrouvent respectivement: Assyrie et Kush dans Isa. xiv 25, xxxi 9 et xviii 2, 7, quelques allusions sonores à Ninive dans les oracles de Nahum, où les rapprochements euphoniques sont très voilés mais, par contre, renforcés par les renvois à des signifiés étymologiques, comme p. ex. *nin^ewê — yônim*, ii 8,[23] et plusieurs jeux sonores sur Tyr en Ezéchiel, p. ex. *ṣor — ṣorî*, xxvii 17 ou *ṣor — soḥarim*, xxvii 21 (2x), 36.

Une telle variété d'échos sonores des noms propres ressort du besoin de décoder leur sens et de le communiquer dans le message. Il ne s'agit pas ici uniquement du sens des noms propres, du remplissage de leur vide significatif, mais avant tout du sens des événements, du rôle historique des nations, de leur destin, du déroulement de l'histoire se developpant sur le canevas des pays, des villes et des souverains qui y participent, reconnus par leurs noms. Le recours des prophètes à ces ressources puissantes qui reposent sur la force magique des noms propres, veut déterminer, d'une certaine faççon, la nature et le destin de leurs porteurs et, avant tout, veut faire comprendre à l'auditeur/lecteur, moyennant des récits développés autour de ces noms, pourquoi leurs porteurs sont

---

[22] L'antithèse ressort de l'opposition *har ṣiyyon — har ^ceśaw*; le correspondant sonore de *har ^ceśaw* se transforme en signifié fonctionnel de *har ṣiyyon*: vainqueurs (*môšī^cim*>*yaša^c-^ceśaw*) au Mont Sion jugeront le Mont Esaü.

[23] Une conjecture textuelle au *v.* 8, *haṣṣ^ebi* (*ḥṣb/nwh*), proposée par R. Tournay, *RB* 72 (1965), p. 428, renforcerait la paronomase par une allusion étymologique à Ninive.

tels et non autres, et où conduit leur cheminement à travers les événements racontés.

3. *Le nom de Sennachérib comme générateur du sens en Isa. xxxvi-xxxvii*

Les divisions usuelles de la péricope en question, basée sur l'alternance des actions et des personnages, subissent une certaine modification si l'on prend en considération la présence du protagoniste central, le roi d'Assyrie, indiquée par son nom. Sa personne revient plusieurs fois dans le récit, marquée tantôt par son nom, *sanḥerib*, tantôt par ses titres royaux. De surcroît, le nom du roi d'Assyrie, transparent dans sa forme qui est réductible à deux groupes morphologiques, *san* et *ḥerib*,[24] retentit à plusieurs reprises, à travers des signifiants qui lui rendent des échos sonores, tout au long de la péricope.

Commençons par le nom propre et ses substituts, les titres royaux. Le nom de Sennachérib apparaît quatre fois, une fois tout simplement *sanḥerib*, xxxvii 17, et trois autres fois avec le titre adjoint, *sanḥerib melek 'aššur*, xxxvi 1, xxxvii 21, 37. On y reconnaît un double mode d'emploi de ce nom: la formule officielle caractérisée par le nom accompagné du titre royal, employée au commencement et à la fin du récit ainsi que dans l'introduction de l'oracle d'Isaïe; la formule simple limitée au nom propre, comme s'il s'agissait d'une personne quelconque, formule trouvée dans la prière d'Ezéchias. Le titre royal *melek 'aššur* est employé un peu partout, mais les trois titres royaux réunis, *melek 'aššur*, *hammelek haggadol melek 'aššur* et *'adonî hammelēk 'aššur*, alternent uniquement dans le discours du grand échanson. Les premières observations étant faites, on est amené à formuler deux remarques.

a) Tout d'abord, le nom de Sennachérib souligne quatre parties du récit mises en relief: deux petits morceaux narratifs, xxxvi 1-3 et xxxvii 36-38, qui encadrent le déroulement de toutes les actions, la prière d'Ezéchias, xxxvi, 16-20 et l'oracle d'Isaïe, xxxvii 21-35. Les titres royaux éparpillés dans tous les discours, mettent au premier plan le discours du grand échanson, xxxvi 4-20. De cette façon nous repérons au sein des huit parties composant la péricope,[25] cinq unités qui se distinguent par l'usage onomastique: l'introduction et la conclusion du récit, le discours du grand échanson, la prière d'Ezéchias et l'oracle d'Isaïe.

---

[24] C'est d'après ce critère que le nom *sanḥerib* est interprété par les onomastica anciens: πειρασμός de *nasah* (=SAN) et ξηρασία *ḥoreb* (=ḤERIB), cf. *Onomastica Sacra*, p. 222.

[25] Ce sont les parties de la structure de surface: l'introduction et la conclusion du récit, le discours du grand échanson, la réaction d'Ezéchias, la réponse d'Isaïe, le second message de Sennachérib, la prière d'Ezéchias et l'oracle d'Isaïe.

b) Ensuite, le mode d'emploi inégal du nom propre et de ses substituts prouve que les acteurs prennent leur distance de manière différente à l'égard de Sennachérib.[26] Le narrateur se montre neutre et respectueux dans l'introduction et la conclusion du récit en appelant le souverain par la formule officielle; pareillement le prophète Isaïe dans l'introduction de l'oracle. Le roi Ezéchias n'emploie pas, dans sa prière, le titre royal d'Assyrien, marquant ainsi son dédain et son refus de reconnaître le pouvoir de l'adversaire, ce que fait, d'ailleurs, le grand échanson à l'égard d'Ezéchias. Au contraire, le grand échanson tente de niveler toute différence entre lui et son souverain en multipliant les titres qui marquent son respect, son attachement et sa servilité.[27]

Il devient manifeste, d'après ces premières informations, que l'auteur fait participer Sennachérib au récit, non par les actions, mais à travers les discours des acteurs, notamment celui du grand échanson, celui d'Ezéchias et celui de Yahvé lui-même par la bouche d'Isaïe. Le cadre général de cette présence décrite par les acteurs est constitué de la triple indication de sa personne par la formule officielle: Sennachérib, roi d'Assyrie, monte contre Jérusalem, il y reçoit l'oracle de Yahvé, puis il repart chez lui. C'est autour de ces trois éléments, indiqués par l'usage particulier du nom du protagoniste, que les actions se déroulent dans le récit. Là encore, le nom propre sert de clé à la compréhension qui ouvre l'accès à d'autres informations possibles grâce aux connexions et aux renvois sonores. Le récit analysé abonde en interprétations de la forme *sanḥerib*, qui ne sont pas indiquées par la structure syntaxique, mais qui comblent, par la poétique sonore, son vide significatif. Puisque nous avons noté que ce sont les acteurs qui parlent du roi d'Assyrie et qui ont des rapports inégaux avec lui, nous allons voir comment chacun d'eux interprète son nom.

Quant à l'introduction du narrateur, le signifiant *habb^{e}rekâ*, *v.* 2, est un renvoi paronomastique (ḤE-RIB = B^e-REK) qui lie la personne du roi avec le lieu de la rencontre. Nous ne nions pas qu'il s'agisse là d'une information topographique, mais au-delà de l'information, nous y voyons le lieu, *topos*, d'une rencontre particulière, importante, le lieu de la "rencontre de l'oracle".[28] Près de *b^{e}rekâ*, le roi *sanḥerib* se dresse devant le Dieu vivant à Sion pour le défier et pour se voir défait.

---

[26] Les rapports émotionnels de l'auteur avec les personnages de son récit, traduits moyennant le changement de leurs noms et de leurs titres, ont été mis au point par B. Uspeński, "Poétique de la composition", *Poétique* 9 (1972), pp. 124-34.

[27] La fréquence des titres est significative dans cette unité; elle rehausse la figure de Sennachérib, le vrai auteur du discours.

[28] Rappellons que la *b^{e}rekâ* du canal est le lieu de la rencontre d'Isaïe avec Achaz et de l'oracle de l'Emmanuel, Isa. vii 3, et qu'encore l'expression *mê haššiloaḥ* en Isa. viii 6 constitue le renvoi topographique au second oracle de l'Emmanuel.

Dans le discours du grand échanson, les échos sonores retentissent en deux endroits; aux *vv.* 8-9: paronomase dans *hit-ʿareb-na'* (ḤE-RIB = ʿA-REB), déclinaison des syllabes en *rokebim lerekeb* (ḤE-RIB = RO-KeB-Le-RE-KEB); aux *vv.* 16-17: paronomase et metathèse dans *berakâ* (ḤE-RIB = Be-RAK)[29] et allusion par syllabisation en *mê-borô*, *keramim* (ḤE-RIB = ME-BOR, Ke-REM). Dans le premier cas, discours aux fonctionnaires d'Ezéchias, le grand échanson interprète le nom de son souverain à l'aide de termes militaires (chars, cavaliers) et s'en sert pour ironiser sur les forces militares d'Ezéchias ("fais un pari avec le roi d'Assyrie!");[30] dans le deuxième, en s'adressant au peuple, il donne à ce nom une signification de bienveillance: Sennachérib est votre bienfaiteur, faites la paix avec lui, il vous donnera à manger et à boire.

Les derniers renvois sonores laissent démêler les autres éléments constituant l'axe sémantique du discours du grand échanson, à savoir l'*expression polaire* "manger-boire", employée en relation oppositionnelle. Le "manger-boire" dans le territoire d'Ezéchias est, d'après une peu élégante expression au *v.* 12,[31] le synonyme de destruction, *ḥarap*, mais "manger-boire" sous la protection, *berakâ*, de Sennachérib et dans son pays, sera repos et paix, *mê-borô*, *keramim.*

La réaction d'Ezéchias contient un jeu paronomastique dans *leḥarep*, prolongé par la syllabisation de *haššeʾerit hannimṣaʾa* (SAN-ḤE-RIB = Še-'E-RIT, NIM-ṢA), xxxvii 4. Cet *omen* du nom du roi d'Assyrie dans la bouche d'Ezéchias est significatif: Sennachérib est "insulteur du Dieu vivant" et "menace pour le reste" qui subsiste à Jérusalem.

Mais l'interprétation que lui donne Yahvé par la bouche du prophète indique un autre sens; elle sonne: *wehippaltiyu baḥereb beʾarṣô*, xxxvii 7. L'insistance sur le signifiant *'arṣô* (2x) qui fait écho à la première partie du nom propre (ṢÔ = SAN-ḥerib) et la paronomase sur la deuxième (ḤE-RIB = ḤE-REB) en donnent l'interprétation authentique, voire divine, et déterminent le destin de son porteur: Sennachérib signifie "retour à son pays" et "mort sous l'épée".

Puis, c'est au tour d'Ezéchias de reprendre, dans sa prière, l'épithète d'insulteur dans l'expression *sanḥerib šalaḥ leḥarep*, xxxvii 17, et d'en tirer une autre signification, élargie à d'autres rois d'Assyrie: *heḥeribu malkê 'aššur*, xxxvii 18.

---

[29] On attendrait ici le mot *šalom*; en effet, l'expression *ʿaśu 'itti berakâ* n'est employée qu'ici (=2 R. xviii 31), ce qui prouve l'intérêt particulier de l'auteur pour *berakâ.*

[30] L'expression n'est pas à interpréter comme une proposition de se lier d'amitié, comme le suggère P. Auvray, *Isaïe 1-39* (Paris, 1972), p. 305, mais comme un défi ironique.

[31] Selon la lecture du Ketib, *ḥr'yhm* et *šynyhm*, l'expression devait être grossière; le Qere corrige en *ṣo'atam* = "excréments" et *mêmê raglêhem* = "l'eau des pieds".

Il ne reste que la seconde réponse d'Isaïe, la série de trois oracles, dont la richesse en figures poétiques, en images et en métaphores sonores, dépasse, en nombre et en créativité, les exemples repérés ci-dessus. Voici l'orchestration sur la forme du nom *sanḥerib*:

v. 22 — allusion par une consonance dans *ṣiyyon 'aḥarêka* (ṢN 'HR);

v. 23 — paronomase dans *ḥerapta*, *harimota*, renforcée par la déclinaison des syllabes *mi-*, *mi-*, *tiś-śa'*, *ma-rom*;

v. 24 — paronomase dans *ḥerapta*, *m^erom harim*, *mibḥar*, prolongée dans les syllabes *b^e-rob*, *rik-bê*, *'ek-rot*, *b^e-roš-*, et renforcée par l'allitération de R (14x), M (9x) et B (8x);

v. 25 — paronomase dans *'aḥrib* plus syllabisation *qar-ti*, *y^e-'or*, *ma-ṣor*,[32]

v. 26 — paraphrase du nom propre par la consonance dans *l^emeraḥoq* (MRḤQ) et la syllabisation *gal-lim*, *niṣ-ṣim*, *ʿa-rim*, *ṣu-rot*;

v. 29 — les échos à la première partie de *sanḥerib* dans les syllabes *ša-'a-nan-'oz-nay*;

v. 30 — paronomase sur *san-* dans *šanâ* (4x) et allusion à *-ḥereb* dans *k^eramim* et *piryam*;

v. 31 — orchestration euphonique dans *hanniš'arâ* et *ʿaśâ p^erî* et syllabisation évoquant *sanḥerib* dans *teṣe' š^e'erit* (SAN-ḤERIB = ṢE' Š^e-'E-RIT);

v. 32 — allusion en métathèse par la consonance dans *mehar ṣiyyon* (MHR ṢN).

C'est une véritable biographie sonore de *sanḥerib* qui se déploie en un riche éventail de figures engendrées par ce nom. De ce bref documentaire sonore, qui à l'époque devait jouer le rôle de nos documentaires filmés, on relève le thème essentiel, la réponse de Yahvé à l'audacieux défi du roi d'Assyrie, et ensuite les motifs qui lui sont subordonnés tels que la valorisation du rôle des deux partenaires, Yahvé et Sennachérib, la qualification du défi comme insulte, les grands exploits de l'Assyrien, leur véritable origine et leur rôle dans l'histoire, et, par suite de l'incompréhension par Sennachérib de ces signifiés inscrits dans son nom, la vraie signification de celui-ci: *ša'anan ḥorep* = "insolent — insulteur". L'oracle est donc une sentence de Yahvé sur le nom *sanḥerib*: il sera enlevé, avec toute sa signifiance, à son porteur, et sera confié, avec un autre sens, aux Israélites comme signe de leur prospérité. En effet, dans le deuxième oracle, *vv.* 30-32, les jeux paronomastiques et les paraphrases sonores concourent dans une métaphore qui transpose la signification polyvalente du nom *sanḥerib* sur le peuple d'Israël, et la réduit à une annonce joyeuse: *te-*

---

32 Puisque la même expression apparaît en Isa. xix 6-7, il semble qu'elle devait être usuelle à l'époque du prophète. Ici les renvois sonores aux noms de Sennachérib et de l'Egypte se fondent sur le même procédé poétique.

ṣe' še'erit ... mehar ṣiyyon. Là encore, la sonorité touche la lisière d'une autre structure sous-jacente au récit et construite sur l'expression polaire "manger-boire". Les signifiants de "manger" reviennent ici, de concert avec les échos sonores, et retablissent le vrai sens de l'expression falsifiée dans le discours du grand échanson.

Quant à Sennachérib, le destin qui s'accomplira sur lui au moyen de *ḥereb*, et dont parle la conclusion du récit, *v.* 38, constitue le dernier jeu, ou mieux, le dernier mot du programme de sa vie inscrit dans son propre nom.

Pour conclure, nous tenons à dire que la lecture des signifiés et du sens codifiés dans la texture sonore du récit ne veut pas remplacer l'analyse littéraire, critique et historique. Tout au contraire, elle la complète en éclairant certains aspects nouveaux non encore explorés. Le motif du défi de Sennachérib à Yahvé est transparent dans le texte, mais ses composants tels l'insulte, la destruction, l'épée, le reste de Sion, constituent les point cardinaux du récit et demandent à être reconnus dans le système référentiel de l'ensemble. Les renvois sonores, les rapports entre les jeux paronomastiques, laissent entrevoir dès l'abord une structure compacte des éléments réciproquement subordonnés, encadrés par les morceaux narratifs et développés autour de l'oracle d'Isaïe qui vient en contrepoint du discours du grand échanson.[33]

Mais c'est surtout la force transformatrice de la parole de Yahvé qui jaillit de l'euphonie sur le nom de Sennachérib. Dans chaque discours il est dit quelque chose de son porteur, chaque acteur en propose son interprétation, mais la vraie et la plus efficace est celle de Yahvé. Toute la force magique cachée dans ce nom, toute sa signification cèdent la place devant la sentence du Seigneur qui annule le nom pour le roi d'Assyrie et le transforme en faveur des Israélites. *Nomen* est *omen*, il est vrai, mais c'est à Yahvé seul qu'est laissé d'en inscrire la signification dans les événements historiques.

---

[33] Même si l'on accepte différentes sources sous-jacentes à cette péricope, cf. p. ex. P. Auvray, *Isaïe 1-39*, pp. 329-33, on doit constater que sa composition implique des critères unificateurs. Par conséquent l'hypothèse de deux récits en Isa. xxxvi-xxxvii est de nouveau remise en question.

DAS KLAGEGEBET IN LITERATUR UND LEBEN DER EXILSGENERATION AM BEISPIEL EINIGER PROSATEXTE

VON

TIMO VEIJOLA

Helsinki

I

Das babylonische Exil bedeutet den Tiefpunkt in der bisherigen Geschichte des Verhältnisses zwischen Jahwe und seinem Volk, und die Klage stellt die ihm am meisten angemessene und charakteristische Ausdrucksform dar. Wir wissen, daß die Mehrzahl der kollektiven Klagepsalmen und -liturgien aus dieser Epoche des Leidens stammen,[1] wie ebenso doch wohl auch der Grundstock der eigentlichen Klagelieder (Threni).[2] Bekannt ist weiter, daß Deuterojesaja seine Heilsverkündigung als befreiende göttliche Antwort auf die vorausgehenden Klagen seiner Zeitgenossen ausrichtet. Angesichts der extensiven kollektiven Klage ist kaum zu bezweifeln, daß die Individualklage im Zeitalter des Exils nicht weniger verbreitet war, obwohl die zeitliche Fixierung ihrer konkreten Äußerungen mangels eindeutiger historischer Anspielungen in den meisten Fällen offen bleiben muß. Weniger bekannt ist hingegen, in welchem Umfang die sonst gut bezeugte exilische Klage ihren Niederschlag bereits in den Prosatexten gefunden hat, die in dieser Zeit verfaßt oder redigiert wurden. Gewöhnlich wird in diesem Zusammenhang auf das umfangreiche dtr Tempelweihgebet Salomos (1 Reg. viii 14ff.) hingewiesen,[3] dessen Mittelstück (V. 31-51) in seiner festgeprägten Struktur

---

[1] Von den eigentlichen Klagepsalmen des Volkes Ps. xliv, lx, lxxiv, lxxix, lxxx, lxxxiii, lxxxix (vgl. C. Westermann, *Der Psalter* [Stuttgart, ^{3}1974], S. 29) sind alle, ausgenommen vielleicht Ps. lxxxiii, exilischen Ursprungs, s. Verf., *Verheißung in der Krise. Studien zur Literatur und Theologie der Exilszeit anhand des 89. Psalms* (Helsinki, 1982), S. 55 (mit Literatur) und S. 117f. Das Gleiche gilt auch von dem Klagelied in Jes. lxiii 7-lxiv 11 (S. 57) sowie von den Klageliturgien in Mi. vii 8-20 (ebd.) und in Jer. xiv 1-xv 4 (W. Thiel, *Die deuteronomistische Redaktion von Jeremia 1-25* [Neukirchen-Vluyn, 1973], S. 178-94).

[2] Trotz der neuerdings geschehenen Bestreitung durch O. Kaiser, *Klagelieder*, in H. Ringgren-W. Zimmerli-O. Kaiser, *Sprüche/Prediger/Das Hohe Lied/Klagelieder/Das Buch Esther* (Göttingen, ^{3}1981), S. 301f.

[3] Vgl. etwa J. Hempel, *Gebet und Frömmigkeit* (Göttingen, 1922), S. 43f., und O. Plöger, Reden und Gebete im deuteronomistischen und chronistischen Geschichtswerk, *FS G. Dehn* (Neukirchen, 1957), S. 36 (= *Aus der Spätzeit des AT* [Göttingen, 1971], S. 51).

offenbar den Ablauf eines exilischen Bitt- und Klagegottesdienstes widerspiegelt.[4] Die Bezugnahme auf diesen Text ist legitim, läßt jedoch leicht übersehen, daß seine barocke Form die Existenz weiterer ähnlicher Klagetexte von kleinerem Format voraussetzen könnte. Im folgenden geht es darum, einige vergessene Klagegebete in Prosa ausfindig zu machen und ihren Charakter auf dem Hintergrund der exilischen Klagepraxis zu erörtern.

II

Zuerst wollen wir uns einem Gebet Davids zuwenden, das in 1 Sam. xxiii 10-11a überliefert ist. Es wird von David in dem Moment ausgesprochen, als er die Stadt Keïla von den Philistern befreit hat (V. 5), kurz danach jedoch Gefahr läuft, von Saul und seinem Heer überfallen zu werden (V. 7-8). In dieser Notsituation fordert David seinen Priester Abjatar auf, das Ephod herbeizubringen (V. 9), und spricht dann selber ein Gebet (V. 10-11a), das auf den ersten Blick einen durchaus plastischen Eindruck macht und deshalb auch von den meisten Kommentatoren — wenigstens zum größten Teil — für authentisch gehalten wird. So meint auch A. Wendel, dem wir die klassische Darstellung des Laiengebets im vorexilischen Israel verdanken, daß hier ein früher Vertreter des sog. Orakel-Frage-Gebets vorliege.[5] Freilich muß er zugleich feststellen, daß dieser Text der einzige seiner Art im AT sei (S. 240). Die sonstigen in den geschichtlichen Büchern erzählten Gottesbefragungen sind von einer lapidaren Kürze: Es wird Jahwe eine gezielte Frage gestellt, auf die er eine ebenso prägnante Antwort gibt (Ri. i 1-2, xx 18,23,28; 1 Sam. x 22, xxiii 2,4, xxx 8; 2 Sam. ii 1, v 19) — oder sie verweigert (1 Sam. xiv 37). Gebetet wird bei den Orakelbefragungen nie — abgesehen von unserem Text.

Als "bemerkenswert" muß auch Wendel den Sachverhalt bezeichnen, "daß gerade auf dieses ausgeführte Gebet hin ganz kurze 'technische' Antworten berichtet werden" (S. 246). Das Gebet wird in der zweifachen göttlichen Antwort (V. 11b-12) in keiner Weise berücksichtigt. Zudem fällt die Reihenfolge der Anfragen in Davids Orakelgebet auf: Er erkundigt sich *zuerst* danach, ob die Bürger von Keïla ihn an Saul ausliefern werden (V. 11aα^1), und erst später danach, ob Saul überhaupt nach Keïla herabkommen wird (V. 11aα^2), obwohl genau die umgekehrte Reihenfolge die einzig logische, in der Situation begründete wäre. Außerdem wird in V. 12 Davids erste Anfrage noch nach dem Gebet wie-

---

[4] Hempel, S. 43; Verf., S. 182f. (dort auch weitere Literatur).

[5] A. Wendel, *Das freie Laiengebet im vorexilischen Israel* (Leipzig, 1931), S. 240, 246-8.

derholt und erst dort beantwortet, ein sicherer Beweis dafür, daß sie in V. 11 eine unsachgemäße Vorwegnahme derselben Frage in V. 12 ist.[6]

Diese Beobachtung darf jedoch nicht zu der Schlußfolgerung führen, daß Davids Gebet nach der Beseitigung dieses störenden Elements in Ordnung sei.[7] Denn auch die Zielrichtung des Gebets ist ins Auge zu fassen: David motiviert sein Gebetsanliegen vor allem mit dem Schicksal der Stadt Keïla. Er habe gehört, daß Saul nach Keïla zu kommen beabsichtige, *um die Stadt seinetwegen zu vernichten* (V. 10). Das war aber nach der voraufgehenden Erzählung (V. 7-9) keineswegs die Absicht Sauls, der vielmehr die Gunst der Situation nutzen wollte, daß David in einer befestigten Stadt eingeschlossen war, und sein Heer gegen ihn und seine Männer aufbot. Auch David wußte sehr wohl, daß Sauls Kriegszug auf ihn persönlich zielte (V. 9), und betrachtete deshalb die Bewohner von Keïla als seine potentiellen Verräter. Aus diesem Grund wollte er sich durch die Orakelanfrage Klarheit vor allem darüber verschaffen, ob die Bürger von Keïla ihn im kritischen Moment auslieferten, womit nach Jahwes Antwort wirklich zu rechnen war (V. 12). Also besteht zwischen David und den Bewohnern von Keïla auf der einen Seite eine herzliche, schicksalhafte Verbundenheit, die David für die Stadt beten läßt, auf der anderen aber eine indifferente, wenn nicht gar feindselige Haltung, die keine Solidarität in der Stunde der Krise kennt.

Die Gegenprobe bestätigt die Vermutung, daß Davids Gebet insgesamt einer sek. Erweiterung der alten Textgrundlage entstammt. Nach der Beseitigung des Gebets — d.h. V. 10 (ohne die Redeeinleitung) und V. 11a (ohne *hyrd šʾwl*) — bleibt ein Text übrig, der die gängige Struktur einer Orakelszene aufweist: David fragt Jahwe durch die Vermittlung des Ephods: "Wird Saul herabkommen?" (V. 11aα^2) und erhält die Antwort: "Er wird herabkommen" (V. 11bβ), worauf die andere Frage folgt: "Werden die Bürger von Keïla mich und meine Männer an Saul ausliefern?" (V. 12aβ) mit der göttlichen Antwort: "Sie werden ausliefern" (V. 12bβ). Auf diesen Bescheid hin verläßt David mit seinen Männern Keïla, und auch Saul gibt seinen Kriegszug auf (V. 13). Die erzählerische Struktur dieser Szene, die aus jeweils zwei aufeinander bezogenen Orakelanfragen und -antworten sowie aus der entsprechenden Reak-

---

[6] Daß V. 11aα^1 in 4Q Sam^b offenbar fehlt (vgl. F. M. Crosss, *JBL* 74 [1955], S. 169f.), besagt nur, daß die Doppelung schon früh als solche empfunden wurde. Auch LXX bietet einen scheinbar glatten Text, indem sie V. 11b-12a gänzlich fallen läßt, jedoch infolge des homark *wyʾmr yhwh*, vgl. D. Barthélemy, "La qualité du Texte Massorétique de Samuel", in *The Hebrew and Greek Texts of Samuel, 1980 Proceedings IOSCS - Vienna* (Jerusalem, 1980), S. 7,12.

[7] Etwa gegen Wendel, *Laiengebet*, S. 246f.; *Jer-B*, ad loc., und P. K. McCarter, *I Samuel* (Garden City, New York, 1980), S. 370-2.

tion des Befragenden besteht, hat ein genaues Gegenstück in 2 Sam. ii *1-3,[8] was unsere Analyse augenfällig bestätigt.

Was die Herkunft des sek. Gebets betrifft, ist kaum zu bezweifeln, daß es von dem dtr Geschichtsschreiber (DtrH) stammt, somit also exilischen Ursprungs ist. Dafür spricht der Umstand, daß es sich hier nicht um eine isolierte Eintragung, sondern ein Stück aus einer breiteren dtr Bearbeitungsschicht handelt, was hier freilich nicht näher erläutert werden kann.[9] Aber die dtr Abstammung des Gebets geht auch daraus hervor, daß es ausgerechnet im Munde Davids begegnet. Damit fügt es sich in die Reihe der anderen dtr Zeugnisse ein, nach denen das Gebet eine wichtige Rolle in Davids Leben spielt. Das beredteste Beispiel dafür ist das ausgeführte Dankgebet Davids nach dem Empfang des Nathanorakels (2 Sam. vii 18-29).[10] Die alte geschichtliche Überlieferung dagegen kennt kein einziges Gebet von David.[11] Das Bild von dem betenden David entstammt offensichtlich dem dtr Frömmigkeitsideal, nach dem ein frommer König — nicht nur David, sondern auch Salomo (1 Reg. iii 6-9, viii 14ff.)[12] und Hiskija (2 Reg. xx 2b-3a)[13] — auf die göttliche Offenbarung bzw. eine Notsituation mit einem Gebet reagiert.

---

[8] In 2 Sam. ii 1-3 ist der Text sekundär erweitert worden, was bereits die brüchige Syntax verrät. Ursprünglich lautete er m.E. folgendermaßen: V. 1,2aα, 3aα (*wʾ nšyw ʾšr ʿmw*), 3b.

[9] Dazu gehören vor allem die Retterformeln in V. 2bβ,5b und als deren Vorbereitung V. 1bβ sowie wahrscheinlich auch die Ephod-Parenthese V. 6. Den Nachweis erbringe ich in dem Aufsatz "David in Keïla. Tradition und Interpretation in 1 Sam 23, 1-13", *RB* 91 (1984), S. 51-87.

[10] Zur dtr Herkunft und Schichtung dieses Gebets s. Verf., *Die ewige Dynastie. David und die Entstehung seiner Dynastie nach der deuteronomistischen Darstellung* (Helsinki, 1975), S. 72-9, und ders., *Verheißung*, S. 62-5. Neben 2 Sam. vii 18-29 sind aber auch die anderen, kürzeren Passagen zu berücksichtigen, nach denen David betet: 1 Sam. xxv 32,*39; 2 Sam. xii 13, xxiv 10,17; 1 Reg. i 47b-48 (zu allen diesen Stellen s. *Ewige Dynastie*, S. 17,26f.,52f., 109-13). Dagegen sind die Schwurformeln in 1 Sam. xxv 22; 2 Sam. xix 14 und der Vergeltungswunsch in 2 Sam. iii 39 kaum als *Gebete* einzuordnen (gegen Wendel, *Laiengebet*, S. 11,76f., der sie etwas künstlich "Fluch-Gebetswünsche" nennt).

[11] Als historisch sehr zweifelhaft erscheint mir auch die traditionelle Annahme von David als Urheber *poetischer* Gebete, nachdem sich auch "die letzten Worte Davids" 2 Sam. xxiii 1-7 als späte Überlieferung erwiesen haben, s. T.N.D. Mettinger, *King and Messiah* (Lund, 1976), S. 257f., 279-82, und R. J. Tournay, "Les 'dernières paroles de David', II Samuel, xxiii, 1-7", *RB* 88 (1981), S. 481-504.

[12] Dtr (d.h. in diesem Fall: DtrN) ist in dem Gebet 1 Reg. iii 6-9: V. 6 (abgesehen von der Redeeinleitung), V. 7 (*wʿth*), V. 8 und V. 9aα².b (s. Verf., *Verheißung*, S. 146, Anm. 8). Das salomonische Tempelweihgebet 1 Reg. viii 14ff. ist hingegen Ergebnis sukzessiver dtr Arbeit (S. 150-4).

[13] Zu 2 Reg. xx 2b-3a s. Verf., "Hiskian sairaus", in *Suomen Eksegeettisen Seuran vuosikirja 1971*, S. 72f. Von Hiskijas früherem Gebet in 2 Reg. xix 14-19 ist in diesem Zusammenhang abzusehen, weil es eine große Anzahl Züge enthält, die charakteristisch für die nachexilischen Gebete sind (zu ihnen s. B. Hornig, *Das Prosagebet der nachexilischen Zeit, Diss. Leipzig*, 1957).

In 1 Sam. xxiii 10-11a handelt es sich um ein Gebet in einer Notsituation, die durch eine feindliche Bedrohung verursacht ist. Im Psalter ist dies der häufigste Anlaß der Individualklage,[14] und bei näherem Zusehen zeigt sich, daß auch Davids Gebet genau den Aufbau eines Klagelieds des Einzelnen aufweist:

Jahwe, Gott Israels,	Anrede + Gottesprädikat
dein Knecht hat gehört, daß Saul beabsichtigt, nach Keïla zu kommen, um die Stadt meinetwegen zu vernichten.	Klagender Bericht
Werden die Bürger von Keïla mich ihm ausliefern? Wird Saul herabkommen,	Orakelanfragen
wie dein Knecht gehört hat?	Klagender Bericht
Jahwe, Gott Israels,	Anrede + Gottesprädikat
gib deinem Knechte Auskunft!	Bitte

Inhaltlich besteht das Gebet aus den drei wesentlichen Faktoren der Klage: Jahwe, dem Klagenden und dem Feind.[15] Formal sind in ihm die drei wichtigsten Elemente der Klage vorhanden: Anrede, Klage und Bitte (vgl. Gunkel-Begrich, *Einleitung*, S. 240). Die am Anfang stehenden Glieder, Anrede und Gottesprädikat, die stilgemäß vor der abschließenden Bitte wiederholt werden (vgl. S. 212), haben die seit der Exilszeit üblich gewordene Form "Jahwe, Gott Israels", die eine besonders weite Verbreitung in der dtr Literatur, auch in den Gebeten (vgl. Ri. xxi 3; 2 Sam. vii 27; 1 Reg. viii 15,23), gefunden hat.[16] Zudem sei vermerkt, daß das Gottesprädikat "Gott Israels" einmal auch in einem (nachexilischen) Klagelied des Einzelnen im Psalter vorkommt (Ps. lxix 7). Durch die Anwendung dieses Gottesprädikats bekommt Davids Gebet eine nationale Dimension. "Seine persönliche Angelegenheit (wird) im gewissen Sinne als Volks-Sache vorgetragen", wie Wendel durchaus zutreffend kommentiert (S. 247). Wir werden später sehen, daß die Tendenz zur Nationalisierung und Kollektivierung einen wesentlichen Zug in der exilischen Gebetsliteratur und Theologie überhaupt darstellt.

---

[14] Vgl. H. Gunkel-J. Begrich, *Einleitung in die Psalmen* (Göttingen, 1933), S. 196,215.

[15] Vgl. C. Westermann, "Struktur und Geschichte der Klage", *ZAW* 66 (1954), S. 47,57f. (= *Forschung am Alten Testament, Gesammelte Studien* [*I*] [München, 1964], S. 269, 280f.).

[16] Vgl. etwa A. Jepsen, *Die Quellen des Königsbuches* (Halle, 1953), S. 6, Anm. 2, und J. C. Trebolle Barrera, *Salomon y Jeroboan* (Salamanca-Jerusalem, 1980), S. 150. Zur dtr Herkunft von Ri. xxi 3 s. K.-D. Schunck, *Benjamin* (Berlin, 1963), S. 59-62. Die Anredeform "Jahwe, Gott Israels" ist sonst typisch für die nachexilischen Gebete, vgl. 2 Reg. xix 15 (//Jes. xxxvii 16); Ps. lix 6 (textlich und zeitlich unsicher), Ps. lxix 7; Esr. ix 15; 1 Chr. xxix 10; 2 Chr. vi 4,14,16 (//1 Reg. viii 15,23,25), 2 Chr. vi 17.

Die kollektivierende Tendenz kommt in diesem Gebet darin zum Ausdruck, daß David seine Klage — die des näheren als klagender Bericht über den drohenden Anschlag des Feindes zu bezeichnen ist[17] — mit dem Hinweis auf das Schicksal der Stadt Keïla motiviert (V. 10b). Damit versucht er Jahwe zum Einschreiten zu bewegen ("Beweggrund"). Ein anderes Motiv im Dienste desselben Interesses ist die von David gebrauchte Selbstbezeichnung "dein Knecht" (*ᶜbdk*), die in dem kurzen Gebet insgesamt dreimal vorkommt und Davids devote Haltung vor Jahwe zum Ausdruck bringt. "Dein Knecht" ist als Selbstbezeichnung des Beters verbreitet einerseits im Psalter, wo sie 26mal, vorwiegend in den Klagepsalmen, begegnet,[18] und andererseits in den dtr Prosagebeten, unter denen Davids Dankgebet 2 Sam. vii 18-29 mit seinen 10 Belegen an der Spitze steht[19] — auch dies ein Beweis für die gemeinsame Provenienz dieser Gebete.

Als befremdlich mag zunächst wirken, daß die Klage des Einzelnen in diesem Gebet mit zwei Orakelanfragen verbunden ist. Diese Besonderheit erklärt sich jedoch ungezwungen aus dem Umstand, daß der Bearbeiter die Orakelanfragen — wie wir gesehen haben — in dem alten Text vorgefunden und mit seinem eigenen Gebet gerahmt hat. Zudem ist in Betracht zu ziehen, daß die Gattung der Gottesbefragung und die der Klage, so verschieden sie ihrem Ursprung nach auch sind, insofern doch eine gewisse gegenseitige Anziehungskraft besitzen, als die Klage — sowohl in ihrer individuellen wie auch kollektiven Form — in der Regel durch ein Heilsorakel beantwortet wurde.[20] Der exilische Bearbeiter sah sich offensichtlich durch die alte Orakelszene veranlaßt, die Gottesbefragung durch eine Klage zu ergänzen, die in der *Bitte* um das Orakel gipfelt ("Gib deinem Knechte Auskunft!"). Während in der alten Erzählung

---

[17] Den Begriff "klagender Bericht" habe ich bei J. Kühlewein gefunden, der ihn freilich nur im Zusammenhang der Volksklage verwendet (*Geschichte in den Psalmen* [Stuttgart, 1973], S. 33-44). Der drohende Anschlag des Feindes ist wiederum der häufigste Anlaß der Individualklage im Psalter (Westermann, *Ges. Studien* [*I*], S. 286).

[18] Vgl. C. Lindhagen, *The Servant Motif in the Old Testament* (Uppsala, 1950), S. 262-75 (Lindhagen gibt als Gesamtzahl 27 an, weil er auch Ps. lxxxix 40 als Selbstaussage des Sängers betrachtet).

[19] Andere dtr Belege in Gebeten, wo sie auf David verwendet wird, sind: 2 Sam. xxiv 10; 1 Reg. iii 6, viii 24,25,26. Sonst begegnet *ᶜbdk* in den dtr Gebeten Nu. xi 11 (vgl. H. H. Schmid, *Der sogenannte Jahwist* [Zürich, 1976], S. 70-5); Dtn. iii 24; 1 Reg. viii 28,29,52, xviii 36; vgl. auch Gen. xxxii 11 (später Sprachgebrauch nach C. Westermann, *Genesis* 2 [Neukirchen-Vluyn, 1981], S. 620f.) und Ri. xv 18 (das Gebet V. 18a$\alpha^2\beta$.b ist wahrscheinlich eine sek. Erweiterung). Eindeutig jünger sind hingegen Dan. ix 17 und Neh. i 6,11bis. Nach dieser Durchsicht kämen allein 1 Reg. iii 7,9 als vor-dtr Belege für *ᶜbdk* als Selbstbezeichnung des Beters in der Prosaliteratur in Frage.

[20] Gunkel-Begrich, *Einleitung*, S. 136f.,177,246f., und J. Begrich, "Das priesterliche Heilsorakel", *ZAW* 52 (1934), S. 81-92 (= *Gesammelte Studien zum Alten Testament* [München, 1964], S. 217-31).

die Gottesbefragung ganz automatisch mit einer nachgerade technischen Perfektion funktionierte, ist sie in der exilischen Neuinterpretation Gegenstand eines intensiven Gebets geworden.

Das dürfte seine Gründe letztlich in der exilischen Wirklichkeit haben, wo das Heilsorakel seine Selbstverständlichkeit verloren hatte. Damals wurde geklagt: "Unsere Zeichen (*ʾwttynw*) sehen wir nimmer, kein Prophet ist mehr da; niemand unter uns weiß, wie lange" (Ps. lxxiv 9).[21] Das Orakelwesen mußte angesichts der Größe der Katastrophe versagen, und auch die Propheten empfingen keine Gesichte mehr von Jahwe (Thr. ii 9). Folglich mußte auch der Einzelne in seiner persönlichen Not besonders intensiv um Erhörung beten (vgl. Ps. lxxvii 2-3, cii 2-3).[22] Ausdruck derselben trostlosen Stimmung sind wohl auch die in die Vergangenheit und in die Zukunft projizierten Aussagen der Deuteronomisten, nach denen das Volk in seiner Drangsal zu Gott schreit, dieser ihm jedoch die Erhörung verweigert (1 Sam. viii 18; Jer. xi 11,14, xiv 12, xv 1).[23] Jetzt waren die Tage gekommen, da "die Menschen von Meer zu Meer wanken, von Norden nach Osten ziehen, um das Wort Jahwes zu suchen, es jedoch nicht finden" (Amos viii 12).[24] So hatte die Exilsgeneration die peinigende, aber auch wertvolle Erfahrung zu machen, daß zur Kontingenz der Offenbarung Jahwes wesentlich auch sein Schweigen und seine Verborgenheit[25] gehören. Hier liegt m.E. der zeitgeschichtliche und theologische Hintergrund auch für Davids Klagegebet in 1 Sam. xxiii 10-11a.

III

Aus dem gleichen geschichtlichen Milieu stammt auch die Klage, die Gideon vor seiner Berufung zum Retter Israels ausspricht (Ri. vi 13). Die exilische Herkunft dieser Passage — deren Klagecharakter Wendel

---

[21] Daß diese Klage auf das exilische Versagen der Orakelpraxis Bezug nimmt, hat J. J. M. Roberts nachgewiesen ("Of Signs, Prophets, and Time Limits", *CBQ* 39 [1977], S. 474-81).

[22] Beide Psalmen sind exilisch, zu Ps. lxxvii s. H.-J. Kraus, *Psalmen* (Neukirchen-Vluyn, [5]1978), S. 694, und zu Ps. cii E. Janssen, *Juda in der Exilszeit* (Göttingen, 1956), S. 20.

[23] Vgl. weiter auch Ri. x 14; 1 Sam. iii 1b; Ez. viii 18, xx 3,31 und Verf., *Verheißung*, S. 205 mit Anm. 31.

[24] Amos viii 11-12 ist in Wirklichkeit Zeugnis der schon eingetroffenen Katastrophe, s. H.W. Wolff, *Dodekapropheton 2* (Neukirchen-Vluyn, [2]1975), s. 374f., 379f.

[25] Vgl. aus diesem Zeitalter auch Dtn. xxxi 16-18 (vgl. xxxii 20); Jes. lxiv 6; Ps. xliv 25, lxxxix 47 und zur theologischen Deutung L. Perlitt, "Die Verborgenheit Gottes", *Probleme biblischer Theologie, FS G. von Rad* (München, 1971), S. 367-82 (besonders S. 379f.).

völlig übersehen hat[26] — bedarf freilich in der gegenwärtigen Forschungslage eines kurzen Nachweises.

Früher wurde die zweite Vershälfte (V. 13b) wegen ihres Sprachgebrauchs häufig für sek. gehalten,[27] aber heute gilt der ganze Vers den meisten als integrierender Bestandteil von Gideons Berufungsgeschichte (Ri. vi *11-17).[28] Die einzige Ausnahme bildet, soweit ich sehe, W. Dietrich, der in einer Fußnote seiner Arbeit *Prophetie und Geschichte* (Göttingen, 1972) die Vermutung äußert, daß Gideons Klage (V. 13) mit der darauffolgenden Überleitung (V. 14aα) ein Einschub aus der Hand eines jüngeren Deuteronomisten (DtrN) sein dürfte (S. 74, Anm. 37). Er beruft sich dabei auf den Kontext, der ohne diese Versteile einen ganz lückenlosen Erzählungszusammenhang aufwiese (V. 12bβ + V. 14aβ), weiter auf den Inhalt der Klage, der aus der Exilszeit gut verständlich wäre, und weist schließlich darauf hin, daß "alle auffälligen Begriffe entweder aus dem Kontext entlehnt oder typisch dtr zu sein scheinen".[29] Alle diese Argumente halten einer genaueren Nachprüfung stand und lassen sich zudem um ein paar weitere vermehren:

Gideons Klage "Wenn Jahwe mit uns ist (*wyš yhwh ᶜmnw*), warum..." knüpft wörtlich an den vorangehenden Gruß des Engels "Jahwe *sei* mit dir (*yhwh ᶜmk*), starker Held" (V. 12bβ) an, dessen Sinn sie jedoch als eine assertorische Aussage (d.h. "Jahwe *ist* mit dir") (miß-)versteht und zugleich generalisierend auf ganz Israel überträgt ("mit uns"). Es läßt sich hier besser vorstellen, daß die gängige Grußformel[30] (vgl. Ruth ii 4) von einer *zweiten* Hand als Anknüpfungspunkt für eine neue theologische

---

[26] *Laiengebet*, S. 123. Stattdessen behandelt Wendel aber Ri. vi 22b unter den Klagegebeten (S. 123-43), was jedoch unbegründet ist, weil Ri. vi 22b in Wirklichkeit ein Weheruf ist (die abwehrende Interjektion *ᵓahāh* erscheint hier in genau derselben Funktion wie *ᵓōy* in Jes. vi 5 u.ö.), vgl. Westermann, *Ges. Studien* [*I*] S. 291, Anm. 82.

[27] So z.B. von W. Böhme, "Die älteste Darstellung in Richt. 6,11-24 und 13,2-24 und ihre Verwandtschaft mit der Jahweurkunde des Pentateuch", *ZAW* 5 (1885), S. 257, und K. Budde, *Das Buch der Richter* (Leipzig-Tübingen, 1897), S. 54.

[28] Siehe u.a. E. Kutsch, "Gideons Berufung und Altarbau Jdc 6,11-24", *ThLZ* 81 (1956), Sp. 78, Anm. 17, Sp. 29; W. Beyerlin, "Geschichte und heilsgeschichtliche Traditionsbildung im Alten Testament", *VT* 13 (1963), S. 6-9; W. Richter, *Traditionsgeschichtliche Untersuchungen zum Richterbuch* (Bonn, 1963), S. 127; N. Habel, "The Form and Significance of the Call Narratives", *ZAW* 77 (1965), S. 298f., und L. Schmidt, *Menschlicher Erfolg und Jahwes Initiative* (Neukirchen-Vluyn, 1970), S. 36,40,44f.

[29] Außerdem erwähnt er als zusätzliches Argument für seine These, daß "in der Rückleitung zum alten Text (14aα) der Engel unpassend mit Jahwe identifiziert wird". Das hat jedoch keine Beweiskraft, weil bereits in dem Grundtext diese Identifikation vollzogen wird (V. 15-17).

[30] Vgl. dazu I. Lande, *Formelhafte Wendungen der Umgangssprache im Alten Testament* (Leiden, 1949), S. 11f.

Aussage verwendet wird, als daß ein und derselbe Verfasser sie einmal als Wunsch, ein anderes Mal als Feststellung versteht.[31]

Dazu kommt die problematische Stellung von Gideons Klage innerhalb der Erzählung von seiner Berufung. Sie ist nach dem gängigen *Berufungsschema* verfaßt, dessen Bestandteile *Auftrag, Einwand, Zusicherung des Beistandes* und *Zeichen* ab V. 14 deutlich erkennbar sind (V. 14-17).[32] Weniger deutlich ist hingegen, ob auch Gideons Klage (V. 13) eine Funktion innerhalb dieses Schemas hat. W. Richter vertrat 1963 die Ansicht, "daß Ri 6,13 nicht dem Schema der Berufung zugehört haben kann" (S. 154),[33] weil nämlich die anderen Textvertreter des Berufungsschemas keine Parallelen für die heilsgeschichtlichen Familientraditionen bieten, wie sie in Ri. vi 13 zutagetreten. Sieben Jahre später (1970) hat Richter jedoch seine Ansicht insofern revidiert, als er nun Ri. vi 13 dem Berufungsschema integriert und in ihm die zum Schema gehörende *Andeutung der Not* erblickt.[34] Freilich muß er zugeben, daß Ri. vi 13 durch die Anwendung der sog. Übereignungsformel ("er hat uns in die Hand Midians gegeben") in dieser Funktion vollständig von den anderen vorprophetischen Berufungsberichten abweicht (S. 140). In ihnen wird nämlich auf die Not des Volkes durch eine gleichbleibende Aussage Bezug genommen, die besagt, daß Jahwe/Gott die Not seines Volkes gesehen habe und daß dessen Hilferuf (*ṣᶜqh*) zu ihm gekommen sei (Ex. iii 7,9; 1 Sam. ix 16 LXX). Die Berufung des Retters ist die göttliche Antwort auf den Hilferuf des Volkes. In dieser Hinsicht weicht Gideons Klage nicht unerheblich von den anderen Berufungsberichten ab, und es stellt sich die Frage, ob sie sich überhaupt auf die gleiche Ebene mit den sonstigen Lagehinweisen stellen läßt.

Gideons Berufung geschieht jedoch nicht ohne eine stilgemäße Andeutung der Not. Sie liegt nur nicht in V. 13 vor, sondern bereits in V. 6, wo man in V. 6b dem für die anderen Lagehinweise konstitutiven "Hilfeschrei" begegnet, hier ausgedrückt durch das Verb *zᶜq*: "und die Israeliten *schrien* zu Jahwe".[35] Dazu kommt, daß dieser Vers einst unmittelbar

---

[31] So müssen jedoch diejenigen postulieren, die beide Aussagen demselben Verfasser zuschreiben (vgl. Budde, *Richter*, S. 54; Lande, *Formelhafte Wendungen*, S. 11; Richter, *Untersuchungen*, S. 148f.), oder sie fassen schon V. 12bβ als Feststellung auf (vgl. Kutsch, *ThLZ* 81, Sp. 78 Anm. 16; Beyerlin, *VT* 13, S. 6 mit Anm. 3; Habel, *ZAW* 77, S. 299).

[32] Vgl. Kutsch, *ThLZ* 81, Sp. 79; Richter, *Untersuchungen*, S. 149-55; Habel, *ZAW* 77, S. 299-301.

[33] Auch bei Kutsch (*ThLZ* 81, Sp. 79) steht V. 13 außerhalb des Schemas. Habel hingegen definiert V. 12b-13 als "introductory word" (*ZAW* 77, S. 298f.), was jedoch eine zu vage Bezeichnung ist, um V. 13 in dem Berufungsschema zu rechtfertigen.

[34] W. Richter, *Die sogenannten vorprophetischen Berufungsberichte* (Göttingen, 1970), S. 139. Ähnlich auch Schmidt, *Menschlicher Erfolg*, S. 44-9.

[35] Bezeichnenderweise trägt dieses Element des Berufungsschemas bei Schmidt den Namen "Hinweis auf das Schreien des Volkes" (*Menschlicher Erfolg*, S. 49). Um so mehr befremdet, daß Schmidt diesen "Hinweis" in V. 6 völlig übersieht.

vor der Engelerscheinung (V. 11) stand — V. 7-10 sind bekanntlich ein junger Zusatz[36] — und damit den direkten Hintergrund für Gideons Berufung bildete. Die Unfähigkeit Richters und anderer, den formgemäßen Hinweis auf die Notlage in V. 6b — und nicht in V. 13 — zu erkennen, beruht letztlich darauf, daß dieser Versteil anerkanntermaßen dtr Herkunft ist[37] und die Berufungsgeschichte Gideons gewöhnlich als vor-dtr gilt. Durch dieses Postulat entsteht freilich die nicht geringe Schwierigkeit, daß man dann mit verlorengegangenen Textstücken operieren muß, weil nämlich die Geschichte von Gideons Berufung (V. 11ff.) unbedingt eine vorangehende Information über die Midianiternot erfordert, und diese ausschließlich in den dtr Rahmenangaben am Anfang des Kapitels zu finden sind (V. 1,2a,3a.bα^1, 4,6).[38] Die Schwierigkeit löst sich m.E. nur durch die Annahme auf, daß derjenige, der für die Schilderung der Midianiternot zuständig war, auch die Geschichte von Gideons Berufung zum Retter aus dieser Not verfaßt hat; d.h. die Berufungsgeschichte (V. *11-24) samt ihrer Einleitung (V. *1-6) stammt von DtrH, der sie aufgrund einer älteren Altarätiologie konzipierte.[39] Für Gideons Klage V. 13 (und V. 14aα) besagen diese Beobachtungen, daß sie sek. nicht nur im Blick auf die Grunderzählung, sondern sek. sogar im Blick auf die erste dtr Bearbeitung ist, damit also aller Wahrscheinlichkeit nach in die jüngere dtr Bearbeitungsphase (DtrN) gehört, wie schon Dietrich aus anderen Gründen angenommen hatte.

Durch die eingeschobene Klage (V. 13) hat Gideons Berufung (V. 14-17) einen neuen Charakter erhalten. Sie wird jetzt als Heilsorakel er-

---

[36] So auch nach Richter, *Die Bearbeitung des "Retterbuches" in der deuteronomistischen Epoche* (Bonn, 1964), S. 108.

[37] M. Noth, *Überlieferungsgeschichtliche Studien* (Tübingen, ^{3}1967), S. 51. Auch Richter sieht V. 6a und 6b als redaktionell, wenngleich noch vor-dtr an (*Bearbeitungen*, S. 10,61). M. E. stammt V. 6 insgesamt von DtrH.

[38] Richter sagt einerseits, daß Ri. vi 11b-17 als seinen Hintergrund V. 2b-5 voraussetzt (*Untersuchungen*, S. 127,155), stellt aber andererseits fest, daß V. 2b-5 nicht mit V. 2b angefangen haben kann, da eine allgemeine Notiz der Bedrängnis zu erwarten gewesen wäre, die jedoch der Bearbeitung eines Redaktors Rdt zum Opfer gefallen sei (S. 155). Näher liegt es jedoch, die führende, dtr Schicht (d.h. V. 1,2a,3a.bα^1,4,6) als *Grundlage* zu betrachten, die nachträglich durch jüngere Zusätze (d.h. V. 2b,3bα^{2}β,5) erweitert worden ist.

[39] Zu dieser Überlieferung rechne ich V. 11aα.bα (ohne *bnw* und *bgt*), 12,17a,18aα.b, 19aα.b, 21,22a,24aα. Die erste, vor-dtr Erweiterung umfaßt Gideons Weheruf und die Namensätiologie in V. 22b,23,24aβ. Die nächste Stufe repräsentiert DtrH, der die vorgegebenen Traditionen zu einer Berufungsgeschichte umformte; von ihm stammen in V. 11-24 die folgenden Elemente: V. 11aβ.bα (*bnw* und *bgt*), 11bβ, 14aβ.b,15,16,17b,18aβ,24b. Danach kam die von DtrN eingeschobene Klage V. 13 mit ihrer Überleitung in V. 14aα (bis einschließlich zu dem Wort *wyʾmr*). Jüngere Zusätze unbekannter Herkunft sind schließlich V. 19aβ,20. Die hier vertretene Sicht hat, was die Schichtenabfolge — aber nicht ihre Herkunft! — betrifft, die größte Affinität zu der literarkritischen Analyse von Schmidt, *Menschlicher Erfolg*, S. 22-57.

zählt, mit dem Jahwe auf Gideons Klage antwortet. Dies geht u.a. aus dem Verb *pnh ʾl* "sich zu jemandem wenden" hervor, das in der Rückleitung von der Klage zur Berufung verwendet wird (V. 14aα). Nach K. Budde erscheint der Satz "Da wandte sich Jahwe zu ihm" in diesem Zusammenhang auffällig.[40] Der Grund für seine Verwendung erhellt jedoch unschwer, wenn man einen Blick in die Psalmen tut, wo *pnh ʾl* in der Bitte um das Erhörungsorakel erscheint, z.B. in Ps. lxix 17-18:

> Erhöre mich, Jahwe (*ʿnny yhwh*)...
> wende dich zu mir (*pny ʾly*).
> Verbirg nicht dein Gesicht vor deinem Knecht...
> Erhöre mich bald (*mhr ʿnny*)!
> Vgl. auch Ps. xxv 16, lxxxvi 17 (s. *BHK*/*BHS*), cii 18, cxix 132.

Daß für DtrN diese Verwendung von *pnh ʾl* geläufig ist, zeigt auch die folgende Bitte in Salomos Tempelweihgebet: "Wende dich (*wpnyt*), Jahwe, mein Gott, zu dem Beten und Flehen deines Knechtes! Höre auf das Rufen und auf das Gebet...!" (1 Reg. viii 28).[41] Was hier und in den Psalmen erbeten wird, erscheint in Ri. vi 14 als Wirklichkeit: Jahwe nimmt sich der Klage Gideons gnädig an und beantwortet sie durch ein Heilsorakel, dessen Inhalt der Redaktor in der nun folgenden Berufung Gideons erblickte.

Die Klage selbst (V. 13) ist als Kollektivklage in Wir-Form verfaßt, was allein schon in diesem Kontext auffällig ist; denn es versteht sich keineswegs von selbst, daß Gideon den ihn persönlich betreffenden Gruß des Engels (V. 12bβ) auf ganz Israel überträgt. Die engsten Entsprechungen dafür finden sich einerseits in der Poesie in den Klageliedern des Volkes, wo "wir" die normale Redeform der Klage repräsentiert (vgl. Gunkel-Begrich, *Einleitung*, S. 123), und andererseits in der Prosa ausschließlich in den exilischen und nachexilischen Klage- und Bußgebeten, wo ein Einzelner in der 1.P.Pl. die Sache des ganzen Volkes vor Jahwe bringt.[42] Diese Form ist nicht eine zufällige Erscheinung, sondern Ausdruck einer breiten kollektivierenden Tendenz, die in der

---

[40] *Richter*, s. 54. Ähnlich äußert sich auch Böhme: "Zu einem *pnh 'l* lag meines Erachtens kein rechter Grund vor" (*ZAW* 5, S. 258).

[41] Zur Herkunft von 1 Reg. viii 28 s. Verf., *Verheißung*, S. 152f. Vgl. weiter auch 2 Reg. xiii 23 DtrN (dazu Dietrich, *Prophetie und Geschichte*, S. 34, Anm. 51, S. 74, Anm. 37, S. 76).

[42] Ex. xxxiii 15-16, xxxiv 9 (zu beiden Stellen s. J. Scharbert, *Heilsmittler im Alten Testament und im Alten Orient* [Freiburg, 1964], S. 86f.); Jos. vii 7-9 (s.u.); 2 Reg. xix 15-19 (s.o. Anm. 13); Esr. ix 6-15; Neh. i 5-11, ix 5-37; Dan. ix 4-19, vgl. auch 2 Chr. xiv 10, xx 6-12; 3 Makk. ii 1-20 und vi 2-15 (in Bittgebeten). E. Lipiński hat diese Tendenz in den späten Gebeten klar erkannt (*La liturgie pénitentielle dans la Bible* [Paris, 1969], S. 38,56f.,68,105) und deshalb Bedenken auch hinsichtlich des hohen Alters der jetzigen Form von Ri. vi 13 geäußert (S. 68).

exilischen Literatur immer stärker hervortritt und auch in der Forschung der letzten Jahre zunehmend Beachtung gefunden hat. So macht J. Becker auf kollektivierende Tendenzen innerhalb der exilisch-nachexilischen Psalmen aufmerksam: Ehemals individuelle Klagelieder werden zu dieser Zeit in einem national-theokratischen Interesse kollektiv neuinterpretiert (z.B. Ps. xxii, lix und cii)[43] und die Königspsalmen auf das Volk Israel übertragen.[44] Um das gleiche Phänomen geht es auch in den Arbeiten von H. Vorländer und R. Albertz, die beide darauf hinweisen, wie das persönliche "Ich" sowohl in der exilischen Klage wie auch in der zeitgenössischen Prophetie (Deuterojesaja!) immer häufiger die Rolle des Volkes übernimmt und damit in Wirklichkeit zu einem kollektiven "Ich" wird.[45] Ähnliche Tendenzen treten auf breiter Front auch in den jüngeren Schichten des DtrG in Erscheinung, wie ich im Zusammenhang meiner Arbeit über den kollektiven Klagepsalm Ps. lxxxix nachzuweisen versucht habe (*Verheißung*, S. 135-61). Das nationale "Wir" in Gideons Mund ist somit keine isolierte Erscheinung, sondern entspricht einem allgemeinen Trend innerhalb der spätexilischen Theologie.

Nach ihrer formalen Struktur ist Gideons Klage nach dem üblichen Schema der Volksklage aufgebaut, das in diesem Fall aus den folgenden Elementen besteht:

Mit Verlaub, mein Herr,	Ausruf + Anrede
wenn Jahwe mit uns ist, *warum* hat uns all dies getroffen?	Anklage Gottes I
Wo sind alle seine Wundertaten, von denen uns unsere Väter erzählten, indem sie sagten: "Hat uns Jahwe nicht aus Ägypten heraufgeführt?" Und nun hat Jahwe uns verlassen und uns in die Hand Midians gegeben.	Anklage Gottes II

Der Hauptteil der Klage besteht aus zwei vehementen Anklagen Gottes, die seine frühere Zusage (Beistandsformel) bzw. Heilstat (Heraufführungsformel) provokativ der gegenwärtigen Misere gegenüberstellen und dadurch Jahwe zur Aktion zu bewegen versuchen. Für beide Anklagen sind die gattungstypischen Fragen *lāmmā* (I) und *ʾayyē* (II) konstitutiv. Die Frage "Warum" hat eine überaus große Verbreitung in der exilischen Klageliteratur, sowohl in den Prosagebeten wie auch in den kol-

[43] *Israel deutet seine Psalmen* (Stuttgart, 1966), S. 22-4; ders., *Wege der Psalmenexegese* (Stuttgart, 1975), S. 85-98.

[44] J. Becker, "Die kollektive Deutung der Königspsalmen", *ThPh* 52 (1977), S. 561-78.

[45] H. Vorländer, *Mein Gott. Die Vorstellungen vom persönlichen Gott im Alten Orient und im Alten Testament* (Neukirchen-Vluyn, 1975), S. 293-304; R. Albertz, *Persönliche Frömmigkeit und offizielle Religion* (Stuttgart, 1978), S. 178-89.

lektiven Klagepsalmen.[46] Es ist von der spezifischen Situation der Exilszeit her verständlich, daß damals die Warum-Frage eine besonders hohe Aktualität besaß; denn sie ist eine Äußerung der Verzweiflung von Menschen, die wie im Dunkeln tappen und nicht mehr weiter wissen (Westermann, *Ges. Studien* [*I*], S. 276). Die Exilskatastrophe bedeutete für Israel den Einbruch eines heilsgeschichtlichen Dunkels. Davon zeugt auch die andere Frage "Wo sind alle seine Wundertaten, von denen uns unsere Väter erzählten...?", die ihre engsten Parallelen auf der einen Seite in dem dtr Geschichtspsalm Ps. lxxviii (V. 3) und auf der anderen in dem exilischen Volksklagelied Ps. xliv (V. 2) hat. Überhaupt taucht die *ʾayyē*-Frage zum ersten Mal in der Exilszeit in der Volksklage auf (Ps. lxxix 10, lxxxix 50; Jes. lxiii 11,15; Mi. vii 10, später in Ps. cxv 2 und Jl. ii 17). Sie betrifft hier wie auch in Ps. lxxxix 50 und Jes. lxiii 11,15 die Gültigkeit der vergangenen Heilstaten Jahwes, die in der gegenwärtigen Lage ihre Evidenz eingebüßt und damit Jahwes ureigenstes Gebiet, seine Wirksamkeit in der Geschichte, in Frage gestellt haben.[47] Pars pro toto wird hier auf den zentralen Glaubenssatz von der Heraufführung aus Ägypten verwiesen[48] und ihm — eingeführt durch das kontrastierende *wʿth*[49] — die augenblickliche Not entgegengestellt, die Jahwe durch Verlassen (*nṭš*) und Preisgabe seines Volkes in die Feindeshand verursacht habe.

Das exilische Israel besaß ein tiefes Bewußtsein davon, von Jahwe "verlassen" (*nṭš*), "verstoßen" (*znḥ*) und "verworfen" (*mʾs*) zu sein.[50] Unter den zahlreichen Äußerungen dieser trostlosen Stimmung verdient eine Stelle in Salomos Tempelweihgebet ausdrückliche Erwähnung, 1 Reg. viii 57 "Jahwe, unser Gott, sei mit uns (*yhy ʿmnw*), wie er mit unseren Vätern war. Er verstoße uns nicht und verlasse uns nicht (*wʾl yṭšnw*)!", weil sie von demselben Verfasser stammt wie Ri. vi 13 (vgl. Verf., *Verheißung*, S. 153) und zudem in ganz ähnlicher Funktion die Beistandsformel und das Verb *nṭš* verwendet. Was in 1 Reg. viii 57 als Bitt-

---

[46] Für exilisch halte ich die folgenden Belege (a) in der Prosa: Ex. v 22bis, xvii 3, xxxii 11,12; Nu. xi 11, xiv 3, xxi 5; Jos. vii 7; Ri. xxi 3, (b) in der Poesie: Ps. xliv 24,25, lxxiv 1,11, lxxix 10, lxxx 13; Thr. v 20. Vgl. weiter auch Jer. xiv 8,9 und Jes. lxiii 17.

[47] Vgl. zu dieser Anfechtung der Exilsgeneration L. Perlitt, "Anklage und Freispruch Gottes. Theologische Motive in der Zeit des Exils", *ZThK* 69 (1972), S. 296f.

[48] Die dtr Heraufführungsformel (dazu Verf., *Das Königtum in der Beurteilung der deuteronomistischen Historiographie* [Helsinki, 1977], S. 42) erscheint auch in Ex. xvii 3 und Nu. xxi 5 in der Klage des Volkes.

[49] Vgl. *wʿth* in der gleichen Funktion auch in Gen. xxxii 11 (spät); Nu. xi 6 (dtr); Ri. xv 18 (dtr?); Hi. xxx 1, und H. A. Brongers, "Bemerkungen zum Gebrauch des adverbialen *weʿattāh* im Alten Testament", *VT* 15 (1965), S. 291f.

[50] Vgl. *nṭš*: 1 Sam. xii 22 DtrN; 1 Reg. viii 57 DtrN; 2 Reg. xxi 14 DtrN; Jer. vii 29 (exilisch); Ps. lxxviii 60, *znḥ*: Ps. xliv 10,24, lx 3,12, lxxiv 1, lxxvii 8, lxxxix 39; Thr. ii 7, iii 17,31 *mʾs*: 2 Reg. xvii 20 DtrN, xxiii 27 DtrN; Jer. xiv 19, xxxiii 24,26 (alle exilisch); Ps. lxxviii 59,67, lxxxix 39; Thr. v 22.

gebet im Blick auf die Zukunft ausgesprochen wird, erscheint in Ri. vi 13 als eingetroffene Wirklichkeit, freilich übertragen in eine weit zurückliegende Vergangenheit, die jedoch den Lesern die eigene exilische Situation transparent machen soll.

IV

Als drittes Prosagebet möchte ich noch auf die Klage aufmerksam machen, die Josua nach dem ersten, mißlungenen Eroberungsversuch der Stadt Ai ausspricht (Jos. vii 6-9). Auch in diesem Gebet handelt es sich um eine fürbittende Klage in Wir-Form, die von dem Anführer des Volkes in einer Krisensituation für ganz Israel ausgesprochen wird. Im Unterschied zu Gideons Klage weist Josuas Gebet jedoch einen erheblich größeren Wortreichtum auf, weshalb gelegentlich schon Bedenken gegen die Ursprünglichkeit seines heutigen Wortlauts geäußert worden sind.[51]

Josuas Gebet wird in V. 6 durch die üblichen Klageriten vorbereitet: Er zerreißt seine Kleider, fällt nieder zur Erde vor der Lade Jahwes und bleibt dort bis zum Abend (V. 6aα). Die Erwähnung der Ältesten und ihrer Trauergesten (V. 6aβ.b) dürfte hingegen einer sek. Erweiterung des Textes zugehören, weil die Ältesten in der Fortsetzung keine Rolle mehr spielen (vgl. V. 10).[52] In dem verbleibenden Grundtext deuten auf eine relativ junge Entstehungszeit die Lokalisierung des Ritus vor der Lade sowie seine Dauer "bis zum Abend"; denn nur in einem späten Zusatz (Ri. xx 27b-28aα, vgl. Budde, *Richter*, S. 136) wird die Klage vor der Lade durchgeführt und erst in dtr Texten begegnet die Vorstellung, nach der sie "bis zum Abend" dauert (Ri. xx 23,26, xxi 2; 2 Sam. i 12)[53] — was offenbar die Sitte bei den exilischen Klagebegehungen war.

Das Gebet selbst (V. 7-9)[54] läßt sich folgendermaßen gliedern:

Ach, Herr Jahwe,	Ausruf + Anrede
warum hast du dieses Volk über den Jordan geführt, um uns in die Hand der Amoriter zu geben und uns zu vernichten? Wären wir doch jenseits des Jordan geblieben!	Anklage Gottes

---

[51] Vgl. Wendel, *Laiengebet*, S. 125-7; B. J. Alfrink, "Die Achan-Erzählung (Jos. 7)", *StAns* 27/28, *Miscellanea Biblica et Orientalia A. Miller oblata* (Rom, 1951), S. 116; F. Hesse, *Die Fürbitte im Alten Testament, Diss. theol. Erlangen*, 1951, S. 35,139; Westermann, *Ges. Studien* [*I*], S. 292; Lipiński, *Liturgie pénitentielle*, S. 69.

[52] Vgl. H. Holzinger, *Das Buch Josua* (Tübingen-Leipzig, 1901), S. 20, und auch Wendel, *Laiengebet*, S. 127. Ein Zusatz mit dem gleichen Wortlaut wie V. 6aβ findet sich in Jos. viii 10.

[53] Zu den Belegen im Richterbuch s. Verf., *Verheißung*, S. 187f. Der in 2 Sam. i 11f. berichtete Klageritus ist ein den Dialog (V. 3-10,13-15) unterbrechender Zusatz, der in die Reihe der oben erwähnten Texte (des DtrN) gehört. Vgl. später Esr. ix 4-5.

[54] Als spätere Zusätze in ihm sind auszuscheiden: *by ʾdny* in V. 8 (vgl. LXX und Lande, *Formelhafte Wendungen*, S. 18) sowie *hknʿny w* in V. 9 (vgl. M. Noth, *Das Buch Josua* [Tübingen, ³1971], S. 38).

Was soll ich sagen, nachdem Israel seinen Feinden den Rücken gekehrt? Wenn das alle Bewohner des Landes hören, so werden sie uns umzingeln und unseren Namen von der Erde ausrotten.	Klagender Bericht
Was wirst du für deinen großen Namen tun?	Frage (Bitte)

Nach der Einleitung (Ausruf und Anrede), die in die um die Exilszeit übliche Gebetseröffnungsformel *ʾhh ʾdny yhwh* gefaßt ist (vgl. Jer. iv 10, xxxii 17; Ez. ix 8, xi 13, xxi 5), gliedert sich die Klage deutlich in drei Teile, die alle mit einer *Frage* beginnen. Der zweite und dritte Teil sind ganz gleichmäßig gebaut — sie enthalten 21 bzw. 20 Wörter —, der Akzent liegt jedoch auf der abschließenden kurzen Frage, die de facto einer *Bitte* entspricht: Tue doch etwas für deinen großen Namen!

Die durch die *lāmā*-Frage eingeleitete Anklage in V. 7 folgt dem gleichen Schema wie die entsprechende in Ri. vi 13: Sie fragt nach dem Sinn des früheren Heilshandelns Gottes — in diesem Fall, bedingt durch den Kontext, nach dem der Führung über den Jordan (vgl. Jos. iii-iv) — und stellt ihm die gegenwärtige Not als Kontrast gegenüber. Es wird Jahwe unterstellt, er habe seine Heilstat in böser Absicht vollbracht. Diese Argumentation hat ihr exaktes formales und sachliches Gegenstück in der dtr Einleitung des Dtn., wo es in einer Klage des Volkes heißt: "Aus Haß gegen uns hat uns Jahwe aus dem Lande Ägypten herausgeführt, um uns in die Hand der Amoriter zu geben und uns zu vernichten" (Dtn. i 27). Weitere Parallelen finden sich in den dtr Klagen des Mose in Ex. xxxii 12 und Nu. xiv 16, wo derselbe Vorwurf als hämische Feststellung der Feinde erscheint.[55]

Die zweite, durch *mā* formulierte Frage leitet einen klagenden Bericht ein, der Israels Versagen vor seinen Feinden und dessen Wirkung auf die Landesbewohner zum Inhalt hat. Gattungsmäßig entspricht dieser Abschnitt dem in den exilischen Klageliedern häufigen Hinweis auf die Reaktion der Feinde, die Israels Schicksal mit offenem Spott und Hohn begleiten (vgl. Ps. xliv 14-17, lxxix 4,10,12, lxxx 7, lxxxix 42,51-52; Thr. i 9, iii 45-46). In den Prosagebeten begegnet dieser Hinweis in den oben erwähnten dtr Klagen des Mose, der die Befürchtung ausspricht, daß die Ägypter und die Landesbewohner erfahren werden, was Israel geschehen ist, und dies zum Anlaß des Spottes gegen Jahwe nehmen (Ex. xxxii 12; Nu. xiv 13-16, vgl. Dtn. ix 28). Die Anspielung auf die Reaktion der umliegenden Nationen erfolgt hier überall in der Absicht, Jahwe zum Einschreiten für sein Volk zu bewegen. Genau das ist das Ziel auch von Jos. vii 9, wo die abschließende Frage ("Was wirst du für deinen großen Na-

---

[55] Zu Ex. xxxii 7-14 s. Dietrich, *Prophetie und Geschichte*, S. 96, und zu Nu. xiv 11b-23a M. Noth, *Numeri* (Göttingen, ²1973), S. 97. Vgl. auch Dtn. ix 28 (eine Kombination von Dtn. i 27 und Nu. xiv 16) und weiter Ex. xiv 11 dtr, xvi 3 P; Nu. xiv 3 P.

men tun?") stichwortartig (durch *lšmk*) an die vorangehende Klage (*šmnw*) anknüpft und damit Israels und Jahwes Namen in eine fast bedenklich enge Verbindung miteinander bringt. Damit *Israels Name* nicht von der Erde ausgerottet werde, solle Jahwe etwas für *seinen eigenen Namen* tun!

Der Appell an Jahwes "Namen" als Manifestation seiner Ehre ist eine gerade für die exilische Theologie charakteristische Erscheinung.[56] Nach dem Ezechielbuch, wie auch gelegentlich bei Deuterojesaja, handelt Jahwe um seines (heiligen) Namens willen, damit er nicht (mehr) unter den Heiden entweiht werde (Ez. xx 9,14,22,44, xxxvi 21-23, xxxix 7,25 u.ö.; Jes. xlviii 9,11 LXX, lii 5,6). In den zeitgenössischen Volksklagen erscheint "der Name" Jahwes als eine Appellationsinstanz, die angesichts des Spottes der Feinde immer wieder angerufen wird (Ps. lxxiv 7,10,18, lxxix 9; Jer. xiv 7,9,21; Jes. lxiii 14, lxiv 1). Die Namenstheologie ist natürlich auch den Deuteronomisten bekannt, die zudem auch die Verbindung *šm gdwl* (vgl. Jos. vii 9) kennen: Samuel versichert nach 1 Sam. xii 22 DtrN: "Jahwe wird um seines großen Namens willen sein Volk nicht verstoßen" und David in seinem Dankgebet 2 Sam. vii 26 DtrN: "Dein Name wird für immer groß sein." Auch das salomonische Tempelweihgebet kennt diesen Ausdruck (1 Reg. viii 42), der ein Kennzeichen der jüngeren dtr Schichten ist.[57] Die starke Hervorhebung des Namens Jahwes als Motiv seines Handelns in den exilischen Schriften ist kaum unabhängig von der dtn Namenstheologie entstanden, und zusammen mit den anderen exilischen Indizien in Josuas Klage spricht sie sehr deutlich dafür, daß auch dieses Prosagebet seinen zeitgeschichtlichen Ort in der Theologie der Exilszeit hat.

Mit der Untersuchung des Wortlauts ist der Sinn von Josuas Gebet jedoch noch nicht voll erfaßt. Wie es nicht möglich ist, in Josuas Klage eine alte Grundlage vor ihrer angeblich sek. Bearbeitung zu befreien, so ist es gleichfalls abwegig, sie insgesamt zu entfernen und die Achangeschichte ganz ohne sie verstehen zu wollen (so u.a. Alfrink, *StAns* 27/28, S. 116); denn Josuas Gebet bildet einen unentbehrlichen Bestandteil in ihr. Die göttliche Reaktion, die in V. *10-15[58] berichtet wird, hat quasi den Stellenwert eines Heilsorakels, mit dem die vorangehende Klage beantwortet

---

[56] Vgl. J. Köberle, "Die Motive des Glaubens an die Gebetserhörung im Alten Testament", *FS der Universität Erlangen* (Erlangen-Leipzig, 1901) I, S. 269,274.

[57] Zu 1 Sam. xii 22 DtrN s. Verf., *Königtum*, S. 83-92, zu 2 Sam. vii 26 DtrN und 1 Reg. viii 42 spät-dtr (vgl. auch V. 41) Verf., *Verheißung*, S. 64f.,144f.,151-4. Vgl. weiter auch 2 Sam. vii 9b DtrN (mit *ʿśh*, aber in bezug auf David). Sonst ist die Verbindung *šm gdwl* belegt in Jer. x 6; Ez. xxxvi 23; Mal. i 11bis und Ps. lxxvi 2.

[58] Unmotivierte Personenwechsel, Wiederholungen und andere syntaktische Brüche weisen in diesem Abschnitt als späte Zusätze die Versteile V. 11aβ.b,12b und 13b aus.

(vgl. Gunkel-Begrich, *Einleitung*, S. 137) und der Grund für Israels Niederlage vor Ai angegeben wird: In seiner Mitte befindet sich Banngut, das ausfindig gemacht und beseitigt werden soll. Auf den göttlichen Befehl hin (V. *13-15) wird ein Losverfahren durchgeführt (V. 16-18) — das übrigens seine engste Entsprechung in dem dtr Bericht über Sauls Königswahl in Mizpa hat (1 Sam. x 19b-21bα DtrH)[59] — und der Schuldige angezeigt. Ihm wird ein Sündenbekenntnis abverlangt (V. 19-20),[60] und anschließend werden er und seine Familie gesteinigt (V. *24-26).[61] Ließe man nun das einleitende Gebet Josuas fallen, würde die ganze Geschichte ihre innere Logik verlieren, oder aber man müßte eine völlig anders aussehende Vorform der Geschichte postulieren. Weitaus geringere Schwierigkeiten bereitet die umgekehrte Annahme: Die gesamte Achangeschichte, deren integrierender Bestandteil Josuas Gebet ist, stellt bereits in ihrer ältesten Fassung eine exilisch-dtr Lehrerzählung dar.[62]

Diese Annahme wird durch die Beobachtung bestätigt, daß die Achangeschichte nur ganz oberflächlich mit ihrem Kontext verbunden ist: Sie wird durch eine isolierte red. Notiz in Jos. vii 1 vorbereitet, die Israels Versündigung am Bann bei der Eroberung von Jericho post festum konstatiert und den Inhalt der nachfolgenden Erzählung vorwegnimmt. Danach folgt in V. 2-5 der ältere Bericht über Israels gescheiterten Versuch, die Stadt Ai mit 3000 Mann einzunehmen. Er findet seine Fortsetzung in Jos. viii 1ff., wo Josua von Jahwe ermutigt und aufgefordert wird, nun mit dem *ganzen* Heer gegen Ai auszuziehen (V. 1). Zwischen diesen Angaben ist die Achangeschichte nachträglich eingeschaltet worden; und was in diesem Zusammenhang besonders wichtig ist: Bereits der Rahmen, an den Josuas Klage anknüpft, stammt von einem — und zwar dem ersten — Deuteronomisten (DtrH), der in V. 5b sagt, daß "das Herz des Volkes zerfloß und zu Wasser wurde" (vgl. Dtn. i 28, xx 8; Jos. ii 11, v 1), und dazu als Kontrastaussage in Jos. viii 1 die Ermutigung ausspricht: "Fürchte dich nicht und sei unverzagt!" (vgl. Dtn. i 21, xxxi

---

[59] Vgl. dazu Noth, *Überlieferungsgeschichtliche Studien*, S. 58 (freilich dürfte Jos. vii 16ff. nicht als Vorbild für 1 Sam. x 19ff., sondern umgekehrt 1 Sam. x 19ff. als Vorbild für Jos. vii 16ff. gedient haben).

[60] Achans Bekenntnis V. 20 hat in V. 21-23 eine nachexilische, midrašartige Erweiterung erfahren. Das beweist nicht allein der Inhalt dieser Verse, sondern auch die Formel *kzʾt wkzʾt* in V. 20, die auf etwas schon Bekanntes (vgl. V. 1) Bezug nimmt (vgl. 2 Sam. xvii 15; 2 Reg. v 4, ix 12 [s. *BHK*]) und keine so detaillierte Beschreibung wie die in V. 21-23 hinter sich duldet.

[61] Für sek. halte ich in diesem Abschnitt: in V. 24aα die ausführliche Liste des Bannguts (nur Achan, "seine Söhne und Töchter" sind ursprünglich), weiter V. 25bα und 26b.

[62] Eine ähnliche Vermutung äußert — freilich etwas zögernd und mit dem Postulat einer älteren ätiologischen Grundüberlieferung — J. A. Soggin, *Le Livre de Josué* (Neuchâtel, 1970), S. 81.

8; Jos. x 25; Jer. xxx 10//xlvi 27).[63] Damit stellt sich die Achangeschichte als eine Überlieferung heraus, die erst von einem jüngeren Deuteronomisten in Hinblick auf den heutigen Kontext geschaffen wurde.[64] Das Ergebnis erinnert in kompositionstechnischer Hinsicht sehr eng an das bei Gideons Klage (Ri. vi 13) erzielte, und zudem legt auch die große Ähnlichkeit der beiden kollektiven Prosagebete die gemeinsame Verfasserschaft (DtrN) nahe.

Nach dieser Horizonterweiterung wird es möglich, Josuas Klage aus der Perspektive der *ganzen* Achangeschichte zu betrachten. Dabei verdienen die Angaben des Rahmens Aufmerksamkeit, nach denen als Folge von Achans Diebstahl der Zorn Jahwes gegen die Israeliten entbrennt (vii 1: *wyḥr ʾp yhwh bbny yśrʾl*) und Jahwe sich nach Achans Bestrafung von seinem Zorn wieder abwendet (vii 26a: *wyšb yhwh mḥrwn ʾpw*). Die beiden aufeinander bezogenen Aussagen, die in dieser sprachlichen Form erst um die Exilszeit auftauchen,[65] bringen die zentrale Bedeutung des göttlichen Zornes für das Selbstverständnis der damaligen Generation zum Ausdruck. Im DtrG wird das zukünftige Schicksal des Volkes bereits jenseits des Jordan im Rahmen des Dtn. sorgfältig vorbereitet und der Tag ins Auge gefaßt, wo Jahwes Zorn gegen sein Volk entbrennen und er sein Gesicht vor ihm verbergen wird (Dtn. xxxi 17).[66] Diese düstere Prognose geht in Erfüllung in der Verbannung der beiden Staaten, die als Folge des göttlichen Zornes gesehen wird, der gegen Israel und Juda entbrannt war (2 Reg. xvii 18, xxiii 26, xxiv 20). Die exilischen

[63] Es geht nicht an, mit Noth (*Josua*, S. 43) V. 5b zur Achangeschichte zu rechnen — für die er schon Teil der zur redaktionellen Anknüpfung geeigneten Vorlage ist —; denn die Angst (V. 5b) und ihre Beseitigung (viii 1) sind komplementär aufeinander bezogen (vgl. Dtn. i 28f.).

[64] Die "Wirkungsgeschichte" der Achanerzählung bestätigt ihr junges Alter: Vorbereitet wird sie durch die offensichtlichen Zusätze Jos. vi 17-20abα[1], 24b (V. 19 und 24b vertreten dieselbe Stufe wie Jos. vii 21-23,24aα* und weisen durch die anachronistische Erwähnung des "Tempelschatzes" auf ein chronistisch-priesterliches Entstehungsmilieu hin, vgl. 1 Chr. xxix 8; Nu. xxxi 50-54). Später wird auf sie ausschließlich in Jos. xxii 20 innerhalb eines nach-dtr, priesterlichen Einschubs (Jos. xxii 7-37) angespielt.

[65] Zusammen in: Ex. xxxii 10,11,12 DtrN; Nu. xxv 3-4 spät (Verf., *Ewige Dynastie*, S. 114 Anm. 54); Jos. vii 1,26a DtrN und 2 Reg. xxiii 26 DtrN, getrennt in: Ex. xxii 23 (im Zusatz V. 22-23); Nu. xi 1,10,33 dtr, xxxii 10,13 nach-dtr; Dtn. vi 15, vii 4, xi 17, xxix 26, xxxi 17; Jos. xxiii 16 DtrN; Ri. ii 14 DtrH, ii 20 DtrN, iii 8 DtrH, x 7 DtrH; 2 Sam. xxiv 1 DtrH; 2 Reg. xiii 3 DtrN; Jes. v 25 spät (O. Kaiser, *Das Buch des Propheten Jesaja. Kapitel 1-12* [Göttingen, [5]1981], S. 115); Hos. viii 5 (falls echt, handelt es sich um den frühesten Beleg für *ḥrh ʾp b* + Israel); Ps. cvi 40 (nachexilisch) auf der einen, Dtn. xiii 18; Jer. iv 8, xxx 24; Jon. iii 9; Ps. lxxxv 4 (nachexilisch); 2 Chr. xxix 10, xxx 8 und Esr. x 14 (Hi.) auf der anderen Seite.

[66] Vgl. weiter Dtn. iv 25-26, vi 15, vii 4, xi 17, xxix 26-27, xxxi 29; Jos. xxiii 16; 1 Reg. viii 46 und dazu D. J. McCarthy, "The Wrath of Yahweh and the Structural Unity of the Deuteronomistic History", *Essays in Old Testament Ethics, J. P. Hyatt In Memoriam* (New York, 1974), S. 100f.,106.

Klagelieder schließen sich an dieses Verständnis an und deuten die Exilskatastrophe als eine gewaltige Manifestation des göttlichen Zornes (vgl. Ps. lx 3, lxxxix 39; Thr. i 12, ii 2,3,4,6,21,22, iv 11; Jes. lxiv 4 u.ö.). Der gegenwärtige Zustand wird als Sein unter diesem Zorn beschrieben: Jahwe hat sich in seinem Zorn wie in Wolken gehüllt, durch die kein Gebet zu dringen vermag (Thr. iii 43f., vgl. Thr. ii 1; Ps. lxxvii 10, lxxx 5). Trotzdem klagt und fragt man um so intensiver: "Wie lange wirst du noch zürnen?" (Ps. lxxix 5, vgl. Ps. lxxiv 1, lxxx 5; Thr. v 22). Bevor darauf die befreiende Antwort durch Deuterojesaja verkündet wird (Jes. xlviii 9, li 22, liv 8-9), weiß die Exilsgeneration, daß sie den Zorn Jahwes tragen muß (Mi. vii 9).

Man blieb dieser Situation gegenüber jedoch nicht tatenlos, sondern sah offenbar in dem Klagegebet ein Mittel, dem göttlichen Zorn entgegenzuwirken, und deshalb berichten die Deuteronomisten auch von verschiedenen Fällen, wo Jahwes Zorn durch intensives Klagen und Beten beschwichtigt wurde.[67] Dieselbe Funktion hat offenbar auch Josuas Klage in der Achangeschichte. Die Geschichte ist somit ein Stück narrativer Theologie, das als Paradigma für etwas dient, was auch in der gegenwärtigen Not praktiziert werden kann und soll.

Allerdings wendet sich der göttliche Zorn in diesem Fall nicht allein kraft der fürbittenden Klage Josuas ab, sondern dazu bedarf es außerdem noch eines Sündenbekenntnisses (V. 19-20). Das Sündenbekenntnis ist ein Phänomen, das die jungen Gebete charakterisiert. Im nachexilischen Zeitalter kommt die Anklage Gottes fast ganz zum Schweigen, und an ihre Stelle tritt das Bußgebet (vgl. Ps. cvi; Esr. ix 6-15; Neh. i 5-11, ix 5-37; Dan. ix 4-19).[68] Ein wesentliches Merkmal der nachexilischen Bußgebete ist, daß sie die Gerechtigkeit Jahwes als Kehrseite der menschlichen Schuld stark betonen: "In allem, was über uns kam, bist du gerecht. Denn du hast Treue geübt, wir aber haben Frevel begangen" (Neh. ix 33).[69] Die Wurzel dieser Entwicklung, die in theologischer Hinsicht auf der einen Seite die Bereitschaft, die verschiedenen Formen des Unheils zu akzeptieren, erhöhte,[70] auf der anderen aber die

---

[67] Vgl. Nu. xi 1-3,10ff. (dazu Schmid, *Der sog. Jahwist*, S. 70-5); Ex. xxxii 10-14; 2 Sam. xxiv (dazu Verf., *Ewige Dynastie*, S. 108-17; ders., *Verheißung*, S. 202, Anm. 20); 1 Reg. viii 46-50; 2 Reg. xiii 3-5 und außerhalb des dtr Bereichs Jer. iv 8, xviii 20; Jon. iii 9; Ps. cvi 23.

[68] Vgl. weiter Jes. lix 12-13; Bar. i 15-iii 8; 3 Esr. viii 73-89; Or.Man.; Ps.Sal. ix und z.B. Westermann, *Ges. Studien [I]*, S. 296-304.

[69] Vgl. weiter Esr. ix 15; Dan. ix 7,14,16; Bar. i 15, ii 6,9; Zus.Est. iii 18; Ps.Sal. ii 18, viii 7-8,25-26.

[70] M. Limbeck, "Die Klage — eine verschwundene Gebetsgatttung", *ThQ* 157 (1977), S. 13.

Gefahr der Verobjektivierung Gottes nach sich zog,[71] liegen bereits in der Theologie der Exilszeit. Obwohl in den damaligen Klageliedern sporadisch auch die sture Behauptung der eigenen Unschuld begegnet (Ps. xliv 18-23), überwiegt in ihnen doch das Bewußtsein der eigenen Schuld, die als eigentliche Ursache der Katastrophe empfunden wird (vgl. Ps. lxxix 9; Thr. i 8,14,18,20,22, ii 14, iii 42, iv 6, v 16; Jes. lxiv 4-6; Mi. vii 9). Das gilt ganz ähnlich auch für das DtrG,[72] auf das W. Zimmerli den Begriff "die Generalbeichte Israels" verwendet und das G. von Rad "eine große, aus dem Kultischen ins Literarische transponierte Gerichtsdoxologie" nennt.[73] Weder Zimmerli noch von Rad haben geahnt, daß die Gültigkeit beider Begriffe im Blick auf das dtr Kerygma gerade durch die Achangeschichte vortrefflich illustriert wird. Der göttliche Zorn hat ja in ihr — wie wir gesehen haben — als seinen Hintergrund die Verfehlung Israels (vii 1), die Josuas Klage allein nicht zu besänftigen vermag (V. 11aα), wozu es vielmehr einer "Gerichtsdoxologie" bedarf: Achan muß Jahwe die Ehre in der Form geben, daß er ihm seine Sünde bekennt (V. 19-20) und damit die Rechtmäßigkeit der göttlichen Strafe bestätigt. In diesem Akt, der Doxologie und Confessio in einem ist,[74] sind in Wirklichkeit schon die Elemente vorhanden, die sich als kennzeichnend für die nachexilischen Bußgebete erwiesen haben. In Jos. vii haben sie jedoch die Klage noch nicht verdrängt, sondern diese hat ihre eigenständige Rolle in dem Verfahren behalten, das auf die Abwendung des göttlichen Zornes zielt. Offenbar waren Klage und Sündenbekenntnis, deren Entwicklung später auf getrennten Wegen verlief, in der exilischen Klagepraxis noch kompatibel.

V

Ich komme zum Schluß. Die Absicht der vorangegangenen Erörterungen war, einige wenig beachtete Klagegebete in Prosa ans Licht zu bringen und zeigen, daß sie erst auf ihrem zeitgeschichtlichen Hintergrund im Exil voll verständlich werden. Die Auswahl der behandelten Texte geschah eher willkürlich; das Ergebnis hat m.E. jedoch exemplarischen Charakter: Die Mehrzahl der in älteren Prosaschriften überlieferten Gebete unterliegt nämlich dem Verdacht, daß sie keine originären Bestandteile der betreffenden Überlieferungen sind, sondern vielmehr sek. Bear-

---

[71] O. Fuchs, *Die Klage als Gebet* (München, 1982), S. 343.

[72] Vgl. Dtn. i 41 DtrH(?); Ri. x 10,15 DtrN; 1 Sam. vii 6 DtrH; xii 10,19 DtrN, xv 24 DtrN, xv 30 DtrP; 2 Sam. xii 13 DtrP, xxiv 10,17 DtrP; 1 Reg. viii 33,35,47 spät-dtr.

[73] W. Zimmerli, *Grundriß der atl. Theologie* (Stuttgart, 1972), S. 158; G. von Rad, *Theologie des AT I* (München, [5]1966), S. 355.

[74] Vgl. F. Horst, "Die Doxologien im Amosbuch", *ZAW* 47 [N.F. 6] (1929), S. 51.

beitungen entstammen oder insgesamt Teile von jüngeren Überlieferungen darstellen; denn ganz ähnlich wie die Rede bot auch das Gebet als ausgesprochen religiöse Redeform den späteren, reflektierenden Interpreten der alten Texte vorzüglich Gelegenheit, ihre eigenen Akzente in die alten Texte einzutragen. An dieser Stelle denke ich vor allem an die zahlreichen Klagen und Fürbitten des Mose im Pentateuch,[75] die oben gelegentlich nur gestreift wurden, in der zukünftigen Forschung aber gezielt untersucht werden sollten. Es wird kein Zufall sein, daß der dtr Redaktor des Jeremiabuches in Jer. xv 1 gerade Mose als den paradigmatischen Fürbitter neben Samuel anführt. Es steht fest, daß Samuel sein Fürbitteamt vollständig der dtr Redaktion verdankt (1 Sam. vii 5-11, xii 19,23), und ein näheres Eingehen auf die Gebete des Mose könnte ein ähnliches Ergebnis zeitigen. Freilich ist gerade bei Mose auch die Möglichkeit offenzuhalten, daß ihm Gebete auch im nachexilischen Zeitalter in den Mund gelegt wurden; denn im nachexilischen Judentum wurde sicherlich nicht weniger gebetet als in der Exilszeit. Die Grenze zwischen exilischer und nachexilischer Entstehung — die allerdings fließend ist — muß bei jedem Einzeltext sorgfältig geprüft werden.

Bei den oben besprochenen drei Klagegebeten möchte ich jedoch auf ihrer exilischen Herkunft bestehen und für diese Datierung einen Beweis darin sehen, daß sie sowohl inhaltlich wie auch sprachlich in engster Verbindung mit den damaligen Klageliedern und -psalmen stehen, wie oben immer wieder festgestellt werden konnte. Zudem wissen wir — was für die kollektiven Klagegebete von Belang ist —, daß im Juda der Exilszeit regelmäßige Klagefeiern veranstaltet wurden (Sach. vii 3, viii 19). Als ihre Orte werden in den zeitgenössischen Quellen Bet-El (Sach. vii 2-3) und Mizpa (Jer. xli 4-9) erwähnt.[76] Es dürfte weiter kein Zufall sein, daß gerade diese beiden Orte, wo M. Noth die geographische Heimat des DtrG vermutete (*Überlieferungsgeschichtliche Studien*, S. 97, Anm. 6, und S. 110, Anm. 1), mit großer Regelmäßigkeit als Schauplätze der dtr Klagefeste dienen (Bet-El in Ri. ii 1-5, xx 18,23,26-28, xxi 2-4 und Mizpa in Ri. xx 1b,3a, xxi 1,5,8; 1 Sam. vii 5-11). So werden die in die Vergangenheit projizierten dtr Klagegebete keine rein literarische Fiktion sein, sondern von der tatsächlichen Praxis der damaligen Zeit Zeugnis ablegen. Zugleich weisen sie auf die hohe Bedeutung hin, welche die Klage für diese "Generation seines Zornes" (Jer. vii 29) besaß: Sie bot ein Mit-

[75] Vgl. die zitierten Gebete in Ex. v 22f., xxxii 11-13,31f., xxxiii 12-17, xxxiv 8f.; Nu. xi 11-15, xii 13, xiv 13-19; Dtn. i 11, iii 23-25, ix 25-29 und die Hinweise auf Gebete in Ex. viii 4-9,24-27, ix 28f.,33, x 16-19, xv 25; Nu. xi 2, xxi 7; Dtn. ix 18f.; Ps. xcix 6.

[76] Zur Deutung dieser und der im folgenden genannten Texte s. Verf., *Verheißung*, S. 183-98.

tel, das Israel dazu verhalf, ganz an der Realität Gottes festzuhalten, ohne daß es seine eigene Leiderfahrung hätte verleugnen müssen. Und indem diese Spannung im Sprechakt der Klage als einer Art Krisengespräch durchgehalten und artikuliert wurde, wuchs aus ihr eine sehr intensive Begegnung mit diesem Gott, die neue, bisher unbekannte Tiefen in seinem Wesen eröffnete und Israel den Weg in die Zukunft wies.[77, 78]

---

77 Vgl. Fuchs, *Die Klage als Gebet*, S. 331,335,338f.

78 Sprachlich durchgesehen wurde dieser Aufsatz von Herrn Dr H. Spieckermann, dem ich dafür einen herzlichen Dank ausspreche.